Psychology Revivals

Psychology and the Poetics of Growth

In this volume, originally published in 1977, the authors describe the relevance of figurative language for the psychology of language and present a methodological approach best described as naturalistic in orientation. The first section presents the idea of figurative language in terms of linguistic, aesthetic, and philosophical background. Also included is a description of empirical techniques used to assess figurative language and findings from an analysis of widely differing spoken and written contexts.

The second section of this volume deals with the occurrence and significance of figurative language within the specific context of psychotherapy. The use of such language is shown to be crucial in patient insight. The third section deals with children, their understanding and use of figurative expressions, specifically within the school. Here is a volume that was an outstanding addition to the literature at the time and still a valuable resource today.

Psychology and the Poetics of Growth

Figurative Language in Psychology, Psychotherapy, and Education

Howard R. Pollio, Jack M. Barlow, Harold J. Fine and Marilyn R. Pollio

LONDON AND NEW YORK

First published in 1977
by Lawrence Erlbaum Associates, Inc.

This edition first published in 2024 by Routledge
4 Park Square, Milton Park, Abingdon, Oxon, OX14 4RN

and by Routledge
605 Third Avenue, New York, NY 10017

Routledge is an imprint of the Taylor & Francis Group, an informa business

© 1977 by Lawrence Erlbaum Associates, Inc.

All rights reserved. No part of this book may be reprinted or reproduced or utilised in any form or by any electronic, mechanical, or other means, now known or hereafter invented, including photocopying and recording, or in any information storage or retrieval system, without permission in writing from the publishers.

Publisher's Note
The publisher has gone to great lengths to ensure the quality of this reprint but points out that some imperfections in the original copies may be apparent.

Disclaimer
The publisher has made every effort to trace copyright holders and welcomes correspondence from those they have been unable to contact.

A Library of Congress record exists under ISBN: 0470991585

ISBN: 978-1-032-59384-5 (hbk)
ISBN: 978-1-003-45465-6 (ebk)
ISBN: 978-1-032-59433-0 (pbk)

Book DOI 10.4324/9781003454656

PSYCHOLOGY AND THE POETICS OF GROWTH:

Figurative Language in Psychology, Psychotherapy, and Education

HOWARD R. POLLIO
University of Tennessee

JACK M. BARLOW
Private practice, Knoxville, Tennessee

HAROLD J. FINE
University of Tennessee

MARILYN R. POLLIO
Maryville College

 LAWRENCE ERLBAUM ASSOCIATES, PUBLISHERS
1977   Hillsdale, New Jersey

DISTRIBUTED BY THE HALSTED PRESS DIVISION OF
JOHN WILEY & SONS

New York   Toronto   London   Sydney

Copyright © 1977 by Lawrence Erlbaum Associates, Inc.
All rights reserved. No part of this book may be reproduced in any form, by photostat, microform, retrieval system, or any other means, without the prior written permission of the publisher.

Lawrence Erlbaum Associates, Inc., Publishers
62 Maria Drive
Hillsdale, New Jersey 07642

Distributed solely by Halsted Press Division
John Wiley & Sons, Inc., New York

Library of Congress Cataloging in Publication Data

Main entry under title:

Psychology and the poetics of growth.

Includes bibliographical references and indexes.
1. Psycholinguistics.   2. Figures of speech.
3. Psychotherapy.   4. Children--Language.   5. Language arts.   I. Pollio, Howard R. [DNLM: 1. Psycholinguistics.   2. Psychotherapy.   3. Language development.   4. Symbolism. BF455 P9745]
BF455 .P79   153   77-9880
ISBN 0-470-99158-5

Printed in the United States of America

Contents

Preface   ix

PART I: FIGURATIVE LANGUAGE

1. Why Figurative Language? 3

   The Functions of Figurative Language   9
   How Does Poetic Language Mean?   18
   Summary and Conclusions   29

2. Models of the Metaphoric Process 32

   Some Formal Categories of Figurative Expression   37
   The Mechanics of Metaphor   40
   Feature Models of Metaphor   45
   Perceptual Models of Metaphor   58
   Evaluation and Summary   64

3. The Measurement of Metaphor and Some Preliminary Findings 67

   Some Preliminary Findings   73
   Summary and Conclusion   96

vi   Contents

PART II: FIGURATIVE LANGUAGE AND THE PROCESS OF PSYCHOTHERAPY

4. Metaphor in Psychotherapy 101

    Psychoanalytic Approaches to Figurative
       Expression   104
    Summary and Conclusion   114

5. Insight in Psychotherapy 116

    Insight as the Consequence of Interpretation:
       The Early Analysts   116
    Insight as a Complex Patient Process   118
    A Contemporary View of Insight   124
    Some Summary Comments on Insight   129
    Insight and Metaphor in Psychotherapy:
       A Tentative Hypothesis   129

6. Metaphor and Insight in Psychotherapy: Some Empirical Results 132

    Metaphoric Themes in the Five Interviews   142
    Some Summary Speculations and a General
       Conclusion   155

PART III: FIGURATIVE LANGUAGE, CHILDREN, AND THE EDUCATIONAL CONTEXT

7. The Development of Figurative Language 161

    Developmental Trends in Figurative
       Language Use   162
    Developmental Course of Figurative Language:
       Socio-Cultural Effects   170
    Developmental Course of Figurative Language:
       Comprehension and Explanation   187
    Summary and Conclusions   192

8. Figurative Language and the Educational Process 194

    Student Textbooks and the Teaching of
       Figurative Language   196

Teacher-Education Texts and the Teaching
  of Figurative Language   200
Reading and the Teaching of Figurative Language   202
Figurative Language and Writing   206
Summary and Conclusions   208

9. **Making It More: Evaluating Methods for Teaching
    Figurative Language** 210

Experimental Procedures for Teaching
  Figurative Language   211
Making it Strange Training Procedures   215
Making it Strange Across Socio-Economic Levels   219
Teachers, Teaching, and Teaching Techniques   231
Summary and Conclusions   233

References 235

Author Index   249
Subject Index   253

Preface

There is a peculiar Janus-like quality to the human use of human language: It is both for us and for the people to whom we speak. Were it only for us, we could give language its fullest scope as individual expression; as it is, each of us is also responsible for maintaining the use of language as communication among individuals. The tension between personal and communicative expression is probably nowhere more significantly at issue than in poets practicing their craft or in more ordinary people speaking poetically. Poetic language is the fine line between subjective expression and interpersonal communication.

Despite, or perhaps because of, its crucial position, empirically minded social scientists have tried to keep figurative language at a safe distance, for after all, poetry is poetry and science is science. Part of the problem has to do with the general difficulty social science has in measuring qualitative aspects of human behavior, while another has to do with the preconception that figurative expression is not really all that common. As a matter of fact, this work is meant to show not only that it is possible to measure figurative language quite reliably but that, once measured, such expression is quite frequent even in the most ordinary interactions among people. From data such as these, it is but a short step to try to determine when and where people use figurative language and, when used, what consequences it has for both the speaker and the listener.

The plan of this book is quite a simple one, consisting of three parts. In the first section the idea of figurative language is presented in terms of its linguistic, aesthetic, and philosophical backgrounds. Also included is a description of the techniques used to assess such language as well as some preliminary findings emerging from an analysis of widely differing spoken and written contexts.

The second major section of the book deals with the occurrence and significance of figurative language within the specific context of psychotherapy. The major conclusion of this section is that figurative language represents a very important aspect of the specific process of patient insight so crucial to personal growth.

The final section deals with children and their understanding and use of figurative expression within that special social institution known as the school. Again, as in prior sections, the role of figurative expression in promoting intellectual and personal growth is stressed for children ranging in age from kindergarten through high school. In both the second and third sections our emphasis is always on the poetics of personal growth; in one case, for patients in psychotherapy; in the other, for children at school.

At one point we ask the reader to view this work as a series of tentative steps along some unknown path. For this reason, we really do not offer firm answers to any of the questions we pose. To tell the truth, we are much better at posing questions than at providing answers. Although we wish we could, and though we do feel we have uncovered a number of new "facts," firm answers are not easy to come by in so curiously worked an area as that of figurative language. After all, any such answer would have to satisfy not only the psycholinguist, but also the therapist, the educator, the poet, the philosopher, the linguist, and almost anybody who has ever been touched by poetic language—all of which makes for a pretty large and heterogeneous group. In the end we have been content to try and satisfy ourselves, and even here we have not always been completely successful.

This book, as well as every other book, reflects the personalities of the people who wrote it. In this case, they are a variegated collection of individuals, which may perhaps explain why they were so difficult to satisfy. Of the four authors, one is an experimental psychologist, two are clinicians, one in the town, the other in the tower, and one is an expert in reading and the language arts. Their various points of view and expertise color each of the three major sections. Although each author or group of authors took primary responsibility for writing one or another section, the final result is the outcome of a genuinely collaborative effort.

In addition to the collaborative effort involved in this work, the thinking of a number of present and former students is also reflected in the various chapters. Although we have referenced them where appropriate, we would like to list the following people who were of particular importance in helping us work out some of the implications of figurative language for human growth: Charles A. Simpkinson, Rita B. Schoenberg, Roy Kersey, R. Bruce Lockwood, James Pickens, Edward Francisco, and James Kerlin. In addition, there are colleagues at other institutions, such as Howard Gardner of Harvard, Jean Aitchison of The London School of Economics, Brian Butterworth of Cambridge University, and an anonymous reviewer whose wise counsel is reflected in many places in this work.

Howard and Marilyn Pollio would like to thank the United States Public Health Service, Cambridge University, and The London School of Economics for their financial and educational support during the fall semester of 1975, during which time much of the present work was put into its final form. Sally McCauley and Sandra Todd did the endless typing and retyping of the manuscript with skill and, perhaps even more importantly, with charity toward all and malice toward none. Some of the earlier work on child-figurative usage was supported by Grant PEG-7-71-0066 from the United States Office of Education whose support is gratefully acknowledged.

In addition, there is a debt we all owe to the many people who participated in our empirical work. These include the children, teachers, and administrators of the Knoxville public school system as well as the patients and therapists of various therapy centers around the country. Together with John F. Kennedy and Richard M. Nixon, they spoke and wrote the data on which we worked our statistical magic and tried to discover, or more exactly, to recover some of what, we hope was there in the first place. We can consider our job reasonably well done if we were successful in capturing only a small part of the richness that is human speech, figurative or otherwise.

Part I
FIGURATIVE LANGUAGE

1
Why Figurative Language?

In the late summer of 1957 of Cuernavaca, Mexico, a conference was held on the rather surprising topics of psychoanalysis and Zen Buddism. Not surprisingly, however, the major paper was delivered by D. T. Suzuki who attempted to spell out the implications for psychoanalysis of Zen theory. Since psychoanalysis is so clearly a child of Western thought, Suzuki faced the rather tricky and demanding problem of explaining an intricate and complicated Eastern philosophy of Being to his very Western colleagues. How he did this is of importance not only for psychoanalysis but for the study of figurative language as well.

Suzuki (1960) begins by quoting the following haiku poem by the seventeenth century Japanese poet Basho:

> When I look carefully
> I see the nazuna blooming
> By the hedge!

This, he follows in short order with a poem by Tennyson:

> Flower in the crannied wall,
> I pluck you out of the crannies;
> Hold you here, root and all, in my hand,
> Little flower—but if I could understand
> What you are, root and all, and all in all,
> I should know what God and man is.

Obviously, Suzuki continues, both poets are dealing with a similar situation, and just as obviously both are dealing with it in extremely different ways. Tennyson plucks the flower, while Basho simply looks at it, as he says, carefully, and in so doing both reveal a basic difference between East and West: whereas East is able to leave things alone and try to grasp them in their entirety, West is analytic, and by its analysis, destructive. Suzuki further points out that Tennyson is filled with a desire to understand ("what God and man is") while Basho is content simply to experience without any explicit reflection on his experience.

In addition to differences in content there is also a difference in style. Basho accepts the constraints of a 17-syllable form and expresses his relationship to the world simply. Tennyson uses an intricate and complicated rhyming scheme involving over 50 syllables, and as Suzuki says "transforms the word into flesh and makes this flesh too voluptuous."

There are obviously a great many other aspects to Suzuki's contrast between the two poems, and through them, the two cultures, but there seems to be no real reason to pursue the matter further. All that needs to be noted here is the tremendous economy of communication achieved by making use of poetic discourse. Suzuki teaches—and his Western audience understands and learns—on the basis of a relatively straightforward discussion of two short poems. Learning and understanding are engendered by the simple juxtaposition of two poetic images.

As a second example of how poetic language can be used in human communication, let us turn to a locale where poetry seems strangely out of place: in politics. Here let us look at an exchange between John F. Kennedy and Richard M. Nixon in the course of their famous televised debates. In the very first debate both Kennedy and Nixon began with an opening statement. Very early in his statement, Kennedy used the following words:

> "In the election of 1960... the question is whether the world... will *move* in the direction of freedom; in the direction of the road that we are taking, or whether it will *move* in the direction of slavery..." "I think it's time America started *moving* again."

Throughout almost all of his opening remarks Kennedy contrasted some form of *moving* with some form of the phrase *standing still,* and therefore it came as no surprise when Nixon's opening remarks took this contrast into account:

> "There is no question but that this nation cannot *stand still* because we are in a deadly competition... We're ahead of this competition... We're ahead in this competition as Senator Kennedy, I think, has implied, but when you're in a *race* the only way to stay ahead is to *move* ahead... [Kraus, 1962]"

The significant addition made by Nixon to the idea of movement figuratively conveyed by Kennedy was to talk about that movement in terms of international competition. On this basis, he particularized the idea of movement plus competition into the obvious metaphor of a race – a race which the United States was in need of winning – and it was this figure that Nixon developed in the opening moments of his initial statement.

Both teachers and politicians seem to have an affinity for teaching and politicating in terms of figurative language. As an antidote to such fancy speaking, consider the following interchange taken from the transcript of a psychotherapy interview:

Therapist: Right (pause). Yeah, I think I felt a little of your sadness, then ... and what came to mind to me was this idea of somehow deep inside of not wanting to change ... like it's better to keep on wearing the white hat ... that sort of confirms the suspicion you had about yourself all along ... it's hard to take it off [the white hat].
Patient: It seems like it's sort of turned grey [faint laugh].
T: Your white hat, you mean?
P: Yeah [both chuckle]. A little dirty.
T: Getting a little dirty, huh?
P: I find myself on ... like uh ... when you know, like, selling my car. It's sort of like [unclear] I'm not the nice little ... uh ... I don't find myself wearing a white hat ... [pause] I don't know.
T: Are you afraid if you take your white hat off you are gonna end up being the angry monster?
P: Yeah, I think I might.
T: Yeah, let's look at it this way ... maybe the angry monster ...
P: [Interrupts] ... Is a little mouse about that big [holds index and thumb close together, laughs nervously]. The mouse that roared.
T: That would be scary, wouldn't it? Maybe the angry monster is just as much an illusion as the white hat. The mouse that roared.

In this particular case the patient was an undergraduate college student while the therapist was a graduate student not particularly interested in the role of figurative language in psychotherapy. Despite this, both patient and therapist knew a good thing when they heard one and both made good use of the figures — the white hat and the mouse that roared — in trying to deal with the patient's problem.

In three separate settings, having three separate purposes, speakers and writers seem automatically to reach for nonliteral or figurative language. In none of these cases did the usage seem strange or forced and in no case was the language difficult to produce or understand. Examples such as these are not hard to find, and it seems a reasonable starting point to assume that figurative language is a rather ubiquitous aspect of human communication. But how ubiquitous is ubiquitous? In order to answer this question on other than a purely impressionistic basis, it is necessary to look at a great many different and fairly extensive language samples gathered in a great many different speaking and writing situations. Table 1.1 presents some preliminary quantitative data dealing with just this issue. The data presented in this table were culled from a number of different analyses carried out at the University of Tennessee and comprise speaking situations as diverse as patients talking in psychotherapy interviews to the Kennedy—Nixon debates of over a decade ago. Values for written material were obtained from a number of different situations ranging from compositions done by children to Thematic Apperception Test (TAT) protocols written by adults.

Across the whole table one conclusion is clear and does accord with a less quantitative intuition: human beings, when speaking or writing, and regardless of

TABLE 1.1
Sample Figurative Rates for Various Spoken and Written Samples

Situation	Total number of words sampled	Rate/100 words		Source of sample
		Novel	Frozen	
A. Psychotherapy interviews (patient and therapist)				
Psychoanalytic (5 sessions)	23,622	1.70	4.01	Barlow (1973)
Gestalt (1 session)	5,602	3.07	2.37	Pollio and Barlow (1975)
Student therapists (2 patients: 5 sessions each)	54,312	1.26	1.41	Simpkinson (1972)
B. Kennedy–Nixon debates[a]				
Prepared statements (Kennedy)	4,681	1.40	4.79	Pollio and Francisco (1974)
Answers to questions (Kennedy)	17,246	.56	3.06	Pollio and Francisco (1974)
Prepared statements (Nixon)	3,896	1.52	4.61	Pollio and Francisco (1974)
Answers to questions (Nixon)	16,294	1.20	3.64	Pollio and Francisco (1974)
		1.53	3.41	
C. Written works[b]				
Children compositions (high SES school)				
Grade 3	5,247	1.31	1.69	Pollio (1971)
Grade 4	9,052	.82	1.20	Pollio (1971)
Grade 5	9,617	.72	1.44	Pollio (1971)
Adolescent compositions	9,209	.44	6.73	Schonberg (1974)
Adult compositions	34,680	1.56	4.68	Lockwood (1974)

[a] For the Kennedy–Nixon debates the total number of words is an estimate rather than a direct count. After all figures of speech had been recorded, the first sentences were counted and an average word value per sentence compiled. All rate/100 word values were then estimated on the basis of these average sentence length values.

[b] The total number of words reported represents a summation of all the individual compositions written by 53 children in Grade 3, 62 in Grade 4, and 59 in Grade 5. Adult figures were taken from TAT protocols written by college students.

their purpose in speaking or writing, do make use of a great deal of figurative language, both novel and frozen. Frozen figurative language, of course, represents those nonliteral instances that have become cliched in the language, such as the "mouth" of a river, or a "head" of beer, and so on; while novel figurative language represents new linguistic creations developed or applied specifically to or for a given situation and never (or rarely) before encountered by a group of native speakers in that context, for example, the figure of a "white hat."

The figures presented in Table 1.1 show that for spoken language sources, novel usage ranges from a high of 3.07 figures per 100 words produced to a low of .56 (per 100). The comparable values for written sources range from a high of 1.56 to a low of .44. Frozen figurative usage, on the other hand, shows a range from 4.79 to 1.41 in speech and from 1.20 to 6.73 in writing. Considering both novel and frozen usage, the combined totals for speaking range from 2.67 to 6.19 with a mean value at about 4.90. For written sources, these values range from 2.12 to 7.17 with a mean of about 4.12.

Even simple numerical data such as these suggest a number of preliminary implications. One of these concerns differences in the rate of figurative language for the three different types of psychotherapy interviews analyzed (see part A of Table 1.1). In general, these results indicate that a typical therapy session contains about 5,000 words. A more fine-grained description of each of the specific interviews has shown the ratio of patient to therapist words to be about 3:1 for student therapists, about 4:1 for Gestalt therapists, and about 1:1 for psychoanalytic therapists (see appropriate references cited in the table). Further examination also reveals that for psychoanalytic and Gestalt therapy sessions, the total amount of figurative language used comes to about 5.5 figures per 100 words while the comparable value for student therapy sessions is about 2.2 per 100. Taken in conjunction with other descriptions of these particular sessions (see the appropriate references) present results suggest that experienced therapists are more sensitive to, and make more extensive use of, figurative language than do less experienced therapists.

Pollio and Barlow (1975) point out that the very high rates of novel figurative usage for Gestalt therapy is due in large measure to one special property of Gestalt technique: that it specifically makes disciplined use of personifications, such as "talk to your anger," "talk to your fist," etc. For this reason an estimate somewhat less than 3.00 novel figures per 100 words spoken is probably a more reasonable one.

The values reported in Part B of Table 1.1 for Kennedy and Nixon allow for an evaluation of the rate of figurative usage by highly skilled speakers in that complicated speaking situation known as the debate. Compared to psychotherapy, results indicate low—average to low values for novel figures and inflated values for frozen figures. Both of these results would seem to confirm everybody's attitude about political rhetoric. One other effect obvious in these data concerns the relatively lower rates of both novel and frozen figurative language for question and answer periods when compared to rates obtained for prepared statements. If both politicians were careful in their use of *strange* novel figurative language during their prepared statements, it is clear that they were even more careful in their use of *funny* language when responding under less constrained conditions.

A more fine-grained analysis of these debates by Pollio and Francisco (1974) revealed that over the four debates Kennedy's novel rates tended to increase slightly while Nixon's tended to increase more dramatically, with figurative usage in the last session approximately 3 times as great as in the first. This would seem to imply either that as they both became more comfortable in the debate situation they used more figurative language or that they used figurative language in later debates as one aspect of a dramatic finish. In addition, Pollio and Francisco were able to document the fact that both speakers freely borrowed each other's figures and that this tendency was more marked for Nixon than for Kennedy. By the fourth debate Nixon's novel rate rose to 2.70 per hundred words spoken, while his frozen rate rose to 6.84 per 100 words spoken. Comparable values produced during the fourth debate for Kennedy were 0.88, novel, and 4.35, frozen.

The values presented in Table 1.1 for written discourse also show some interesting trends. First, there seems to be a progressive decrease in children's use of novel figurative language over the three elementary school grades studied. Since adult values for written work seem to fall within the same range as spoken discourse (see Lockwood, 1974), one possible implication must be that there is an initial suppression of figurative language in elementary school and that an upswing in figurative language occurs between the end of elementary school and the beginning of college. Exactly when in the life cycle this might happen is unknown. It does, however, make sense to expect such an increase during adolescence as children pass into the so-called stage of formal operations. (For a more complete discussion of developmental trends in figurative usage, see results presented in Chapter 7, pages 161–193 in this volume.)

A final obvious, yet significant, implication that can be drawn from the data contained in Table 1.1 concerns the simple volume of figurative language in human speech (and writing). If we take an average rate across the seven different speaking situations (which admittedly are not completely ordinary), results indicate that this varied group of speakers used about 1.50 novel and 3.40 frozen figures per 100 words spoken. Although speech rates vary, Goldman-Eisler's data (1968, Table 3, p. 20) provide an average speech rate of about 242 syllables per minute. If we assume that an average word has two syllables (see Miller, 1951, p. 81, for data on this point) then the usual rate of speaking would be about 120 words per minute. Taking this value as a possible unit means that speakers would use about an average of 1.80 novel and 4.08 frozen figures per minute. Further multiplication gives values of 108 and 245 per speaking hour, and although it is not known how many hours per day people speak, the rate for a 4-hr speaking day would be 432 and 980, respectively. The comparable values would be 3,024 and 6,860 per week and 157,248 and 356,720 per year. Figuring 60 speaking years, the estimates approach almost 9.5 million novel and 21.4 million frozen figures. Even if we allow only two speaking hours per day the values are still around 4.7 and 10.5 million instances, respectively. Either estimate represents a lot of behavior in two language categories that often have been considered as esoteric rather than ordinary.

This exercise in arithmetic, however, only confirms what by now should be quite obvious: figurative language is an ubiquitous aspect of human language usage. Somehow or other, speakers cannot control themselves when it comes to figures of speech; they borrow or invent them, good and bad, by the hundreds, literally by the millions. In terms of parts of the body we have frozen figures such as: the "head" (foot) of a bed, the "mouth" of a river, the "finger" of fate, being "nosey," having "eyes" for someone or thing, "male" plugs and "female" sockets, "hairy" problems, and a list as long as your arm. Sensory experiences also provide an ear full: mood "indigo," true "blue," a "cool" manner, a "red"-letter day, "frigid," "purple"-passion prose or what have you, "green" with envy, "bright eyed," as well as many other colorful examples. Treating animals as people is still another fertile source of figurative language: "goose," "hawks" and "doves," to "wolf" food or girls, a "whale" of a time, a "snake" in the grass, as well as a flock of others. The list is enough to make the stout hearted blanch, or at least turn slightly green.

In addition, authors of fiction often christen their characters with names describing their character or importance. Thus, the main character in each volume of Durrell's *Alexandria Quartet* provides some hint as to how reality will be presented in that particular volume: Justine (the sexual heroine), Balthazer (the mystical), Mountolive (the political), and Clea (the artistic). Even less esoteric fiction features characters such as Terry Southern's Candy or Ian Fleming's Pussy Galore.

The general conclusion to all of this must be that whether used in a controlled debating situation or in a seemingly more haphazard spontaneous one, figurative language is not the special privilege of a few specially gifted speakers. Rather, we all use a great deal of figurative language and this simple empirical fact needs explaining. In a sense, the three instances of figurative language used to open this chapter suggest that one profitable way of doing this would be to look at the role of figurative language in a wide variety of different settings and it is to this task which we now turn.

THE FUNCTIONS OF FIGURATIVE LANGUAGE

To speak figuratively is to speak in a somewhat unusual or strange way, and it seems appropriate to ask exactly what purpose is achieved when a speaker moves from ordinary to figurative discourse. In the case of the three examples presented above the functions seem clear enough: for Suzuki, the purpose was to instruct; for Kennedy as well as for Nixon, the purpose was to sell a president; while for the "mouse that roared," the purpose was to solve personally perplexing problems in living. Figurative language shows up at least in those cases in which a speaker intends to teach and/or learn, to convince or to sell, as well as those in which the intention is to solve problems.

To list the functions or purposes of figurative language and simply let it go at that seems a bit inappropriate as such a list entails at least two different types of problems: (1) no single phrase or use of language ever seems to have just a single function; while (2) it is not clear whose point of view we ought to be taking in talking about what figurative language can or cannot do. So, for example, in regard to the "mouse that roared," it is clear that our patient did want to capture an extraordinary experience in somewhat unusual terms, yet it is also clear that without the help of the therapist he would not have been able to make much further use of the figure in coming to some new awareness of his personal situation. The same piece of figurative language, then, had at least two different functions one which surely was obscure to the speaker when he produced it for the first time.

An observation such as this leads to a second problem. Is it reasonable to call something a function of figurative language if it is not specifically so intended by the speaker? It seems clear that Nixon did intend to use the figure of a race as standing in contradistinction to Kennedy's more open-ended figure of diffuse movement but it is not quite so clear that he intended to invoke the idea of losing as well. Thus, Nixon's implicit concern with losing was certainly not something he necessarily wanted to share with his audience, yet this associated idea nonetheless did appear as a consequence of the race metaphor. His strategic purpose involved only one of these two implications — to concretize movement plus competition into vivid language: the second implication just sort of came along uninvited.

In the case of Suzuki, however, we find more of the possible functions of figurative expression clearly under the speaker's strategic command. Not only did Suzuki make the appropriate distinctions between Eastern and Western philosophies of man, but he also did so in an elegant and poetic style. It would be difficult to miss Suzuki's understated and totally invidious comparison between Basho's simple poetic image and Tennyson's more wordy one. For Suzuki, figurative usage clearly served many different ends all of which were under his strategic control.

Given these complications, what strategy can we use in describing the functions of figurative language? Probably the best way in which to do this is to recognize that figurative usage always has many functions and that to talk about them one at a time is simply a convenient fiction. Only, however, if we present them in such a relatively unencumbered way will it be possible for us to look at any possible interaction among the various functions that might emerge in any specific speech situation. Although such a perspective will never be exactly right for any given speech act, it should serve to provide a reasonable set of categories for looking more generally at the functions of figurative expression in specific speech contexts.

Metaphor as Additional Vocabulary

One of the first and probably most obvious functions of figurative language is that it is often used to express an idea or feeling for which there is no clear or unique expression already available in the language. In this sense, metaphor provides the possibility for talking about things, events or ideas we have never before talked about nor perhaps even thought of.

The idea of metaphor as additional vocabulary is also given support by the existence of clichéd or frozen figurative usage. As is quite obvious, frozen figures were not always frozen and it is only the best of a generation's expressions that gets to be frozen; that is, which get to provide a new word for a new idea or a new way of looking at an old idea. Only those figures which were unique and which brought about, and continue to bring about what Brown (1958) has called "a click of comprehension" are usually good enough to be retained and, therefore, good enough to be frozen into the standard vocabulary of a language.

Not surprisingly, it often turns out that frozen figures come to take over a meaning so completely that it is difficult to see the figurative origin of a given expression. How else, for example, could the "arm of chair" or the "leg of a piano" be called? The fact that these uses become so fixed indicates not only that figurative expression extends the range of things that can be talked about by a speaker but that it can do so for a total language community as well.

The difficulty we now have in seeing the "arm of a chair" as figurative tells us that for a figure to remain figurative the parts joined must not be absorbed into one another. Only if the individual parts – arm and chair, for example – remain distinct will we have the experience of novel usage. A clichéd or frozen figure can be defined as one in which the constituent parts have lost their unique identities and all that remains is a (new) single item which can be analyzed into its parts only with great difficulty.

Metaphor as Intellectual History

Despite the fact that frozen figures lose their vitality with repeated use we should not overlook that frozen figures do enter the language and that they must at one time have represented an absolutely unique bit of linguistic play. If we extend this view a bit, it is quite clear that an historical analysis of metaphoric usage might help to highlight the particular interests and ideas of a particular historical period or epoch. Thus, an age often can be defined in terms of its salient metaphors and such metaphors not only influence the subject areas to which they are applied but may also help shape the problems and solutions of that age. "As a form of comparative analysis then, metaphors can structure inquiry, establish relevance and provide an interpretive system" (Stelzer, 1965, p. 53).

In an attempt to evaluate this hypothesis in a specific substantive domain, Stelzer examined the figures used in speech texts to characterize the process of human communication. A somewhat impressionistic review revealed that a mechanical model of human communication which used figures such as "the power of speech", "the speaker's craft," and so on, has given way to a more biological one employing figures such as "living speech," "adaptable communication," "the vital process of communication," and so on. With specific regard to speech, Stelzer asked whether or not an uncritical acceptance of mechanical metaphors did not lead speech teachers to an overemphasis on technique, such as voice and diction, at the expense of an emphasis on content and meaningful communication; or just those aspects of speech suggested by more biological and/or psychological metaphors. The more general point to be made here is that the figures used to talk about a given topic not only help the speaker describe that topic they may also serve to alter his or her perspective of what it is that is to be selected and what it is that is to be rejected in that domain.

This insight — that metaphors reveal and describe a particular historical way of looking at a problem — has been legitimatized in language circles in the form of Sperber's law. Basically, Sperber's law states that an area of intense interest in a culture and/or period will become a center for metaphorical expansion. As Ullmann (1966) expressed it:

> If at a certain time a complex of ideas is so strongly charged with feeling that it causes one word to extend its sphere and change its meaning, we may confidently expect that other words belonging to the same emotional complex will also shift their meaning. (p. 240)

A more dramatic and somewhat more radical view of the role of metaphor in changing language and thought has been taken by Schon (1963) who feels that the processes involved in figurative language, which he calls the displacement of concepts, are essential processes in the development of new theories, scientific or otherwise. He sees the displacement of concepts as "the functioning of older theories as metaphors or projective models for new situations." In order to function as a projective model, older concepts come to be seen in a new manner and it is in this way that a new(er) concept emerges. Given this orientation Schon (1963) goes on to propose a kind of historical analysis based in part on Sperber's law:

> There is here the possibility of a new kind of inquiry — an intellectual history which would consider not the manifest content of theories; but the development of their underlying metaphors; a history of the displacement of theories... It would attempt to describe the patterns of interaction and change in metaphor and theory. (p. 192).

If Schon's hypothesis is even partially correct we ought be able to discern the role of metaphor and analogy in many of the greatest scientific and mathematical discoveries of this, or any other, age. Dreisdadt (1968), in his review of metaphoric thinking in the arts and sciences, points out that Einstein sometimes visualized himself as a passenger riding on a ray of light holding a mirror in front of him. Such a situation would cause no image in the mirror for the light and the mirror would be traveling in the same direction at the same speed. Since Einstein's mirror would be just slightly ahead, light could never catch up to the mirror and, therefore, could not provide for any reflected image. This, however, would apply only to Einstein's mirror; a stationary observer, also equipped with a mirror and watching the rider flash by, would be able to catch the rider's image. A bit of fancy such as this captured the idea that optical events are relative. Since it was intended as analogous to physical events, Einstein was able to make informal deductions from this fanciful situation and assume that such deductions could be more rigorously developed should they prove interesting (Driesdadt, 1968, p. 107).

The use of figurative expression is also obvious in biology. As any introductory text will show, evolutionary development and differentiation are almost always portrayed as a living tree — or as Darwin called it "The Great Tree of Life." In commenting on this, Dreistadt noted that Darwin did not invent the figure of the great tree in biology; rather he simply borrowed it from other biologists. Darwin's insight consisted in seeing more in the metaphor than others did. Thus, for a metaphor to be scientifically useful it need not be original: all the thinker need to do is to see the world in its light and thereby see the world anew.

Figurative language has also played an important historical role in the development of certain concepts in philosophy and psychology, particularly in regard to mental events. Talking specifically about Descartes and his influence on psychology, Ryle (1949) set up his rejection of Cartesian dualism by the "deliberately abrasive phrase: the ghost in the machine." After successfully doing in anyone in psychology or philosophy who was still likely to believe in this "myth" and its attendant metaphors of "inside" and "outside," Ryle then went on to concede that when the metaphor was new it did have a certain significance to it. As a matter of fact, Ryle conceded that metaphoric expression is almost unavoidable in philosophical and psychological work. What he meant to emphasize, however, was that metaphoric statements should be used only with the greatest of care and that they should be discarded when of no further heuristic value.

In a similar analysis, emerging this time from phenomenological rather than from linguistic analysis, Edie (1963) also stressed the unavoidability of figurative expression in philosophical discourse. This occurs because as he put it: "Man is not pure consciousness; he becomes conscious, little by little," and it is through the agency of language that more and more of the world becomes accessible to him. Metaphors are useful in this regard because they help put difficult abstract concepts back in contact with the lived world, and in this way help us make contact with the concept. With specific regard to thinking and mental operations, Edie cites Sartre's analysis of the "alimentary" epistemology of empiricism in which thinkers were described as "digesting an idea" or as "assimilating reality." In addition, Edie also discussed Plato's use of sexual–generative words in his analysis of thinking: "conceiving" an idea, "having intercourse" with the world, "knowing" (in the carnal sense), and so on.

Metaphor as Heuristic

All of the preceding historical analyses suggest that figurative language often serves to organize as well as to restrict the way in which events are thought about, and this suggests that such language ought play an important role in creative human problem solving. The most straightforward, even if somewhat quixotic, presentation of this viewpoint has been made by Gordon (1961) under his banner of "synectics," a neologism based on two Greek words meaning the fitting together of diverse elements. Synectic theory is concerned with creativity and invention particularly in industrial settings. Most specifically for Gordon (1961) it applies to the integration of diverse individuals into a "problem-stating, problem-solving" group and is "an operational theory for the conscious use of the preconscious psychological mechanisms present in all of man's creative activity" (p. 3).

In order to discover the specific nature of these mechanisms, Gordon and his co-workers examined the biographies and autobiographies of numerous creative thinkers as well as reports of people in the process of invention. From these data they concluded that the essential process in any and all creative acts involved trying to make the strange familiar (understanding a problem as given with all of its various ramifications) or in trying to make the familiar strange (taking a problem and distorting so that it could be viewed from a new angle).

For Gordon and his co-workers, there are four basic mechanisms used to make the familiar strange or the strange familiar and each of these is essentially figurative in nature:

1. Personal analogy, which is becoming yourself, one of the objects looked at and then feeling, thinking, and acting like that object. It goes beyond mere role playing in that the thinker can be an inanimate, as well as an animate, object or being. In terms of figurative language, this involves the category of personification.

2. Direct analogy, which is an actual comparison of parallel facts, knowledge or technology. In problem-stating, problem-solving situations the synectics group has found that analogies from the biological sciences appear to be the most fruitful.

3. Symbolic analogy, which is a compressed description of the function or elements of a problem as the problem solver views it. It is the poetic response

that sums up what has been said in the personal and direct analogy phases and it most often takes the form of a direct metaphor or of an oxymoron.

4. Fantasy analogy, which is an attempt to solve a problem by wish fulfillment, that is, by wishing the problem solved in any manner whatsoever.

Although parts of the synectics process as described by Gordon sound like a magical, ritualistic incantation to the goddess Creativity, selected research has in fact shown it to work. The synectic approach has been used extensively in industry (in which the standard of evaluation was the new or improved product or invention) as well as in science education (in which grades and student comfort have been the standards of evaluation). In both cases results have been impressive − better products and better teaching (Gordon, 1965).

In an attempt to define the synectics process in a somewhat more objective and rigorous way, Mawardi (1959) analyzed the patterns of communication in a highly successful industrial consultation group using synectic methods. Her analysis revealed that metaphors and other nonliteral items often played a pivotal role in bringing about problem definition and problem solution. She came to this conclusion by categorizing all instances of communication occurring within four 3-hr problem-solving sessions. After repeatedly coalescing her rather unwieldy original category system, Mawardi found that every communication could be meaningfully placed into one of four different groupings: orientational (O), instrumental (I), abstract (A), and metaphorical (M). An orientational response was any communication intended to praise, scold, redirect or instruct the group; An instrumental statement dealt with the group's attempt to engineer a possible solution; while abstract responses dealt with any intangible notion. Metaphoric responses, though usually personifications of nature, originally involved 12 subcategories, later reduced into the general category of figurative language. As a consequence of a lengthy and somewhat involved pattern analysis Mawardi concluded that the tetrad AMIO was repeatedly the most successful sequence of communications producing a viable solution to the problem at hand. For this one industrial consulting group, solving the problem involved a process Mawardi termed "the taming of metaphors."

The notion that figurative language plays an important role in structuring and ultimately in solving problems should and does have application beyond the industrial setting. The major additional locale in which this insight has been used is the psychotherapist's office (e.g., Ekstein, 1966; Leedy, 1969; Lenrow, 1966; Fine, Pollio, & Simpkinson, 1973). In his version of this position Leedy (1969) suggested that it is possible to facilitate communication in psychotherapy by giving patients poetry that parallels or matches their psychological condition or by encouraging them to write their own poems. In the case of providing poetry to his patients, Leedy is obviously using the vocabulary augmenting aspect of metaphor in psychotherapy. There is, however, another aspect to the use of poetry in psychotherapy and this deals with the ability of a poem to serve as teaching−learning device that allows the patient, by puzzling out the meaning of an appropriate poem, to puzzle out the meaning of his own problem—situation.

The idea that poetry and all figurative language can function as a teaching—learning heuristic in psychotherapy has also been developed by the psychoanalyst, Ekstein. Basically, Ekstein (1966) feels that interpretation within the patient's metaphor provides an effective way of dealing with a personally dangerous idea in a playful and somewhat disguised form. He uses this method with borderline schizophrenic patients where he notes that if the relations expressed in a metaphor are interpreted by the therapist within the context of the metaphor itself, it is likely to be less threatening to the patient than if interpreted directly and thereby to engender communication so vital to the therapeutic process.

There has been a great deal more work describing the relationship of figurative expression of therapeutic change. Part II of this volume presents a series of specific hypotheses and results dealing with just this issue; suffice it to note here that such application is made; the specifics are dealt with subsequently.

Metaphor as Mask

The optomistic view of figurative language presented to this point has not been agreed to by all. In a series of papers dating back to the beginning of this century psychoanalysts such as Sharpe (1950) described figurative expression in somewhat less friendly terms. The basic hypothesis here was a simple one: figurative language, like all symbolic expression, may represent a mask for unacceptable urges. Like other symbols, the metaphoric use of ordinary vocabulary items clothes the unacceptable impulse in respectability and thereby allows the indulged motivational source to go undetected and unrecognized. By clever use of ordinary language, a patient can keep his or her therapist from problem areas and it is only through a careful analysis of asking the patient why he or she employed such language that the therapist could come to unmask what was being hidden.

We need not take only the psychoanalytic viewpoint to realize that figurative language can abet hiding. The use of figurative expression in public debate does sometimes also seem to have a similar effect. A politician put on the spot often resorts to platitudes (frozen figures) so as to cover an embarrassing situation. In addition, public rhetoric often explicitly encourages the use of language which evokes an expected response in the listener (Osborn & Ehninger, 1962) and in this way new ideas are pushed aside in favor of those that can be counted on to arouse the audience in predictable ways.

There is, however, a further consequence to this negative aspect of figurative expression and that is that a speaker or listener may be misled by a false analogy. Psychoanalytic writers are here fond of noting that if figures do mask unacceptable urges, one particularly good way of avoiding a difficult problem area is to draw a false conclusion from a particular way of talking about a particular topic. Nash (1962), in his discussion of one of Freud's metaphors, notes how even the master was trapped by his own figure of a "play within a play," and thereby prevented from resolving the difficult problem of how to proceed in certain types of therapeutic situations. In this case, figurative language not only masked the difficulty, it actually misdirected the thinker from a proper evaluation. From the psychoanalytic point of view the motto governing the use of figurative language surely must be: let the user beware — we never know what is being masked by a given figurative expression.

Metaphor as Ornament

We come, finally, to a very obvious, yet somehow misunderstood function of figurative expression — that metaphors lend beauty and interest to all writing whether it be scientific, artistic, or otherwise. Unfortunately, the idea that figurative language can be interesting or beautiful has come perversely to suggest that such expression is only ornamental and that ornaments are neither functional nor useful. This view runs contrary to those analyses of figurative expression which attribute far more useful consequences to such language. The issue, however, is easily resolvable. All we need do is note that the ornamental quality of figurative language serves, at a minimum, to call attention to itself and that only because some piece of language has been highlighted as interesting or beautiful (or whatever) do other functions of figurative expression have the possibility of emerging.

This ornamental quality of figurative language then is not something extra, something extrisinic; rather it would seem to be at the very center of figurative expression. It is precisely because a figure is beautiful that it compels our attention and only because our attention has been caught do some or all of the other functions have an opportunity to bring about their effects. This insight has a further implication for as we noted in the very beginning, no single function really ever operates alone. In looking carefully at the ornamental function of figurative expression do we see how the functions combine and mutually support one another. Being compelling, ornamental, or interesting is not *just* a function of figurative expression, rather it is the condition by which figures work.

This is true whether we look at the socially useful functions such as vocabulary additions, heuristics, and so on, or at the socially difficult ones such as masking and misdirecting. In both cases, a figure has first of all to call attention to itself before the speaker/listener/thinker will devote extra time to it. In discussing the joint functions of analogy and ornament in figurative language Hester (1967) wondered if the assumption of both functions "did not suggest inconsistency rather than catholicity of mind" (p. 14). The answer to this question is that linguistic beauty and function are not incompatible and that it is precisely in the case of figurative expression that the two come together to complement one another.

Such a conclusion also suggests that while it may be useful for purposes of exposition to list separate functions, such an enumeration does violence to the operation of figurative expression in living speech contexts. For this reason, it is necessary at the end of this section to reemphasize that the various functions interrelate with one another and that no one function ought to be considered as a "cause" for any other. Rather the various functions are better thought of as in constant interaction and for this reason, we must never speak of one function as prior to or even as independent of any other. To a greater or lesser extent all functions are possible in any figurative expression; it is the speaker in his or her situation who gives prominence to one or another. Speaking figuratively is a human action and subject, like all other such actions, to the choices and constraints which operate more generally in determining significant human behavior, linguistic or otherwise.

HOW DOES POETIC LANGUAGE MEAN?

When philosophers, literary critics, or poets deal with figurative language they usually concern themselves with one of two questions: (1) how does a figure produce its effect, and (2) how does the effect produced alter our subsequent view of reality? Although such questions have as yet to be resolved by philosophical or literary analysis they do provide a number of issues and suggestions that must be considered in any specific attempt at understanding the *how* of poetic expression. In a very important sense, they set a background of knowledge and speculation against which any specific theory of figurative expression must be evaluated.

The Role of Transfer and Analogy in Figurative Expression

In approaching the first of these questions it would seem appropriate to begin at precisely that same point at which all Western philosophy begins — with Aristotle. In his *Poetics* (translation, 1909), Aristotle introduced the following definition—description of the metaphoric process:

> Metaphor consists in giving the thing a name that belongs to something else; the transference being either from genus to species, or from species to genus, or from species to species, or on grounds of analogy . . . (p. 7).

> That from analogy is possible whenever there are four terms so related that the second (B) is to the first (A), as the fourth (D) to the third (C); for one may then metaphorically put D in lieu of B, and B in lieu of D. (p. 18)

For Aristotle, as for many subsequent analysts, the essence of the metaphoric process involves a transfer of meaning between two or more items, particularly when such transfer has its own style or grace. One extension of this view leads to a more formal position which entails the idea of analogy in its strict logical sense. So, for example, Brown (1966) described the process of metaphor in terms of a transfer between analogic proportions. For Brown, a sentence such as "His brilliance dimmed the sun" must be analyzed as follows:

$$A : B :: \text{Cause 1} : \text{Effect 1}$$
$$X : Y :: \text{Cause 2} : \text{Effect 2}$$

Thus, the subject's superior intelligence (A) overpowers the intelligence of others (B) as Cause 1 is related to its Effect 1. This is similar to some luminous brilliance (X) overpowering the brilliance of the sun (Y) just as Cause 2 is to its Effect 2.

Although Brown describes metaphor as a type of formal analogy, it need be emphasized that he does not rob it of its emotional aspects; rather he simply makes them subservient to the cognitive act of analogic metaphor making. Indeed Brown (1966) describes figurative language as the outcome of a poetic struggle to express a powerful emotional state:

> Metaphor ... would seem to be the outcome of an emotional mood reacting on the imagination. Such a mood, when it achieves adequate expression, issues forth in poetry. ... The primary aim of such mood is not clearness of logical statement, but force, vigor and intensity, so that the outward expression may bear some resemblance and proportion to the inner frame of mind. (p. 56)

With this statement does Brown present a further complication for any transfer analysis of figurative language. Figurative transfer is not to be taken as logical or informative in any usual sense of these terms: rather it provides for an outward expression of a strong internal state. The idea of an absolute division between so-called rational and emotional language and the relegation of figurative language to emotion receives its clearest and most articulate statement not in Brown but in the work of Ogden and Richards. In their well-known book, *The Meaning of Meaning* (1960), Ogden and Richards hold very strongly to the idea that poetic usage is capable of dealing only with expressive experience while symbolic or referential language is what is needed for dealing with truth and correctness. To be sure, Richards subsequently softened this extreme stand in *The Philosophy of Rhetoric* (1936) as well as in other later works, but the message contained in *The Meaning of Meaning* is still quite characteristic:

> A poem ... has no concern with limited and directed reference. It tells us, or should tell us nothing. It has a different though an equally and far more vital function — to use an evocative term in connection with an evocative matter. What it does, or should do, is to induce a fitting attitude to experience. (Ogden & Richards, 1960, pp. 158–159)

In his later work it is as if Richards seeks to avoid downgrading poetic language by increasing its importance; in truth this maneuver does little to change the basic spirit of his approach.

The truth of the matter — and one response to Richards' dichotomy — would seem to be that rational language, no matter how hard we try, is never free from some sort of emotional aspect. At the same time, poetic language is never free of rational constraints for even poetry itself always involves the use of formal systems such as rhyme or prosody both of which impose constraint on the poet's so-called license. The use of language then is never one sided, for whether in poetry or mathematics all language entails both "the truthtelling of rationalism and the persuasiveness of elocutionism. Try as we may, we cannot frame an utterance in such a way that it will be totally informative or totally affective" (Winterowd, 1967, p. 2).

Even if we now grant that figurative transfer from Aristotle's A to Aristotle's B (and beyond) is best described as involving both informative and affective aspects we still need some way of describing which A ought to go with which B for best effect. Here Isenberg (1963) among others, offers the idea that metaphor is best to the degree that the transfer between A and B involves a "resemblance in difference." For Isenberg, as for Leibniz, the recipe for a good metaphor is the maximum resemblance combined with the greatest possible difference. Even though resemblance in difference might seem to be an important aspect of metaphor, such a definition does not seem very useful as a general formula for producing or even for evaluating metaphors. Indeed, as Welsh (1962) has noted, this formula does not fit all cases of figurative language as metaphoric transference often arises because of the felt appropriateness, rather than inappropriateness, of a pair of images. Although resemblance in difference may capture one aspect of figurative expression it does not seem to be the only basis on which to describe the process by which figures emerge and have their effects.

Despite some advance then, we are still left with the problem of how the "right" A is to get together with the "right" B for maximum effect. In a charming article entitled "Metaphor as Mistake" (1958), Percy considers the possibility that it all occurs quite by chance. So, for example, there are some language errors which clearly tumble into poetic metaphor; like mistakingly thinking the name of the *Blue Darter Hawk* to be the *Blue Dollar Hawk*; or mistakingly reading *un*passioned as *impassioned* in the poetic line: "The keen/impassioned beauty of a great machine" (Empson, 1955). In addition, there is the frankly experimental use of words by surrealist poets in whose poems astoundingly good images often result on the basis of random pairing.

Despite the teasing possibility that poetic transfer might in the end result from nothing other than random combinations of words, Percy comes out quite firmly against it. As he notes:

> [T]here is missing (in such an explanation) one essential element of the meaning situation: the authority and intention of the Namer. Where the Namer means nothing or does not know what he means or the Hearer does not think he knows what he means, the Hearer can hardly participate in a co-intention.... Once the good faith of the Namer is so much called into question, the jig is up. There is no celebration of a thing beheld in common. One is only trafficking in the stored-up energies of words, hard won by meaningful usage. It is a pastime, this rolling out the pretty marbles of word-things to see one catch and reflect the fire of another, a pleasant enough game but one which must eventually go stale. (Percy, 1958, p. 93)

What Percy is saying is that figurative language, like all language, always requires a tacit bond between speaker and listener. The listener, in most contexts, assumes the speaker intends to say something and if this trust is misplaced "the jig is up." All language, figurative included, depends upon an implicit contract between Namer and Hearer: the Namer promises to try and not speak non-sense while the Hearer pledges to try and understand what is said. If a language game is done in bad faith either by Namer or Hearer not only is communication impossible, the whole structure of interpersonal dialogue is endangered.

Thus figurative language cannot be the result of conjoining any two elements at random. There clearly is some requirement that the elements make sense intellectually and emotionally and it is precisely this criterion of intention that distinguishes figurative usage from gibberish. Figurative language must be interpretable and although the ability of a human language user to interpret the juxtaposition of almost any two words is awesome we must always remember that *figurative* language is after all, figurative *language*.

Although Percy's analysis again provides some new insight into the process, we still do not have any specific idea as to how the process of figurative transfer might work; we are left with the problem of model or mechanism. Perhaps the clearest approach to this problem within what we have called the transfer-analogy position has been presented by Black (1962) in his book *Models and Metaphors*. Black begins his analysis with the restriction that he will discuss metaphors only as they occur in the contex of a sentence(s) rather than in a phrase or in a single word units. A prototype sentence such as: *The chairman plowed through the discussion,* is analyzed into *frame,* its literal sentence components, and *focus,* its metaphorical sentence components. While this analysis uses terms reminiscent of I. A. Richards' (1936) *vehicle* and *tenor,* the major difference here is that Black views the literal element (tenor) in a much broader context than Richards. For Richards the tenor is given by a literal reading of the meaning of the sentence; for Black, the frame is given by an understanding of the unabstracted, literal components of the sentence; namely, *The chairman* and *the discussion* without the sentence's specific (figurative) focus, *plowed through.* In order to understand a metaphor then, the problem becomes one of knowing how to treat the (metaphoric) focus.

Black begins his analysis by describing various attempts at answering this question; attempts which have resulted in corresponding theories of metaphor. One such account leads to a substitution view of metaphor in which metaphoric expressions are understandable only in so far as an equivalent literal translation can be found. For this view metaphor becomes a more decorative or, perhaps, a more persuasive way of making a literal statement. Another description of how to treat the focus is offered by the comparison or similarity view in which the underlying process of figurative expression is seen as analogy or similarity. Here, it is assumed that the conjunction of two language elements is brought about by means of an awareness of an a priori similarity between the two objects or situations compared and it only behooves the would-be metaphor maker (or interpreter) to find those similarities.

Black contends that the first view can be dismissed by the existence of metaphoric expressions which lose their fullness once they are literalized, while the second view can be rejected since the author of a metaphor establishes rather than finds the various senses of an analogy. In addition, Black feels that the preexistence of "similar features" is entirely too vague and difficult a criterion to be applied rigorously at least in informal literary analysis.

Black's own answer to the puzzle of metaphoric meaning involves more than an extension of a simple transfer position. Rather, he prefers to view the relationship between A and B as interactive: that is, a situation in which the reader attends both to the old and the new meanings of the words involved. The words or ideas paired by an author are "active together and interact to produce a meaning that is a resultant from that interaction." When a word is used in a sentence context in a literal way, its use is governed by syntactical and semantic rules. In this situation, meaning is derived from the application of these rules to the sentence, with any serious violation of one or another rule system producing gibberish or nonsense. The process of metaphor involves pairing what Black calls two "literal use systems," with one system operating as the focus and the other as the frame. In Black's scheme the focus functions as a filter serving to organize and, to some extent, construct (or reconstruct) the perception of the frame.

A literal use system, however, is a far more complicated affair than the simple literal use of a word. Such a system consists of associated commonplaces, or those culturally agreed-upon lexical meanings which combine with the culturally agreed-upon myths, half-truths and mistakes of a particular society during a particular era. For Black, focus and frame comprise two systems with the critical aspect to metaphor having to do with the manner in which they interrelate. The process works, as a filter works, to insure the selective contrast of certain aspects of the associated commonplaces as well as the selective suppression of others. In general, the principle subject of a metaphoric expression is filtered by the action of a subsidiary subject or focus of the sentence.

On the basis of this analysis, Black has extended the transfer notion to one of interaction. It is not so much that one word or phrase transfers anything from itself to something else: rather both work on each other at one and the same time. A figure means to the degree that the elements joined are dealt with simultaneously; if one comes to dominate the other, selective emphasis so crucial to figurative expression does not obtain. The rule for a good figure, then, is one which recognizes that two items must be simultaneously held in relationship in order for one to serve as ground against which to see (understand) the other.

The process of figure interpretation is thus a wholistic process in which two or more items are contrasted against one another. For this reason, there are many figure—ground relationships possible and it is reasonable to suggest that two items linked metaphorically can either be in the relationship of same to same or of same to different. In the latter case, resemblance in difference, the critical aspect of the figure emerges as a contrast; in the former case, resemblance in similarity, the critical aspect emerges as in a summation. In either case, it is the qualities of the total figure that give selective emphasis to one or another of its constituent parts. It is not so much that figures transfer something from A to B; rather they produce a selective heightening or contrast of certain elements by forcing us to consider both A and B at one and the same time.

"Tension" as a Factor in Figurative Expression

With the realization that figures have their effect by requiring the reader or listener to consider two or more images simultaneous, it is clear that some kind of dynamic principle is needed to hold the combination together. Just such a principle has been proposed by Foss (1949) and extended by Wheelwright (1959, 1962) under the hypothesis of poetic tension. In order to understand this hypothesis in its larger context, however, it is first necessary to consider a prior question discussed by Wheelwright in his book *The Burning Fountain*. Wheelwright (1959) begins his discussion of figurative expression by considering the question: What does language mean in relation to the world? As a partial answer, he suggests that language has two complementary possibilities: (1) it is involved in the efficient communication of meaning, and (2) it attempts to communicate with maximum fullness of expression. In so far as the communicative efficiency of language is emphasized, the speaker uses what Wheelwright calls "steno-language." If, however, primary importance is placed on the fullness of expression, the speaker uses "depth-language."

Even though these distinctions seem to echo a difference between "rational" and "expressive" statements as described by Richards (1936), Wheelwright disavows any allegiance to this position:

> The position I have been defending is that steno-language . . . should be regarded as a limiting case of expressive language . . . and that steno-statements, therefore, . . . are limiting cases of expressive statements. . . . Scientific truth (verification as this is understood in the laboratory) is a limiting case of truth in general — a special type of what ought to be intellectually assented to. (Wheelwright, 1959, p. 298)

In giving expressive language this more inclusive status, Wheelwright sets the stage for his view that a metaphor, as a cognitive process, is an essential way of interacting with and understanding our world or what he calls reality. Here he argues that the most general property of both figurative language and poetry is that they partly create and partly disclose unguessed aspects of reality. For this reason every effective figure represents a perspective that is "individual and cannot be put into a class with other similar perspectives ... [it] is capable of eliciting a fresh response and fresh insight on the part of every attentive hearer or reader" (Wheelwright, 1962, p. 50). If reality is everchanging, so too is an appropriate figurative understanding of it.

Turning specifically to the process by which figures achieve their effect, Wheelwright (1962) begins by assuming that the essence of figurative language, "consists in the nature of the tension which is maintained among the heterogeneous elements brought together in one commanding image or expression (p. 57)." In this context, he draws heavily upon an earlier analysis by Martin Foss (1949) who described metaphor as a tensive process running through the texture of (all) expressive language and not confined to single words and phrases. In order to bring about such tension, Foss argued, the metaphor maker has to sacrifice the established senses of the words involved and it is precisely this semantic destruction which gives the metaphor its power to bring about novel understanding and insight.

While Wheelwright readily accepts Foss' notion of tension, he rejects the idea that metaphor involves semantic sacrifice or destruction; rather he opts for the idea of a vital synthesis instead. Such a synthesis occurs when the metaphor maker is able to integrate or make sense of the semantic and syntactical violations he has introduced with the understanding that these violations were undertaken in the first place with just this synthesis in mind. In this stance he reiterates the position put forward by Percy (1958) that figurative expression is not an accidental combination of words or images conveyed by words: rather, such a combination must always bear the intention and authority of a metaphor maker.

Dealing now with the tensive character of poetic language, Wheelwright (1962) suggests that metaphor can be divided into two types: epiphor and diaphor. Epiphor expresses a metaphor's capacity to extend meaning through comparison, that is, by expressing a similarity between something relatively well known or concretely known, and something which, although of greater worth or importance, is less known. Diaphor, on the other hand, creates new meaning by juxtaposing discrete images (which need not be epiphors) thereby leading to a new whole not decomposable into its linguistic elements. This new whole allows the user to see in a novel way.

Epiphor and diaphor are thus seen as complementary principles of figurative expression. Hester (1967) develops the epiphor—diaphor position in the following way:

> Epiphor means that metaphors are contagious. They tend to implicate wider and wider contexts in their semantic plenitude of implication. Diaphor, on the other hand, is a type of inward focus, an internal juxtaposition of qualities which gives the poem the concrete status of a presented object. The best metaphors display a fusion of diaphor and epiphor, the tension of which gives the metaphor its power. (p. 16)

Here then is just the dynamic principle required by Wheelwright's (1962) analysis — a metaphor works to the degree that it forces the reader to see some A both in a more profound (deeper) and in a more extended (wider) sense. It is the reader's oscillation between these two somewhat contradictory demands that keeps him involved with the successful figure, and it is this tension which ultimately enables him to come to some new personal understanding of A. Thus, the heuristic function of figurative expression can be derived as a consequence of poetic tension which leads the reader/listener to new insights. Such insights involve both the implication of wider contexts and the attainment of a more focused and detailed understanding of the particular issue at hand.

Poems, Poets, and Poetic Vision

Carried to its inevitable conclusion, any discussion of figurative language must end with a discussion of poetry. The pieces appropriate to this task have been assembled and all that now remains is to fit them into a single reasonable picture. Unfortunately, the pieces do not fall easily into place and it is difficult to describe precisely the nature of the bond relating figurative language to poetry.

To begin: a poem is always meant to present a description of some particular situation and, at the same time, to go beyond that situation to more universal concerns. Wimsatt (1958b) has dealt with this aspect of the problem in terms of what he calls the concrete–universal aspect of poetry. Although he never makes himself entirely clear as to whether a poem is a concrete–universal or simply makes use of concrete–universals, it is clear that for Wimsatt the descriptive aspects of poetry serve to reveal its concreteness while its semantic content produces its universality. This relationship is developed further by comparing poetic symbolism to a sculpture in stone:

> Poetic symbols ... call attention to themselves as symbols and in themselves invite evaluation .... The verbal symbol in calling attention to itself must also call attention to the difference between itself and the reality which it resembles and symbolizes .... In most discourse we look right through this disparity ... but poetry by thickening the medium increases the disparity between itself and its referents .... As a stone sculpture of a human head in a sense *means* a human head but in another sense *is* a carved mass of stone and a metaphor of a head, so a poem in its various levels and relations of meaning has a kind of rounded being or substance and a metaphoric relation to reality. (Wimsatt, 1958b, p. 217)

For this reason, all language has an interesting double function: to call attention to what it is about and to call attention to itself. Thus, poetry forces the reader to attend both to content and to style and a poem can be defined as great precisely to the degree that both content and style are in the service of a single purpose. In lesser poems, style or content dominates with the tension between the two dissipated in favor of one or the other.

Perhaps the most ambitious attempt to understand the interaction of poetry and figurative language has been presented by M. B. Hester (1967) in his book *The Meaning of Poetic Metaphor.* In this work Hester draws upon three major sources: Wittgenstein, Wheelwright, and Wimsatt. Hester summarizes the principal convergence found in their theories and this consensus leads him, following Wimsatt, to describe a poem as a concrete-universal. For Hester, one or all of three different things are implied by the term "concrete":

1. Reading poetry is a down-to-earth feeling experience.
2. Poetic language uses a very (concrete) particularity of detail.
3. Sound qualities present in a poem function iconically.

By the term "universal," Hester suggests that poetic language is related to a wider context than itself and that the logical elements of poetry must function iconically.

Accepting these generalizations about poetry, Hester relates them to the process of poetic metaphorizing which he considers an art form using language as its medium. But the medium of language has special qualities all its own and one of these is *sense*; that is, language communicates meaning and often does so in an abstract fashion. It is this quality of sense that gives poetic metaphor its universal feature.

Language as a medium also possesses the quality of *sensa*; that is, it is capable of generating images that evoke sensations relevant to all sense modalities. This notion of sensa adds a new dimension to the theory of metaphor and here Hester (1967) assumes that reading (and reacting to) poetry always involves a multisensory experience in the present tense; as we read it. Sensa not only includes auditory sensations specific to spoken or read language; it also produces sensations relevant to other sense modalities as well. In metaphor this broader understanding of the sensuous elements in the poem is essential:

> *Sensa* is a broader term and includes not only sound, that is, auditory sensations, but sensations relevant to all the senses. With regard to metaphor this broader understanding of the sensuous elements in the poem is essential. Metaphors will prove sensory in senses in addition to auditory sensations. I have in mind the ability of metaphors to arouse imagery. Imagery may appeal to any one of the senses. Metaphor will be seen to involve imagery which appeals to each of the senses and often to several senses at once in the phenomenon of synesthesia. (Hester, 1967, p. 119)

Drawing some inspiration from Wittgenstein (1953), Hester does not mean images in the sense that they are to be considered as ghostly internal events. Instead, he means the rather usual experience of having images during that special situation known as reading poetry. For Hester, as for Wittgenstein, the poetry game is often set up just so as to produce imagery and thus meaning has not been pushed "inside" (as Wittgenstein argued against doing) but is understood as the subsequent activity of imagining brought about by an intentionally evocative use of words.

The fusion of sense and sensa so essential to this task is achieved through the process of reading or as Hester calls it, "that stance appropriate to metaphor." The special sense of reading intended by Hester (1967) represents an amplification of Husserl's (1931) concept of *epoche*: a mode of consciousness in which, "consciousness in itself has a being of its own which in its absolute uniqueness of nature remains unaffected by the phenomenological disconnexion [p. 113]." Reading metaphor then involves a special state of consciousness – a special situation, as Wittgenstein might say it – in which questions of fact and fancy, reality and unreality are held in abeyance for the time being. For this reason, reading considered as an epoche "allows for the original right of all data presented by the metaphor during the act of reading [Hester, 1967, p. 119]."

If this is the case, how are the metaphoric images to be controlled when "the original right of all data" is respected? For Hester, such images are controlled in four ways: (1) by a common shared language which forces a limit on the number of images possible within a given language community; (2) by the common body of historical associations shared by words and images; (3) by the intention and stylization of the author; and (4) by the experience—act of *seeing as*.

This final element of control, seeing as, Hester considers to be the "fundamental distinguishing characteristic of metaphor in poetry." Seeing as is that part of the intentional structure of metaphor which selects the relevant aspect of metaphoric imagery. This concept is drawn from Wittgenstein (1953) who defined seeing as as a process of "noticing an aspect" of various language usages rather than as "seeing in the mind's eye." It is, however, more than that for Hester who describes it as a process "based upon the ability to execute a technique" and it is this execution which distinguishes seeing as from simply *seeing*, a process which he describes as relatively passive and nonconstructive. Poetry then requires work for its understanding and this work is best captured in terms of the active process termed "seeing as."

All of this talk about work leads one to ask: work for what? Is there anything to be gained from poetic work other than work itself? Here we must turn again to the poets for guidance and the overriding conclusion seems to be that poets often sense an interpersonal and epistemic significance to figurative language. So, for example, Wallace Stevens (see Sheehan, 1966) believes that poetic metaphor serves as a mimic for, and of, the structure of reality. The poet only discovers resemblances between real and imagined things and it is these imagined things which the poet tries to "fit" to reality. For Stevens, the interaction between reality and imagination defines the only mode by which we can know reality at all and the method by which such imagination works is metaphor.

Another poet sharing a similar point of view is James Dickey. In a speech delivered at the Library of Congress in 1967 Dickey offered some ideas quite similar to those presented by Stevens. The major difference between the two was Dickey's strong emphasis on the poet's role in transfiguring and recreating reality by a "deliberate conjunction" of disparate items in the real world rather than in simply perceiving it. Dickey, however, went even further in his explanation of the metaphoric process. Metaphor, for Dickey, begins with an image (an "iconic thread") which poetic intelligence sees as pervading one or another aspect of reality. The poet's job is to seek out such threads of continuity and find some way of recombining them in a fruitful and literate structure. The final structure, achieved in combination with apt and salient language comes to define poetry and poetic language.

For Dickey and for Stevens, as for many other poets, poetic language does more than simply concretize, emphasize, or entertain. It creates a tension whereby the reader or listener is compelled to move forward with the poetic image and thereby to redefine his or her world or some aspect of that world. All thinking operates on the basis of a similar "poetic plan" which, in turn, suggests that poetic analysis is concerned not only with poetry but with the more significant task of how universe and mind are fitted to one another (Sewell, 1964).

One rendering of this relationship has been made by assuming a reciprocal correspondence between intelligence and world, with the world yielding patterns and structures of perception and understanding to intelligence, which, in turn, is shaped and formed by intelligence's typical structures and operations (Sewell, 1964). Under this analysis, epistemology and poetic diction are finally joined and any analysis of mind comes down to an analysis of the processes it exhibits. In the end, mind is method, and one clear method of mind is poetic metaphor.

The view that language shapes reality and vice versa has its proper philosophical ancestry in the analysis of symbolic forms proposed originally by Cassirer (1953) and made more accessible by Langer (1957). For Langer, as for Cassirer, metaphor represents only one special application of a more general human tendency to symbolic transformation; that is, the tendency to "see" one thing as another with no direct utilitarian purpose in mind. Although Langer has sometimes gone so far as to propose a "need for symbolization" her basic premise in regard to metaphor is much less radical: that metaphor is in some way a fundamental process by which language and thought grow and that such mutual growth allows for an evernew description and understanding of the world. To this line of approach, metaphoric thinking applies not only to poets and scientists but serves as a means by which all people sort their perceptions, evaluate their ideas, and guide their actions. Metaphoric activity is not the treasured possession of a few specially tuned geniuses; rather it is basic to thinking and speaking at any level and in any thinker and speaker.

If figurative language represents a basic expression of human symbolic activity, then the essence of language is not denotation, but connotation. Langer, following the same general lines of analysis as Cassirer (1953), sees the development of language as involving a transition from emotional to propositional language, where both flow from the basic human act of symbolic transformation. The construction of reality begins with nondiscursive or figurative expression and on this basis it is easy to see how a theory of metaphor automatically implies a theory of the world. The metaphoric process is the law by which language grows while discursive or rational speech is only a later development in this life. As Langer (1957) puts it: "Speech becomes increasingly discursive, practical, prosaic, until human beings can actually believe that it was invented as a utility and was later embellished with metaphors for the sake of a cultural product called poetry [p. 126]." According to Langer, in the beginning there was the poetic metaphor; only later was there the scientific word.

We could do no better than conclude this discussion of the difference between the scientific word and poetic diction than with a quotation from the poet–critic Paul Valery. In this extended quote Valery (1961) describes the poet as a person who has decided to change the function of language — to change as he put it, "the walking of prose to the dancing of poetry":

> Walking, like prose, has a definite aim. It is an act directed at something we wish to reach. Actual circumstances, such as the need for some object, the impulse of my desire, the state of my body, my sight, the terrain, etc., which order the manner of walking, prescribe its direction and its speed, and give it a *definite end.* All the characteristics of walking derive from these instantaneous conditions, which combine *in a novel way* each time. There are no movements in walking that are not special adaptations, but, each time, they are abolished and, as it were, absorbed by the accomplishment of the act, and by the attainment of the goal.
>
> The dance is quite another matter. It is, of course, a system of actions; but of actions whose end is in themselves. It goes nowhere. If it pursues an object, it is only an ideal object, a state, an enchantment, the phantom of a flower, an extreme of life, a smile — which forms at last on the face of one who summoned it from empty space [p. 70].

SUMMARY AND CONCLUSIONS

Metaphor suggests poetry: poetry, literary criticism; literary criticism, philosophy; and philosophy, a world. The world, in its turn, suggests metaphoric and poetic perception and on this basis the cycle completes itself. The close association existing among all of these disciplinary pieces suggests that there is no one way in which to talk meaningfully about figurative language and that we must consider it from a great many different points of view. For this reason the clean metallic lines of disciplinary analysis must be blurred if the phenomenon of figurative expression is to be clearly presented. Figurative language always implies something beyond itself and it is this conceptual play that explains its appeal, its function and its ubiquity.

From a wide variety of different spoken and written samples we have seen just how ubiquitous figurative language actually is. Although the number 20 million is a large one, it does not seem large enough to capture how many individual figures a speaker will produce in a lifetime and any analysis of human language which does not take figurative usage into account must now be, and is destined to remain, an incomplete one. Simply stated, human beings use an enormous amount of figurative language and 20 million is only a low estimate.

Given such extensive usage it seems reasonable to ask why speakers resort to figurative language when they always would seem to have available a much less ambiguous possibility in literal expression. The issue here revolves around the idea of literal language and the conclusion must be that literal language is not all that literal. It is perhaps too strong to say that a philosophy of meaning which can only ask, "to what do words refer?" is at fault, yet this seems to be the case. The naming function of all language changes both our view and our way of talking about reality and it remained for Wittgenstein (1953) to overthrow the referential theory of meaning by asking "how do speakers use language," rather than "to what do words refer."

With the idea that meaning is better construed as use rather than reference, the notions of literal and figurative must change in character. Although it may be going too far to say that all language is at base figurative, it does not seem to be going too far to say that language structures reality and that the poet as well as the scientist bring a world into being through their varied language games. It is perhaps most important to keep in mind that discursive scientific language is quite probably a later development than figurative language and that before the detached, cool denotative use of language can occur the speaker must already have used language in a much more excited and connotative way. This, of course, is the point made both by Cassirer (1953) and by Langer (1957).

With this as a basic premise, it is not at all difficult to see why a seemingly ornamental aspect of language such as metaphor can be so useful in so many different contexts. Although it is unnecessary to list all of its functions some are quite surprising at least when considered from a simple ornamental point of view. Foremost among these is the heuristic value of figurative language. In situations ranging from a psychotherapist's couch to an industrial consultant's laboratory, figurative language has been shown to promote innovative problem setting and problem solving. Similarly, analogic thinking has been shown to operate in the model-building enterprise so crucial to scientific work. Finally, there is the vocabulary augmenting role of figurative language and here the notions of frozen figurative language and Sperber's law come to mind. Only those figures which once blazed brightly for a particular age find their way into the dictionary of future ages and the history of a prior age would seem to be writeable in terms of its more salient metaphors.

Figurative language also seems to have some less desirable functions as well. Here we need only think of the strategic use of a clever figure to end a political argument or the possible use of a figure to mask an improper impulse in a psychotherapeutic interview. In both of these cases, the speaker calls attention to his or her language rather than to its content, thereby seeking to divert the listener from a clear understanding of what is being said.

But most figurative expression is more benign than this and it seems reasonable to ask into the process or processes by which figurative language operates.

Although a great many different theories have been proposed all seem to agree that a figure works to the degree that it provides the listener with an exciting experience as he or she encounters the figure in speaking or writing. The basis for such excitement comes, according to Wheelwright (1959) and others (Foss, 1949), from the tension brought about by combining heterogeneous elements. Such tension is seen as the result of two complementary processes, epiphor and diaphor, which force the reader to deal with the elements of the figure in both a wider and narrower (more focused) sense. The method of metaphor, then, comes down to one of simultaneous interaction where the elements paired must form a new whole having unique properties of selective emphasis and contrast. Only if such a new gestalt emerges from the combination is it possible for a figure to bring about its varied effects.

Poetic language forces tension in still another way and this has to do with the distinction between form and content. For most speaking situations form remains submerged in content: we are usually aware of what is said rather than how it is said. Figurative expression calls attention to the medium itself and in this way forces the listener or reader to pay simultaneous attention to both medium and message. In good figurative usage form and content fulfil a single intention; in lesser usage one or the other dominates. In all cases, however, it is the tendency of poetic language to demand its due that makes us stop and ponder not only content, but style, as well as style and content.

On the basis of these analyses it does not seem as if good poets and good literary critics take their work or their criticism too seriously. To solve the riddle of poetic language would be to solve one aspect of the riddle of human symbolic activity. Regardless of the view, and whether it derives its orientation from philosophy or poetry, the conclusion seems to be that not only does a theory of metaphor grow out of a theory of aesthetics (and vice versa) but metaphor and aesthetics must also have close ties to a theory of epistemology. Poetry is an everfresh way of dealing with reality and of coming to grips with that reality. What we have here is the view that figurative language in conjunction with other nonliteral symbols represents a primary human mode of dealing with the world. This occurs because in each of us there is a touch of the poet, a touch which makes its inevitable presence felt in the widespread use of figurative expression in every language, as well as in every language user, no matter what the context or how varied the purpose.

2
Models of the Metaphoric Process

In her dissertation dealing with the role of metaphor in creative problem solving, Mawardi (1959) noted that it was often quite difficult to distinguish between remarks intended to evoke laughter and instances of figurative language. Although perhaps surprising at first, such a finding seems quite reasonable for a number of different reasons: For one, groaning laughter often follows that special category of figurative language known as puns; for another, triumphant and/or appreciative laughter often accompanies a particular figure that just exactly captures whatever it was that needed capturing; and finally condescending laughter often goes along with that awkwardly graceful creature known as the mixed metaphor.

Puns, as Arthur Koestler (1964) reminds, represent the tying together of two ideas by way of a single phonemic knot and the combination either can be well balanced and clever or awkward and forced. A simply pun like "I'm descended from a very old line my mother fell for" works precisely because all parts of the pun combine easily and well. The change from one meaning of "an old line" to another, while dramatic, still deals with the same basic generational—sexual issue and here the phonemic knot makes a clever and balanced package. On the other hand, there are a number of puns, many of which have been assembled by Bennett Cerf (1966) in his *Treasury of Atrocious Puns,* which evoke a groan (if that) mostly because atrocious puns seem to force rather than tie together originally disparate elements.

Consider the following rather random selection, contained incidentally in a section entitled, "Pundemonium: Short Puns For People In A Hurry":

1. An eccentric bachelor passed away and left a nephew nothing but 392 clocks. The nephew is busy winding up the estate.

2. I know a dermatologist who built his practice very deliberately: he started from scratch.

3. One of those currently popular Indian guru's hops around a great deal more than his fellow contemplators — that's why he's known as a Kan-guru.

The third of these three puns is obviously the worst: there is no intrinsic, or for that matter, extrinsic relationship between kangaroos and gurus other than that the verb hop was applied to both and that with coercion both can be made to sound alike.

From one point of view, however, the Kan-guru pun is of more than quickly passing interest because of the somewhat nonliteral use of the word "hops"; and it is this somewhat figurative usage that brings the pun into being in the first place. More explicit figurative usage is involved in the first and second puns where frozen expressions — "winding up an estate" and "starting from scratch" — create the joke. In both cases, the pun comes about from playing on the literal and frozen figurative uses of these two phrases. In a sense, both puns are somewhat more clever than the Kan-guru joke mainly, it would seem, because a meaning rather than simply a sound combination is involved.

But not all puns are forced to this extent. Sometimes as in the case of the "descended old-line" pun previously described a number of different themes are presented, combined, and resolved with an apt and abrupt change of focus. Since changing focus is one of the characteristics of useful figurative language, puns of this sort do represent innovative linguistic usage. As a matter of fact, puns seem to have a reputation much worse than they deserve. There is almost no language in which they do not occur and often some of the greatest writers in that language have made use of this particular linguistic structure. Shakespeare, and lesser early poets such as Thomas Hood ("They went and told the sexton, and the sexton toll'd the bell") all used this device as have more contemporary light poets such as Ogden Nash. In general, Boswell's attitude seems reasonable: "A good pun may be admitted among the excellence of lively conversation."

But what exactly is a good pun? Probably because most puns are not good, an early etymological dictionary (Skeat, 1898) derived the word *pun* as an obsolete variation of the verb "pound;" as in the expression, "to pound words; to beat them into new senses; to hammer at forced similes" (p. 120). The idea of forcing seems to be the one that gives puns a bad name for, as we have said before, atrocious puns force combinations and show little understanding or respect for the connotations of the constituent words. Not so with good puns where all parts combine to form a coherent, well-balanced and appropriate whole. As a matter of fact, a good pun which also has some significant topical substance in addition to its more formal properties clearly deserves recognition as a clever and innovative piece of language usage on a par with that of other figures of speech. The only difference here is that the intent is to make someone laugh other than one or more of the functions usually expressed through figurative usage.

Although there is no completely satisfactory explanation as to what makes any event or statement funny, it does seem clear that some aspect of superiority or self-glory is often involved. This is as true on a theoretical basis — it was Hobbes who said, "Sudden glory ... maketh those grimaces called laughter" — as on an empirical one — we laugh when the clown gets hit in the face with a pie or when one comedian successfully puts down another via the verbal thrust. In terms of this analysis, two of the three situations in which Mawardi (1959) noted that figurative language was confused with humorous remarks (puns and mixed metaphor) are somewhat demeaning to the speaker while the remaining situation (a really good figure) involves a clear statement of superiority for the speaker as well as for the clever enough listener.

What all of this would seem to mean in the context of puns (and figurative language more generally) is that there are two types of superiority possible: (1) when I appreciate the pun (it makes me feel clever to understand such a complex combination); and (2) when the pun is so bad that by groaning I (gently) put down the person making it. In the case of appreciation—understanding, there is a very old observation which notes that a listener generally enjoys any joke — but especially a pun — better when it is told in a foreign language, for here there is double achievement: getting the double meaning and getting it in the foreign language (Ludovici, 1932).

There is still one further case of figurative expression in which humor results because the speaker is demeaned. This deals, of course, with that awkward literary construction known as a mixed metaphor. In order to locate some examples of this somewhat esoteric breed it is necessary to step outside of a more strictly literary context and look instead at the prose of high-school and college students. Here, in addition to agrammaticisms and misspellings, we often find prime examples of this genre, one of which is presented by Owen Thomas (1969) in his book on metaphor: "A virgin forest is one in which the hand of man has never set foot."

The humor in this sentence basically revolves around a number of different (metaphoric) words and phrases: *virgin, hand of man,* and *never set foot.* Leaving, as we should, the first of these alone for the moment, we note that *hand of man* and *never set foot* are both frozen figures that draw whatever inspiration they have left from parts of the body: unfortunately for our would-be writer, different parts of the body, but body parts nonetheless. The idea of *virgin* similarly has a body referent and although the metaphor is confused as a literary structure it works as a kind of joke precisely because of the confused, but still interrelated, set of words and images evoked. Since as we have said, part of a humorous response often comes from some feeling of superiority on the part of the laugher there is really a double superiority here: (1) in the reader's ability to find a common thread; and (2) in seeing the undoing of a possibly pretentious, or at least, inexperienced writer.

Probably the most widespread use of puns and other intentional word play is to be found not in high-school or freshman college compositions but in that special variety of childish game known as a riddle. Who has not cringed at riddles of the following type (as before, Bennett Cerf, 1966, is to thank for this collection):

Q: What's a crick?
A: The noise made by a Japanese camera.

Q: What's the best way to drive a baby buggy?
A: Tickle its feet.

Q: What did Paul Revere say when he passed a London Barber Shop?
A: The British are combing.

As in the case of atrocious puns, we've saved the worst for last. Even in this case there is something of interest: the riddle can only be understood if we are familiar with the admittedly trite phrase "the British are coming." In the absence of such knowledge the riddle (and the pun derived from it) cannot be understood.

The first riddle, however, really is probably closest to what is usually meant by a (bad) pun with a simple phonetic alteration producing the effect. Yet even here some prior knowledge is required about Japanese pronunciation of English. The second riddle involves a piece of frozen figurative language for its effect: only if *buggy* is understood as *crazy* or *agitated* in some way does the pun come off. In any case it is clear that puns and other less sound-related word play do figure in riddles and this is a possibly significant observation. Although riddles cease to have any great appeal for most adult speakers (Bennett Cerf excluded) their widespread occurrence and appreciation among children does seem to indicate that there may be a close relationship between puns, figurative language, humor, and problem solving.

In a sense, then, these examples suggest that the lowly pun can be found at one early nexus of a number of significant intellectual operations: figurative language, humor, and problem solving. The implicit, and often explicit, word play involved in childish riddles suggests that such play is not without developmental or cognitive implication, and it was none less than the austere Gestalt psychologist Koffka who began his section on problem solving with an analysis of a joke based on a pun (Koffka, 1935, Chapter 13). For Koffka, as for Koestler (1964), jokes have much in common with many different kinds of problem-solving and poetic activities (and vice versa), and the problem becomes one of describing these relationships in some kind of reasonable detail. For Koestler (1964), the essential process involved in seeing the point of a joke, understanding a poetic image, or in solving a difficult problem is a combinatorial one he has called the bisociation of ideas. The major difference between these three activities is not cognitive; rather it is motivational: jokes involve what Koestler calls "self-assertive motive systems" such as aggression or sexuality; poetry involves "transcendent emotional systems" such as awe or sympathy; while "rational" problem solving involves a blend of emotional states derived in large measure from the self-asserting and self-transcending varieties.

For Koffka, as for Maier (1932) before him, the issue was not one of motivation but one of set or attitude. Koffka sees the essential aspect of understanding a joke, a poem or a problem as involving a perceptual–conceptual reorganization of parts presently not forming a single coherent whole, as for example, the vehicle and tenor of a particular figure of speech or the stem and punch line of a joke. Such reorganization, however, is determined by the wider connotations of the words or images involved so that the resulting combination is not due to the simple addition of contiguous elements but to an ongoing process which builds a new structure capable of encompassing the original component pieces.

Although Koffka (1935) does not directly discuss the aesthetics of poetic imagery, he does note that jokes are not problems and that this difference is best captured in terms of what he calls the context of the joke or problem. Jokes, and presumably poems, work by setting up a particular context — in the case of humor what Maier has called the *joke attitude* — and such context moderates or modifies any and all combinations occurring within it. By joke attitude, Maier simply means that in order to understand a joke the listener must suspend, or at least vary, his or her everyday attitude so that sensibly, nonsensical combinations and situations can be dealt with and understood.

Thus, for Koestler as for Koffka there is nothing really very surprising about Mawardi's (1959) observations. There often is a profound relationship between figurative language and humor as well as between both of them and the more respectable phenomenon of creative human problem solving. Although it does seem to be going a bit too far to see all problem solving as identical with humor and figurative expression, it does not seem to be going too far to note that figurative language (and humor) are significant intellectual operations and that one way in which a child comes to be able to do all three is through the (incessant) telling and retelling of riddles at a particular development level.

Although there is no really secure data on this point, recent work by Shultz (1972, 1974; Shultz & Horibe, 1974; Shultz & Pilon, 1973) does bear on the issue. Following an earlier lead provided by McGhee (1971), who found a positive relationship between some aspects of concrete–operational thinking and a child's ability to understand jokes, Shultz looked at the developmental course of joke appreciation for many different kinds of joke ambiguities. All of these ambiguities involved an incongruity of one or another type, with the major types involving ambiguities of sound, grammar, or word meaning. Results showed that even though six-year-olds could understand why certain items were incongruous, they could not understand many of the resolutions presented, and therefore did not find many of the incongruities funny.

More relevant to cognitive development, older children could understand both joke incongruity and joke resolution. There were, however, differences among the various types of incongruities studied. Word jokes were understood developmentally sooner than syntactic jokes, which in turn were understood somewhat later than simple puns or other kinds of lexical substitutions. In general, the greatest increase in laughing and smiling at any and all jokes occurred at about eight years of age — or just about at the same time riddles run riot.

The conclusion to all of this work on joke appreciation must be that there is a strong relationship between understanding a joke and the development of more general problem-solving abilities. Since many of the jokes used involved an appreciation of various types of figurative usage, it seems reasonable to propose that such usage also follows a similar developmental course. A more complete evaluation of developmental trends in figurative language use and comprehension as well as their relationship to problem solving is presented in Chapters 7, 8, and 9; at this point suffice it to note that developmental trends in figurative language are compatible with those reported for joke appreciation. Joking and speaking figuratively would seem to have much in common, not only for the adult but for the child as well. This conclusion seems warranted, whether we approach it from the joke or figurative-language point of view.

SOME FORMAL CATEGORIES OF FIGURATIVE EXPRESSION

There are really two quite different ways in which to use the word metaphor. In one of these, the word is used in a generic sense and can be considered as a synonym for words and phrases such as figures of speech, figurative language, poetic diction, and so on. This is basically the way in which it has been used to this point. There is, however, another more technical sense in which the word can, and often is, used and this is as one of a much larger set of figures of speech most of which have fairly exotic and esoteric sounding Greek names. The need to provide a somewhat more formal definition for the various categories of figurative expression — metaphor and puns included — is a debt long overdue and the following discussion is meant to provide some feeling for the range and variety of figurative expression delineated by grammarians and rhetoriticians.

Metaphor, Simile, Oxymoron, and Personification

Perhaps the major reason metaphor is used as the generic label for all figurative expression is that it most clearly exhibits the combinatorial nature of such usage. Whether in its mixed or unmixed form metaphor seems descriptively to involve the putting together of a number of different pieces even if some of the pieces do not always go together all that well. But what of other figures? Do they share this same relational property? Metaphors and similes can both be defined somewhat more formally as linguistic devices which make an explicit or implicit conjunction or comparison between two ideas; ideas that share some common, though often highly imaginative, feature. A *simile* is an explicit comparison between two things and is signaled specifically by words such as "like," "as," and "as if." In the case of both metaphor and simile the same pattern is descriptively obvious: two initially unlike words or phrases are likened to one another.

A different way of linking one thing to another is through *oxymoron,* or by pairing two terms that are ordinarily thought of as contradictory. The oxymoron is thus a unique form of figurative language in which normally opposed terms are used to express a single idea. For example, in the phrase: *love is such sweet pain, sweet* and *pain* are both equated to *love* as a single idea. Normally these terms would not be used together; they do, however, express the idea that love, while being very good, can also hurt.

Although this first group of figures does function on the basis of comparing one thing to another a special subcategory of comparison, *personification,* does this in a rather special way; namely, by investing abstract ideas or concepts with human qualities, vices or virtues. In such cases as *the sea beckoned me* an inanimate object is described by a mode of acting usually found only among the animate. *Apostrophe* represents an even more special case of personification. It occurs when an absent person or a personified abstraction is addressed: *"Death, where is your string?"* or *"Courage, do not fail me!"*

Synecdoche and Periphrasis

Synechdoche and periphrasis represent figures of speech which can be described best by the phrase, "the part for the whole, or, the whole for the part." *Synecdoche* is a substitution of an attribute or suggestive word for what is meant; it is a figure of speech in which a part stands for a whole or the whole for a part:

1. If you are serious about betting, let's see some *green*.
2. Let's take a *head count* to see how many showed up.

In each of these examples the word used is actually a part of a larger whole: green for money, head for people.

Periphrasis is defined as the "substitution of a descriptive word or phrase for a proper name or a proper name for a quality associated with the name" (Corbett, 1965, p. 443). Using phrases such as "Uncle Tom" and "Jim Crowe" are modern examples of periphrasis; calling someone "Brutus" or "Apollo" would be a literary or historical bit of periphrasis. A final example might be: "Tom is helpful, but he always *leaves a silver bullet* when he departs." *Silver bullets* refer to Tom's theatrical manner of casting the limelight upon himself much in the style of the Lone Ranger.

Hyperbole, Litote, and Irony

For purposes of convenience the next set of figures are grouped together because they presuppose that the speaker and listener share some knowledge of the subject matter under discussion. They work not by comparing one thing to one or any other but by a deliberate use of over, under, or opposite statement.

Hyperbole involves the use of exaggeration, whereas *litote* is a conscious understatement designed not to deceive but to emphasize. The third type of figurative language considered here involves the use of a word to convey meaning opposite to the literal meaning of the word and this, of course, is *irony*; like, "General Custer was a *brilliant strategist* at the Little Big Horn." This basic idea of irony is clearly apparent in that the listener must be aware of the actual events upon which its use is based.

Puns and Onomatopoeia

Finally there are those figures of speech which depend upon sound, and play with sound and meaning, for their effectiveness: *puns* and *onomatopoeia*. Although we have discussed puns previously, it is clear that pun is a very broad term often used to cover a variety of ways that people make a play on words. The grammarian usually differentiates at least three distinct categories of puns (Corbett, 1965):

1. *Antanaclasis* occurs when one word is used or repeated in the same context in two different senses:

    a. *Watch* your *watch*!
    b. The pot party was to be held on *High* Street.

2. *Paronomasia* is a play on word sounds. Two or more different words that sound alike are used in the same context:

Knock, Knock. Who's there? Adolf. *Adolf* who? *A dolf* ball hit me in the head — that's why I talk like dis.

3. *Syllepsis* is the use of a word in relation to two or more words, which it modifies or governs. However, the word is understood differently in each relation:

    a. He *lost* his hat and his temper.
    b. *Turn on* your radios and your minds.

Finally *onomatopoeia* is an unusual form of figurative language in that its only definite identification is the sound value of the words used to produce an effect on the reader or listener. The onomatopoeic word not only conveys a meaning but also produces sound in the language appropriate to the item intended. Examples of this class of figurative language that can be found in an ordinary dictionary include words such as "hiss," "crunch," "bang," and so on.

The problem with schematic definitions of this sort is that although they do tell how to recognize figurative language, they do not specify in any detail what happens psychologically (or even linguistically) when two or more different linguistic pieces are combined. Although philosophers and poets have had something to say about the nature of the combinatorial process involved in figurative language and poetry (see Chapter 1, pages 18–25), the specific mechanisms, both within the person as well as within the language system, have yet to be described in any real detail. In the case of the person, the question is largely psychological; in the case of the language system, the question is largely linguistic. For this reason it is not surprising to find that most theories of how figurative language works are given from the perspective of the psychologist, the linguist, or from some combination of both. For the psychologist, the problem has been seen as one of describing the mechanism by which a combination between two or more originally disparate elements is mediated; for the linguist, the question of mechanism comes down to one of describing how the rules of language use need to be modified (if at all) to account for figurative expression. In either case it is clear that any description of the psychological or linguistic mechanisms by which figurative language works will not only have to encompass each of the various types of figures discussed but will also have to provide some provision for describing its relationship to more general cognitive abilities such as are involved in understanding jokes or in solving problems. With this as a general framework we can now turn to a more detailed and specific presentation of the mechanics of metaphor.

THE MECHANICS OF METAPHOR

Recent psychological interest in the topics of human symbolic activity — most especially language and meaning — certainly begins with Osgood, and, therefore, it is not surprising to find that Osgood (1952, 1953) should have begun his work with an analysis of synesthesia and metaphor. As a matter of fact, interest in these topics seems to have led fairly directly to the consideration of meaning as a mediational process and this too is not surprising: both synesthesia and metaphor (as well as a great many other psychological processes) can be seen to involve combining responses from two separate domains. In the case of synesthesia, the domains involve separate sensory modalities while for metaphor they involve separate words, phrases, or ideas. In both cases, the associative principle of response mediation seemed to Osgood (1953) to provide a basic operational device, and all that was required to explicate metaphor (as well as synesthesia) was some technique to assess the underlying mediational response(s). As is well known, the semantic differential provided just the technique needed (Osgood, Suci, & Tannenbaum, 1957).

But metaphor also figures in Osgood's approach in yet another way, and this is in terms of the way in which flesh and blood subjects make use of the semantic differential. Brown (1958b) in his review of Osgood's work asked whether "a boulder was sweet or sour" and by this meant to imply that it was highly unlikely that subjects using a semantic differential (SD) scale did not often, if not entirely, use scalar adjectives in some metaphorical sense. Indeed most sets of instructions provided to subjects using the SD such as those used by Jenkins, Russell, and Suci (1958) stress the fact that metaphoric usage is appropriate: as they say, both trains and girls can be rated "fast," and although this use of the word does not represent great metaphorical usage, it is metaphorical, nonetheless.

For Osgood, synesthesia and metaphor are comparable phenomena and both can be taken as more particular instances of mediated generalization. Although the specific way in which this occurs was handled quite informally by Osgood (1953; Osgood, Suci, & Tannenbaum, 1957) the rudiments of his argument can be simply stated: two domains of experience can be tied together to the degree that they evoke a common mediator. Although Osgood specified fractional mediation responses as of prime importance in carrying the mediation function, other investigators have stressed word associates (Deese, 1965), imagery (Paivio, 1971), or some combination of all three as of crucial importance (Pollio, 1966, 1974).

With specific regard to metaphor, mediational analysis have been provided for the word-associates approach by Koen (1965) and for more general mediational responses by Osborn and Ehninger (1962). Since Koen's model is conceptually the simpler of the two, it seems wise to begin with it. Basically, Koen assumes that words or phrases used metaphorically have associative connections with one another as well as with other words, and that such associative halos provides much of the meaning evoked by a given metaphoric expression. In order to test one prediction from this position — that context words associatively related to metaphoric usage will cue metaphoric choices and context words associatively related to literal usage will cue literal choices — Koen performed the following experiment. In this experiment, the subject's task was to listen to five words and then choose one of the two possible words or phrases in a sentence of the form: "The sandpiper ran along the beach leaving a row of tiny STITCHES/MARKS in the sand." The five words preceding the presentation of the target sentence were free associates to either the literal word in the sentence (MARKS) or to the metaphorical one (STITCHES).

Three groups were given these tasks: Group 1 heard associates appropriate to the literal term; Group 2 heard associates appropriate to the metaphorical term; while Group 3 heard a mixture of both. The results were in the expected directions: Group 1 consistently (75%) chose the literal word, Group 2 chose (67%) the metaphorical usage, while Group 3 showed no special preference.

Koen's interpretation assumed that the five preliminary words served to set a frame of semantic reference prior to the subject's task. Unfortunately, he presented no data as to what would have happened had he not established any of these contexts. In addition, Koen evaluated the goodness of metaphoric choice and found a slight negative correlation ($r = -.33$) between frequency of metaphoric word choice and goodness. He also found that figures which stayed in the same modality were judged as less good that synesthetic figures; that is, where the words joined crossed dimensions.

Despite such preliminary results, no one has taken up the word-association approach and Koen's study remains the single example of this particular type of mediational analysis. Such a seeming lack of interest is really not all that surprising especially in view of the extremely simple nature of the experiment and of its underlying conceptual basis. Without going into an extended analysis it is clear that this experiment really has very little to do with figurative usage in more ordinary speaking and listening contexts. While it is a reasonably clear experimental demonstration of the role of prior context in word choice, it is not really very clear how word contexts such as those used in this experiment make contact with linguistic and interpersonal situations appropriate to the production or understanding of figurative language in poetic, as well as in ordinary, speech contexts.

A somewhat more broadly based approach, drawing in equal measure from Osgood and Ogden-Richards, has been proposed by Osborn and Ehninger (1962) and extended somewhat by Reinsch (1971) and Jordan (1972). In their view of mediation theory, which is aimed specifically at metaphoric usage in public address, Osborn and Ehninger begin by considering metaphor as both a "communicative stimulus" and a "mental response." Although the metaphoric process involves both aspects only the listener's response is described in any detail. For Osborn and Ehninger, the mental activity involved in interpreting a metaphor is composed of three phases: error, puzzlement, and resolution. The process begins when a listener first erroneously interprets the figurative word in its usual sense. This is then followed by a period of puzzlement in which the ordinary meaning of words contained in the figure are found not to apply and this period is then followed by a period of resolution in which the actual metaphoric work goes on.

Although Osborn and Ehninger introduce a great many different terms designed to explicate the process, the major aspects of this process and their structural relations are probably best presented in Figure 2.1. The *subject* and *item for association* appearing in Figure 2.1 refer respectively to what the metaphor is about and to the related idea by which it is expressed. So, for example, in the phrase: "The British Constitution is our foundation," "British Constitution" is the subject and "foundation" is the item for association. The terms tenor and vehicle, borrowed very loosely from Ogden and Richards, represent the mental concomitants of subject and associated item, respectively, and it is the interaction of these two ideas that gets the metaphoric job done. The line of x's in Figure 2.1a represent the semantic distance between tenor and vehicle at the beginning of resolution while the vertical lines in Figure 2.1b represent the bond linking elements of the figure after resolution.

In addition to these four components, another group of events called *qualifiers*

2. MODELS OF THE METAPHORIC PROCESS   43

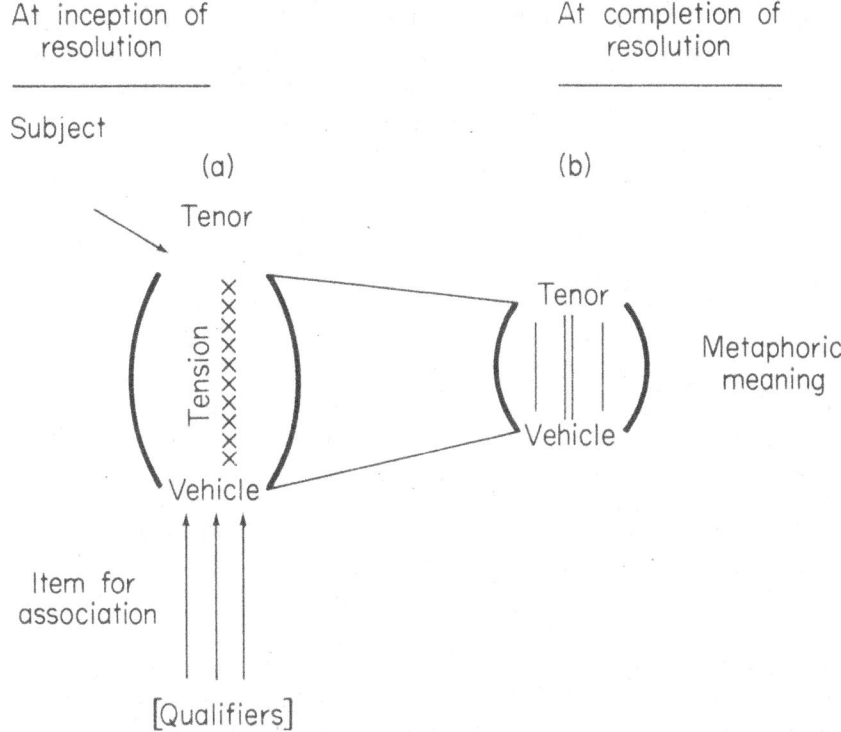

FIGURE 2.1   Osborn and Ehninger's (1962) model of metaphoric interpretation.

helps to give some direction to the final resolution of a particular figure. For this reason qualifiers are referred to as "forces which formulate lines of association" between figured elements. As their name would suggest, qualifiers serve to distinguish which of the many possible similarities two items may have in common will actually be responded to; that is in the figure, "he was a lion in combat," the phrase "in combat" specifies courage, ferocity, power, and so on, as the relevant aspects, while implicitly rejecting as irrelevant such things as hairy, four legged, having a tail, and so on.

Within this approach, it is possible to distinguish among various degrees of metaphor usage ranging from fresh, living figures, through to dead, frozen ones. Fresh, or living, figures occur when the distance between tenor and vehicle is large (but not so large such that no points of contact can be made); frozen metaphors occur where there is no resolution required: tenor and vehicle are already perfectly associated so that the vehicle seems absolutely the only word choice possible as the arm of a chair, and so on.

In the context of associationistic theory, it is clear that all three models considered thus far (Osgood's, Koen's and that by Osborn and Ehninger) involve pairing and mediated generalization as basic operations. In addition all three models revolve about the idea of a transfer of meaning from vehicle to tenor. These models, in so far as they go, are true both to the description of a metaphor as involving pairing and to the idea of a transfer of meaning. Unfortunately, exactly how such transfer might take place is not specified very fully; nor, for that matter, do they deal with some of the more dynamic interaction effects suggested by philosophical analysis. Transfer, for these models, always seems unidirectional — from vehicle to tenor — and there is no real provision for how figurative language could serve any of the functions figures usually serve.

The one aspect to this class of models that is interesting, however, is that they tend to describe figurative language as involving processes no different, in principle, from those involved in other psychological processes. Although the principle of mediated transfer surely does not capture all there is to be captured about figurative usage, it does at least have the value of allowing us to consider figurative language as continuous with other cognitive and linguistic operations. This class of models then, would have no real problem with the fact that ordinary speech exhibits an enormous quantity of figurative language, and that such usage seems to have something to do with helping us form concepts and/or solve problems.

This potential strength, however, would seem to be a liability in talking specifically about the case of poetry. In mediational theory, there are no principles that deal directly with language considered as a system. In order to extend this position to handle some of the more ordinary problems posed by literal language use, Osgood (1968) found it necessary to import principles from other disciplines such as linguistics and computor science. For this reason it is not surprising to find the mediational approach somewhat unprepared to deal directly with poetry. Such a conclusion, need not necessarily be a very damaging criticism largely because mediation theory operates on the explicit assumption that the proper order in which to handle behavioral phenomena is from simple to complex. With this as an underlying principle, the complexities of poetry must wait their turn; that is, until the relatively simpler issues of ordinary language use have been worked out.

Not all models that deal with the semantic aspects of language use share this particular point of view. Perhaps the major approach to the problems of semantics which does not share this simple-to-complex strategy involves what have come to be called semantic feature models. These models all have their origin to a greater or lesser degree in linguistic rather than in psychological analysis and for this reason deal with features rather than responses, although as Osgood (1968) and others (e.g., Pollio, 1974) have pointed out, meaning responses considered from a mediational perspective can be considered equivalent to semantic features. For this reason, it seems appropriate and reasonable to consider featural models as a further development of the more general class of models which involve elementwise combination as the basic process involved in figurative expression.

FEATURE MODELS OF METAPHOR

If Osgood is the father of psychological analyses of meaning and metaphor, then Katz and Fodor (1963) must take responsibility for a similar paternity of semantic-feature models. The basic outlines of their position are too well known to be described in detail; for our purposes it is enough to note that the problem of metaphoric usage intruded itself into the very first featural analysis of that seemingly innocent word, "bachelor." In his critique of this model, Bolinger (1965) noted that it was not accidental that "bachelor" had at least four distinctly different, but related meanings:

(1) Young male fur seal without mate during breeding season.
(2) Young male knight serving under the banner of another knight.
(3) A person having the first or lowest academic degree.
(4) A male who has never married.

While the markers and distinguishers found in the Katz and Fodor (1963) system do serve to denote specific senses of the term "bachelor," there are no real rules for figurative relationships among the various senses of the term. And it is quite clear that all four senses are in fact related by meanings deeper than simple markers and distinguishers.

One of the more troublesome parts of the Katz–Fodor model, regarding figurative language, concerns their notion of selection restriction. Generally speaking, selection restrictions determine which word can properly go with which other word. So, for example, "drinks" is marked as a verb [+ verb] with the restriction that it can only be used with a human subject [+ human], as in the sentence

He [+ human] drinks water.

The difficulty with holding to the idea of strict selection restrictions appears in a very low level figurative expression such as

My car [− human] drinks gasoline.

In a sense, figurative expression often involves the violation of selection restrictions thereby rendering the whole idea of restriction empty of any real significance.

On two counts then — that different dictionary meanings of the same word can be coordinated by figurative relations and that figurative language regularly violates selection restrictions — the original Katz–Fodor model falls into difficulty. Largely because the original model fit so well into Chomskian theory, much subsequent work in transformational semantics can be considered as one or another attempt at repairing some or all of these initial difficulties. Although such repair work did not always directly concern itself with figurative expression, many of the changes suggested do have strong implications for such usage. In one early attempt to improve this state of affairs Weinreich (1966) proposed what he called a *construal rule* which was thought to provide a theoretical device whereby speakers and listeners would be able to handle seeming violations such as those that occur in figurative usage. Take, for example, the sentence

He trues the theorem.

Since "trues" is not in the dictionary with the grammatical category making [+ verb] Katz and Fodor would not allow the sentence, and, therefore, would have to consider it as agrammatical. Such a conclusion is obviously false: the sentence can be meaningfully and consistently interpreted. Weinreich's (1966) construal rule operates, as he put it: "in construing a new semantic entity with a more elaborate structure in which the transferred feature is decisive, but in which the contradictory feature can be accommodated" (p. 462). For this analysis, the contradiction brought about by dictionary restrictions can be resolved by restating the sentence in the following way:

He proved the theorem to be true.

Although a procedure such as this does resolve the difficulty, it is quite cumbersome to apply. Despite this, it represents a genuine attempt to accommodate figurative usage (as well as language flexibility more generally) within the confines of a featural approach to meaning.

A more direct linguistic approach to metaphor via a semantic features model has been presented by Thomas (1969). This approach assumes that all noun definitions, such as for the word "boy," etc., are given implicitly or explicitly by a simple declarative sentence of the general form

Boy is a noun.
Boy is an animal.
Boy is a human.

Words, therefore, are defined by a specific sentence type which presents the specific set of features defining the word. As an example consider the following dictionary definitions of the word "child," and Thomas' (1969) proposed featural analysis of it:

1. an infant; baby. 2. an unborn offspring. 3. a boy or girl in the period before puberty. 4. a son or daughter. 5. a descendant. 6. a person like a child in interests, judgment, etc., or regarded as a child; immature of childish adult. 7. a person regarded as the product of a specified place, time, etc.: as, a *child* of the Renaissance. 8. a thing that springs from a specified source; a product: as a *child* of one's imagination. [Thomas, 1969, p. 20]

As is obvious, Definitions 1–5 are literal while Definitions 6–8 are clearly more figurative in nature. On the basis of Definitions 1–5 Thomas proposes the following *feature matrix* as appropriate for "child":

Child
+ noun
+ common
+ countable
+ animal
+ human
+ infant / unborn offspring
+ boy / girl
+ time before puberty
+ son / daughter
+ descendant

In actual language use, not all features occur each and every time a word is used even when the word is used literally. For example, the sentence:

My child likes ice cream.

immediately precludes [unborn] as a feature and presupposes [+ alive] as one. The sentence:

My child has three children.

presupposes not only [+ alive] but [+ pubescent] as well. What this means is that for certain uses, certain features (usually low level) are ruled out by the logic of the sentence and that not all features are used everytime the word is used.

The situation, however, is quite different in the case of figurative language: the features that need to be ruled out (or "blocked," as Thomas calls it) usually are not low level or slightly redundant ones; rather they are among the most pervasive and far reaching of the total set. For example, in Definition 8 (a child of one's imagination) almost all high-level features would have to be blocked. For this reason, blocking does not seem a reasonable mechanism by which to include figurative usage in a feature model. Instead of blocking Thomas suggests that certain syntactic devices, such as the use of words like *like* or *as*, allow the reader "to tolerate" rather than block inappropriate high level features. By tolerate, Thomas seems to suggest that the listener/speaker still has, so to speak, both the appropriate and inappropriate features available to him or her during figurative expression. Unlike more literal usage where certain lower-level features are excluded (or blocked), figurative usage represents a selective emphasis of one feature at the expense of certain others. In the case of child, Definition 8 selectively emphasizes the feature [+ something created] at the expense of the features [+ animate] [+ human], and so on. The process of metaphor then becomes one of transferring features from one matrix to another, with emphasis for some and tolerance for all the major operations by which metaphors are brought into being and understood.

But figurative language always occurs within some syntactical frame and for this reason, Thomas also analyzes the role of syntactic factors in figurative usage. Within the grammar of a language there are two types of errors that can occur in talking or writing, taxonomic and operational, and both of these provide some possibilities for those "intentional" mistakes known as figurative expression.

Taxonomic features within the grammar include such things as a word being a noun or a verb, or perhaps more particularly, a mass noun or a transitive verb. In addition there are taxonomic semantic features such as markings for [animate] or [human] or more particularly, for [male] and [female]. As is true of syntactic markings, semantic features are also thought by Thomas (1969) to be hierarchically arranged so that if a morpheme or word is marked as [+ male] it must automatically also be marked as [+ human] and further on up the line as [+ animate].

Operational errors are errors of sentence formation and here the most familiar ones are the usual bugaboos of high school and college composition writers: sentence fragments, improper agreement, as well as faulty subordination, coordination and/or modification.

With all of this grammatical and semantic machinery in hand, Thomas (1969) deals with the major categories of figurative language — metaphor, simile, personification, and so on — as taxonomic violations of either the semantic and/or syntactic systems. Semantic violations, of course, are more usual: for example, in the case of transferring animate features to inanimate matrices (personification), or as in transferring concrete features to abstract ones as in the line "Shame is a pink shawl" (Emily Dickinson). Syntactic violations, being less frequent are usually more shocking as, for example in e.e. cummings': "he sang his didn't/he danced his did," in which *didn't* and *did* are treated as nouns, rather than as verbs.

The joint ideas of featural hierarchy and grammatical violation are central to Thomas' analysis. Both arise from the cardinal linguistic assumption that language is a well-organized system and that any and all aspects of language usage must make use of the system in highly determinate ways. Featural hierarchies are essential because they provide for great conceptual economy. If we know

2. MODELS OF THE METAPHORIC PROCESS   49

some morpheme is marked as [+ female], we also know that it is marked as [+ human] and as [+ animate]. Syntactic order is necessary if we are to distinguish grammatical from ungrammatical sentences in the simplest and most elegant way. Within a theory such as this, violations of the usual system, either semantic or syntactic, are essential to figurative language and in fact represent the basic source of novelty found in figurative expression. As a final remark Thomas (1969) notes: "When a writer uses figurative language he is asking his reader for the privilege of violating normal linguistic structure: he therefore assumes the responsibility of rewarding the reader for his permission by making such violations significant" (p. 62)."

Not all linguistic theories of metaphor agree with all aspects of Thomas' analysis. Although Bickerton (1969) does agree that language is a system and that figurative language involves an intentional violation of the system, he explicitly denies the hierarchy notion espoused initially by Katz and Fodor (1963) and more recently by Thomas (1969). Most especially damaging in this regard is the fact that certain metaphoric expressions such as "bachelor girl" (wherein lower order markers such as [+ single] are able to override higher order markers such as [+ male]) are recognized as sensible even if impossible or inappropriate on the basis of a hierarchical analysis.

Even in regard to the issue of rule violation, Bickerton (1969) notes that while metaphors can be represented as violations of one or another rule, not all rule violations are figurative in any clear-cut sense: "Poverty gripped the town" is easily and obviously figurative, while "Ability gripped the town" is not, upper-case letters notwithstanding. This is true despite the fact that the same subcategory restrictions have been violated in both cases. After a few further examples of this type, Bickerton (1969) concludes: "Thus there is no level of rule violation at which metaphor and non-metaphor cannot co-exist, and no means ... (at present) ... for distinguishing between them at any level" (p. 41).

For Bickerton, the solution to these problems would seem to be to abandon a hierarchical notion and come instead of recognize a multidimensional feature grid having no fixed ordering for semantic categories. In addition, he proposes that we recognize a scale of possible figurative usage ranging from (1) literal expressions at one end to (4) possible anomaly at the other. Intermediary positions of figurativeness would include (2) permanent assignments, and (3) temporary assignments, with both of these categories corresponding to frozen and novel usage, respectively. On this basis it is clear that certain words become marked with certain properties as critical. In English, iron is marked as [+ hard], diamond as [+ expensive], bachelor as [+ unmarried], and that these words carry this property into any combinatorial situation, metaphoric or otherwise.

Although such a suggestion is not carried out in any great formal detail, Bickerton (1969) does provide the following informal illustration of how this approach might work. Consider the two oppositions, Married/Single and Male/

Female, and form an appropriate 2 × 2 table as follows:

		Feature A	
		[+ Married]	[+ Single]
Feature B	[+ Male]	(a) husband	(b) bachelor
	[+ Female]	(c) wife	(d) spinster

Of the four words (a), (b), (c), and (d), contained in the table, only the marked word "bachelor" seems able to cross the Male/Female categorization and produce an acceptable expression such as *bachelor girl.* All other possible crossings (*Unmarried wife, *Unmarried husband, *spinster boy), while producing interesting social and linguistic possibilities, do not have the proper feel to them and must, according to Bickerton (1969), be assigned to the category of potentially metaphoric but presently anomalous.

In this example, only one of the four words was able to cross a feature boundary and produce an acceptable figurative expression. The point to this must be that natural language is able to tolerate two different kinds of rules operating over even the same set of examples. In the case of *spinster* no such cross-feature movement is possible; in the case of *bachelor* such movement is not only possible, but has already occurred and been accepted into common (frozen) usage by most speakers. Such a state of affairs suggests more generally that semantic feature combination must be talked of in terms of at least the following two different rules:

Rule 1: There exist two features, A and B (each having a + and − marking) such that the intersection of $[+A]$ and $[-A]$ and $[+B]$ and $[-B]$ is mutually subdividing and sets up four discrete categories $[+A]$, $[+B]$; $[+A]$, $[-B]$; $[-A]$ $[+B]$; and $[-A]$ $[-B]$.

Rule 2: There exist two features, A and B, wherein certain combinations are compatible across one feature $[+B]$ and $[-B]$, while incompatible on the other $[+A]$ and $[-A]$. Thus, some combinations simultaneously can be compatible and incompatible.

To return now to the bachelor-girl example it seems reasonable to suppose that bachelor is marked + for [single] and + for [male]. The word "girl;" which is marked for + female (or [− male]) and + for [single] therefore ought not to be able to take the word *bachelor* as an appropriate adjective. On the basis of Rule 2, or some similar rule, Bickerton (1969) proposes that *bachelor* is able to cross the [Male/Female] feature, but not the [Single/Married] one. On this basis, bachelor girl is an acceptable combination, whereas none of the other combinations (such as *spinster-boy) are acceptable. Rule 2, therefore, is suggested by Bickerton as a theoretical mechanism whereby a nonhierarchal featural approach would be able to handle figurative expression.

As Bickerton notes, language, most especially literal language, runs according to Rule 1 while figurative language seems to run according to Rule 2. A conceptual frame of mutually exclusive subcategories as implied by Rule 1, according to Bickerton (1969), is

> far too rigid to accommodate the Heraclitean flux which is our day-to-day experience... while we can hardly begin to think without setting up categories, we need, for many practical purposes, to be able to make connections between them, connections which a strict adherence to [Rule] (1) would make impossible. Thus the system of [Rule] (2) has to be invoked; and, as we shall see, this system rules the attachment of attributes, and the superstructure of true metaphor which is erected on it. (p. 45)

For Bickerton, then, figurative language necessitates the introduction of a rule which allows for cross-category crossings. Literal language is seen to require distinct markings as in the original (and subsequent) model, while figurative language is seen to require a loosening of such a strong and inflexible system of binary categories. Still within the spirit of a feature model, Bickerton has suggested not only that figurative language requires its own rule of composition but that the idea of a strict featural hierarchy must be given up. The reasons for these changes are motivated not only by strictly linguistic concerns but by some psychological ones as well. It is as much a matter of suggesting a theoretical mechanisms capable of encompassing a constantly changing set of Heraclitean categories as it is a matter of accounting for *bachelor girl* in purely linguistic terms that gives direction to much of Bickerton's attempt at revising semantic feature theory.

Metaphor, Presuppositions and Some New Features for Semantic Theory

Bickerton is not alone in his attempt to recast semantic feature theory by taking more of the speaker/hearer's context to account. While it would be inaccurate to say that presupposition theory came about primarily because linguists were unable to handle figurative language in any consistent or reasonable sort of way, it is true that such considerations did play a minor role in their dissatisfaction with early feature models. As we have already noted, two of the earliest critical analyses of the Katz–Fodor model – one by Bolinger (1965) and the other by Weinreich (1966) – did, in fact, emphasize its difficulty with figurative usage. More serious and far-reaching criticisms, however, were raised on purely linguistic grounds so that it now seems fair to say that most attempts to deal with semantic problems from a featural point of view consist of nothing less than a complete revamping of the structure of such theory within the generative–transformational approach to language (see Maclay, 1971, for a clear and well-developed historical presentation).

The single major conceptual innovation involved in such attempts at repair concerned the notion of a presupposition, and for a while in the early 1970s it seemed as if the psycholinguistics world was going to overrun with papers on presuppositions. (See Fillmore & Langedoen, 1971; or the linguistic section of Steinberg & Jakobavitz, 1971, for examples of the coming deluge.) Despite this extensive outpouring, it is now clear that presupposition was not a clear concept and seemed to have been used in at least two quite different senses: (1) as a logical device designed to answer questions of entailment, truth value, synonomy, and the like; and (2) as a pragmatic device designed to provide some possible ways of taking speech contexts into account (Wilson, 1975).

Characteristic of its first use is some work by Leech; first in an original contribution dealing with verbs (Leech, 1971) and second within the context of his text on semantics (Leech, 1974). Much of this work stemmed from earlier philosophical analyses in which an attempt was made to see what was, or was not, presupposed in the form of implicit propositions so as to make a given sentence understandable. So, for example, a sentence such as

The earth goes around the sun.

presupposes the proposition that the earth moves. Although a number of formal statements have been made to describe what is meant by logical presupposition, a reasonable and simple definition describes it as a relationship between two propositions, X and Y, such that anyone who utters X takes for granted the truth of Y (Leech, 1974, p. 292).

For psychological purposes, however, the role of contextual presuppositions in speech acts seems more directly related to figurative expression than to the description of presupposition as a logical device. Here the major treatment was provided by Fillmore (1971) who used the sentence:

Please open the door.

as an example of this approach. In analyzing this sentence, Fillmore makes a distinction between its presuppositions and its meaning. Included in its presuppositions are those that relate to the hearer's knowledge of what door was intended and that the particular door in question was not open at the time the request was made. The distinction between meaning and presupposition is given by the fact that the same set of presuppositions apply to the sentence

Please don't open the door.

even though the "meaning" is quite different in terms of what is being requested.

Thus, for Fillmore (1971); as for Lakoff, 1971; and McCawley, 1968) presuppositions reintroduced the speaker's world into semantic analysis. Although it would take us too far afield to discuss the more general implications of this approach for linguistic theory (see Maclay, 1971, for some discussion on this point) it is necessary to tie this work on both aspects of presupposition theory to the topic of figurative expression. In its speech act or context stance, presupposition theory seems to suggest that there is an implicit presupposition made by every Hearer that the Speaker listened to is trying to "make sense" and is not trying to speak nonsense. What this means vis-à-vis figurative language is that infrequent or even odd word and sentence usage will not immediately be dismissed as non-sense; rather the Hearer will attempt to provide some interpretation for almost any and all utterances no matter how deviant they may appear when considered in isolation from the total speaking situation. Sentences and phrases would seem to be anomalous only within the abstracted context of linguistic analysis, hardly ever within the context of speaking human beings. All that limits the Hearer's understanding is the Hearer's "imagination" or knowledge; hardly ever the oddness or infrequency of a given bit of language use.

Presupposition also enters the picture in terms of its logical aspects. In one sense, a sentence or phrase can only be seen as metaphoric if there is some contradiction, or at least some strangeness, in one or another of its constituent propositions. From the viewpoint of logical analysis, the philosopher Michael (1974) has suggested that the recognition of nonliteral speech depends on the presence of certain semantic conditions which lead to rejecting the literal usage or meaning of an expression. For this purpose, six conditions seem most important:

1. No literal meaning is possible; that is, words are not used in their dictionary senses ("he drinks power").
2. A literal meaning is obviously false ("the black cloud carried the sun away").
3. A literal meaning is rejected because it is self-contradictory ("I'm there but absent").
4. A literal meaning is rejected because it is a pointless truism ("a dollar is a dollar").
5. A literal meaning is rejected because it is contextually unacceptable ("a light walks around the dark towers").
6. A literal meaning is rejected upon instruction ("I wasn't talking about that . . .").

In order to exclude anomolous sentences — that is, sentences which juxtapose words leading to seemingly uninterpretable meanings — it is necessary to meet one further condition in defining a usage as metaphorical and this condition, according to Michael (1974), is that the metaphor bear "some . . . relation to one of the [possible] literal readings [of the expression] . . . which . . . provides a [consistent] interpretation for it" [p. 60].

The addition of presupposition as a theoretical concept in linguistics would seem to have added a major new dimension to the nature of semantic analysis. Within the context of featural analysis it is necessary not only to take featural combinations into account but their logical and communicative aspects as well. These new theoretical endeavors all take issue with one of the basic assumptions of the original Katz—Fodor model: that semantics had to be dealt with theoretically as independent of what can best, but crudely, be called the world of the speaker; that is, in a particular sociolinguistic context. The work of Fillmore

(1971), McCawley (1968; 1971), Lakoff (1972), and others all seems geared to put linguistics back into the speaking context of the world, and the way in which this has been done is through the use of the theoretical notion of presupposition.

A word of caution, however, need be sounded not only in regard to figurative language but more literal language usage as well. Not everybody is satisfied with the theoretical status of presupposition theory. So, for example, Wilson (1975) has attacked the whole endeavor in both its logical and contextual aspects as being unwieldy and confusing. More to the psychological point, however, has been the work of Rommetveit (1974) in which he deals specifically with the assumption that logical form and presupposition are somehow separate from one another and that in the end the meaning of a sentence is to be understood on the basis of analyzing its constituent propositions:

> The games of ordinary language are often very subtle and composite games, with multifaceted and fluctuating premises for intersubjectivity. A model of linguistic competence in terms of abstract propositional structures and invariant semantic features may still be useful, however, even when inappropriate as judged from the subtle meta-contracts and contracts of actual use: it may, for instance, allow us to reveal contradiction... The outcome is primarily an explication of anomalies, however: actual use is only indirectly described, as deviance from some hypothetical (or 'ideal') standard based upon an erroneously postulated separation of reasoning from... [interpersonal] orientations... (Rommetveit, 1974, p. 83)

Despite these objections the attempt to handle contextual aspects of the speech act represents a genuine advance for semantic theory. In terms of figurative language such emphasis suggests that figurative expression can only be understood on the basis of changing the order of features suggested by two or more words as well as on the basis of changing our presuppositions about the conditions of the speech act itself. In this latter regard it is useful to keep in mind that figurative language is figurative only to the extent that we recognize the speaker's intention to speak figuratively. As Rommetveit (1974) noted, there is nothing particularly poetic about the statement "a grief ago" when produced by a student learning English as a second language. When the same expression is encountered in a poem by Dylan Thomas we not only accept the phrase as meaningful, we are even likely to feel that we have been party to a very special experience in human life. Only the newer linguistic approaches, which (however primitively) put semantics back in language and language back in the world, seem able to encompass facts such as these; and it is the significance of facts such as these that are suggested by a sensitive attitude toward figurative expression.

A Psychological Feature Model

Not all feature models, however, have been developed by linguists. Although a number of different psychological feature models have been developed to deal with a wide variety of cognitive processes such as learning, remembering, and so on, there is only one such model directly concerned with the topic of figurative language and that was proposed by Michael Johnson in 1972. As is true for linguistic models of the metaphoric process, Johnson assumes a multidimensional feature grid, although in this case concepts (or meanings) are broken down into purely theoretical components known as *elementary cognitive characteristics* (ECCs) (Johnson, 1970). Given this assumption, the structure of one part of the lexicon can be represented as shown in Figure 2.2. The part labeled Register indicates the ECC pattern of that concept, word, or morpheme at present being held in mind.

Actually Johnson's model, as is true for most models, is concerned with interpreting figurative language rather than in describing how it is created in the first place. For this model, the meaning of a word is given by its pattern of ECC entries. Thus, Concepts 1 and 2 in Figure 2.2 are more similar in meaning than Concepts 1 and 3. That this assumption has some experimental validity to it has been shown by Deese (1965) in an extensive series of word-association studies as well as by Johnson in the context of a compound-associations task (1970).

In terms of metaphor, Johnson (1972) suggests that the effective meaning of a combination of nouns such as occur in a metaphor or simile of the form *A is B*,

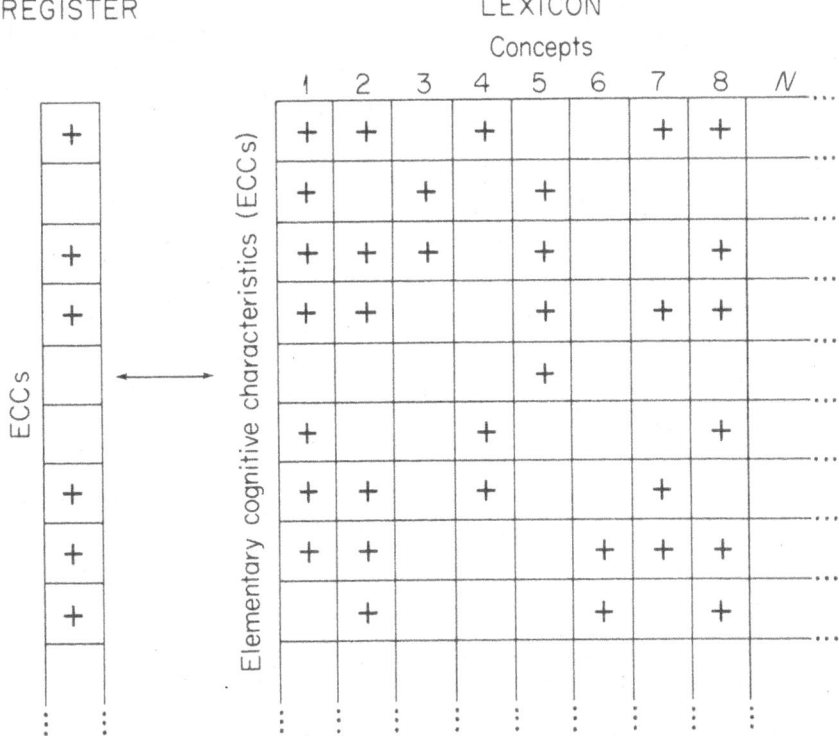

FIGURE 2.2 A schematic representation of Johnson's model. (From Johnson, 1970).

or A is like B, is an additive summation of the ECCs defining each word. This means that those features which both words share are raised in salience for the compound; that is, they become more important in determining the effective meaning of the compound, while nonshared features, although still present in the cognitive register are less salient, and, therefore, less significant.

In order to explore some of the implications of these ideas within the context of an experimental study Johnson (1972) first selected 28 literary metaphors, ranging from Shakespeare to McKuen, and then asked different groups of subjects to respond to them in a number of different ways. One of his tasks required subjects to rate the metaphors on a 1–5 scale of goodness while a second required them to interpret the metaphor. The second task served as the basis on which Johnson developed a measure of interpretability for all of the figures presented. Other procedures involved the following five tasks:

1. association to words used figuratively within the context of the metaphor;
2. association to words used figuratively without metaphoric context;
3. similarity judgments, in context, of words linked in the figure;
4. similarity judgments, without context, of words linked the figure; and
5. a listing of common properties for key words given out of context.

The results of these procedures allowed Johnson (1972) to intercorrelate all seven measures across all 28 figures, and his results are presented in Table 2.1. The overall impression emerging from an examination of these data is the relatively large number of significant correlations: almost everything seems to

TABLE 2.1
Correlations between Various Characteristics of Metaphors and Words Used to Form Metaphors[a]

	Interp.	Unc. in	Unc. out	Sim. in	Sim. out	Entropy of shared properties	Number of shared properties
Goodness	.593[b]	−.006	−.165	.365	.567	.465	.397
Interpretability	–	−.424	−.474	.768	.819	.571	.395
Associative uncertainty in context[c]	–	–	.802	−.682	−.479	−.832	−.500
Associative uncertainty out context[c]	–	–	–	−.657	−.523	−.779	−.409
Similarity in context	–	–	–	–	.815	.772	.434
Similarity out of context	–	–	–	–	–	.565	.417
Shared properties: Entropy measure Numerical measure	–	–	–	–	–	–	.609

[a]From Johnson (1972).
[b]Any value above .317 is statistically significant ($p = .05$).
[c]Associative uncertainty value for each word set computed on the basis of Garner's uncertainty analysis (see Johnson, 1970, for details).

correlate with almost everything else. Perhaps the most relevant result concerns the high correlation between interpretability and goodness and that over all measures the best predictor seems to be similarity out of context, although almost all measures do intercorrelate well. Johnson also looked at multiple correlations and found that it was possible to predict figure goodness from everything else at a level where $R = .73$ and figure interpretability from everything else at a value of $R = .89$.

What do these results mean? On the face of it the easy implication is that metaphor is dependent on similarity, and that's all there is to it. Johnson, however, is careful to make the point that correlation and causality are two different things and that while metaphor goodness is related to similarity it probably is best not to consider it as causality related in any direct way. What seems more reasonable to suppose, Johnson argues, is that whenever words are put together in a situation where the listener feels he is not being tricked — that is, where he presupposes a genuine attempt at communication — there is the possibility for metaphoric interpretation. The act of looking for similarities is an interpretative act and like the act of judging metaphors is performed on a meaning created out of a linguistic situation in which two words are put together.

By this device, Johnson means to explain that both word to word similarity and good metaphor involve a constructive meaning-seeking act on the part of the listener. In this way, the seemingly static, almost computerlike, nature of his version of the feature model is given a bit of life. This device and its attendant theorizing really represent one way in which to come to grips with some fundamental aspects of figurative language: words do seem to have usual meanings, and, either singly or in combination, also seem to be capable of having their meanings modified, changed or selectively reorganized. It is just this amoebalike quality to word meaning that is so difficult to conceptualize and which seems to require a much less structured lexicon than originally proposed by Katz and co-workers.

In one sense, Johnson's (1972) model yields quite satisfactory results: it not only is theoretically neat and operationally testable; the data obtained also are in agreement with theoretical expectations. In another sense, however, there is a sharp discontinuity between the model as stated and tested and Johnson's speculations about interpretive acts, the creation of meaning and so on. Like many of the more purely linguistic featural approaches discussed earlier. Johnson's model seems to run into the problem of activating an essentially inert vocabulary. While words do seem to have partially fixed meanings, speaking (and most especially figurative speaking) seems to require a much more dynamic and fluid conception of the speaking vocabulary. Speakers often seem to deviate from established usage and this is especially noticeable in the case of figurative language.

All of these considerations raise the very difficult question of what does it mean to say that a person "knows" a word or "has" a word in his or her vocabulary? Traditionally a question such as this is usually answered by reference to something static like an "internal dictionary" or a "lexicon of attributes." In either case, a word is considered a possession of the speaker in somewhat the same sense that the speaker owns a bound dictionary or thesaurus. But "to have a word" isn't the same as that: to "have" a word is to be able to use a linguistic unit with both a history and a future; and in which present usage is only partially constrained by past use. Words provide the raw material out of which speaking is constructed — but it is the speaker who continues to offer old uses or to develop and create new ones as appropriate to the speaking situation.

Given these considerations it is clear why somewhat static feature models must have difficulty in dealing with creative-language usage such as involved in figurative expression. From this review of a wide variety of different featural approaches it is clear that such theory usually comes to handle figurative language as somehow or other violating the rules of one or another component of the language system — be this component, syntactic or (more usually) semantic. Figurative language, then, is construed as a violation of literal language, a conclusion quite at variance with many of the philosophical and poetic conclusions represented in the previous chapter. For a poet such as Valery, figurative language is a natural aspect of ordinary language use. It is always a purposeful extension of the language system; never a capricious violation lightly undertaken.

The idea that figurative language may require us to consider new meanings as emerging in a particular context suggests that Gestalt psychology might have something to say about the processes involved. Although Gestalt Theorie has concerned itself with the topic of figurative expression from time to time, the references are widely dispersed in the gestalt literature and often cryptic in nature. For these reasons, it is not always immediately clear what gestalt psychology says about the processes involved in figurative language and, therefore, it is necessary to look at a number of different Gestalt authorities in coming to some possibly coherent picture. It is this collative task which forms the topic of the following section.

PERCEPTUAL MODELS OF METAPHOR

The prototypic statement dealing with figurative language by a significant gestalt theorist has been made by Kohler (1929) when he quoted the following line of poetry:

Die Möwen sehen alle aus, als ob sie Emma hiessen.
[All seagulls look as though their name were Emma.]

To which Kohler (1929) adds: "[the poet] I find was quite right — all seagulls do look as though their name were Emma [p. 133]." Following this, Kohler then presents his famous demonstration example of "maluma" and "tuckatee"

FIGURE 2.3 (a and b) Kohler's *maluma–tuckatee* figures. In Kohler's demonstration, subjects are asked to match the nonsense words *maluma* and *tuckatee* with the two constructed figures presented above. The invariable match is between *maluma* and (a) and between *tuckatee* and (b). (From Kohler 1929, p. 135.)

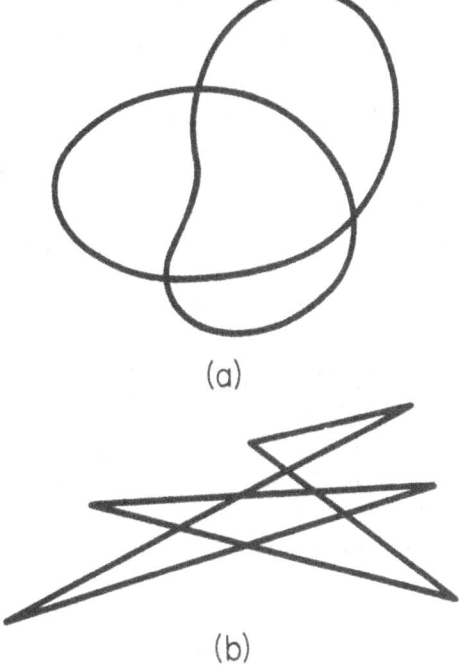

(see Figure 2.3a and b) and proceeds to discuss more structured metaphoric usages such as "bitter feelings," "bright joy," "hot wrath," and so on.

What Kohler argues in all of this, is that seeing one thing as another is a regular and naturally occurring experience undoubtedly at the heart of the linguistic device known as figurative language. This "seeing one thing as another," in addition to its naturalness, is thought to emerge from common perceptual experience and that such experience underlies both poetic imagery and its verbal expression. The seagull and its name share much in common and it is this commonality of perceptual experience, rather than of atomized detail or feature, which enables the human observer to match not only Emma with seagulls, but *maluma* and *tuckatee* to their respective shapes.

Given the significance and power of such experiences, one question, which suggests itself, concerns the generality of metaphoric usage across different language families. In an attempt to answer this question Asch, in two separate papers (1955, 1958), examined cross-cultural and cross-language use of words that relate both to perceptual and personality domains; that is, double-function terms such as "cold," "warm," "crooked," and so on. Basically, Asch's studies dealt with two different questions:

1. Do historically independent languages employ the same morphemes to designate both physical and psychological properties?

2. Do languages belonging to different language families agree in the detailed couplings they make?

Operationally, the second question can be phrased: Do different languages use the word "straight," for example, to designate both the true alignment of an object and the honesty of a person; and if they do, do they make use of this particular coupling?

For his sample, Asch (1955) chose five languages that differed markedly in terms of language family and historical epoch: Ancient Hebrew (Semitic), Ancient Homeric Greek (Indo-European), Modern Chinese (Sino-Tibetian), Modern Thai (Sino-Tibetian), and Malayalam (Davidian). On the basis of his analysis, Asch reports:

1. All five languages use dual-function expression; that is, use certain words to express both a physical and psychological property.
2. All languages possess *some* morphemes of a physical–psychological pairing similar to, or identical with, English couplings.
3. A morpheme referring to a given physical property may develop psychological meanings not identical in all five languages.
4. A morpheme is often used solely in a physical sense but never only in a metaphorical sense.

Thus, the answer to his first question is "yes" while the answer to his second question must be "sometimes."

In a somewhat different type of linguistically motivated study, Ullmann (1946, 1957) examined metaphoric transfer between components of synesthetic–perceptual imagery used by 11 different English and French poets of the 19th century. His basic question was to find out if there was any regularity in the "source" and "destination" of such imagery. So, for example, in Keats' line in "Isabella," "Taste the music of that pale vision," Ullmann (1957) reckons two transfers: "one from taste to sound, the other from sound to sight" (p. 278). In order to present his results somewhat more systematically, Ullmann organized the senses in the form of a hierarchy, with what he termed the least differentiating senses such as *touch* and *temperature* at the bottom, and with the most differentiating ones such as *sound* and *vision,* at the top.

Given this arrangement, results showed that of 2009 transfers, 1665 (83%) involved a transfer from lower to higher, for example, from touch to sight, while only 344 (17%) involved a transfer from higher to lower. Although Ullmann then went on to discuss the relevance of his work for semantic analysis, it remained for Werner (1952), in his review of Ullmann's earlier book, to suggest that such findings might have significance for a more general theory of thinking and figurative language. For Werner, this pattern of results suggested that the more differentiated senses such as sight and hearing are put back in contact with the "primordial unity" of all the senses (in which sensory experiences are not parceled out into a number of different modalities) when explicitly linked to less differentiated ones such as touch and temperature. In just this way does the poet try to bring about a more compelling and immediate response than might have been possible by appealing to the higher senses alone.

Werner's early and continuing interest in synesthesia and metaphor, as a matter of fact, was only part and parcel of his more general interest in language and language development. For this reason it is not surprising to find that the most well-articulated statement of the Gestalt position about language and symbol development is to be found in Werner and Kaplan's (1963) book on symbol formation and in their specific application of the idea of physiognomic perception to language and expression. Physiognomic perception (and the family of related concepts that go along with it) represents one of those concept families which everyone inside the Gestalt camp finds quite easy to understand and one which everyone outside the group finds most puzzling if not indeed incomprehensible. Perhaps the best way to approach the idea of a physiognomic process is to begin with Werner and Kaplan's (1963) notion of a symbol and then move on more specifically to their analysis of the physiognomic process and its relationship to symbols and symbol formation.

For Werner and Kaplan, the relationship between a word (or any other speech form) and its referent does not depend upon a contiguity-based bond established between the two. Rather the essence of this relationship is to be found in the so-called process of dynamic schematization; that is, where it is understood that both a word and its referent are related by a schematizing process which does not operate on already established similarities between word and referent. Rather the similarity between word and referent are jointly created in the process of learning (actually, of constructing) the meaning of the word. Strictly speaking, there is always a correspondence between word and referent; a correspondence which emerges from the original schematizing activity serving to bring both word and referent into phenomenal existence for the first time.

The reference example of this relationship would seem to be provided by onomatopoeia in which the relationship appears to rest on purely objective aspects of words and the world. In this regard, however, Werner and Kaplan (1963) note that:

> onomatopoeia is not a simple mirroring of an independently given 'reality.' The onomatopoetic relationship involves the *establishment* of a bond of similarity between an object formed in the medium of perception and a vehicle shaped in the medium of sound or vocalization. There is an unwitting 'translation' from perception into a phonemic medium, or better, a concurrent shaping of material in two media, perception and vocal articulation. There is no more an independently given similarity between onomatopoetic forms and their referents than there is between conventional forms and the objects to which they refer. In both cases, there is an establishment of 'similarity.' (p. 206)

According to a further development, once structuring between vehicle and referent takes place there occurs a second stage during which a progressive "distancing" intervenes between symbol and referent. Finally the relationship becomes so remote as to make it appear in the adult that the two are linked only by external relationships and that there is no intrinsic similarity between the two.

The deeper ontogenetic similarity between word and referent can be appreciated only under a number of different and rather special conditions. Sometimes a poet can force the relationship with ordinary words and ordinary objects — like Emma and the seagull. At other times, however, special and extraordinary forms are needed to cut across ordinary boundaries — Kohler's *maluma* and *tuckatee* — while at still other times the observer is required to adopt a special attitude toward word and referent. In this latter case, known as *physiognomic definition,* the observer is asked to describe a word or other symbol in terms of more tangible modalities such as are involved in movement or in sound.

The physiognomic-definition task (see Hormann, 1965, for a review of relevant work) is critical for Werner and Kaplan (1963) largely because it affords an opportunity to examine the dynamic schematization process at work in an adult. As an example of the type of data produced by respondents in these experiments, consider the following protocol given to the word *Holz* [wood] (Werner & Kaplan, 1963):

> Something crude, raw, uncouth. One gets stuck at its splinters if one moves over the word with one's eyes. This quality seems to be (visually and articulatory—auditorily) centered particularly in the o and the z. (p. 209)

In this case, the physiognomized word assumes a quasisubstantial, thing-like character.

In the next example, Werner and Kaplan (1963) see the "dynamic expressive features of the (word) pattern as vividly . . . depicting what it means":

> One subject remarked that *Seife* (soap) 'has for me the character of something viscous, smeary, gelatinous, something spreading without definite form and consistency. It is particularly in the broadly spreading *ei* and the gelatine-like flowing sound, *f,* where these characteristics are centered. (p. 211)

Finally, physiognomized words often reveal a fusion with bodily activity. It is this latter property which is so important for sensory—tonic perceptual theory. To the word *hart* [hard] a subject responded:

> At the sight of the word I immediately experience a definite 'steellike' structuring of my body with the center in the back and the neck, particularly strong around the uppermost vertebrae. This structure coalesces fully with the visual structure of the word. Now, the organization dissolves and with it the pictorial expression is lost for a while. I gain it back, however, rather quickly by emphasizing the vertical structure of the *h* and the *t*: but now what previously was all in me, is now partly before me: a visual pattern structured in stern and stiff vertical strokes. The word now has an external existence, out there, rigid, angular, unbendable. (Werner & Kaplan, 1963, pp. 211–212)

In addition to these studies on physiognomic perception, other data also bear on the issue of how word and referent form a single unity. Here, we need mention Werner and Kaplan's (1963; Chapters 20–24) work in relating linguistic and pictorial forms; Harrower's (1932) work in relating joke endings to line drawings; and finally much of the cross-cultural work reported earlier by Werner (1948) on syncretic organization in natural language. The purpose of all this work is to elucidate the dynamic qualities of symbol—referent interaction for in the end, as in the beginning, it must be as Kohler says: "Die Möwen sehen alle aus, als ob sie Emma hiessen."

But where is figurative language in all of this? Although Werner and Kaplan, and Kohler before them, do talk about figurative language they generally treat it only as a further example of the dynamic schematizing process. That is, metaphors come about because of created relationships inherent in the expressive properties of constituent elements. Metaphor, far from being a recondite or esoteric phenomenon deriving from literal language, represents a more basic mode of relating different aspects of experience. In this, the Gestalt hypothesis relates back to Cassirer (1953) and Langer's (1957) more philosophical view that human mentality operates on the basis of "need to symbolize" wherein the incessant seeing or thinking of one thing as another is an intrinsic property of human cognitive activity. For this view, metaphor represents the primary linguistic expression of this process.

Although such an approach is certainly within the spirit of Gestalt Sprachtheorie, it does seem possible to provide a somewhat less philosophical analysis if we take Koffka's (1935) discussion of joke-completion and problem-solving activity as our starting point. Basically, Koffka casts his analysis into a discussion of how and where new processes originate and suggests that the structure of any given problem sets up a process within the person which communicates with other traces relating to the same topic. A problem is resolved when the appropriate structure, including an appropriate completion, emerges from the combination of traces, the generation of a new trace, or from an adaptation of an already existing one. In any event, both the active process set up by the problem situation and the resolution subsequently arrived at must combine to satisfy the demands of the situation. This end state is reached when all systems are back in equilibrium such as would occur when a problem is solved.

In the case of figurative language we may say that there is some aspect of experience in need of expression or, alternatively, that an aspect of experience has been expressed in an unfamiliar way (figuratively). Both situations are analogous to the problem situation, and either understanding a figure presented or creating a genuinely new one will take place only to the degree that elements of the figure make contact with appropriate preexisting traces or, alternatively, initiate new processes capable of resolving the ambiguity created. To be sure, all of the words in a figure are no longer the same as they were in isolation and it is the structure of this new situation, rather than of the component pieces, that is in need of being understood if the figure itself is to be understood.

This admittedly tentative proposal regarding figurative language from a perceptual viewpoint clearly does make contact with combinatorial-feature theories in a number of places. The differences between the two, however, relate to certain fundamental questions and these differences must color the similarities as well. For perceptual theory, there are no preexisting, wholly circumscribed, units such as features or meanings to combine; rather what is preexisting is a much more flexible and dynamic process, profoundly affected by the specific nature of the present novel configuration of words and phrases. For perceptual theory, figurative language is not a derived process that somehow or other plays off of literal language; rather, under rather special attitudes (such as are associated with physiognomization), the originary nature of figurative language comes to the fore and suggests again that literal, not figurative, language is the derived second-order expression.

These, and other, differences between perceptual and combinatorial models have been summarized by Werner and Kaplan (1963) who note (in specific regard to their theory):

> The view presented here may seem, at least superficially, to have some similarity to the well-known 'mediation hypothesis' of Osgood. As we understand it, Osgood's theory holds that words (e.g., 'apple') are essentially signs that come to signify their objects by evoking in the organism some fraction of the total response evoked by the stimulus object (e.g., apple); it is thus by virtue of sharing some common response properties that sign (word) and object are related to each other. Thus, both our view and Osgood's hold that there is "similarity" (partial identity) between "reaction" to the referent and "reaction" to the vehicle. But here the agreement of the two viewpoints ends. Osgood's view, rooted in a stimulus–response psychology, is agenetic and does not distinguish fundamentally between mere *reacting* and *knowing;* representational activity is treated as a response essentially no different from other responses. Our view, on the other hand, is genetically oriented and makes a fundamental distinction between *reacting to* and *knowing about*; representation is thus an emergent activity not reducible to the overlap of responses. Finally, for us, but apparently not for Osgood, representational activity goes hand in hand with the *construction* of a world of objects ("knowables"). (p. 24)

In any case, although figurative language can be described as involving a combination of two or more words, it is quite clear that combinatorial and Gestalt theories approach the deeper nature of this process in quite different ways. For combinatorial theories, figurative language serves selectively to suppress certain features while emphasizing others, whereas for Gestalt theory there is a certain *Verstandlicher Zusummenhang* [an understandable relationship]: about those aspects selectively emphasized or suppressed. Such selection is governed not by a convergence or shifting of specific features; rather it is intrinsic to mental activity itself: after all, all seagulls do look like Emma.

EVALUATION AND SUMMARY

In a very real sense, any attempt to evaluate any or all of the various approaches to figurative language requires nothing less than a complete evaluation of a number of vastly different approaches to behavioral phenomenon in general.

Rather than do this, however, it seems far wiser to render unto combinatorial models of either the linguistic or psychological variety what is rightfully theirs, and unto Gestalt models what is rightfully theirs. In this way do we recognize that both contain valuable, although partial, insights into the metaphoric process.

What does seem clear is that, for the adult, words are used in fairly regular ways to refer to aspects of reality as well as to other words, and it is this insight that is captured by featural models. What also seems clear is that words not only can be, but very often are, used in nonordinary ways and that such uses are not always violations of the usual linguistic system.

The situation here is very much like that discussed by Neisser (1967) in regard to perceptual phenomenon: that although perceiving is an active, ongoing, and constructive process it must operate on something; and this something must be input from the world. In the case of metaphor, however, this something must be the ordinary meanings regularly evoked by a given word. In terms of many of the models described in this chapter, this somewhat common-sense notion of "ordinary meaning" has been made theoretically more precise via the hypothesis of semantic features and their associated rules of use. What these approaches all mean to suggest is not that these theoretical fictions exist, but that they help capture the very reasonable idea that, in the adult, certain core features can be expected to go along with the use of a given word in a given speech context.

Hypotheses such as these, however, do not require the evocation of a full set of features each and every time a particular word is used. As a matter of fact, even in nonfigurative speech we would expect only a few very general properties of a word, having little or no hierarchical structure, to be evoked. In addition, we would expect the order of features to vary depending upon the total situation within which a word is used and this is as true for literal as for figurative usage. The idea that word meaning can be represented as an extensive set of features seems to result from considering too seriously the thesaurus as the most appropriate model for word meaning. Many features would seem better construed as created within the specific context within which they are used, rather than as having been there prior to the particular language act under consideration. In addition, as Bolinger (1965) noted, features ought have sfumato rather than outline contours.

Does this mean that we are vacillating between two incompatible views while pretending to offer a synthesis? Hopefully, the answer is no: rather, what we are trying to say is that metaphors work both by making use of preexisting information (perhaps, on the basis of "features" or "traces") as well as by creating new meanings for use in a specific situation. The larger question that seems to be involved, however, is one of deciding what ought to be meant by the idea of an internal dictionary or lexicon. The conclusion vis-à-vis featural and Gestalt approaches would seem to be that feature theories give it too much structure while dynamic theories give it too little. Both, however, agree that words (and other "meaningful" units) do have a preexisting "something" associated with them. Given this agreement as a starting point it seems reasonable to suggest that the lexicon might profitably be considered as a continuously updating summary of a given speaker's contact with, and use of, the words in the speaker's language. In this way words have some preexisting structure that can be modified in accordance with the demands of the present situation. Thus, it seems reasonable to propose that a word has a past, a present, and future — with its past being given by a thesaurus or dictionary, its present by speaking, and its future by figurative use.

What all of this then suggests, somewhat more prosaically, is that the metaphoric process involves both preexisting structure and ongoing construction, and that any theory predicated exclusively, or even primarily, on the basis of one or the other of these assumptions is necessarily incomplete. Preexisting structure is necessary if we are to be able to talk about anything at all, but the idea that that is all there is, is simply too limited. Creative use of language is necessary if we are to explain not only Kohler's gulls or Werner's hart but all sorts of figurative language as well. Creative elaboration must always depend upon some prior process evoked by the words in question (traces, features, and so on) and this also needs to be considered. The heart of the metaphoric process would seem to necessitate both a loosening of featural organization by combinatorial theories and an acceptance of preexisting structure by dynamic theories. Only in this way can we hope to accommodate the insights motivating both classes of model.

But how much "loosening" and/or "acceptance" is enough? Here the answer must not be prejudged. Instead it seems best to adopt an open attitude to theory and to seek guidance from the phenomenon itself. What this means is that we ought look at when, where, and why human beings use figurative language rather than attempt to prove or disprove extant theories of the metaphoric process. Indeed the remainder of this volume may be viewed as a series of tentative steps (gropings, if you will) designed to provide some empirical foundation on which to build a theory of figurative language and then to examine its relationship to significant phenomena occurring in other contexts such as psychotherapy and/or education. Needless to say, we do not consider these tentative steps without direction (Chapters 1 and 2 provide direction enough); rather it is our feeling that a problem-oriented and basically descriptive program represents a viable and meaningful approach to a topic that only infrequently has been studied by a straightforward combination of empirical and theoretical means. In this way, we plan to be sensitive to larger (and smaller) theoretical concerns as these emerge in the course of our investigations but not to be needlessly constrained by them at the outset.

3
The Measurement of Metaphor and Some Preliminary Findings

In order to own a phenomenon philosphically all we need do is think clearly and well; in order to own a phenomenon theoretically all we need do is provide a potentially workable model; and in order to own a phenomenon empirically all we need do is measure it. The usual procedure employed in literary analyses of figurative language (e.g., Brooke-Rose, 1958) involves a single scholar working alone over a text, and this seems a perfectly reasonable strategy for an analysis of texts. Fortunately or unfortunately, the niceties of psychological measurement often will not sit still for a single rater — no matter how well trained — and for this reason a different approach is required for psychological and psycholinguistic research.

In order to meet, even partially, the reliability requirements usually imposed by psychological measurement, Barlow, Kerlin, and Pollio (1971) developed a training manual designed to teach raters to identify figurative language in contexts ranging from therapy interviews to children's compositions by way of political speeches. Basically their manual is composed of a number of different parts, each part presenting a general definition of one or another class of figurative language such as presented in Chapter 2. In addition to specifically didactic exposition, each part also contains a programed instruction component designed to help a rater evaluate his newly acquired knowledge. Following each bit of programmed instruction is a practice–discussion section involving other raters. This section is designed to serve as a further practice session for identifying and categorizing figures of speech from conversational prose, and as a basis for a discussion session(s) designed to iron out discrepancies between raters.

In actual practice the training procedure consists of two steps: first, three different raters are trained to recognize 15 specific types of figurative language; and second, they are asked to rate independently 4 prose passages provided in the manual. Of these 4 passages, 2 are literary selections, 1 is a speech, and 1 is a transcript of a psychotherapy interview.

After each of these selections is rated independently, the three judges meet together to talk about their ratings and to discuss differences. Raters not only are trained to recognize the occurrence of figurative language, but also are asked to decide whether a given instance represents a frozen (clichéd) or novel usage.

Once training is completed, and all raters feel confident that they could (and do) agree on their rating of these passages 80% of the time, they are then given the experimental materials of interest and asked to rate them independently of one another. Rater's judgments are tallied on the basis of the following coding scheme:

3 + 0: all three raters independently judged this instance as figurative.

2 + 1: two of the three raters independently judged this instance to be figurative, and during group discussion the third rater agreed.

1 + 2: only one of the raters independently judged the instance to be figurative, but after group discussion the other two raters agreed.

2 − 1: two raters independently chose an instance as figurative, but the third judge after discussion did not agree.

1 − 2: one rater independently chose an instance as figurative, but the other two raters still disagreed even after discussion.

Although there are other possibilities these can usually all be assigned to one of these five categories, for example, if one rater judges an instance as figurative and manages to persuade only one of the other two, the resulting judgment would be coded as 2 − 1. Outcomes other than those presented above, however, are extremely rare.

Thus, by using this coding system, an instance might be coded 1 + 2 F. This would be a case in which the instance was first independently chosen by only one rater as figurative and after discussion the other two raters agreed. This code also reveals that the instance was judged to be frozen. Only those instances rated as 1 + 2 or better are considered as countable instances of figurative language in any given language sample. Items scored as 2 − 1 or 1 − 2 are never used as instances of figurative usage. Novel or frozen judgments are made on the basis of a majority vote; two out of three or three out of three raters must have judged the figure in one or another of these categories.

Using raters trained by this procedure, Pollio and Barlow (1975) examined in detail the ebb and flow of figurative language as it occurred in the course of a single, highly successful hour of Gestalt therapy. A typed manuscript as well as an audio tape of the case study were obtained from the tape library of the American Academy of Psychotherapists in Philadelphia. Transcripts for a wide variety of different cases are commercially available from this group and are meant to be used for didactic purposes.

Although we present some specifics of the clinical data obtained from the Case of Audrey subsequently in this chapter, what is of importance in this context is the general scoring procedure used — the way in which agreements and disagreements among raters are figured – and these data are presented in Table 3.1. Probably the best way in which to read this table is from the bottom up. For the patient, all three raters scored a total of 298 different words or phrases as figurative. Of these, 272 (19%) were agreed upon by all raters after their discussion sessions, while 26 (9%) were never agreed upon. These 272 instances were further divided up into 122 frozen figures and 150 novel ones. An examination of the ratings show that of the 150 novel figures, 88% were picked up by 2 of the 3 judges during their independent ratings. The additional 12% were picked up by only 1 rater, although both of the remaining raters did agree with this judgment during a post rating discussion session. The values obtained for frozen figures showed that 82% of the instances were picked up by 2 of the 3 raters independently and 18% picked up by only 1 rater during the independent rating session.

For the therapist, raters scored a total of 41 items of which 35 (85%) were used as data (ultimately agreed upon after discussion) and 6 (15%) were not. It is also clear that 2 of the 3 raters independently agreed upon 100% of the frozen figures and 91% of the novel figures. In all cases – for both frozen and novel figures – raters did attain a 2 + 1 criterion value of greater than 80% for communications produced by both patient and therapist. If we combine the values for patient and therapist, the 3 + 0 and 2 + 1 judgments go to 112/134 or

TABLE 3.1
Reliability of Rater Judgments: Patient and Therapist[a]

	Speaker							
	Patient				Therapist			
	Frozen		Novel		Frozen		Novel	
Rater scoring category	N	%	N	%	N	%	N	%
3 + 0	52	43	91	61	10	83	15	65
2 + 1	48	39	40	27	2	17	6	26
1 + 2	22	18	19	12	0	0	2	9
Subtotals	122		150		12		23	
Subtotal (both accepted)	272		91%		35		85%	
1 – 2	23				2			
2 – 1	3				4			
Subtotal (rejected)	26		9%		6		15%	
Total items rated	298		100%		41		100%	

[a]From Pollio and Barlow (1975).

84% for frozen and 152/173 or 88% for novel. This figure is of some interest because it indicates one usual criterion imposed on rating data; namely, where 2 of 3 or 3 of 3 raters must agree independently on the occurrence of a given behavioral category. Similarly the $1-2$ and $2-1$ categories represent a rejection range indicating how often 1 or 2 of the raters disagreed with the remaining rater(s) and provides a measure of how many of the total words or phrases picked by one or another rater were idiosyncratic to that rater; that is, it provides a rough measure of how well the various categories were defined.

A different way in which to measure reliability is to count the pattern of agreements between pairs of raters. In order to do this, 3 different 2 × 2 tables were set up for each rater pair with the basic form of this table as follows:

	Rater 1	
Rater 2	Figure: yes	Figure: no
Figure: yes	a	b
Figure: no	c	d

For each of the 3 tables the unit of analysis was the sentence produced by therapist and patient. On this basis, the percentage of agreement obtained between any pair of raters is given by the number of entries in cells a and d divided by the number of entries in the total table. If more than a single figure appeared in a given sentence for either rater, it was entered in the appropriate cell the appropriate number of times. So, for example, if Rater 1 rated 2 figures in a single sentence and Rater 2 no figures in the same sentence, a 2 would have been entered in the appropriate Yes–No cell. Using this procedure, the proportions of agreement were .84 between Raters 1 and 2; .74 between Raters 1 and 3; and .78 between Raters 2 and 3. In general, Rater 1 tended to score the smallest number of figures.

At least for this one case of spoken language reliabilities do seem reasonably good: raters do not agree on about 10% of the total items rated; but of the remaining 90% or so do agree about 85% of the time at a 2 of 3 or better rate. In addition to reliability data for the Pollio–Barlow (1975) study, reliability values have been computed for all studies to be reported in this book, as well as for some unpublished dissertations done at the University of Tennessee between 1971 and the present. Table 3.2 presents a listing of these dissertations as well as the appropriate agreement and disagreement figures for the 16 different situations in which we have gathered data. These are divided, in Table 3.2, into spoken and written language samples.

The column headings in this table perhaps require a word of explanation. The heading, "Total items independently selected," refers to the bottom line of tables identical in construction to Table 3.1, and represent, as the name implies, the total number of words and/or phrases selected by all three raters regardless of whether or not the other raters agreed. The next column, "Rejection rate,"

TABLE 3.2
Pattern of Rater Reliabilities for Various Language Samples

Type of material related	Total items independently selected	Rejection rate (1 − 2; 2 − 1) (%)	Acceptance rate 2 + 1 or better (%)	
			Frozen	Novel
A. Spoken language samples				
1. Case study: Gestalt (Pollio & Barlow, 1975)	339	10	84	88
2. Case study: Rational–emotive Chapter 3[a]	297	8	65	82
3. Case study: Child–analytic Chapter 3[a]	231	13	76	84
4. Case study: Existential Chapter 3[a]	337	7	66	87
5. Case study: Student therapist (5 sessions) (Simpkinson, 1972)	1079	15	76	81
6. Case study: Behavior therapy (5 sessions) (Simpkinson, 1972)	502	23	66	73
7. Case study: Psychoanalytic (5 sessions) Chapter 6[a]	1506	12	60	78
8. Kennedy–Nixon debates (Pollio & Francisco, 1974)	1514	14	82	92
B. Written language samples				
1. Children's compositions: 3 grades (Pollio & Pollio, 1974)	626	13	55	73
2. Children's sentences: 3 grades (Pollio & Pollio, 1974)	451	4	76	84
3. Children's similarities: 3 grades (Pollio & Pollio, 1974)	569	6	45	80
4. Adolescent compositions (Schonberg, 1974)	1363	2	89	97
5. TAT protocols (Lockwood, 1974)	2527	17	73	82
6. Children's compositions Chapter 7[a]	2095	2	78	87
7. Children's sentences Chapter 7[a]	625	1	93	95
8. Children's sentences Chapter 7[a]	823	1	95	96

[a] All chapter numbers refer to reliabilities for material presented in various chapters of this volume.

presents the 1 — 2 and 2 — 1 columns of such agreement tables while the final 2 columns represent the 2/3 or 3/3 rates for frozen and novel figures separately. Under each specific sample is the reference from which present values were taken. Where a chapter number appears, these values represent reliability figures for data to be reported in the appropriate chapter(s) of this book.

As can be seen from Table 3.2, the first 7 entries represent case studies involving a wide variety of different therapists, patients, and therapeutic techniques. In addition, Samples 5, 6, and 7 involve results for 5 separate sessions of 3 different types of psychotherapeutic techniques. Sample 8 presents the data for answers given by Kennedy and Nixon in response to questions posed in their television debates of 1960. We examined answers to questions since prepared statements probably fall closer to written than spontaneous (unprepared) speech and therefore ought to be more comparable to the second set of examples considered (see the discussion by Pollio & Francisco, 1974, on this point).

In terms of written language, the samples described in Table 3.2 were gathered from a number of different age groups ranging from child writers in the third through sixth grades producing "creative" compositions, to college students responding to Thematic Apperception Test (TAT) cards. In addition, values also are presented for a series of tasks specifically designed by Pollio and Pollio 1974) to be evocative of figurative usage.

Even a cursory examination of this table reveals that only in a very few situations does the rejection rate exceed 15% and that these situations involve spoken rather than written-language contexts. As a matter of fact, there is some indication that the rejection rate is higher for spoken than written language (with six of the eight rejection values for spoken language exceeding those for written) although absolute values are not large in any significant sense. Perhaps the more critical and more obvious differences to be noted in Table 3.2 concern those between acceptance rates for frozen and novel figurative language. In all eight written and in all eight spoken samples, the values are from a little to a lot higher for novel than frozen language. This would seem to indicate that raters, not surprisingly, more often agree on the occurrence of novel than frozen figures.

Such a finding, while of some importance for reliability aspects of this procedure, is also of some importance regarding the perception of figurative usage. To be sure, observers trained for, and looking for, instances of figurative language are not the ordinary run-of-the-mill listener; yet just as surely, the data do make the rather sensible point that novel figurative language is perceptually more compelling (more readily recognized when looked for) than frozen language. Although all theories of metaphor, particularly those emphasizing its unique aspects, would expect such a result, raters in this set of studies often noted that the salience of a novel figure was due to a certain surprise or a certain incongruity of expectation in a particular language sample.

To help understand why this might happen, let us start with the case of frozen usage. For example, if the patient says, "he sure cut me down," how else could that meaning be expressed except in terms of a long and cumbersome phrase, or exactly the linguistic motivation causing a particular figure to be frozen in the first place? On the other hand, if a patient says "my anger *screams* inside of me" there already exists a regular and fairly simple way of saying the same thing: "I'm really very angry" (which the patient in question had said many times before). The novel figure is all the more compelling precisely because it does not represent the only, or even the most usual, way of saying something; quite the contrary, it represents this speaker's unique attempt, for whatever reason, to move away from an ordinary phrase and from ordinary usage. For this reason, novel figurative language is uniquely compelling to the listener and, if of sufficient interest, ought (as we noted in regard to the ornamental function of figurative language) to set some unusual and/or creative things going inside his or her head (see Chapter 1, pages 17–18).

One more point needs to be made in regard to figurative language, and this concerns absolute differences in raters. The total number of figures produced is a reflection not only of the verbal sample being considered but also of how carefully and well a given rating group did its job. All cross-sample comparisons, therefore, must be interpreted with some degree of caution. Any rating team is a social group of sorts and as such is influenced by all of those factors involved in group interactions. Although, in many cases, groups of peers have been used, it was necessary in some cases (those in which teenage or black respondents were used) to use a rater familiar with slang appropriate to that particular group. Exactly what effect a group composed of two graduate students and one teenage rater has on the absolute values recorded cannot be known for sure; what we do know, however, is that this could be a possible confounding factor and, well, let the reader take heed.

Actually, no single results should ever be taken in isolation in coming to some conclusion or other; for this reason, it is the pattern of all our results that will support or refute any particular cross-sample comparison. The work is of a piece and it is the total entity, including interrelationships both within and across samples, that will or will not make sense. No single bit of theory or data, by itself, can or ought ever make or break a particular argument.

SOME PRELIMINARY FINDINGS

Figures in Speech: Clinical Results

The major reason for presenting reliability data, however, was not to examine the way in which figurative language is perceived, but to set the stage for an analysis of how figurative language is used in speaking and writing. Perhaps one rather direct way with which to come to grips with this question is to look carefully at figurative-language outputs in situations in which two people are talking about issues of importance to one or both of them. Such a situation would seem to be provided by a patient and therapist talking to one another in the context of a psychotherapy interview and here a relevant study has been presented by Pollio and Barlow (1975).

In their work, cumulative output curves were plotted for both patient and therapist. In this context two different pairs of curves were drawn; one presenting the output rates for novel figures for both patient and therapist and the other presenting these values for frozen figures. In their work, each successive utterance, that is, whenever there was a change in speaker regardless of length, was used as the unit of interest. Figure 3.1 presents the patient and therapist output curves for frozen figures and Figure 3.2 presents these data for novel figures. Since there is little articulation in either of the therapist's curves we need look instead at both patient curves in some detail. An examination of Figure 3.1 shows that there is only a single point at which the patient's output curve changed rate significantly, and that this occurred at about Communication 62. Both prior to, and following, this communication there are only slight and nonsystematic changes in rate. With the exception of this point the overall rate in each of the two segments appears to be fairly constant.

An examination of Figure 3.2, on the other hand, shows that the total output curve seems to divide itself into 3 segments with each segment defined by a dramatic and highly articulated change in rate. The first of these segments runs from Communication 1 to 71, the second from Communication 72 to 108, while the final segment runs from Communication 109 to 136.

Although Pollio and Barlow (1975) then went on to do a content analysis of each of these three bursts, for our purposes all we need note is that, in this case, novel figurative language seemed to occur in bursts and that, if we believe Pollio

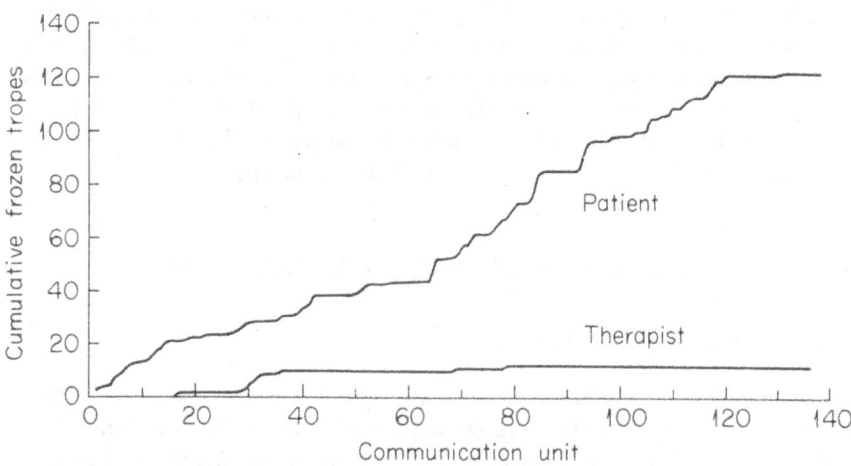

FIGURE 3.1 Rate of frozen figurative output for patient and therapist. (from Pollio & Barlow, 1975.)

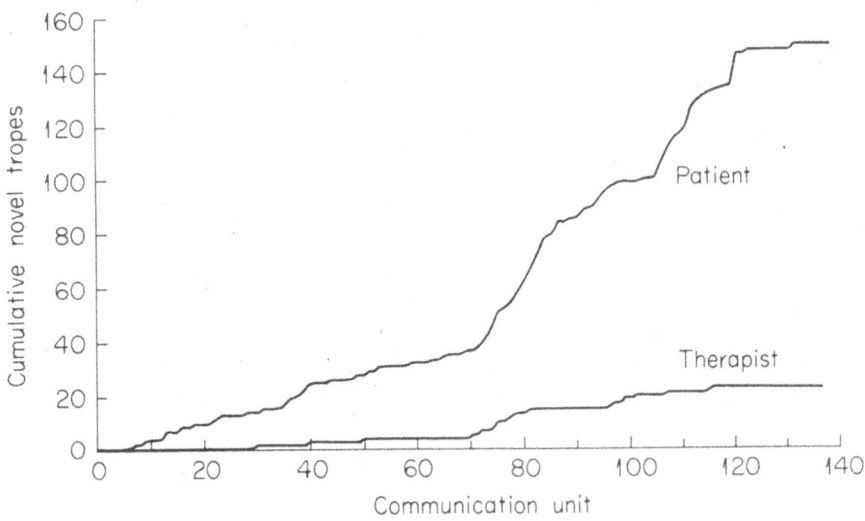

FIGURE 3.2 Rate of novel figurative output for patient and therapist. (from Pollio & Barlow, 1975.)

and Barlow's analysis, such bursts relate meaningfully to patient problem areas (see Chapter 4 for more on this point). Frozen figurative language, on the other hand, seemed to be much more regular in occurrence and as Pollio and Barlow note much less involved in the therapeutic process.

Although novel figurative language did play a significant role in this particular case study, we should be aware that these results are open to a number of obvious limitations and these need to be talked about rather directly. For one, the type of therapy presented by this tape is a variety of Gestalt therapy and one of the principle tenets of this position is the disciplined use of personification. This aspect of Gestalt therapy was known, of course, when Pollio and Barlow chose to examine the Case of Audrey. Their feeling was that if figurative language — and by implication, figurative thinking — was to be examined by a directly empirical procedure they had to deal with a situation in which such language was commonplace and such was clearly provided by this case. A second rather obvious limitation to these data concerns the fact that Audrey was a highly verbal and highly "practiced" patient. Although this was her first session with this particular therapist, she had been in therapy for some 2 or 3 years and as such was not naive with respect to the therapy context.

What all of this means is that other therapy sessions had to be examined in order to determine if Pollio and Barlow's results would have any generality beyond this single session of a single rather specific type of therapy. In order to do this, three tapes and tapescripts were secured from the American Academy of Psychotherapists and subjected to a similar analysis of figurative language. For our purposes, tapes dealing with existential therapy, child analytic therapy, and rational emotive therapy were chosen. All of these tapes were sent to the American Association of Psychotherapists by the participating therapist as an example of his or her particular brand of therapy. Once these tapescripts were obtained, they were rated by the same procedure as used in the Case of Audrey. The particular patterns of reliability obtained for these tapes can be found in Table 3.2 under the heading "Spoken language samples," Examples 2, 3, and 4.

The novel output curves for each of these three sessions are presented in Figures 3.3a—c. The legend accompanying each describes the nature of therapy employed. The first impression to be gleaned from these additional tapes is that, similar to the Pollio and Barlow (1975) case, all three tapes show strong and sustained bursts of novel figurative activity. A careful examination of Figure 3.3a and b also shows *three* such bursts, and, although Figure 3.3c could also be interpreted to display three bursts as well, the most straightforward conclusion would seem to be that regardless of the type of therapy, novel figurative

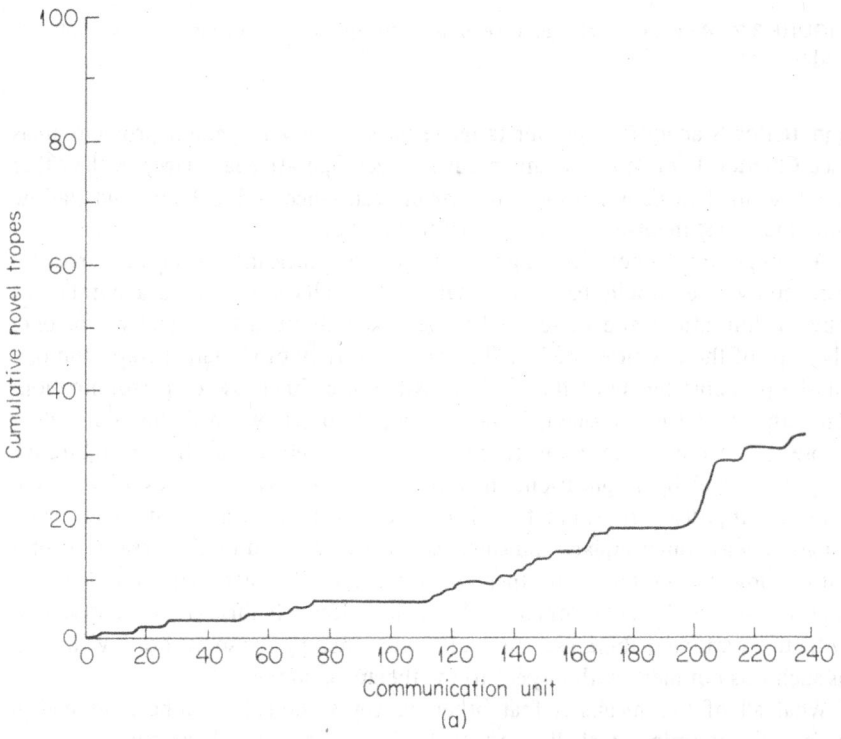

FIGURE 3.3 (a) Rate of novel figurative output for a patient undergoing rational—emotive therapy. (b) Rate of novel figurative output for a patient undergoing existential therapy. (c) Rate of novel figurative output for a patient undergoing child analytic therapy.

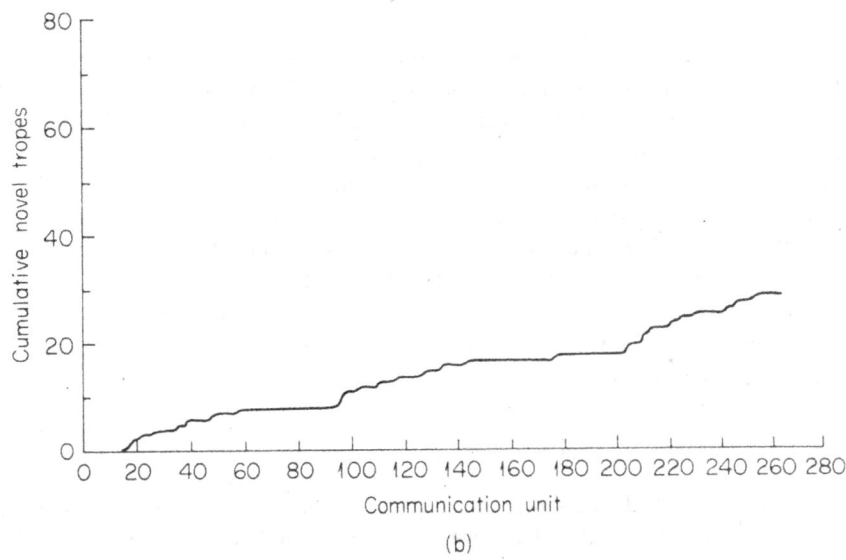

(b)

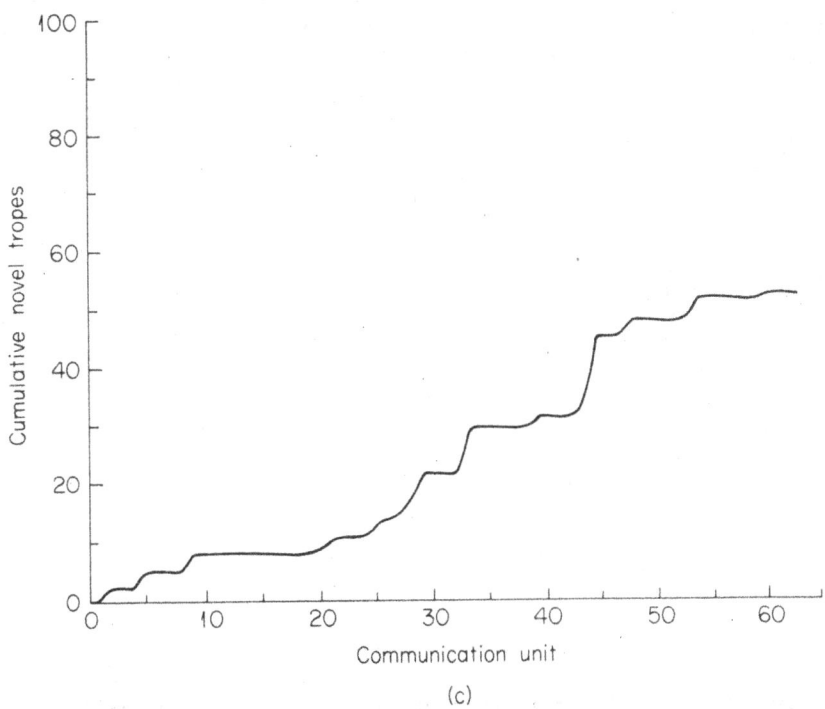

(c)

language is produced in bursts. This conclusion seems to apply equally across four different types of patients and four equally different types of therapists.

Examination of further and different therapeutic interactions by Simpkinson (1972) has also shown that figurative language is usually an episodic phenomenon and that frozen figurative language is generally produced at a fairly uniform rate throughout a given session. Over 14 different sessions — 10 by Simpkinson and the 4 considered here — it seems fair to conclude that frozen figurative language is produced at a fairly regular rate and that novel figurative language occurs in bursts. A question must now be raised as to whether or not such a characterization is unique to therapy situations or whether it also applies to other situations as well.

Figures in Speech: Political Rhetoric

In order to provide data appropriate to this latter question, as well as to examine the occurrence of figurative language in a context where the primary aim was to convince rather than to solve personal problems, Pollio and Francisco (1974) examined figurative language in the Kennedy—Nixon debates of 1960. These debates would seem to represent a good source of data in that both speakers provide samples of prepared and extemporaneous segments of fairly extensive duration. In addition, verbatim transcriptions exist in a number of different places (e.g., Kraus, 1962; *The New York Times* of the appropriate dates, and so

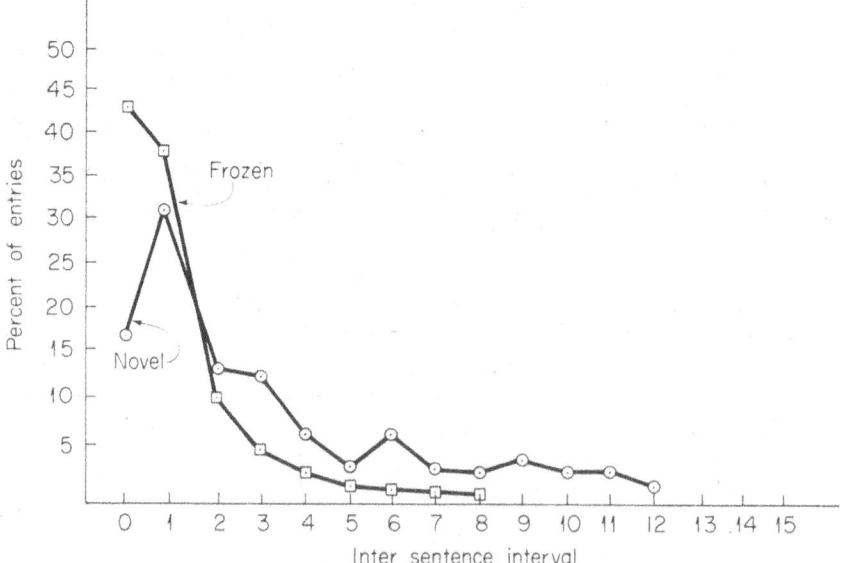

FIGURE 3.3 Frequency distributions of intersentence intervals for novel and frozen figures: Richard M. Nixon.

3. THE MEASUREMENT OF METAPHOR AND SOME FINDINGS 79

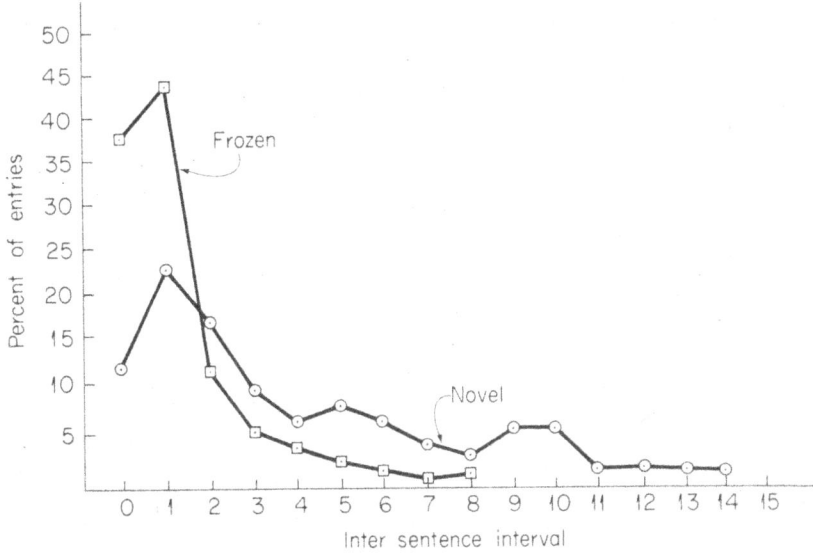

FIGURE 3.4 Frequency distributions of intersentence intervals for novel and Frozen Figures: John F. Kennedy.

on) and it seemed but a simple matter to rate these texts for the occurrence of figurative language. The actual rater reliabilities are contained in Table 3.1, and all were found to fall well within an acceptable range.

The first rather surprising result of this analysis has already been presented in Chapter 1 (Table 1.1, page 6) in which we noted the rather infrequent occurrence of novel figurative language in samples of spontaneous political rhetoric. For both Kennedy (.56 per 100 words) and for Nixon (1.20 per 100 words) novel figurative rates were well below other language samples in which the general average was about 1.53 per 100 words. Frozen rates, however, did fall about the mean of 3.40 per 100 words.

What about output properties: were novel figures in this context produced in bursts? In agreement with results obtained for psychotherapy interviews, novel figurative language in the Kennedy–Nixon debates also seemed to occur in temporally defined clusters whereas frozen figurative language occurred much more frequently and at a much more regular rate. In order to specify these characterizations somewhat more precisely, Pollio and Francisco (1974) examined the intersentence interval separating successive figures for both novel and frozen figures. Once such values were obtained, frequency distributions were plotted for both speakers and both types of figurative language and these data are presented in Figure 3.3 and Figure 3.4.

As can be seen, the intersentence distributions for both novel and frozen figures are remarkably similar across politicians and quite dissimilar within politicians. For both Nixon and Kennedy, the distribution of novel figures is much flatter than the distribution for frozen figures. In addition, the novel distribution covers more intervals and has a small secondary peak at about six for Nixon and at about five and nine for Kennedy.

In order to determine if difference between pairs of these 4 distributions were significant, χ^2 tests were done according to a procedure suggested by McNemar (1969, p. 264). Results of these analyses revealed a consistent pattern: both within Kennedy ($\chi^2 = 124.65; p < .001$) and within Nixon ($\chi^2 = 105.93; p < .001$) distributions for novel and frozen figures differed significantly; cross-speaker differences for novel ($\chi^2 = 6.75; p > .80$) and frozen ($\chi^2 = 9.22; p > .30$) distributions, however, were clearly not significant. What this means is that regardless of speaker, novel and frozen figurative language have the same sequential-output properties and that these properties differ markedly from one another even within the same speaker.

Although not immediately obvious from these distributions, individual cumulative output plots for novel and frozen figurative use produced by both Kennedy and Nixon did again show considerably more bursting for novel, as opposed to frozen figures. In terms of the plots present in Figures 3.3 and 3.4 this fact is captured both in the considerably more flattened distribution for novel, as compared to frozen figures as well as in the occurrence of secondary peaks for both novel distributions. These secondary peaks indicate the occurrence of a number of long intervals between successive novel figures whereas the absence of such secondary peaks in the frozen distribution indicates that these figures were produced at quite regular intersentence intervals spaced close together. Although no specific curve fits were undertaken, the distribution of intervals for frozen figures appears well described as a random Poisson distribution. The distribution for novel figures, on the other hand, seems to contain two distributions: one involving extremely small intervals, and the second involving considerably larger ones. Thus, it seems reasonable, even if not immediately obvious from these distributional data, to conclude that within the context of public oratory novel figures are produced in bursts while frozen figures are produced at a much more regular and faster rate of output.

These data also need to be considered against the background of results uncovered in the various psychotherapy interviews. There, results indicated that novel figures were produced in bursts even where the unit of analysis was a complete communication unit rather than a single sentence. In the present case, using intersentence-interval (ISI) distributions over sets of single rather lengthy answers to questions, bursting was also found for novel but not for frozen figurative usage. On this basis, it would seem reasonable to conclude that bursting is a clear characteristic of novel figurative output and this is as true for therapy as for public oratory contexts.

Given these results for Kennedy and Nixon, it seems reasonable to wonder if a similar ISI pattern would also apply in the therapy situation as well. Unfortunately, none of the individual communications for any of the therapy tapes

3. THE MEASUREMENT OF METAPHOR AND SOME FINDINGS 81

contained more than 6 sentences, with the vast majority containing only one or two sentences. For this reason it seemed neither reasonable nor appropriate to compute ISI distributions over these data. In contrast to such results obtained for therapy interviews, Kennedy's answers contained between 6 and 30 sentences, with a median value of 15, whereas Nixon's answers ranged between 10 and 33 sentences and produced a median value of 16 per answer. Under these conditions, within-answer distributions do make sense and do provide data comparable to those found for the case of individual psychotherapy.

In their analysis of the Case of Audrey, Pollio and Barlow (1975) noted that both of the major bursts were occasioned by the continued use of the same piece(s) of figurative language. Such an observation suggests, more generally, that bursts occur in novel figurative language largely because the speaker is "working out the implications" of a single, or at most, a closely related set of figures. Sequential examples of frozen figurative language, on the other hand, are less likely to be related to a single theme largely because in many cases frozen figurative language represents simple lexical choice rather than a special or unique mode of expression. If this is true we ought expect successive novel figures which occur close to another in spoken discourse to relate to the same theme whereas successive frozen figures ought not relate to the same time.

In order to provide an answer to this question, Pollio and Francisco (1974) examined what they called the thematic interrelatedness of novel and frozen figures occurring within the same sentence for both Kennedy and Nixon. Thematic interrelatedness was measured on the basis of ratings done by two independent judges and a figure was said to relate to the same topic or theme only if both judges agreed. More often than not, the same figure was used when raters judged two adjacent instances to relate to the same theme. The results of this analysis for both Kennedy and Nixon are presented in Table 3.3. The results for both speakers are quite similar: of 35 novel figures appearing in the same sentence for Nixon, 18 related to the same theme while 17 did not. The

TABLE 3.3
Number of Novel and Frozen Figures from the Same Category: Nixon–Kennedy Debates 2 and 3

	Speaker					
	Nixon			Kennedy		
		Theme expressed			Theme expressed	
Type of figure	Total	Same	Different	Total	Same	Different
Novel	35	18	17	11	5	6
Frozen	246	56	190	179	41	138

comparable figures were 5 and 6 for Kennedy. Of the 246 frozen figures produced by Nixon only 56 (23%) related to the same theme, whereas of the 179 frozen figures produced by Kennedy as occurring in the same sentence, only 41 (23%) related to the same theme. Because of the very strong cross-speaker agreement, the data for both men were combined. Results of a 2 × 2, χ^2 test done over these combined data produced a value of 16.15 ($p < .01$) indicating that novel figures which occur in the same sentence in discourse are more likely to relate to the same theme than is true for frozen figures occurring in the same sentence.

There is one further implication arising out of this analysis and concerns the relationship of novel and frozen figurative language to one another and to sentence length. The most straightforward assumption would seem to be that the number of novel and frozen figures produced within the same linguistic unit should be relatively uncorrelated as should the number of novel and frozen figures produced by different individuals. In addition, this analysis suggests that frozen figures ought, in both cases, to correlate quite strongly with output length, however defined, and that novel figurative language ought not correlate quite so strongly, if at all, with output length. Even though such correlations are easy to obtain from much of the material presented thus far, it is also clear that correlations involving length and number of frozen and/or novel figures must be somewhat inflated in that the production of any figure requires some few (or many) words for its expression. For this reason, the meaning of correlations involving length as one of the variables must always be interpreted with some caution.

Table 3.4 presents correlations for eight different sets of speakers and situations. The situations are categorized into speaking and writing situations, although all speaking situations are computed across the speech of a single speaker, while all writing situations involve correlations computed across a group of respondents. For the four different speaker situations, the pattern of correlations obtained between length and frozen figures and between length and novel figures is reasonably comparable: utterance length correlates more strongly (or in one case equally well) with frozen than with novel figures. The range of correlations for frozen is sufficiently narrow and the correlations (even with the caution mentioned previously) sufficiently high as to suggest that it might often be possible to estimate the length of an utterance from the number of frozen figures it contains. While this is not a very significant theoretical finding it is of some practical significance when faced with the rather onerous task of counting words: present data suggest in some instances a simple count of frozen figures might provide an appropriate estimate of utterance length.

The correlations involving words and novel figures, while of lower magnitude, are still fairly significant, even if again we keep our caution in mind. At first glance it would seem to appear that lengthy segments containing a good deal of frozen figurative language ought also contain a good deal of novel figurative

TABLE 3.4
Correlations among Certain Quantitative Properties of Language Samples

	Correlation		
Situation	Novel figures with frozen figures[a]	Number words with number frozen figures	Number words with number novel figures
A. Speaking situation			
1. Case study: Gestalt (Pollio & Barlow, 1975)	.18	.71**	.45*
2. Case study: Psychoanalytic (5 sessions) Chapter 6	−.45	.86**	.79**
3. Kennedy–Nixon debates (Pollio & Francisco, 1974)			
Kennedy	.47**	.73**	.53**
Nixon	.42**	.56**	.58**
B. Written samples			
1. Child compositions (3 grades) (Pollio & Pollio, 1974)	.19*	.49**	.27**
2. TAT protocols (Lockwood, 1974)	.07	.49*	.19
3. Adolescent compositions (Schonberg, 1974)			
Book character	.27	.76**	.27
Self as topic	.24	.79**	.40*

[a] In those cases where there was more than a single correlation median values are reported.
*p < .05.
**p < .01.

language, although correlations computed between novel and frozen figures indicate this is a tenable assumption only for the debate conditions. The essentially zero correlation obtained in Gestalt therapy, and the negative, although not quite significant, correlation obtained in psychoanalytic therapy indicate that this is not the case for all four situations. The most plausible summary description of the data obtained for these four specific situations would seem to be as follows: in the case of public oratory, novel and frozen figurative usage covary with utterance length and with each other. In the case of therapy, particularly of the psychoanalytic variety, there seem to be two different types of lengthy communications, with one being composed mainly of frozen figurative language and with the other composed mainly of novel figurative language.

In a sense this difference between the two situations makes some sense especially if we look at the functions of figurative expression in both contexts. For the politician, unlike the patient (as for other speakers) novel and frozen figures do not seem to represent two different categories of figurative expression. Rather, both must be seen as under the purpose of the public orator, which as Osborn and Ehninger (1962) put it, is to aim at simple "mass reaction" and to minimize, if not ignore completely, complicated private experience. Since public speakers hope to provoke an immediate rather than a more contemplative reaction they often resort to frozen or "slightly" frozen figures. As Osborn and Ehninger (1962) put it: "the orator [must] gamble as little as possible with error (for such error) can easily persist into a genuine puzzlement which might backfire on his intended meaning. Additionally, because of the time problem, attention must be directed as quickly as possible to resolution" (p. 233).

In short what Osborn and Ehninger suggest is that an orator cannot depend upon innovative or idiosyncratic figures but must depend instead upon prosaic and well-known ones. This may account for the rather small number of novel figures in the speech of both Kennedy and Nixon as well as in their tendency to repeat and amplify novel figures within the same answer. What this further suggests is that public orators are often forced by the constraints of their particular speaking situations to use frozen figures as they would, and do, use novel figures in other less public situations. For this reason, the pattern of values obtained seems internally consistent and, of necessity, at some variance with the pattern found in other situations.

The rather special role played by figurative language in public debate probably also accounts somewhat for the view that figures have been primarily thought of as ornamental and masking rather than as innovative and functional. The constraints of the public oratory situation encourage safety and reflexive response at the expense of creative and possibly obscure language usage. When an orator uses figurative language he counts not only on an immediate and expected response but perhaps just as often on a way out of a particularly difficult situation. In such situations metaphors are used to conceal and obscure rather than to illumine and reveal and it is just of these cases of public oratory which give metaphor a tarnished, if not bad, name.

Turning now to the therapy context, correlations reported in Table 3.4 suggest that there are two different types of lengthy utterances: those that contain a great deal of novel figurative language and those that contain a great deal of frozen figurative language. Although a somewhat more detailed and exact analysis of the role of figurative expression in psychotherapy must wait until Chapters 5 and 6, our results do seem interpretable in the following admittedly schematic way. When beginning to talk about personal problems of significance, a patient would seem to have one of two options: either to attempt to avoid talking about them or to attempt to face the problems in a new and possibly constructive way. In the former case we would expect the patient to speak in a fairly clichéd way (to use a great deal of frozen figurative language), while in the latter case we would expect the patient to speak in a novel way. Given these two separate possibilities, we would not expect the number of frozen and novel figures to correlate with one another, or perhaps even negatively.

Turning now to the second half of Table 3.4, which deals with cross-subject correlations, the values seem somewhat more comprehensible and somewhat more in agreement with expectations growing out of prior analyses. In all four cases, there is little or no correlation across individuals between the number of novel and frozen figures they produce. In addition, correlations involving length and frozen figures are all positive and significant while correlations involving length and novel figures are lower and significant in only two of the four cases reported. What this means is that a long composition generally contains many more frozen figures than a short one, and only occasionally more novel figures than a short one. In addition there is no relationship between novel and frozen language outputs across different individuals.

The pattern of results obtained across all eight language samples suggests that different situations call forth different patterns of figurative usage. All four written samples as well as the two therapy samples, agree in part or entirely with earlier analyses of how speakers or writers produce figurative language. Only the debate context suggests a relationship between novel and frozen figures and between novel figures and length. As we have tried to argue, there is very little distinction between novel and frozen figures within the context of public discourse and it is only within the confines of a more private or poetic context that the distinction between novel and frozen figures makes sense, especially as reflected in terms of their different patterns of use.

Personality and Figurative Language

When we listen, even ever so casually, to the conversations of different individuals it soon becomes fairly obvious that certain people produce a great deal of figurative language while others scarcely produce any at all. Fortunately or unfortunately, however, there has been almost no research into the personal characteristics of those people who use relatively more figurative expression and this would seem to be a relevant dimension in any understanding of the metaphoric process. In addition, if stable patterns do exist, an assessment of figurative output might provide a relatively sensitive procedure for the clinician involved in doing psychotherapy.

One way of gaining some understanding as to what types of individuals might use a great deal of figurative language would be to consider what has come to be called their "cognitive style." In using this term, reference is being made to the characteristic manner in which individuals think, perceive and interpret their environment; the manner in which, and the degree to which, they experience their emotions; and, finally, the mode in which they experience things subjectively. Chapman (1971), Harvey (1961, 1963, 1966) and Shapiro (1965) have all stressed this characteristic way of behaving which for them forms the very basis of personality and has great influence upon an individual's so-called character structure. Since the manner in which a person thinks and perceives his environment is such an important determiner of what he does, it might be possible to piece together the personal characteristics of the high metaphorizer by considering various aspects of the individual's cognitive style. Even more important, however, is that it might also be possible to discover which aspects of cognitive style facilitate or impede the metaphorical process, and on this basis begin to approach the closely related topics of creative thinking and creativity.

Although in the past the term cognitive style has been used to label several different, but vaguely related, phenomena in this context it will carry one sure connotation; namely, that characteristic manner in which an individual perceives, thinks about, and reacts to various aspects of the environment. For example, in perceiving and experiencing an event an individual might attend to major details resulting in an accurate picture of what is going on; or perhaps formulate only a vague, impressionistic, and holistic view of things. Alternatively the person might attend only to minute details resulting in a form of tunnel vision and be prevented from seeing the forest for the trees. Another aspect of cognitive style is whether an individual is in touch with his or her feelings and whether or not he or she represses, suppresses, or expresses them. Perhaps reviewing how other theorists have considered the notion of cognitive style might help to clear things up a bit.

Chapman (1971), in discussing cognitive style, considers it to be conceptually similar to Kelly's (1955) earlier concept of cognitive constructs. Kelly felt that people organize and selectively interpret stimuli in such a way as to aid in meeting their own needs. They use these personal hypotheses or constructs to give meaning and structure to their perceptual, emotional, and cognitive experiences. The primary difference between Kelly's cognitive constructs and the concept of cognitive style is that Kelly's concept deals primarily with interpersonal behavior whereas the present focus is on intrapersonal behavior.

Harvey (1961, 1963, 1966), in a series of papers dating from the early 1960s, has studied cognitive style extensively in an attempt to interrelate cognitive functions with theories of motivation and affect, perceptual processes, and value orientations. His conceptual systems theory (CST) assumes that each individual maintains his own necessary level of emotional activation on the basis of his own particular cognitive style. People with low levels of activation develop cognitive styles which are rigid, inflexible and closed, so as to aid them in avoiding excessive stimulation and ambiguity and in maintaining the status quo. Individuals requiring higher levels of stimulation develop cognitive styles which are more open, allowing for greater ambiguity, new awareness, and changes in the status quo. Harvey's This I Believe Test (TIB) was developed as a measure designed to estimate an individual's degree of cognitive flexibility. By having the person write short statements dealing with his attitudes about certain ideas, and then scoring these statements as to their degree of flexibility, Harvey attempted to assess cognitive style. Unfortunately, in his attempt to create an easily administered and reliable technique, he ended up only with being able to tell which of four levels of cognitive flexibility a given subject characteristically exhibited.

While flexibility is probably a quite general and extremely important component of cognitive style, there are also several other aspects which Harvey's system fails to take into account.

Shapiro (1965) has provided an excellent description of how cognitive style relates to individual patterns of personality. He leaves little doubt that the manner of perceiving and experiencing the environment is a major determinant of an individual's characteristic behavior. One example should be sufficient to demonstrate this approach. The particular character style known as the "hysterical style" is defined by the fact that such a person seems to form vague and impressionistic ideas and has a great deal of difficulty in remembering details or factual information. Such individuals tend to perceive what goes on around them in a holistic, impressionistic manner and since facts and details are probably never noticed in the first place, it is difficult for this type of person to recall them later on.

Shapiro also discusses the nautre of cognitive styles associated with several other so-called character disorders and points out how such patterns come to permeate all aspects of a person's behavior. If we know something about how an individual perceives and relates to his environment, it is then a bit easier to make some hypotheses as to what that person will or will not do in a particular situation. This, in effect, is what the skilled clinician does in using a Rorschach profile in making inferences about the person taking the test.

More specific to the case of figurative language, it seems reasonable to talk about a metaphoric style if, and only if, we can delineate the properties of such style in some detail. As we have noted in Chapter 1, much of the literature dealing with metaphorizers has been pursued from a Freudian point of view and in this context figurative language has been conceived primarily as a defense mechanism used to deal with repressed feelings at a sublimated level.

The analytic picture obviously is quite incompatible with expectations derived from other analyses of the metaphorical process (e.g., Gordon, 1961; Koestler, 1964). Here, metaphor users are described as flexible rather than rigid in cognitive style. In addition, such individuals seem to be in touch with, and responsive to, their feelings. Unlike certain types of neurotics they tend not to rely on repression as a defense mechanism. It seems likely that the dark picture painted by the early Freudian was incorrect or at least overdrawn largely because the contours of this picture were derived from an analysis concerned primarily with frozen rather than novel figurative language.

While most theoretical descriptions of a person who would use much figurative language have been taken from a psychoanalytic perspective, in more recent years a brighter, healthier image has appeared. This is particularly true for the existential—humanistic image which is represented by Maslow (1962) in his discussion of what he terms "B—cognition." This form of cognition, which is present in so-called self-actualized individuals, is conceptually flexible and emotionally open to new experiences and to new ways of perceiving. It allows an individual to see the new, the fresh, and the unusual in his environment and in himself. Maslow's description of such cognitive style sounds very much like a description of the metaphorical process. For this reason it appears that Maslow's approach might provide a more accurate picture than that provided by early psychoanalysis.

Only two attempts have been made to study directly the cognitive styles of people who use metaphor easily and frequently. One of these studies, a dissertation by Porter (1969), dealt with the use of divergent thinking in the production of metaphor; while the other, a dissertation by Chapman (1971), is more directly relevant to this context. In his dissertation, Chapman attempted to intercorrelate the variables of intelligence, cognitive style, preference for metaphor, and production of metaphor. As a measure of preference for metaphor, Chapman devised a pencil-and-paper metaphor-preference scale in which pairs of figurative and literal expressions of feelings were presented and in which subjects were asked to choose the statement they most preferred. In order to obtain a measure of metaphor productions, Chapman asked his subjects to write an essay about a particularly meaningful or peak experience (Maslow, 1962). Chapman (1971) felt that in order to describe a peak experience, the subject would need to use metaphoric expressions, and this was found to be the case.

The subjects' scores on these two measures were then correlated with their scores on a pencil-and-paper intelligence test (the Shipley–Hartford scale) as well as with their scores on a paper-and-pencil test of cognitive style (the Harvey TIB). The results of the study showed that there was no correlation between metaphor preference and metaphor production. It also found that while intellectual level was an important variable in preference for metaphor — probably as a result of the range of a subject's vocabulary — it had no direct bearing on the production of metaphor. The ability to communicate with metaphorical expression was found to correlate with only one measure of an individual's cognitive style: the more flexible the style, the more metaphor produced. The fact that intelligence was related to the perception but not to the use of metaphor should have been expected as this had been demonstrated previously by both Carlson (1963) and Horne (1967).

Several difficulties with a simple interpretation of Chapman's results vis-à-vis cognitive style are fairly obvious. First, Harvey's measure of cognitive style actually deals with only one dimension of style, the degree of cognitive flexibility in social–interpersonal situations. In using Harvey's TIB test, Chapman forfeited a great deal of information about other aspects of the cognitive styles characteristic of his subjects. Second, as Chapman himself points out, metaphor would be more effectively elicited by having subjects describe their current emotional states rather than their emotional states at some point in the past.

Aside from this study, Porter (1969) dealt with personality factors and figurative language. In this study, Porter examined the relationship between the incidence of figurative language in written narrative and essay compositions and the divergent thinking factors of fluency, flexibility and originality as measured by a battery of tests developed by Torrance (1966). Results of Porter's analysis showed that all correlations were low positive, with the correlation between originality and the incidence of metaphor being the only significant one. Porter did find that people tend to use more metaphor in narratives than in essays possibly because, as he put it, they viewed narratives as more unstructured and as offering more freedom of expression for creative writing.

Probably the most important reason for Porter's low correlations had to do with his not differentiating between novel and frozen metaphor. Had he controled for the presence of frozen metaphor, and had he weighted the more original or novel metaphors more heavily, his correlations might have been higher.

Both of these studies, but, more importantly, the background theorizing out of which they grow, suggest the following description of the personal characteristics of a person who would use a great deal of figurative language:

> He or she is a flexible individual. He or she is perceptually open and notices and responds to more than other individuals. He or she is able to attend to several diverse things at one time and to integrate and organize these diversities effectively. He or she shows a preference for complexities and is able to tolerate ambiguities and confusion. He or she is unafraid of the unusual and the new, and is therefore willing to experience things in new ways and to be open to change and growth. Such flexibility allows the person to be immature and childlike when desired, but able to respond in a logical, adult manner when needed. Such a person is in touch with him or herself and with his or her own feelings and desires. The metaphorizer can respond to emotion because repression is not used as a defense. He or she can be uninhibited, but can also delay gratifying needs and wishes. Because such a person is not afraid of what is not understood, he or she has access to unconscious and relatively immature, primary process thinking. However, while the person can regress, he or she has sufficient personal strength to "return to reality" when such is wanted or needed. It is this flexible but controlled cognitive style that allows the person to be creative, to produce novelty.

This picture is intended only as a rough sketch and not as a finished drawing. The hypothesis behind this set of observations is that high producers of novel figurative language can be described as having cognitive styles which allow them to function more effectively and more flexibly than is true for low producers of novel figurative language.

In order to test some aspects of this hypothesis, Lockwood (1974) used a double-blind experimental procedure in which stories written to selected cards from the Thematic Apperception Test (TAT) and protocols given in responses to the Roschach Inkblots Test were obtained from 40 student–subjects. The TAT stories were scored by a rating team for the amount of novel figurative language produced by each student. The mean number of novel and frozen figures produced is presented in Table 1.1 while rater reliabilities are presented in Table 3.1. In both cases, values fell within expected and acceptable ranges.

Once reliability data were evaluated, those 10 subjects forming the upper and lower quartiles, in terms of the total number of novel figures produced, were designated as high and low metaphorizers, respectively. Rorschach protocols of these 20 subjects were then scored and interpreted without any information as to whether or not each protocol was that of a high or low metaphorizer. Idiographic descriptions of the cognitive style exhibited on the Rorschach by each of the 20 students were prepared, and following this, Lockwood attempted to identify each subject as a high or low metaphorizer on the basis of expectations derived from an analysis of cognitive styles. Using this method he was able to identify high and low metaphorizers correctly 80% of the time.

By sifting through Rorschach protocols, Lockwood (1974) found that he could provide no consistent characterization of the cognitive style(s) common to high metaphorizers. He did find, however, that low metaphorizers consistently used extensive, constrictive, and repressive defense mechanisms, resulting in, as he put it, "rigid and ineffective use of inner resources." Only 1 of the 10 high metaphorizers could be described as a constricted individual, that is, as one whose cognitive style was similar to that characterizing low metaphorizers. An examination of the subject's TAT stories showed that although he did produce some novel figurative language, these metaphors were not revealing of the high metaphorizer's feelings of personality; instead they seemed to have been produced more for the purpose of hiding. Both in length and content, the stories produced by this subject seemed to fit the description of the high metaphorizer given by the Freudians, as defensive, constricted and as having very little available creative potential. This subject, however, was the exception; all other high metaphorizers exhibiting more open cognitive styles.

In addition to this study by Lockwood dealing with college-age subjects is one by Schonberg (1974) dealing with adolescent subjects between the ages of 16 and 17. Although Schonberg was concerned primarily with the development of figurative language (see Chapter 7 for a further presentation of her findings) she did do a clinical analysis of themes present in compositions written in response to the request, "Write a composition on the topic, Who am I?" These compositions were then rated for number of metaphors as well as for various clinically significant themes (for reliability values, see Table 3.1).

Since her study was undertaken within a combined Eriksonian–Piagetian framework, clinical judgments revolved around the psychosocial level of the adolescent writer as well as around the specific themes treated figuratively. For psychosocial level 3 independent clinical judges produced agreement values ranging between 78 and 88%, respectively. For themes treated figuratively, agreement values between pairs of raters was at 65%; however, only those themes picked out by 2/3 raters were tallied in Schonberg's final analysis of the data.

In terms of psychosocial level, about three-quarters of the high-school students studied were found to be dealing with such appropriate adolescent conflicts as ego diffusion and identity. Only one-quarter were judged to be avoiding such issues or as having prematurely resolved them. In order to examine the relationship of figurative usage to psychosocial level more directly, the final sample of 40 adolescents was divided into quartiles on the basis of how many figures they had used in their compositions. The upper quartile of students was used to define a high-metaphorizer group while the lower quartile used to define a low-metaphorizer group. Of the ten high metaphorizers, all had been judged to be at an age-appropriate adolescent stage, with seven of these students judged to be attempting realistic resolutions of adolescent problems. For eight of these ten students, the theme of their compositions concerned personal integration.

On the surface, there was no clear pattern of results for low metaphorizers: six students, however, were judged as not being at age-appropriate levels, with four judged to be avoiding issues of adolescence and with two judged as having made premature resolutions. The remaining four students were described as experiencing ego diffusion. A fairly clear pattern did emerge, however, when composition themes were compared for their presence and absence across the high or low groups. No student in the low-metaphor group was judged to be dealing with personal integration, which contrasted sharply with eight out of ten students in the high-metaphor group. The only themes present in the low-metaphor group were relationships to others (seven occasions) and to a lesser degree mastery (three occasions), with this latter theme present only in compositions written by females.

In sum, while all ten high metaphorizers were judged to be at age-appropriate levels, only four low metaphorizers were. The most frequent theme for high metaphorizers (eight of ten students) was personal integration. This theme, however, was never present in any of the compositions written by low metaphorizers, where only the themes of relationships to others and to a lesser degree mastery were judged to be of importance.

In this study then, Schonberg (1974) found that high novel-metaphor rates clearly identified those students who were at age-appropriate psychosocial levels of adolescence; and that for these students the use of novel metaphor reflected cognitive flexibility. Ego integration — the normative issue of establishing a sense of identity regardless of the pain — was being dealt with resourcefully by these students. For these students, high novel- metaphor rates reflected their creative and/or insightful movements toward finding solutions for themselves; for those experiencing ego diffusion, high novel-metaphor rates seemed to reflect an awareness of a paradox and an ability to face inconsistencies in themselves and in their world.

Of the low metaphorizers most (six) were not at age-appropriate psychosocial levels and some (four) were experiencing ego diffusion. Not one of the low metaphorizers, however, was primarily concerned with ego integration: two of the four were experiencing what clinically would be called ego diffusion and one of those avoiding adolescence, had the primary concern of mastery. The low-metaphorizer group thus did not utilize their resources in talking about themselves or their problems. While these students may excel when creativity is required in other areas such as school work, it was clear, as Schonberg (1974) concluded, that "cognitive flexibility was blunted," and this was reflected not only in their choice of themes but in their relatively infrequent use of novel figurative language.

In two studies, then, where language users were separated out into high and low producers of novel figurative language certain clear trends emerged: low metaphor users seemed to be personally constricted and incapable of dealing innovatively or flexibly with significant personal concerns. High metaphorizers, on the other hand, while not necessarily presenting a single simple picture, did seem to be better in touch with themselves and did seem to be better able to deal with, even if not resolve, issues of personal concern. On the basis of these results it seems reasonable to conclude that an ability to use novel metaphoric language is probably correlated with an ability to work effectively on personal problems and in this way the picture of a high metaphorizer makes contact and merges with much of the literature relating problem-setting and problem-solving activities to metaphoric productivity. In the end, it would seem to be Maslow's (1962) view rather than Freud's, that better captures the spirit of these results.

An Experiment or Two on Anomaly and a Bit of Speculation

For much of the current work, our methodological strategy can perhaps be best described as an empirical waiting game. That is, we waited until a speaker more or less independently first produced some bit of figurative language and then we dutifully counted it and recorded the conditions under which it occurred. While this strategy is a viable one for many different purposes, there are certain problems that seem to require a much more directed approach. One such problem with regard to figurative language would seem to concern the ability of native speakers and hearers to interpret word sequences never before encountered; or, just that condition serving to define novel figurative expression. In a sense, the purpose of this set of experiments is to see just how far it is possible to push the semantic interpretation system of a speaker–hearer before a given sequence of words will be judged as nonsense.

But why be interested in pushing this particular limit? An answer to this question would seem to have implications not only for a theory of figurative language but also for a theory of the subjective lexicon as well. Generally speaking, previous attempts to determine the limits of sense for word combinations have made a clear distinction between syntactical and semantic eccentricity

3. THE MEASUREMENT OF METAPHOR AND SOME FINDINGS   93

and have focused their attention onto syntactically well found but semantically odd sentences. Although much of the early work on this topic was designed to demonstrate the independence of syntax and semantics, more recent attempts have generally been described as dealing with the topic of anomaly.

One of the earliest psycholinguistic studies on this topic was performed by Miller and Isard (1963), who defined anomaly as occurring when semantic rules were violated; that is, when certain nouns or classes of nouns were chosen that were not appropriate to certain classes of verbs and vice versa. Miller and Isard (1963) contend that when semantic rules are ignored in the selection of words for a sentence "no compound sense can be attached to their concatenation." In defense of this position they point to the meaninglessness of the sentence: "The boy spoke the triangle," in which the verb spoke is seen as inappropriate for use with the noun triangle. They further state than an "adequate semantic theory must incorporate a dictionary that lists for each word all of the syntactic functions and all the senses of the word..." (Miller & Isard, 1963, p. 218). What this means is that certain words can select certain others in a speaker–hearer's dictionary in which each word is already listed in all of its possible meanings.

On this basis, a combination such as *academic liquid* would have no meaning because liquid can't apply to "a person or human activity." Miller and Isard (1963) add that *academic liquid* could have a meaning if an additional semantic property were added, as in the sentence: "The academic liquid filled the universities' ink pots [p. 220]." They do not, however, specifically point out that the additional property added to the initial phrase simply consists of the introduction of an appropriate context. More importantly, they fail to note that an individual speaker–listener always has the option to supply his own context whether particular semantic constraints allow him to or not.

In a different, and somewhat more philosophical context, Pap (1960) follows the same general line of argument and notes that "It is meaningless to say of a stone that it drinks milk," because the predicate "drink [is] restricted to animals" (p. 50). Really? What about "my car guzzles gasoline," and "the ground was thirsty"? Bolinger (1965), also using somewhat the same line of argument as Pap, concludes that the sentence "He walked right through the bachelor" is anomalous; undoubtedly, however, he would accept the juxtaposition, "He looked right through the bachelor" or "She saw right through the bachelor." Although Bolinger quarrels with Katz and Fodor (1963) about how people recognize anomaly, he does not disagree that anomaly is in fact what they are perceiving. Bolinger, who further in his paper, emphasized a speaker's ability to produce metaphor, nonetheless neglects to note that metaphor and anomaly are not as different as most theories (and theorists) would have us expect. Olson (1970), however, correctly notes that although anomalies "...violate selection restrictions,.... the perception of a referent event is a *cognitive* process, not a linguistic one (p. 258).

The crux of the matter seems to be that anomalous sentences no matter by who or how made never manage to look like just empty sentence shells. Witness some sample sentences from Miller and Isard (1963):

(1) Sloppy poetry leaves nuclear minutes.
(2) The popular Latin mare worked tempers.

Far from being empty of meaning, these sentences would seem to be quite readily interpretable. Although we are not always sure *what* the meaning is immediately, we are sure that something meaningful is being said. And why do we feel these sentences are meaningful? Because: (1) they are grammatical and we have learned to look for meaning where there is grammar; and (2) because we are singularly accustomed to metaphoric juxtapositions which "violate" ordinary semantic rules. In the latter case we are very aware that certain classes of words take others that they ordinarily shouldn't. Why? Because the rules that "violate" semantics and make anomalous sentences are the very same ones that make metaphors possible. In one sense it seems reasonable to feel that anomalous expressions are metaphoric precisely for the very reasons they are anomalous: because they conjoin words or phrases which are grammatically arranged but which don't ordinarily go together. The Miller and Isard (1963) example, "The boy spoke the triangle," is more difficult to process meaningfully (though not at all impossible) than an "anomalous" sentence actually used in their experiment, like, "Romantic ink follows wasted games," (p. 227) or than a similarly manufactured anomaly, such as "Snug olives spread splintered subdivisions" (Truscott, 1970, p. 191). It really represents no great stretch of imagination to see the first sentence as dealing with love affairs (sordid or not) and the second as chronicling the effect of dry martinis on a suburban housing development.

The difficulty involved in dealing with anomalous sentences lies not only, nor primarily, in the fact that they break semantic rules but rather in the effort listeners and speakers must expend in discovering the meaning implied by their structure and setting. This then is the nub of the problem: to describe when a juxtaposition of disparate elements is viable and useful and when it is simply anomalous, or even worse, nonsensical.

In order to approach this problem experimentally, Burns (1975) generated a series of sentences on the basis of a well-specified and perfectly arbitrary mechanical production rule. Such a procedure was used in order to insure that words were assigned to positions within a sentence on the basis of form class and not meaning.

In each of three experiments, nine sentences were used. Three of these were actual sentences which had occurred in such places as Southern Appalachian folksongs as well as in readily available children's books. Two mechanically generated sentences were paired with each of these three sentences with the provision that each of the yoked sentences have the same grammatical structure as the model. Control sentences were produced by taking a random sample of the first 1,000 words contained in the Thorndike–Lorge list and then randomly placing these words in empty sentence frames solely on the basis of form class. Only in those cases where artificial sentences were readily interpretable — "The boy picked up silver rings" — were they dropped from the experiment.

Examples of a real and two artificial sentences, taken from the folksong experiment are as follows:

He courted her for seven long years.
**They play us by rapid careful scenes.
**She covers him with rich thin fears.

All of Burns' (1975) experiments involved two different phases: (1) learning all nine sentences as responses in a paired-associates task; and (2) interpreting the meaning of each of the nine sentences. For half of the subjects, learning preceded interpretation, and for the other half, interpretation preceded learning. All subjects were told that the "contrived" sentences were derived from literary sources and that although they might find them difficult to explain that they should try. (All comparisons reported here were within subjects.)

For our purposes, two results are of most importance. In the study dealing with the folksong sentences, Burns found that subjects were able to provide an interpretation for the three actual sentences 100, 92, and 92% of the time, respectively. Results for artificial sentences showed a median value of 75% interpretation (range 92%–50%), with no subject rejecting the task out of hand. In terms of learning, results showed that subjects who learned first and then interpreted correctly anticipated 59% of the words comprising real sentences and 24% of the words comprising the two yoked artificial ones. More importantly, for subjects who interpreted first and learned second, natural sentences produced 75% correct responses while artificial sentences produced 61% correct. What this means is that subjects can and do interpret contrived sentences, and if then asked to learn such sentences are able to do so about as rapidly as is true for natural sentences.

A second study, using different sentences and a slightly different learning procedure, produced values of 68 and 32%, respectively correct for the learn–interpret order and 77 and 75%, respectively for the interpret–learn order for natural and artificial sentences, respectively; while a third study produced values of 39 and 27 and 63 and 59%, respectively. A similar study conducted by Pitts (1975) at the University of Wales also showed that subjects are able to interpret contrived sentences and then use them in a further task. All of these results lead us to question whether the idea of anomaly night not itself be anomalous. In a somewhat more constructive way, these findings argue for the ability of native speakers to tolerate an enormous amount of semantic violation in sentences for which they can still find some (metaphoric) meaning. To be sure, the category of anomalous sentences is probably not empty (see, *The boy spoke the triangle*) but just as surely it is nowhere nearly as large as prior analyses might suggest.

In all of Burns' (1975) experiments, as well as in comparable studies reported by Pitts (1975) there seemed to be two different ways in which subjects were able to interpret the meaning of sentences presented to them: either they invented a context within which the sentence might have been uttered or they interpreted one or another of the words in a figurative sense. Only rarely did subjects in either of the experiments fail to find some interpretation. These three results, taken in combination, suggest that listeners make the tacit supposition, as very many poets and literary critics have suggested, that every speech act is meant to say something even if that something may not be immediately apparent. The interpretation of a given utterance is almost never context free and while the idea of selection restrictions may be useful in a theoretical sense it is not necessarily used by speakers and listeners. Under the tacit assumption that speakers or writers mean to say something, almost any selection restriction can be violated and overcome.

In terms of semantic theory these results argue that any attempt to describe the subjective lexicon independent of existing or invented contexts is likely to be useful only in a logical sense. All speaking takes place in context and any attempt to provide a context-free, selectionally bound lexicon must fall short of being able to describe the nature of an interpretative process for speech. A lexicon is viable only insofar as it provides a situation-free description of how words have been used in the past; it does not necessarily tell us how they are being used or understood in the present. Although revised semantic theory such as that proposed by Lakoff (1972), McCawley (1968, 1971), and others is coming increasingly to recognize the significance of context, figurative language is still described as a violation of one or another semantic rule. Perhaps we need reconsider a position such as this, where so natural a process as figurative language is always considered as an infraction of some rule rather than as an attempt to take account of the changing nature of the world and what it is that needs talking about in that world. Language surely does have semantic rules even though many of the more important things that get said require these rules to change as both the speaker—listener and the world change.

SUMMARY AND CONCLUSIONS

The primary purpose of this chapter was to examine figurative language as she is spoke. In order to do this it was first necessary to develop a well-specified measurement procedure and then determine if this procedure could be used reliably in assessing the occurrence of figurative language in a number of different linguistic contexts. Reliability values, in fact, did show that the procedure developed was a reasonable one; but even more than that, provided some data as to how well and easily figurative language is perceived. Not surprisingly, the overwhelming conclusion of these results is that novel figurative language is much more readily recognized than frozen figurative language.

Differences between novel and frozen figurative language occurred on the output side as well. Not only is frozen figurative language more frequent than novel figurative language in almost all contexts, its distribution properties in speech differ as well. Here, the major conclusion seems to be that whereas frozen figures occur at fairly regular intervals in all kinds of language samples, novel figurative language is much more episodic in output. What this suggests is that when speakers resort to novel language there is something different to be said and that they say as much about it as they can, given the overriding structure and limits imposed by a particular figure and by a particular speech setting. Although the exact properties of a novel burst are somewhat different across different situations, the fact that such episodes occur seems a fairly general one.

Public speaking, however, represents special situations in which these patterns do not emerge as clearly as in many others. Here the conclusion seems to be that frozen figurative language is used in somewhat the same way as novel figurative language is used in other situations. The reason for this is also fairly clear: an oratorical or public-debate situation requires the speaker to use words and figures whose evocative properties are fairly well known and predictable because public speakers cannot allow themselves the luxury of an idiosyncratic figure whose meaning might only confuse rather than convince. No public speaker — at least not any political public speaker — wants his audience to think too much or too deeply and for this reason it seems as if figurative language in the context of political discourse is often used to confuse or hide behind rather than to clarify or reveal. In a sense, it is just this tendency to obfuscate figuratively that has given figurative language its somewhat tarnished reputation.

No analysis of any aspect of speech can be complete without some consideration of the speaker. This is no less true for figurative language than for other more ordinary aspects of language usage. Results of a number of different studies indicate personal differences between speakers who use figurative language a great deal when compared to speakers who use it infrequently. Low users tend to be somewhat constricted not only in their language but in their personal cognitive styles as well. High users, while yielding no perfectly determinate sketch, do seem to be in better touch with themselves and to be better able to work with, even if not solve, issues of strong personal concern.

The speaker—listener also enters the discussion of figurative language in still another way: in terms of an ability to provide some interpretation for almost any syntactically regular word-string. This is usually accomplished either by inventing some context within which the sentence could have been uttered or by providing a figurative "reading" for one or another of the words in the sentence. Although a fact such as this may not be terribly interesting for more formal approaches to semantics, it does suggest that interpretation is a cognitive as well as a linguistic process. Perhaps even more importantly, it shows that there is a tacit agreement among speakers and listeners to try and make sense of what is being said and what is being heard. Given this agreement and our ability to interpret almost any and all sentences, it seems more reasonable to talk not of anomaly but of the relative difficulty we have with a particular utterance in a particular context. Anomaly would seem to be a clear concept only within the confines of logical analysis; within the confines of most speaking situations it seems better to talk of interpretation difficulty rather than of anomaly.

In a sense, this pattern of results has a certain balance to it and seems to agree with some of the philosophical conclusions reached in the two previous chapters. Figurative language is not an esoteric or ill-tempered child of literal language: rather it is a quite pervasive aspect of human language. And this is all to the good, for although figurative language at its ebb may camouflage, distract, or simply decorate, at its crest it reveals, clarifies, and enlarges. And it is this latter set of properties which keeps philosophers, theoreticians, and scientists — not to mention poets — continually employed and continually in its debt.

Part II

FIGURATIVE LANGUAGE AND THE PROCESS OF PSYCHOTHERAPY

4
Metaphor in Psychotherapy

Like the poet, therapists encounter people who want to know about love, suffering, mortality, and the fear of failure. Through the use of figures of speech, myths, allegories and the like, the patient, the therapist, and the poet all try to express their unique understanding of relations among the various aspects of a life. In the case of formal poetry, Bruner (1962b) has described these embodied relations as *models of awareness* largely because they seem to provide the reader or listener with a model of how to understand his or her particular pattern of impulses, emotions, and ideas. Figurative elements, whether in a poem or in speech, all depend for their impact upon images created within the reader or listener: as the person experiences these images he or she can see and know as the poet or speaker has seen and known.

Poetic images, in turn, are important because they provide a vantage point, a horizon or a perspective from which to apply a variety of processes simultaneously (like seeing, hearing, smelling, touching, tasting, feeling, asking, imagining, understanding, reasoning, reflecting, judging, evaluating) so as to allow some or all of the implications of the model to develop. But the model, or more exactly, the figure of speech providing the model, will be able to do this only to the degree that it provides a good representation that has within it the potential for future development. That is, a figure must not only provide a fitting comparison of two ideas; the comparison must work as a heuristic in furthering our understanding of what it is that is involved in either one or both of the ideas compared.

As the poet Elizabeth Sewell (1964) put it:

> [A certain metaphor] though exact will take me no further. I cannot think with it; merely note its exactness and leave it there. A certain amount of metaphor met with in poetry is of this kind. It gives its own pleasure, as Rilke does when he compares the sound of a peal of carillon bells, lingering momentarily in the sky and then vanishing, to

> a bunch of grapes hanging, with Silence eating them off, one by one. It is fitting, but not fertile. In greater poems, and in great poets for the most part, it is harder to find metaphors of this partial sort. All the figures work, have energy or lend the mind energy to work and to work further. That is to say ... they are beautiful, beauty being considered as just such a dynamic heuristic, whether we meet it in the figures of science, those of poetry, or elsewhere. It is exactly such a forward-moving or prophetic energy that the chosen metaphor, within the method in use, has to supply. (p. 59)

The explicit role of poetic language in therapy has been rather slow in being acknowledged even though it has been talked about in different contexts for a fairly long period of time. In Freud's (1905) *Psychopathology of Everyday Life*, especially in his chapter, "Slips of the Tongue," there is a very early statement of the relation between nonliteral language and the movement towards insight. Although not considered metaphoric, Freud's (1905) examples illustrate that many such slips can hardly be considered literal:

> A lady once expressed herself in society — the very words show that they were uttered with fervor and under the pressure of a great many secret emotions: 'Yes, a woman must be pretty if she is to please the men. A man is much better off. As long as he has *five* straight limbs, he needs no more.' (p. 62)

Even though Freud explained the slip in terms of the mechanisms of condensation, contamination, and the fusion of similar modes of expression, he assumed the reader would recognize that the speaker certainly did not mean what she said literally. Freud's understanding of the slip might well run as follows: Men have only four, or less, limbs. A penis is like a limb (especially when erect), and in this way, the lady talked about five rather than four limbs. By interpreting the statement as an implicit simile, an erect penis as a straight limb, Freud was able to read the implicit meaning of her statement. In this case, as in many others, most psychotherapists will attest to the disturbing, but often insightful, consequences of such nonliteral language slips.

Deutsch and Murphy (1955) provide additional unwitting testimony to the efficacy of listening to patient figures. In explaining their interview technique called associative anamnesis they encourage the neophyte interviewer to become familiarized with the patient's language. To do this, the interviewer is advised to focus on key phrases and words which the patient uses most often, especially "somatic language," the transposition of body into figures of speech. It is these key words and phrases that, for Deutsch and Murphy, guide the interview and that the interviewer will repeat many times. It is also around these words and phrases that the interviewer should structure his responses and statements. This technique prepares the patient for identifying with the therapist and serves to facilitate a transference relationship. "However, the essential thing is the intensification and continual guidance of the associations in order to maintain their continuity. Pointing out this continuity to the patient by repetition prepares him for insight into certain connections which he may have to face later" (Deutsch & Murphy, 1955, p. 21). Surprisingly, even a cursory reading of a few illustrative examples reveals a consistent pattern to their approach. Deutsch and Murphy frequently chose metaphors and other figures as their key concepts, but neither realize it nor mention it explicitly.

Bellak and Small (1965) encourage new therapists to facilitate insight in therapy not only by being responsive to figures produced by patients but also suggest that they engage their patients with "colorful language," jokes, humor, and parables. Kris (1956) refers to the same facilitative function of imaginative language without specifically describing such communications as figurative. Similarly, Wolberg (1954) encourages therapists to facilitate insight through the use of "word pictures."

Chessick (1968) reports an excellent example of the unwitting use of metaphor by a psychotherapist to facilitate insight in a female patient, first reporting the patient's dream:

> I am at a dinner party seated between my sister-in-law and my mother-in-law. I feel quite *trapped*. Mother-in-law is a good cook, but sister is taking the credit for her cooking. It is a nasty situation.
>
> [Chessick continues:] One might make a mental note of the oral and homosexual elements in this dream as well as the defensive mechanisms of denial and displacement. They fit previous formulations of the patient. In terms of dealing with the patient, however, I chose the feeling of being *trapped* to discuss. It was the predominant feeling in the dream, and led to a tremendous release of feelings about her husband and the marriage. It opened up a discussion of the patient's contribution to the trap, which was a step forward for this patient. (p. 60)

Chessick claims that his responses to the word "trapped" facilitated a radically novel discussion during which the patient was able to express a great deal of feeling about her real life circumstances—a bit of behavior she found difficult to do in the past. Like his predecessors, Chessick never makes the observation that the "feeling" he selected to work with was, in fact, embedded in a piece of metaphoric language.

But such observations, while never called by their right name, are commonplace in psychotherapy. Consider the following case involving a young soldier confined to a Veteran's Administration Psychiatric Hospital after setting fire to a gasoline depot on an army base in the South Pacific. While talking with his therapist, he remembered his state of mind at the time. His intentions were clear—to destroy an entire army base and himself at a single stroke. This same young man, while recalling a dream he had the previous night about monsters and demons in an elevator shaft, stopped, looked the therapist in the eye, and remarked, "Talking about these things is like seeing a horror movie – it's terrifying to look at, but I know I have to do it." Without a reply from the therapist, he went on to recall the ways in which he felt himself a "monster" as an adolescent. He timidly and cautiously revealed how he sadistically tortured his pets as a young teenager. His simile, "like a horror movie," set the stage for the revelations to follow. It provided a context ("horror movie") within which the patient began to talk about his problems of passivity, weakness, and helplessness and his attempts to make some dramatic, but distorted, assertions about his pain through paranoid delusions, sadomasochism, and stealth.

Most psychotherapists will attest to the rich and disturbingly imaginative metaphoric articulations patients often make in their attempts to solve perplexing problems. One man compared the therapy process to "... using Listerine. You know it works, but it tastes terrible." Another suicidal woman while talking of her relationships with her relatives offered her impression that they saw her as a "pest." From this she moved to a more dramatic understanding of her experience of herself with them. To her, pests were creatures that gnawed away at the foundations of homes and home life, and in turn were attacked by those seeking to protect their homes. She began to sense how it was that she surreptitiously "attacked" those close to her and "asked" for a punishment for her aggression and assertion. Still another middle-aged man lived in a fairly harmless delusional world in which he was a "successful businessman;" when in fact he was a welfare recipient, who through several ingenious, but questionable, maneuvers acquired a substantial welfare income. He fared much better as he began to "see" himself as a "retired gentleman" whose financial status was not really threatened. Another woman who complained, "I carry the world on my shoulders," eventually realized a correspondence between her obsession with familial responsibility and the actual deterioration and calcification of the tendons in her shoulders over the past 25 years. And finally, a middle-aged woman's depiction of her somatic complaints as "beating me to death" set the stage for a gradual realization of her tendency to punish herself for any weakness or self-indulgence.

These clinical examples of metaphoric expression in psychotherapy are hardly unique or uncommon and obviously do not capture the whole of the therapeutic experience for the patients producing them. Nevertheless they do illustrate how imaginative, spontaneously produced figures of speech clearly portray not only specific therapy issues (like the Listerine simile as expressive of the patient— therapist relationship) but more general and pervasive neurotic problems (like the woman who was being beaten to death). What written commentary there is on the occurrence and function of figurative language in psychotherapy is confined primarily to theoretical considerations, and it is to this literature which we now turn.

PSYCHOANALYTIC APPROACHES TO FIGURATIVE EXPRESSION

Anderson (1964) in an able review of the early psychoanalytic literature found three distinct trends emerging:

1. In the early days of psychoanalysis, metaphor was looked upon as an "elaborated symbolic disguise" which seemed to reduce anxiety associated with

repressed libidinal urges. In this dispensation, metaphor highlights points of resistance to interpretation (Silberer, 1951).

2. In the early 1940s Sharpe suggested a somewhat different view of the role of metaphor in psychoanalysis. While still holding to the idea that metaphor can be a disguise for more primitive impulses, she sought to use the metaphoric expressions of her patients in accordance with the following set of assumptions:

   a. Metaphors develop as second-order derivations of the emotions accompanying libidinal discharge.
   b. Spontaneous metaphor used by a patient proves upon examination to be an *epitome* of a forgotten experience.
   c. Since the earliest of all verbal images (preconscious) are the sounds of words, it behooves the analyst to attend to the patient's *phonetic* associations.
   d. Most patients' metaphors center upon pregenital and Oedipal experiences.
   e. Metaphor gives information concerning instinctual tension.
   f. The type of image derived from the patient's metaphors is highly informative; for example, visual imagery versus auditory imagery.

3. In more recent times psychoanalytic explications of metaphor reported by Anderson (1964) center on detailed elucidations of particular metaphors produced by the analysand (Baker, 1948; Erikson, 1954; Fodor, 1956; Issacs, 1952) or upon more sweeping elaborations of technical metaphors used by analysts in their theoretical essays (Brown, 1959; Dreisdadt, 1968; Pederson-Krag, 1956).

Motivating most, if not all, of this psychoanalytic work is the idea that unconscious processes are always present in the production and understanding of metaphor. Knapp (1960), for example, has argued that the metaphorical process must involve primary-process thinking because two objects will be considered equivalent in secondary process if and only if they are substantively identical. Such, however, is not the case for primary process thinking wherein there is no requirement for substantive identity; here things are rendered identical merely by their having certain salient features in common.

In an attempt to examine this assumption experimentally, Knapp (1960) asked subjects to rate the "poetical appropriateness" of lists of metaphoric expressions on a scale from one to seven. His roster of metaphors was random arrangements of instances of figurative language gleaned from Bartlett's *Familiar Quotations*, representing six abstract categories: time, conscience, death, success, love, and self-image. Knapp attempted to illustrate how a "scale of metaphors" could function as a measure of (unconscious) attitude. He assumed that a metaphor, through its ability "to equate two widely divergent objects or situations by virtue of a common attribute," effects an alliance between deep-lying and unconscious attitudes and the covert expression of these in language. By asking people to judge the poetic appropriateness of a metaphor, Knapp hypothesized that he would be able to capture the person's deep-seated attitudes relating to the six categories sampled.

Following each subject's ratings, a cluster analysis of these responses showed significant intercorrelations among the love, self-image, conscience, and success scales, with these four scales producing essentially zero correlation with the time and death scales. On the basis of these and other results, Knapp (1960) concluded that this central grouping of four scales serves to circumscribe a cognitive complex that:

> ...associated positive and buoyant self-acceptance with images of a benign conscience, a joyous and victorious success, [and] a supportive conscience...[all of which] represent a general quality of wholesome life attitude. The converse [of this complex]...would characterize a generally neurotic or disturbed character structure (p. 394)

Although Knapp's study did not contribute much to an understanding of how metaphors function in language and thought, he did demonstrate that how people rate poetic figures might prove to be useful as a semiprojective technique. In general, however, these results can guide the clinician no further than his assumption that figurative expressions are somehow "attached" to unconscious processes.

Downey (1919), in a much earlier article, was also concerned with the relation of unconscious processes to poetic language in her comparison of dream and poetic symbolism. As a starting point, she felt that both were related to deep-seated, unconscious impulses, and that both consisted of substituting one "mental object" for another. She found, however, that the motivation for dream symbolism was an attempt at disguise — the gratifying of one's forbidden wishes by masking them — while the motivation for poetic symbolism was held to be a desire for novel expression of feelings or subtle conceptualizations. Downey (1919) also points out that:

> The substitution occurring in dreams is often cryptic in nature. The underlying meaning can at times be penetrated only after the most far-reaching analysis, an analysis of the intimate life of the dreamer. Literary or poetic symbolism must be more obvious in nature else the poet's song may be sung for his ear alone. Yet, too, the allegories, the metaphors in which he delights must, for the most part, well spontaneously from his spirit and he must trust to their appealing to those among his readers whose life of instinct and emotion is similar to his own. This basal similarity in the instinctive and temperamental life constitutes native rapport. (p. 104)

As might be expected, other Freudians such as Sharpe (1950) and Silberer (1951) did not agree with Downey. In their rendition of analytic theory, there is no difference in the motivations of poetic and dream symbolism, and the usual dictum still holds that the function of metaphor is similar to that of the dream: "a form of elaborated symbolic disguise that reduces the 'psychic tension' associated with repressed libidinal urges" (Anderson, 1964, p. 55).

Despite generally good coverage of the early Freudian sources, Anderson's (1964) review is somewhat short on more recent analysis of metaphor from the analytic camp. Cain and Maupin (1961), for example, amplify and cultivate some proposals made by Ekstein (1956) on the use of metaphors with borderline and psychotic children. By using a technique termed "interpretation within the metaphor" the child therapist or analyst is able to preserve the tenuous ego organization of the borderline child. Cain and Maupin report an instance in which a child on the verge of a frenetic panic, because the red paint on his canvas began to run, was gently subdued by the therapist who, interpreting the red paint as being fire, quickly drew a fire engine, thereby reassuring the child that the fire would be extinguished.

The major theoretical statement of this position, however, had been made not by Cain and Maupin (1961), but rather by Ekstein (1966) who claimed that active focusing on the productions of schizophrenic patients in early analytic interviews facilitates the surfacing of primary process material in which such material is safely couched in, or displaced to, the symbols and conceptualizations of secondary process. More generally, he views the whole process of metaphor making as an ego function and as providing viable inroads into more adaptive ego functions for severely disturbed patients. For Ekstein (1956), metaphoric expression creates a desirable distance between the figure's latent meaning, derived from primary process sources, and its manifest meaning as it appears in the metaphor. By this method, a fearful patient can come to work with anxiety-arousing material safely and at a safe distance.

Aleksandrowicz (1962), addressing himself specifically to the psychological aspects of metaphors created by schizophrenic patients, notes that a semantic or logical interpretation of these elements will lead the therapist and patient nowhere. He senses that the affective connotations of the patient's metaphoric communications are essential elements in understanding schizophrenic communication; hence, "empathetic resonance" becomes the pathway by which lines of communication can be opened between patient and therapist.

Although not a psychotherapist in any sense of the term, Rommetveit (1974) has also tried to analyze schizophrenic language — figures of speech and all — in terms of its communicative intent rather than its semantic intent. Suppose, for example, we are talking to a schizophrenic patient in a mental hospital who says: "I too was invited, I went to the ball . . . and it rolled and rolled away . . ." The therapist's initial reaction to this is likely to be one of confusion. Although we seem to understand perfectly the two phrases *I went to the ball* and *it [the ball] rolled and rolled away*, the total statement seems to make no sense, even if we try to understand it figuratively. It is as if we have been deceived or rejected — no real communication takes place and the notion that speaker and listener share a common world, untrue. In discussing this case specifically, Rommetveit makes the point that far from making no "sense" at all, the communication expressed by this statement tells us that the speaker does not share the same world or even the same set of rules for speaking as we do. This particular act of speaking reveals the interperson break between the schizophrenic and listener, and it has little or nothing to do with a fancy party or an errant ball. The communication has meaning even if the words may not, and it is this fact that is stressed by both Aleksandrowicz (1962) and Rommetveit (1974).

Figurative Language in Psychotherapy: Some Data and a Bit of Theory

From a completely different viewpoint, Goldiamond and Dryud (1968) have dramatically illustrated the therapeutic potential of an apt metaphor in the following case report of a suicidal adolescent being seen in therapy:

> One of the discussions centered around the fact that there was little communication between the boy and his father. When either spoke, the other made some comment which terminated the conversation.... The boy commented that he did not wish his father to control him, but wished to maintain his own autonomy and would not engage in a conversation. The metaphor of a tennis game was then brought up by the therapist. If one wished to control the other player in tennis, one had to put oneself under control of the oncoming ball. Hitting the ball left made the opponent run left. Then hitting it right made him run right, and so on. But, said the young man, I can choose not to hit the ball back. Then you lose, was the reply. You're a loser. This discussion continued with vigor and the patient raised it several times since. (p. 80)

Lenrow (1966) notes that "experienced therapists, and wise men generally, are often distinguished by their gift for finding a few metaphorical words, sometimes with a touch of humor, that open new possibilities for troubled persons" (p. 145). He cites earlier discussions of the use of metaphor in psychotherapy by Butler, Rice, Laure, & Wagstaff (1962) and Weissman (1965), all of whom argued that the introduction of metaphor into a therapy interview generates a multiplicity of meanings and possibilities from which the therapist ought to be able to develop new diagnostic and therapeutic strategies, and the patient new thoughts and interpretations of his or her problems.

More specifically, Lenrow (1966) sees psychotherapy as a special case of social influence and expands this notion into seven specific functions of figurative language in therapy:

1. Metaphors provide a model of willingness to try out novel ways of looking at behavior; that is, the patient may model the therapist in using metaphors.
2. Metaphors function to simplify events in terms of a scheme or model that emphasizes some elements more than others.
3. An intimate or personal quality is achieved by the concrete referents of figurative language.
4. Metaphors have a half playful, half serious quality that permits the therapist to communicate about intimate characteristics of the patient without appearing intrusive.
5. The form of the metaphor is especially well suited for asserting the equivalence of apparently dissimilar concepts or events.

6. To the extent that metaphors refer to an interaction between an object and its environment, they are well suited for highlighting subtle social roles that a patient takes.
7. Metaphoric concepts, once learned, are likely to transfer readily to new situations that the person enters or to old ones he reenters.

Throughout his discussion Lenrow (1966) assumes that it is the therapist or analyst who provides, guides, and creates metaphors that help patients to achieve these ends. He seems to disregard the ubiquitous stature of figurative language and the everyday functioning of metaphoric expressions in facilitating creative problem solving. Fine, Pollio, and Simpkinson (1973) have looked at this process from the patient's point of view and have suggested that patients often shift to a metaphorical level of communication in therapy because it enables them to draw upon feelings and impulses currently out of awareness. In addition, they see the metaphoric communication as providing a nonthreatening context within which a severely disturbed person can communicate terrifying thoughts to the therapist. For them, this is the other side of the coin emphasized by Lenrow (1966); not only does the patient need distance from an interpretation; but also the distance from his or her own statement of the problem–situation. Both analyses, however, are meant to stress the idea that figurative language is not a defensive maneuver but often is better construed as an ego-process involving a disciplined blend or primary and secondary-level thinking.

For both Lenrow (1966) and Fine, Pollio, and Simpkinson (1973), the distance provided by a metaphor is, therapeutically speaking, a highly desirable aspect of figurative language. Lenrow also emphasizes the distancing function served by humor, and here again we are struck with the similarity between (clever) humorous expression and apt figurative communication. Both would seem to provide a new perspective on an old issue; and it is just this new and nonthreatening perspective which gives both the figure and the genuinely witty remark its impact. It is no accident that in ongoing process, observers often confuse figure and jest, for in ongoing process both may serve the same role and may bring about the same results: a momentary release from a conflictual and seemingly endless present.

A slightly different approach to metaphor has been taken by Leedy (1969) and Harrower (1972), both of whom are interested in the direct therapeutic use of poetry. For Leedy, poetry is useful to the degree that it serves to concretize a particular patient's problem or problem–situation in terms of a specific poetic image or poem. In addition, Leedy encourages his patients to write their own poetry as one way in which to express personal dilemmas. Harrower takes a much stronger stance; for her, poetry *is* therapy and although she does modify the strongest form of this argument in her discussion of adolescent poems, she still sees in poetic diction a self-regulating activity. In a sense, she sees both the content and form of poetry as indivisible, and that both form and expression must be related for poetry qua poetry to have universal as well as personal effects.

Finally Pollio and Barlow (1975), in a much more straightforwardly empirical approach, report the results of an exhaustive analysis of metaphoric expressions within a single hour of psychotherapy. In this work they made use of the Case of Audrey supplied by the American Association of Psychotherapists. The formal properties of this case have been presented in Chapter 3 of this text (see Figures 3.1 and 3.2). The particular patient considered in this case, Audrey, was a 38-year-old woman involved in her second marriage (a marriage that was to end two years after the interview). The patient had previously had two years of individual treatment that included both a male and a female therapist. At the time of the interview in question, she had been in group therapy for two years and the session related here was her first contact with this particular therapist.

The data presented in Table 3.1 indicated that not only was there good interrater reliability on the scoring of metaphoric events but, more specifically, that the patient produced a total of 150 novel figures across the complete session. Of these 150 figures, it was possible to partition all but 22 into 19 major subgroupings. In order to categorize the remaining 128 figures, two judges independently sorted each of them into content categories derived from the data with the provision that they try to minimize the number of categories needed. A specific listing of the themes involved in each of these 19 major groupings is presented in Table 4.1, in which each theme is numbered and a specific example provided to show the typical phrasing used by the patient in communicating it.

Looking first at those themes which occurred only early in the session (roughly in the first half), Pollio and Barlow (1975) noted that such themes included the major presenting complaints mentioned by the patient: her hidden desire to love (11), her harsh will (8), her strong hostility (14 and 16) and her tendency to be a "goody goody" (15). Themes that occurred only in the third quarter of the session seemed to reflect the patient's evaluation of herself as a cold and hard person (6), her inability to face her frail and imperfect human side (12), and a small number of self-deprecating remarks (17 and 18). The major themes that occurred the final quarter of the session concerned a reevaluation of who and what the patient was and is (13, 10, and 7) and more specifically, her ability to be soft and contented (4, 7, and 19). The progression of topics seems to go from a general presentation of her character as she sees it, to an unfavorable self-evaluation of that presentation, and finally to a more realistic reevaluation of herself and her character.

But how does such a change come about? Here we need look at those themes which seem to do therapeutic work (the themes that occurred in the second half of the session) as well as those that did not (those that occurred only in the first half). In addition we need look at those themes which occurred early in the first half only to be suppressed until they reappeared again in the last quarter of the session.

4. METAPHOR IN PSYCHOTHERAPY 111

TABLE 4.1
List of Figurative Themes Used by Audrey[a]

Theme number	Descriptive title	Specific examples
1	Moral Audrey (apostrophic passage)	my moral self; Moral Audrey
2	Human Audrey	the human Audrey, I'm no human self at all
3	I am anger and the anger cloud	this anger cloud I'm nothing but anger
4	I feel like a baby	the way a baby feels
5	Walls hide me and are protective	the walls would go over
6	My moral self is an iceberg	its the coldest, coldest
7	How a real woman is	you just be these qualities, these comforts
8	My will is strict and harsh	I know it's ruining, it's destroying
9	I feel like I have no self-definition	haven't got any form
10	I am discovering myself — attaining self-definition	I'm me
11	Somewhere inside I have a strong desire to love	a big warmth
12	I run from my human side	it just retreats
13	Getting acquainted with oneself	I'm finding out who I am
14	Hostility personified	hostility expressing
15	I act in a perfect way	Miss Goody Goody
16	I'm passively hostile	don't want to say no to it now
17	I have secrets	secret heart
18	I have an exaggerated opinion of me	I am God
19	I am soft like a baby (developed from BABY and REAL WOMAN)	to feel my softness

[a]From Pollio and Barlow (1975).

Perhaps the major figurative theme which does little or no therapeutic work is presented by Theme 5, the idea that Audrey is not an open person in dealing with her anger and that she defends against it by "building a wall around it." Theme 3, on the other hand, represents a theme which occurs both early and late. This theme deals with anger, considered either an intrinsic part of the patient or as a cloud which envelops her. This theme also serves to illustrate how the specific wording of a metaphor can change (for better or worse) in the short period of time involved in a single interview.

The major figurative themes, however, which did almost all of the therapeutic work concerned a division of the patient into two separate personifications, a moral Audrey and a human Audrey. These personifications then provided an enabling metaphor on which all else hinged. In order to get a feel for exactly how this occurred consider a fragment of this session beginning with the sixty-ninth communication produced by Audrey:

A: Uh huh, oh, I'm talking to the anger. [pause] So I won't have to hide it anymore, now, do I? I'm not asking you . . . 'cause it's there. I don't hide it. It's a failure to try and hide it 'cause it can't be hidden, even from myself. So now what am I going to do with it? 'Cause I am going to get angry. This isn't going to solve the problem of anger. I am going to get angry. Well, I think I'll just go in and punch the pillow. That's the best I can do right now though the kids will think I'm kind of silly . . . but they won't really.

T: All right, so who's going to be thinking you're silly? What part of you is going to be calling you silly when you do this?

A: The adult side.

T: Okay, will you be the adult side of you and pretend you're sitting next to the chair and tell yourself how silly you are for doing something like that? Be your . . .

A: Oh, yes. I'm the moral, I'm the moral, I'm the moral Audrey [last name eliminated]. There she's angry, she's punching the pillow: . . . Oh, Audrey, you're silly, you're just acting like a child. And . . . that's how I feel, only much more cold. There's warmth in that and that moral Audrey just hasn't any warmth at all, not any.

T: And what does the human Audrey say back to that? (Sagan, 1962, p. 9)

As can be seen from this fragment, Audrey begins by talking about (and in this case, talking to) her anger, a topic which makes her feel decidedly uncomfortable and "silly." The therapist counters by asking, "Who's going to be thinking you're silly?" which then leads to the idea of an "adult side." With the dichotomy between a moral and a human Audrey set up by the patient, the therapist simply moves in and proposes a dialogue between the two, thereby providing a condition within which Audrey can explore her felt ambivalence both toward herself as an angry person and toward herself as a self-repudiating person.

This fragment also provides some feel for the therapist's use of figurative language. An examination of his novel figurative output revealed that he used only two novel metaphors — the moral and the human Audrey — on more than a single occasion. As a matter of fact, Moral Audrey (or some variation thereof) occurred 15 times while Human Audrey occurred twice. An examination of the specific points at which these figures occurred in the course of this session showed that the greatest number (13) occurred during the late middle part and that they were usually produced in response to the patient's use of these same figures. It must be remembered, however, that Gestalt technique provided this patient with a chance to be harsh with that aspect of herself which already was harsh, as "my moral self is an iceberg," or "You're cold." It is this reversal of patterns which gives the Gestalt approach its punch. Most of the conversations between the patient and her moral self can be seen as figurative attempts to "take the moral Audrey to task."

The detailed analysis presented by Pollio and Barlow (1975) only demonstrates what most experienced therapists must surely already know: that figurative language plays a significant role in the psychotherapeutic process. The one aspect to all of this that is surprising, however, is how readily this conclusion appeared in the quantitative data. As they noted in their report, it was possible to segment this particular therapeutic session into three "acts," with each act defined strictly on the basis of changes in the rate of novel figurative language produced by the patient. As they also noted these acts clearly described the major movements of the session; movements which involved a relatively slow starting segment followed by a rapid burst of metaphoric and interpretive activity, concluded with a temporarily successful resolution of the presenting problems.

Not only did the patient's actions and metaphoric activity validate these divisions, an analysis of the therapist's behavior also made sense in terms of such a division. A careful examination of these behaviors showed that the therapist first encouraged general discussion of the problem, then helped facilitate figurative discovery and finally helped the patient move out of the metaphor into a more realistic resolution of the problem.

Although early psychoanalytic theory may have considered metaphors as dealing with areas of conflict and therefore only useful to the analyst for interpretation, later analysts have begun to consider such expressions as more than a defensive use of symbols. This development derives from a more discriminating and elaborated understanding of the central importance of the ego in development, adaptation, and failure in adaptation. As Breger (1973) has pointed out, Freud's use of a psychosexual model of development represents a transition between biology and psychology. Later therapists coming from within the orthodox or so-called revisionist school further helped reshape the model to a more generally psychological one. So, for example, Sullivan (1947) looked upon development as the result of crucial interpersonal experiences; Erikson (1959) brought in the idea of the psychosocial milieu, retaining and incorporating the psychosexual and the transitional (interpersonal) as a crisis in identity. The writing of Hartmann, Kris, and Lowenstein (1947) — although still tied to certain biological concepts — helped shift the treatment process to where this broadened interpretation of development, including language and communication, came to be labeled as ego psychology. The central role of the ego in mastery, executive functioning and in psychotherapy allows for more emphasis on an individual's ability to cope more adequately with instincts. Within the context of ego psychology, productive psychotherapy takes place at an implicit (or metaphoric) level of communication between patient and therapist.

A later development emerging from this focal shift is an ego psychology divorced from instinct psychology; the so-called object-relations school (Guntrip, 1969). In one aspect of this new tradition, motivations and drives are considered derivative of the person's attempts to establish and maintain personal relationships, whether good or bad, rather than as derivations of threatening or malevolent instincts. Metaphoric productions in this understanding can be viewed not only, or even primarily, as signals to repressed conflicts but as the person's best, present attempts to resolve the conflict.

As an example of this change in perspective, consider the case of a young patient who repeatedly, but cautiously, chastised the therapist for not giving "the formula" for mental health; a formula which the patient was convinced the therapist somehow possessed. In the course of therapy the patient referred to the formula as a mathematical equation which the therapist could simply give and which would surely provide the cure. The patient vehemently rejected a premature interpretation which included the obvious understanding that the word "formula" was a substitute for the phrase "mother's milk" and that this linkage implied an intense experience of helplessness and dependency in his relation to the therapist as well as a need for a good, growth-producing relationship. Months later, less mechanical and more maternal implications of this early metaphor began to emerge, particularly when the patient expressed a concern that the therapist's formula might get "spoiled" if it remained withheld. One way in which to view this metaphor is in terms of the patient's attempts to solve a taxing and terrifying problem of deprivation and ambivalence. The expression was produced not in a vacuum but in a real attempt to understand his powerful feelings for the therapist.

In more conventional terms, the metaphor eventually provided a new and vital perspective both personally and in his relationship to the therapist and others. Interestingly enough, this seems to be the epitome of metaphoric thinking. Metaphoric expressions provide a model, a heuristic, a calculus, or a perspective from which people can consider their lives and, in the case of psychotherapy, the nature of their problematic selves. For this reason it seems appropriate to study figurative language in terms of its capacity to portray and communicate experience in a novel and insightful fashion.

SUMMARY AND CONCLUSION

Although hardly ever called figurative language, experienced therapists, no matter what their orientation, have recognized the significant impact of a funny phrase or an apt figure. Whether wittingly produced or metaphorized by mistake, most commentaries agree that metaphoric expressions are tied to some unconscious or, at least, implicit aspect of the speaker's experience. Early psychoanalysts interpreted metaphoric productions as displaced and distorted fragments of repressed instincts. Within this conceptual model metaphoric production was seen as a defensive ego process with such expression serving to negotiate between emergent instincts and reality. From this attitude developed a technical use of figurative language by psychotherapists and psychoanalysts. The technique of focusing on and interpreting the patient's figurative productions was aimed at guiding a therapy conversation towards successful resolutions of instinctual conflicts. The initial stage of resolution was typically considered an avowal of a wish to act upon a specific instinctual impulse.

Helped by more recent developments in ego psychology, as well as by work in other contexts, therapists have come to see the function of figurative language in a much more positive light. For analysts such as Ekstein (1966) and Alexandrowicz (1962), metaphor represents a type of patient–therapist communication of great import. Perhaps the most seminal theorizing in this area has been done by Lenrow (1966), who not only sees figurative language as providing a somewhat playful way of talking about repressed or at least conflictual material, but who has also insisted on its communicative role as well. Unfortunately, Lenrow focused primarily on the therapist as an initiator of figurative language, and it remained for more recent investigators (Fine, Pollio, & Simpkinson, 1973; Pollio & Barlow, 1975) to reexamine figurative language as a patient process. On the basis of both theoretical and empirical analyses, the overwhelming conclusion seems to be that patients quite frequently resort to figurative language and that a particularly receptive therapist can make good use of such language in helping the patient come to some understanding of himself and his problem. Within the context of therapy, such understanding is usually called awareness, and sometimes insight. And it is the exact nature of the relationship of figurative language to therapeutic insight which forms the content of the next chapter.

5
Insight in Psychotherapy

In his book, *Key Concepts of Psychotherapy,* Singer (1965) sketches out one version of the history of therapeutic insight theory. He begins with Freud, who considered insight as an intellectual act necessary both to break resistances and to resolve transferences and concludes with more modern opinions in which insight is seen primarily as an emotional phenomenon singularly distinct from intellectual activity. According to Singer, all theorists who have dealt with this topic have come to the same conclusion: insight deals with some form of self-knowing. In his attempt to define the features of such self-knowledge Singer (1965) works hard at integrating the polarities of intellectual and emotional insight, noting, "It becomes clear that intellectual and emotional insight go hand in hand and that true intellectual insight cannot develop without its essential emotional precondition: the courage to bear surprise" (p. 271).

This discussion of the evolution of insight theory is, however, somewhat timid. Singer tries to describe such development as unfolding in a gentle and sensible fashion and asks us to believe that the only crucial issue has been whether insight more nearly approximates an intellectual or an emotional experience. In fact, an examination of the insight literature presents a quite different picture. Theories of insight formulated by psychiatrists, psychologists, and others have been quite unsystematic and even a bit haphazard. Despite this, there are some highlights as well as some generalizations which can be extracted from the confusion, and it is to this matter which we now turn.

INSIGHT AS THE CONSEQUENCE OF INTERPRETATION: THE EARLY ANALYSTS

Many analysts in the past, and some even today, conceive of insight as an uncovering — a coming into awareness or consciousness of certain forbidden impulses and/or ideas. The aim of a lengthy psychoanalysis was to make apparent to the analysand the impulses from his instinctual drives which have been long repressed and which now are problematic to him. Early analysts viewed psychopathology as the repression of a significant portion of one's instinctual life with this repression maintained by counterforces called defense mechanisms. The time and energy spent in controlling these impulses cost the patient dearly in flexibility and in the enjoyment of daily living. Periodically such drives would achieve partial, but distorted, discharge (as exigence would have it and without the cooperation of the controlling ego) and it was these discharges that became the symptoms a patient brought into analysis.

At the same time, these symptoms or drive derivatives also revealed something about the instincts repressed. Resistance in analysis was seen as the patient's last ditch effort to guarantee a nonemergence of these drives into behavior. Interpretation of resistance, and later interpretation within the context of transference, therefore, became the chief liberating factors involved in analysis. The analyst's interpretation required the analysand to cooperate in an ego process designed to bring about an emerging awareness of instinctual impulses. Accompanying this new awareness were strong feelings of anxiety expressing the possibility that such newly released instincts might get out of hand. In the early days of psychoanalysis, Wheelis (1950) relates, "... becoming aware of what was repressed constituted insight which — consolidated by working through — is supposed to effect or make possible personality change" (p. 136). It is clear that for this view a crucial focus was upon the interpretive skills of the therapist and its effects upon the patient's ability to gain insight into the aforementioned resistance and to come to some awareness of repressed instincts.

Lasswell's (1936) early comments, perhaps, are representative of this impulse-awareness view of insight. He described insight as an avowal of a present impulse to perform an act which is accompanied by anxiety. The patient's subsequent expressions of certainty to this avowal, even after deciding not to act, represent the final test of insight. What this means in practice is that patient insight always involves stated agreement with the analyst's interpretation.

Like Lasswell, Strachey (1934) also chose to express his understanding of insight from the viewpoint of the therapist's activity in making "mutative interpretations." For him, the goal of psychoanalysis was to enable a patient to begin anew progress towards normal adult development. As Strachey sees it, the patient's whole mental organization is held in check at an infantile stage and in order to break this impasse in development the patient needs to experience a profound modification of the superego. Such agonizing change comes about, according to Strachey (1934), in a series of slight advances which are brought out by "mutative interpretations produced by the analyst in virtue of his position as the object of the patient's id-impulses and as his auxiliary super-ego" (p. 135). For this reason Strachey views the activity of the therapist in making an interpretation as the crucial focus around which change and insight occur. In this analysis, Strachey fails to direct himself to the reality of the patient doing the business of therapy and of the patient's own efforts at achieving insight.

But how does the process of interpretation bring about insight? Wolberg (1954) understands interpretation as an "enabling act" founded upon a patient's capacity to "see beyond the façade of manifest thinking and motivations to thinking, feeling and behaving (at a deeper level)" (p. 483). Furthermore he conceives of various levels or depths of interpretation as measured by the patient's participation in the act, with the most significant interpretive activity occurring when a patient does it for himself and with the least significant occurring when the therapist does it for him. Between these two extremes falls the more mundane activity of the therapist in piecing together the fragments of a patient's story into a meaningful pattern. A patient's acceptance of an interpretation (and thus one measure of insight) is the degree of credibility granted to the therapist. For this view, in Wolberg's (1954) words, insight and interpretation are measured by "... the expression of surprise, enthusiasm, relief, excitement, increased flow of associations, and confirmation of the validity of the interpretation" (p. 486).

What is important for our purposes here is to observe that many therapists see a close relationship between the interpretive activity of the therapist and the experience of insight by the patient. There are others, however, who would reverse the emphasis; that is, insight-producing activities reside primarily in the patient. The focus shifts from the interpretive activity of the therapists to the intellectual and emotional processes of the patient in coming to insight. For this reason, a second view of insight conceives of it as a comprehensive patient process.

INSIGHT AS A COMPLEX PATIENT PROCESS

Leder (1968) represents this new tradition which conceives of insight in terms of the patient's activity rather than in terms of therapist interpretation. Following a modern learning theory approach he implicitly draws a distinction between the emotional components of psychotherapy and its more intellectual processes. It is within the latter domain of human activity that he places the process of insight.

In the first of therapy, according to Leder, the therapist must satisfy the patient's most pressing needs such as for cognitive information, emotional contact, and so on. This is done optimally through the therapist's use of several verbal and nonverbal techniques which may include reassurance, explanation, advice, persuasion, suggestion, acceptance, sympathy and understanding; as well as enabling the patient to unburden himself of emotionally loaded content material. During this initial phase of psychotherapy the patient is "storing up important cognitive and emotional cues in the framework of a therapeutic relationship" (Leder, 1968, p. 115). These interactions lead to increased satisfaction of the patient's needs for emotional support and cognitive information resulting in a "growing feeling of security and a subsequent reduction of symptoms" (Leder, 1968, p. 115) relatively early in therapy.

In this early passive learning stage there hardly ever is a definitive alteration of attitudes and problem-solving strategies. There is no far-reaching integration of new feelings, ideas, and actions. An active relearning consisting of "exploratory activity such as labeling facts and dilemmas, formulating alternative hypotheses and solutions and experimenting with their verification, and drawing conclusions from rewarding and punishing experiences" (Leder, 1968, pp. 116–117) must occur in the next phase of therapy.

During the second phase, the therapist is less directive and active in his interaction with the patient. His role is more that of a catalyst of the activity of the patient than a source of information and his verbal techniques play a smaller role, usually consisting of interpretation and other techniques stimulating the problem-solving activity of the patient. Thus the way of influencing the patient has changed its character. The cues are primarily addressed to the intellect, while emotional support and contact are gradually withdrawn. As a result of these mechanisms, the patient learns greater awareness, understanding, and control. This process is known as "acquiring insight." The content of insight is differently described according to the different concepts of therapists, but all agree that it interprets the causal relationships between psychosocial factors and inadequately maladaptive functioning of the patient. As Leder (1968, pp. 117–118) sees it, in most cases insight seems to facilitate reorientation (the development of new attitudes), which is probably the crucial variable for the outcome of the psychotherapy.

Keeping within the tradition that considers insight as a patient process, Franz Alexander and his successors at the Chicago Psychoanalytic Institute comprise the theoretical representatives promoting the concept of emotional insight. For Alexander (1956, 1963) the course of treatment in psychotherapy ". . . consists in a long series of corrective emotional experiences, which follow one another as the transference situation changes content and different repressed childhood situations are revived and re-experienced in the relationship to the therapist" (1963, p. 443).

Alexander's concepts of "emotional insight" and "corrective emotional experience" are central foci to his understanding of effective change. He relates both concepts to the therapist behaving in a fashion contrary to the patient's transference projection. Once a patient develops a strong transference relationship with the therapist and the therapist acts in ways different from the patient's expectation a contrast is provided. The patient's affective display towards the therapist is similar to his display towards significant past figures. Included in the emotional interaction is the patient's expectation that the therapist will react toward him as others have in the past. When this response does not occur, the therapeutic stage is set for (emotional) insight. The patient becomes aware of the unrealistic patterns of emotional reactivity, interaction, expectation and projection which plague his relationships with and to other people. As insight unfolds so too does tension relief which in turn provides a reinforcing state of affairs to further this kind of activity.

Zilboorg (1952) is also a representative of a newer tradition which conceives of insight as an emotional activity carried on by the patient. According to Zilboorg, insight as an emotional process in the patient has had two different meanings: (1) one in which it was equated with the newly developed ability of a patient to feel appropriately whatever is experienced; and (2) one that viewed insight as the elimination of unconscious affect, which interfered with the ability of the patient to feel what he felt or to see what he saw. In its first use, emotional insight represents a gain or an addition, a positive phenomenon; in the second case, insight becomes a process of being freed from a surplus of unconscious emotions which inhibit or intensify one's conscious intellectual processes or attitudes towards life. Zilboorg views the concept of insight as gradually coming to be described theoretically as an awareness which is gained through a discharge of feelings and emotions, which in turn were associated with or connected to a given character trait or symptom. Once such discharge was accomplished, the symptom or trait could be looked at in light of its respective unconscious origins and could be examined without the impediment of prior unconscious affect.

Zilboorg, however, considers insight as a "process of integration" which the patient does by, and for, himself. In continuing this conceptual development in the light of his understanding of ego processes, Zilboorg (1952) suggests that insight is basically an emotional phenomenon occurring in the context of a person's reliving, and, by reliving, of reintegrating a series of emotional experiences which were problematic and unresolved. Such a process of reintegration must be carried on within the context of a transference relationship with the analyst — the analyst becomes the only reality during the period of treatment with whom the patient's ego can safely experiment through the processes of integration and reintegration:

> The only type of insight which serves the purpose of reorganization and reintegration of the ego is a purely affective process in the wake of which follows rational and affective appreciation of a new orientation of the ego towards the world and towards one's own self. Without transference the process of gaining insight leaves only a series of conceptual props for the ego. (Zilboorg, 1952, p. 24)

Fritz Perls (1947, 1969a,b) also follows an emotive integrative model very closely. His patients achieve "emotional insight" by following through on conflicting dynamic feelings which are warring with one another in his daily living. His "hot seat" technique serves as a prototype for understanding the patient's dilemma and as a suggestion for a way out of the dilemma. In this technique the patient achieves emotional insight by a fantasied confrontation of two or more conflicting aspects of himself that are personified and talked to, or with. Resolution of the conflict is obtained by a forced integration of conflicting aspects or feelings in which the patient must come to recognize and then build upon the compromising elements implicit in the conflict.

Murphy (1965) in his *Tactics of Psychotherapy* describes therapeutic change in terms of reorganization and integration of "chaotic masses of verbalized feelings." Murphy (1965) suggests the therapist must help the patient "recognize-and-express as well as accept-and-control his feelings and understand them in terms of their origins and meanings" (p. 21). From this comment we can extract a kernel of Murphy's orientation toward insight: a process of the patient by which poorly integrated and disarrayed feelings are reintegrated and ordered by recognition, expression, acceptance, control, and understanding.

Emotional expressiveness, however, can be deceiving. Just as the obsessive-compulsive's lack of affective display constitutes an obvious symptom of his pathology, so too the affectualization of the hysteric provides an effective defense. For Valenstein (1962), both constitute defensive maneuvers designed to resist insight. For this reason, he hypothesizes two modes of therapeutic activity capable of leading to insight – but to different kinds of insight. In the first type of therapy, insight is a process in which the patient relives previous events, but one in which he may or may not be aware of the implication of this reliving. For this type of therapy, patients solve problems without ever becoming aware of the processes by which they do this. In the second type of therapy, as in psychoanalysis, the analysand participates in a far more comprehensive experience. Here, the patient is asked to experience directly feelings which lead to firsthand knowledge of the conflicts. This direct, firsthand knowledge defines emotional awareness for Valenstein and the process by which this knowledge is attained is called "experiential acquaintanceship."

Valenstein's terminology, "emotional awareness" and "experiential acquaintanceship," serve to mark his ideas as deriving from a philosophical tradition having its roots in Bertrand Russell's philosophy and as adopted for psychotherapy by A. R. Martin (1952). For Martin, as for Russell before him, there are two types of insight: descriptive and ostensive. The first corresponds to knowing by description while the second represents an extension of the philosophical notion of knowing by acquaintance.

According to Martin (1952), Russell proposed two ways of knowing, with neither the kind of knowing we typically ascribe to intellectual, as distinct from emotional activity. Rather for Russell, and through him, for Martin, knowing is a holistic activity which is more closely akin to what might be called the experience of awareness. Knowing by description is a vicarious knowing we experience whenever we come to understand some referent by having someone else describe it to us. Knowing by acquaintance, on the other hand, is direct knowing with which there is no doubt in our minds that we know – we sense and know spontaneously.

A naive demonstration is easy. Assign someone the task of describing their experience of sailing to you. Usually the description will capture and communicate some of the experience for you; you will know some of what it is like to sail. Should you go sailing yourself, however, you will have a direct experience of the activity of sailing and then you will be able to say, "I know what it is like for me to sail." Such knowing need not necessarily be articulate; it is different from and prior to, the requirement or impulse to communicate the experience.

Martin adopts these same categories in talking about insight in psychotherapy. Interpretations given by a therapist constitute the means whereby a patient is able to come to descriptive insights. The therapist's verbalizations provide symbols or representations which describe and offer novel perspectives about what the patient has said. Ostensive insights are the patient's direct awareness and experiences of feelings and internal states by which direct experience is known. According to Martin (1952), the therapist can facilitate ostensive insights through promoting descriptive insights; that is, by aiding the patient to establish derived relations with internal referents. But it is the ostensive insights which, in the final analysis, are therapeutic because, in psychotherapy, ostensive insights make "knowledge of referents efficacious." Descriptive insights, on the other hand, prepare the patient to "face ostensive insights" and also provide a method "to sustain personality modifications by giving understanding of facts and relations" (Martin, 1952, p. 33).

Martin's application of Russell's more philosophical work serves to promote a view of insight as a complex integrative process. It also added a much needed philosophical foundation to a growing awareness of insight as a deeply personal integrative process. In effect what Martin's work did was to provide a clarification about insight, a clarification which foretold of a possible rapprochement between theories of insight as a purely emotional process and those that emphasized the process as more or less cognitive in nature.

Despite this advance, most theories, then as even now, still continue to assume that insight would be "resisted" by the patient as being something intrusive and unnatural. One of the earliest theorists to hold the contrary opinion that insight is a natural consequence of being human was Rapaport (1967) who described it as a "realm of appearances which turns back on itself and tries to unearth the process underlying itself" (p. 111). Insight becomes a process of becoming aware of oneself, not because one must deny the appearances of things but because appearances reveal their own processes. More to the point, Rapaport's comments provide an early testimonial to the belief that there is something natural about the integrative aspects of insight for he characterized the turning-back process as "integral to the very fabric of thinking."

This notion, that the integrative process involved in insight comes about by a natural inclination of the person rather than by a forced and possibly artificial procedure (such as interpretation by the therapist) forms another nexus in understanding the concept of insight. A somewhat more contemporary psychotherapist who has explored the implications of this idea is E. Kris (1956), who presented his initial ideas in the context of a discussion of the "good analytic hour." As he described it, the good hour was characterized by rapid and massive integrative associations in which many solutions begin to emerge and converge in a meaningful manner. But this type of integration is far too complex to be accounted for by the simple surfacing of repressed material. As Kris put it somewhat figuratively, the analyst can perceive or begin to perceive, however dimly, a battle of forces between emerging conflicts. Over a period of time the analyst is able to see some of the implications of this conflict as well as some intimations of an integrative process taking place out of the patient's current focus of conscious awareness. Kris (1956) sees the analyst as able to observe "the outlines of a larger submerged formation. In the good analytic hour insight comes about as if already prepared, but prepared outside of awareness.... [The good hour is] a confirmation of the view that some and perhaps all significant intellectual achievements are products or at least derivatives of preconscious mentations" (pp. 45–46).

For Kris the concept of insight is also closely allied to his concept of ego. Insight is yet another process of this executive aspect of the person. The ego's capacity to call forth and control temporary and partial regression, to view itself, and to observe its own activity with some objectivity, and; finally, to maintain some measure of control over the discharge of affect is crucial to the development of insight in psychotherapy. Such a process is the growing awareness of the "various parts of the unconscious self and the connections between them" (Kris, 1956, p. 451). Kris even goes so far as to suggest that insight is a naturally occurring phenomenon of the ego and that the processes involved are ever-recurring at both a preconscious and conscious level of awareness.

Up to this point, a number of themes and variations on these theories would seem to highlight the history of our ideas about insight. First, there was the shift from looking only at the effects of a therapist's interpretive activity to a concern for the process by which a patient comes to insight. Out of this new perspective, two new themes evolved: one which claimed to describe insight as a purely emotional process, and a second which understood it as a highly complex integrative activity involving both emotional and intellectual aspects. Both schools of thought, disregarding some of their admittedly important differences, agree that insight is an activity undertaken by the patient rather than simply an affirmation by the patient of a therapist's interpretation. Such a shift in focus led to a major reevaluation of the way in which patients come to awareness and, as a consequence, come to behave differently. The process term that typifies the major thrust of these newer approaches must be *integration.*

The characterization of insight as an integrative personal process which somehow promotes genuine epistemic gains for the patient marks a second departure from the past. Out of this tradition a new epistomology emerged which is distinctly antirationalistic but enthusiastically intelligent. The rationalism of Freud's era gave rise to a somewhat sterile understanding of insight as a logical affirmation; whereas the more contemporary philosophy of knowing by acquaintanceship produced a more extended understanding of emotional awareness as tacit knowledge.

Finally, when insight is considered as an integrative ego activity (an approach which simultaneously accords equal stature to the emotional and intellectual aspects of the process), a third conceptual change occurred. More and more the activity of insight has come to be conceived as an exigent process which unfolds and occurs in a systematic and relatively invariant fashion. No longer is therapeutic insight discussed in terms of the therapist's piercing interpretations which seem to break the patient's resistances. Rather, the therapist is now viewed as providing an interaction matrix within which the patient carries on the naturally restorative and integrative personal process known as insight.

A CONTEMPORARY VIEW OF INSIGHT

The most recent attempt to develop a consistent view of insight in therapy comes from psychotherapists who, steeped in a solid phenomenological tradition, seem to have evolved out of a peculiar mixture of Rogerian client-centered ideas, communications theory, and more traditional psychoanalytic training. These phenomenologists generally describe themselves as experiential psychotherapists whose most important concept is that of experience. In a major article presenting this viewpoint, Gendlin (1970) describes his understanding of how change occurs in psychotherapy. He begins with what he terms two universal observations: (1) most psychotherapists (possibly excluding behavior modification therapists) would agree that significant behavioral change involves some sort of emotional process, and (2) such change can occur only within the context of an ongoing personal relationship. The first of these two universals is concerned with the usual patient experience of significant changes as occurring "from within;" whereas the second refers to the fact that personal change often seems to occur in relation to a significant other, in this case, a therapist.

In accounting for these two universals, Gendlin introduces the notion of "experiencing," a process he describes as a concrete bodily feeling that constitutes the basic matter of psychological and personality phenomena. There are a great variety of experiencing processes possible and the one that is singular to psychotherapy is usually had by the client in making direct reference to inwardly felt meanings having no current symbolization. These felt meanings are implicit in that they contain elements which can become explicit only in symbols or other behavioral events. Prior to symbolized meanings, felt meanings are incomplete and it is only in interaction with verbal symbols that felt meanings are carried into explicitly formed meanings.

This change from implicit to explicit comes about through a process known as *focusing*, the act by which one attends to the direct referents of current experience. Focusing is a kind of attentional turning "inward" to get in touch with oneself and is exhibited by the kinds of responses people make when they express "how they feel" at any moment. Gendlin (1970) defines four different phases of focusing which unfold and characterize the activity in itself. The first phase is the patient's act of making direct reference to vague implicit feelings. Unfolding is the second phase in which these vague, impressionistic meanings become explicit. Usually this happens in an episodic fashion as the person becomes aware of explicit feelings. With this new recognition the patient begins to make global applications and it is during this third phase that patients typically experience a "flooding of associations, memories, situations and circumstances" [Gendlin, 1970, p. 146]. This new awareness then provides the patient with a novel model that is useful in making sense out of a variety of different experiences, past and present. Finally the patient begins a reference movement in which new recognitions are now more explicit and serve to trigger new implicit meanings so that the process reverberates and can continue within the person.

Gendlin's experiencing process is clearly of the knowing-by-acquaintance variety. There is no question to the patient that he has direct and firsthand knowledge of his ongoing experience. Gendlin contrasts this with a nonexperiencing mode in which the patient is little involved in the process of experiencing and is, or becomes, structure bound. When structure bound, the patient is said to be inhibited, repressed, denying, paranoid, and so on. By carrying forward the implicit meanings that are present within a person's structure-bound experience, the patient is able to reconstitute other aspects of living. As Gendlin (1970) put it, "When certain implicitly functioning aspects of experiencing are carried forward by symbols or events, the resulting experiencing *always* involves other, sometimes newly reconstituted, aspects which thereby come to be in process and function implicitly in that experiencing" (p. 156). It is obvious then that a therapist, in order to be effective, *must* respond to the present experience of the patient and not to the structure-bound aspects of his behavior, or according to Gendlin (1970): "No one is greatly changed by responses and analyses of how he does not function" (p. 158).

The psychotherapist, in response to a troubled person, cannot be simplistic in directing his dealings with that person to a partial aspect of the person. Instead, he must be able to relate simultaneously to multiple aspects of the personality system; that is, to environmental interactions, bodily feelings, cognitive meanings, fantasies, object relations, self, and so on. The psychological phenomenon that encompasses all of these systems simultaneously is what Gendlin describes as the experiencing process. It is at this level that psychotherapy is effectively carried on no matter what practicing theoretical stance the therapist may take.

Gendlin's theory of change implicitly comments on the insight process. He never mentions insight by name, only in passing, and then only in referring to the highly intellectualized brands of therapy which offer insight as their outcome. In this context, it is clear he defines insight as an intellectual activity and as an activity antithetical to effective therapy. Such a narrow conceptualization of insight is surprising largely because Gendlin's description of the unfolding phase of focusing unwittingly integrates commentary on insight from a variety of contemporary theorists. Implicit in his comments is the idea that insightlike experiencing is a natural ongoing process from which we can become detached.

Bernard Lonergan, in his massive volume *Insight: A Study of Human Understanding*, as well as in his other writings, provides a powerful epistemology for Gendlin's more practical theorizing. Lonergan (1957) begins with a persuasive commentary of what he understands as the root dynamic of all cognitive activity: the urge to question:

> Name it what you please, alertness of mind, intellectual curiosity, the spirit of inquiry, active intelligence, the drive to know. Under any name, it remains the same. This primordial drive then, is the pure question. It is prior to any insights, any concepts, any words; for insights, concepts, words, have to do with answers; and before we look for answers, we want them; such wanting is the pure question. (p. 9)

What is so important in Lonergan's approach is his attempt to develop the basic terms of human understanding, and once done, to formalize these into a tightly knit metaphysics. His guiding motif throughout is best expressed as follows: "Thoroughly understand what it is to understand, and not only will you understand the broad lines of all there is to be understood but also you will possess a fixed base, an invariant pattern, opening upon all further developments of understanding" (Lonergan, 1957, p. xxviii)."

With questioning as a basis for his "presuppositionless metaphysics" and with "to know knowing" as his guiding motif, Lonergan provides a technical metaphor known as the "horizon" to express the relation between objectivity and subjectivity. For Lonergan, a horizon is defined as the maximum field of vision from a determinate point of view. As such, any horizon is defined by two poles, one objective and one subjective, although both are mutually determined. The subjective pole is given by the subject's primordial drive to question (to know), whereas the objective pole is all that is questionable. The objective pole, therefore, is specified by the subject through the questions he asks; the subjective pole, in turn, is specified by the answers obtained where such answers are possible only within the confines of that particular subjective pole. For this view, reciprocal exchanges between the subjective and objective poles enlarge the horizon where these exchanges can be defined in terms of three different modes of conscious experience: (1) empirical consciousness; (2) intellectual consciousness; and (3) rational consciousness.

Empirical consciousness is the activity of becoming aware of data or experiences in such a way as to provoke questions. Intellectual consciousness is constituted by having an insight into the data questioned — the experience of joyful discovery issued in a unifying concept. But not all joyful ideas are necessarily good, and rational consciousness is the process of questioning whether the answer proposed by intellectual consciousness in fact meets the conditions of empirical consciousness; that is, provides the experience of self-appropriation and verification.

Becoming detached from these modes of experience involves what Lonergan (1957) calls a dramatic bias, and he speaks of this bias in terms of the difficulty experienced by clients in their attempts to talk of problems with a therapist.

What Lonergan offers the therapeutic process is the idea that insight circumvents this dramatic bias and as such is a process which cannot fail. On the basis of this analysis, it is possible to see a rapprochement between the philosopher–theologian Lonergan and the philosopher–psychologist Gendlin. Both advocate psychological processes in persons which invariably lead to reconstitution and growth, even though both focus on these processes in somewhat different terms.

In less dramatic, but equally powerful terms, Hutchinson, in three articles published in the 1940s presented a view of creative insight that is also of relevance here. Not only do Hutchinson's stages of insight closely parallel the three basic terms of cognitive activity proposed by Lonergan; they also bear close resemblance to Gendlin's descriptions of the focusing process. In his analysis, Hutchinson (1949) described some of the stages he felt captured the experience of insight, although he did not confine his comments to insight in psychotherapy but talked more broadly about many different moments of creative insight in a wide variety of contexts.

Hutchinson distinguished four specific stages in coming to creative insight: (1) the period of preparation; (2) the period of renunciation or recession; (3) the moment of insight; and (4) the period of verification, elaboration, and evaluation. It is these last two phases which are especially similar to the middle two phases of focusing in Gendlin's (1970) approach: unfolding and global application.

The period of preparation described by Hutchinson is characterized chiefly by the problem solver's fruitless attempts to find an already existing solution to his problem. In going about this, the problem solver adheres to traditional modes of problem solving according to the mores and dictates of his discipline. In Koestler's terms (1949; 1964), the problem solver confines himself to one sphere (or matrix) of problem-solving activity. Creative, insightful solutions exist in the conjunction of this sphere of activity with some other sphere of activity yet to be encountered. The point(s) of intersection between the two planes may occur frequently but the emotional tenor of the examiner himself often disallows the relevant intersection to be recognized.

Koestler illustrates this by reference to Archimedes who in vain sought a method by which to determine the amount of gold in the emperor's crown without melting it down. Originally, he sought the solution in one sphere that might be called the plane of the crown itself. Concurrently, he often went to the Baths of Athens and many times had witnessed how the water level changed as he and others entered and left the baths. Even though this plane of the displacement of water eventually provided the sphere of activity needed to solve the problem, and even though Archimedes had interacted in both planes innumerable times, he never made the connection during this first stage. This first period of preparation also bears a close resemblance to Lonergan's (1957) empirical consciousness, to Gendlin's (1970) description of structure-bound experiencing and to symptom-ridden behavior which often drives people into therapy.

In the period of renunciation the prolonged struggle to solve the problem at hand leads to a decrease in the energies of the problem solver. His struggle can become so intense that he may develop symptoms analogous to those occurring in neurosis. Finally in frustration he may decide the problem must rest and so must he. During this period the problem solver's activity is characterized by forced distance from the problem and the problem situation. He focuses his energies on some other sphere of activity allowing the problem issue to recede from consciousness (sic; perhaps into the realm of the preconscious). By way of illustration one might imagine Archimedes retreating from his problem by going to the Baths, relaxing in the waters and forcing himself to forget the riddle of the crown.

Hutchinson believes that the period of insight is preceded by an ephemeral awareness that the solution to a problem is at hand. He never delineates the time interval between this intimation and the occurrence of insight but feels it to be an important and integral precursor. Hutchinson (1940) describes the period of insight as follows:

> ... insight consists of more than a simple reorganization of the perceptual field, a new alignment of possible hypotheses. It is often accompanied by a flood of ideas, alternative hypotheses appearing at the same time, many of which are difficult to make explicit owing to the crowded rapidity of their appearances. Noteworthy in this experience are the almost hallucinatory vividness of ideas appearing in connection with any sense department — visual, auditory, kinaesthetic — the emotional release, feelings of exultation, adequacy, finality. The period is integrative, restorative, negating the symptoms of neurotic maladjustment engendered by the preceding periods. The individual steps up to a new level of activity and a new possibility of reaction. Integration opens up new volitional possibilities: reactions, before impossible, now become commonplace. (p. 398)

The similarity of Hutchinson's description to Gendlin's (1970) unfolding and Lonergan's (1957) intellectual consciousness is again clear.

In the period of verification, elaboration, and evaluation, Hutchinson (1939) notes that "all technical and explicit rules of practice are again summoned into use, and all the possible exaggerations and overstatements of the period of insight are checked against external reality. Without such evaluation the insight does not release anything of communicable or social value. It remains otherwise an uncoordinated experience [p. 372]." Gendlin's (1970) phase of global application and Lonergan's (1957) rational consciousness highlight the resemblance here. Although there are other (Gordon, 1961; Kris, 1950, 1956; Koestler, 1949, 1964; Lasswell, 1936) more complicated schemes to describe the process of insight, all stress essentially the same stages as contained in Hutchinson's (1939) analysis and all stress the hedonic tone of the period of insight itself. There is no denying the impact of an insight as it charges into awareness.

SOME SUMMARY COMMENTS ON INSIGHT

The written literature dealing with the problem of insight in psychotherapy is extensive but fragmented. It certainly does not lend itself to as smooth an evolutionary rendition as authors such as Singer (1965) would have us believe. Nevertheless, there are certain highlights that can be useful in organizing a theoretical and research understanding of this process. Clearly it can be argued, and easily agreed to, that insight is an experience for the patient in psychotherapy that has to do with knowing. Any impartial history of insight theory makes it clear that insight has always been considered as a mode of knowing which is very different from what we usually think of by this term in its more detached intellectual sense. Insight in psychotherapy is closely related to what are usually called the emotional aspects of experience, and this brings us to the dilemma of describing what feelings and knowing have in common.

More traditional theories of therapy and insight point to the cooccurrence of emotional and intellectual processes and leave it at that. More contemporary theorists emphasize or deemphasize one or the other of these processes, while a few, such as Lonergan (1957) and Gendlin (1970), seek a new direction. To help in this, they speak of psychotherapy in terms of psychological realities rather than in terms of "internal" entities such as ids, egos, or superegos. For these writers, insight has the texture of something real; that is, the person is certain of his new knowledge and there can be no doubt about it since it makes such "good sense."

Insight is also conceived of as a natural human activity that is essential and unitary to the process of being and acting human. For Lonergan (1957), insight is exigent and invariant in its process. He sees it as following a definite and clearly explicable path to completion and restitution. For Gendlin (1970), insight is presented as a comprehensive experiential process which necessarily affects, and is effected by, various personality systems simultaneously. In the end, insight is such an exciting and compelling experience that we are drawn to follow its lead and thereby achieve some sensible resolution to one or another pressing problem in our lives.

INSIGHT AND METAPHOR IN PSYCHOTHERAPY: A TENTATIVE HYPOTHESIS

To have insight into some situation or other is to understand that situation in such a way that it is no longer problematic in any sense of the term. In the work-a-day world such situations involve the problems of production, design, control, and so on; in the world of psychotherapy the problem, more often than not, is the *me*. Despite this difference it seems reasonable to propose that the process by which insight is achieved in both worlds shares certain points of overlap. Since we have been at great pains in preceding chapters to document the role of novel figurative expression in human problem solving of any and all kinds it will come as no surprise to find that we also view therapeutic insight as sometimes achieved on the basis of using of such expression.

As we noted in Chapter 4, the role of novel figurative usage in facilitating insightful experiences in psychotherapy has its own history in the psychiatric literature although this history is subterranean and hardly ever explicit. Never does a conscientious search of the relevant literature reveal direct reference to figurative language and its relation to insight despite the fact that the possibility for such dialogue is ever present. Although some therapists have hinted at this relation, relatively few have described the processes responsible for the use and/or production of novel figurative language and how such activities might lead to therapeutic insight. The question here is one of providing a transition between the spontaneous production of a novel figure of speech and the subsequent modification of the way in which the patient comes to understand, and, hopefully, to change his or her way of life.

In responding to this question Fine, Pollio, and Simpkinson (1972) describe the production of novel figurative language as an ego process with at least two observable functions: problem solving and wish fulfillment. They attribute some of the motivation for metaphor making to the felt discrepancy between one's evanescent experiences of internal states, impulses, feelings, wishes, and motivations and the difficulty experienced in expressing these states and events. For this view, shifting to a metaphorical way of speaking often permits expression which otherwise would have been impossible. Sometimes this shift is necessitated by the patient's limited vocabulary. In this case, metaphorizing allows the speaker to extend the range of his understanding far beyond the scope of his or her vocabulary. At other times the patient is unable to communicate experiences adequately because of an insufficient awareness of them. In this case the use of metaphor provides an inroad into unconscious impulses, wishes, and feelings.

Conjectures such as these are based on the assumption that for the patient novel figures are often distilled and displaced fragments of unconscious wishes and feelings. In addition, figurative expression allows the patient to talk of certain experiences which may be thought of as frightening, "crazy," or even just unconventional. In this case, the therapist's acceptance and utilization of a patient's metaphors (his willingness to cooperate with the patient's request for a shift in the style of comment) may ease the anxiety common to the therapy situation. Such a shift may also engage an ego process which, if facilitated properly, can lead to realistic attempts at solving those perplexing problems which brought the patient into therapy in the first place.

The manner in which this process operates can be derived from the twofold ability of creative metaphor to: (1) capture and concretize evanescent affective experiences by relating them to observable behaviors and events; and (2) to offer alternative models capable of serving as teaching and learning devices to the metaphor maker. Such a capacity is largely dependent upon the common intersubjective experiences shared by therapist and patient which permit the therapist to understand in an intuitive fashion the experiences and emotions of the patient. By playing back metaphors to the patient, a therapist is often able to initiate a novel experience in which the patient begins to feel understood; and begins to search out new solutions to problems within the context of metaphoric communication.

The patient's search for viable solutions keynotes the problem-solving function of metaphor making within the context of psychotherapy; a process which may encourage such verbalizations to be carried over into action and changes in action. Changes such as these come about because novel metaphors facilitate a progressive approximation of one's seemingly unconscious experiences until such experiences become conscious, explicit, and communicable. Once the patient is able to express his or her personal condition in a manner consonant with his or her experience, the metaphor has served one of its functions and may perhaps give way to more literal statements. Often such a process will not end in a literal statement. Sometimes the patient unconsciously decides that the meaning of his present metaphor is "explicit" enough, and it is up to the patient to determine, reflectively or unreflectively, the degree of self-revelation and disclosure tolerable in that specific situation.

For purposes of this discussion, such a view assumes that self-revelation, disclosure, and increased awareness are instrumental to, if not the *sine qua non* of, efficacious therapy. What all of this suggests is a rather straightforward and empirically testable hypothesis: in psychotherapy, as elsewhere, novel figurative language functions as heuristic for new learning. For this reason it seems appropriate to propose that the unique mode of constructive self-awareness which follows upon the introduction of apt metaphors in therapy is to be understood in terms of what others have called therapeutic insight; that is, as a strongly felt awareness of what to do in a situation which makes sense to the patient: so much sense in fact, that the patient drawn to follow its lead and thereby to develop its implications in changed and more personally satisfying ways of experiencing and acting.

6
Metaphor and Insight in Psychotherapy: Some Empirical Results

Research designed to investigate the cooccurrence of figurative language and psychotherapeutic insight must first lay claim to the phenomena themselves. What this really means is: Can we provide operations that will reliably identify both figurative language and insight within the context of ongoing psychotherapy? The first part of this question can be answered quickly and in the affirmative with procedures described in previous chapters providing the basis for just such a quick and affirmative answer. An answer to the second part, however, poses its own unique problems for it would seem that the person experiencing insight is the most knowledgeable judge of its occurrence or nonoccurrence. In addition, it would also seem that it is one's own insightful experiences which permit recognition of the occurrence of such experiences in others. For these reasons, it would seem most appropriate in assessing insight to appeal to those individuals experienced in observing this process in themselves and in others to tell us when it does or does not occur. Methodologically, this comes down to asking clinical psychologists, psychiatrists, social workers, and so on for judgments as to when a particular patient did or did not experience insight, which was indeed the operational definition used in this analysis.

But such a procedure seems to be a rather loose and willy-nilly way of going about the business of defining insight. Why not just provide a specific definition and ask raters or judges to pick out specific instances of the category? Unfortunately, this seemingly more rigorous procedure has a number of drawbacks, most notably that theoretically motivated definitions of patient insight are usually highly idiosyncratic to the psychotherapist espousing them. There simply is no agreed-upon concept defined and used by any large group of practitioners that would yield an unambiguous criterion definition. Research which has attempted such definition — for example, by comparing insight therapy with noninsight therapy — has had to control an increasingly larger number of variables in order to define insightful experiences rigorously. To ask therapists to select instances of insight according to a preconceived set of criteria would seem overly restrictive for two reasons: (1) there is no guarantee that the criteria would adequately correspond to the actual phenomenon; and (2) appropriately skilled judges would be scarce — only those who could agree with the criteria would be able to participate.

Even though practitioners may disagree on precisely how to define insight theoretically, it can be assumed that the insight process exhibits generic properties which all therapists might agree upon even though such agreement might be covert and inarticulate. If this is the case, then, different therapists asked to select examples of insight without prior specifications, other than their own opinions, ought often to select the same instances. This assumes that most therapists will be able to agree when an insightful experience has occurred for a patient even though they may disagree radically in providing a precise definition of the experience.

A first question to be answered in making use of an approach such as this would be one of agreement: that is, do different therapists, in fact, pick out similar instances of insight when asked to? Some preliminary data gathered on this point suggests both a methodological procedure and some dangers inherent in this type of approach. As a starting point, four psychotherapists working independently were asked to read a transcript of our by now well-worked Gestalt therapy interview (Pollio & Barlow, 1975) and to make some notation whenever insight (however defined) occurred. The total number of insightful instances selected by these four judges was extremely wide, ranging from a high of 15 to a low of 3. It was clear that each therapist had his own understanding of what insight was all about. Despite these differences, however, there were agreements and the important question really comes down to one of deciding what to do with the data, particularly in regard to defining agreements and disagreements.

Table 6.1 presents a roster of the judgments produced by all 4 of our raters. The first thing to note is that while judges did not agree exactly as to where (in which specific unit) the patient had an insightful experience, the raters did agree as to general locale. An examination of the ratings produced by Judge D indicates that he felt that runs of communication units such as 14, 15, 16; 34, 35, 36; and so on, should all be counted as providing separate examples of insight.

This seems to suggest that for Judge D insight is an extended phenomenon not confined to a single utterance. In order to take into account the fact that an insightful experience does not have to be embodied in a single therapeutic interchange, the following procedure was used to select regions of insightful experiences in therapy. First, each instance for which all four raters agreed independently was selected. Next, those for which three of the four agreed independently was chosen. Finally, those instances for which only two agreed

TABLE 6.1
Insight Regions Determined by a Region Rule

Communication units selected as insightful by each therapist judge				
A	B	C	D	Insight region
13	15[a]	13	14[a]	–
13	15[a]	14	14	–
15	15	14[a]	15	–
16	15[a]	14[a]	16	13–16
34[a]	–	34	34	–
34	–	36	35	–
			36	34–36
54	–	54	52[a]	52–54
65	65	65	65	65
82	84[a]	82	84[a]	
84	84	82[a]	84	–
84[a]	84[a]	–	85	82–85
98	–	98	97[a]	97–98
107	–	107	107	–
108	–	107[a]	108	107–108
116[a]	–	115	115	–
116	–	115[a]	116	–
119	–	119	119	115–119
Retained (%)				
59	100	79	44	

[a]Instances of matches made according to the region rule.

independently but where another just missed matching the other two by no more than two communication units in either direction were determined. In this sense therapist–judges' choices were located within a region by allowing for some variability in specific matches.

A specific example may help to clarify the procedure: Even though Raters A and C were the only ones who selected Communication Unit 13 as indicating insight, Therapist–Judge D selected Communication Unit 14, while B selected 15. Since both of these judgments were no more than 2 units away from 13, Unit 13 was considered as a 4 out of 4 agreement. The same rule applies to Communication Unit 14: two raters selected it, while the other raters selected communications within 2 units of it. Instead of reporting these as specific and concrete examples of insight, it would seem better to consider them as representatives of a process which may or may not be obvious in the specific words used by a patient. The therapist–judges' regions of agreement then take on the properties of a marker which tells us that something insightful has occurred, and that it happened within a reasonable proximity to the unit selected.

6. METAPHOR AND INSIGHT IN PSYCHOTHERAPY 135

Using this methodological rule on the transcript of our Gestalt therapy case (see Table 6.1), 17 matches were selected as being representative of all four raters' choices as a group. For these data Judge B was clearly more conservative than any of the other three judges. Using our region rule for the data contained in Table 6.1, it is clear that these four judges felt insight had occurred in eight separate regions of the interview: in Sequence 13 to 16; in and around Units 34–36, 52–54, and 65; and finally in Sequences 82–84, 97–98, 107–108, and 115–119.

Even though the use of a simple region rule such as described above produced a reasonably clear delineation of insightful events, it still leaves something to be desired. For one, a region rule such as this forces an investigator to disregard summarily a large amount of the data generated by our judges. A casual observation of the percentage of insight instances retained in Table 6.1 illustrates this deficiency where Judges A and D were faulted for having been too liberal in their estimation of what constituted an insightful event. In order to account more fully for the data generated by judges a second procedure was used in conjunction with the region rule. Not only was it important that the regions in which an insightful experience occurred be defined; it was also important that a fairly accurate estimate be made of the density of such judgments. In order to do this, the pattern of therapist–judges' insight ratings were examined within each session by summing the total frequency of their ratings within sets of 10 communication units each. For this case this produced 12 distinct regions in which the greatest density occurred, and these involved Regions 11–20, 31–40, 81–90, 91–100, and 111–120. These were then designated as insight regions for this particular hour of therapy.

Given the fact that procedures such as these can be used to identify and locate moments of insight, a direct comparison of the cooccurrence of novel figurative language and regions of insight is possible. To these ends we examined the cooccurrence of insight and novel and frozen figurative language in the Gestalt therapy case presented in Table 6.1 (and elsewhere). Results of this analysis showed that Audrey produced a higher than the median rate of novel figurative language for six of the eight insight regions selected by judges. In addition, she also produced a lower than median rate of novel figurative language for five of the six noninsight regions. In contrast to this, frozen figurative language showed no consistent relationship to regions of insight and noninsight, and there was no clear pattern of relationship between novel and frozen figurative rates.

Because of the rather special nature of Gestalt therapy, these results, while suggestive are not perfectly unambiguous. Gestalt therapy often places special emphasis on resolving conflict through imaginative role playing. The production of highly figurative language in Gestalt therapy would be common. Forcing independent judges to identify insight regions in a Gestalt-therapy interview creates a "special" case study largely due to the structure of Gestalt therapy itself.

In order to examine the relationship of figurative language to insight in a different context, Barlow (1973) studied novel metaphoric communications and therapeutic insight in 5 interviews randomly selected from sets of 30 interviews in a "complete and successful" psychoanalytic-therapy case consisting of over 400 interviews. For this analysis, Interviews 93, 143, 205, 301, and 373 were selected and examined because they seemed to contain a fairly accurate representation of the rate, style, and content of therapeutic exchanges occurring between patient and therapist in this particular case; and because they provided a reasonable time sample of the total case.

By applying techniques described previously, novel and frozen figurative language rates, insight density, and regions of insight were determined and then listed together in a single roster for each session. Such a listing, which locates these measurements within segments of five communication units each, provided the basic data for two quantitative comparisons. These data were examined to determine if, in fact, regions of insight most often coincided with the highest sustained rates of novel metaphoric production. Following this, correlation coefficients were computed for all five sessions between all pairings of novel-figurative rates, insight density, and frozen figurative rates.

In addition to these results a qualitative analysis of themes was undertaken by developing minimal content categories of metaphoric expressions. The minimal content data were computed by asking two judges, working together, to collapse all instances of novel figures into as few groups as seemed necessary without destroying what they felt was the essential content theme in the category. Following this, metaphor themes established for all of the five interviews were compared to themes which occurred only in insight regions. In this way we hoped to be able to recover the topics and content about which the patient experienced insight. In addition, an examination of these insight-themes seemed to describe the progression of events in therapy selected as insightful and to produce a qualitative approach to determining the relationship of figurative language to insight.

Tables 6.2–6.6 present insight density and insight regions in addition to novel and frozen figurative output for each of the five psychotherapy interviews selected. In examining each of these tables separately, our initial interest will be to locate insight regions relative to the various novel figurative rates in each communication unit segment.

In Interview 93 (Table 6.2), novel rates ranged from a low of .00 in two separate segments (Segment 11–15 and 46–49) to a high of 1.35 in Segment 1–5. The five highest novel rates occurred in Segments 1–5, 21–25, 26–30, 31–35, and 41–45, with the five insight regions corresponding to Segments 1–5, 11–15, 16–20, 36–40, and 41–45. Thus, only two of the five regions correspond exactly to two of the five highest novel-figurative rates. The remaining three regions occur within segments of unusually low metaphoric activity. Despite this, the three insight regions in question either immediately precede or follow the highest novel-figurative rates. A correlation coefficient computed

TABLE 6.2
Summary of Results for Interview 93

Segment	Words	Novel-figurative rate	Frozen-figurative rate	Insight density	Insight region
1–5	1331	1.35	2.78	9	1
6–10	224	0.45	3.57	4	–
11–15	335	0.00	6.57	4	1
16–20	725	0.55	3.72	3	1
21–25	291	1.05	4.19	4	–
25–30	610	1.34	3.44	5	–
31–35	100	1.00	0.00	5	–
36–40	322	0.31	1.55	6	1
41–45	283	1.06	2.47	8	1
46–49	28	0.00	7.14	0	–
Total	4349	–	–	48	5
Mean	–	0.87	3.15	4.8	–
SD	–	0.49	2.02	2.4	–

between insight density and novel-figurative rate over all 10 segments indicated a significant relationship between novel expression and insight (.66, $p < .01$) for this particular interview.

In Interview 143 (Table 6.3) only one of the four insight regions corresponded to an unusually high novel rate, that is, in Communication Segment 51–55. The three remaining regions occurred within segments showing an average rate of

TABLE 6.3
Combined Summary for Interview 143

Segment	Words	Novel-figurative rate	Frozen-figurative rate	Insight density	Insight region
1–5	858	1.25	4.08	2	–
6–10	379	0.79	5.53	6	–
11–15	2378	1.45	5.67	6	–
16–20	121	3.30	2.48	0	–
21–25	346	3.76	4.05	5	–
25–30	328	2.44	6.40	6	1
31–35	364	2.48	6.04	4	–
36–40	173	1.74	4.62	0	–
41–45	124	0.81	0.00	6	–
46–50	229	1.75	5.20	6	1
51–55	316	4.45	6.96	5	1
56–59	149	1.35	5.56	3	1
Total	5785	–	–	58	4
Mean	–	1.85	5.32	4.8	–
SD	–	1.13	1.83	3.74	–

novel-figurative activity. The correlation coefficient of .38 obtained between insight density and novel-figurative rate presents a different measure of this rather low degree of relation. On closer examination it is evident that here, as before, insight regions do occur within immediate proximity to regions of high figurative activity. The first insight region (Segment 26–30) follows upon a period of intense figurative activity in Segment 16–25. The combined novel rate during this period almost doubles the overall average rate for the total interview. Turning towards the remaining 3 insight regions involving Segments 36–40, 51–55, and 56–59, we notice a conspicuous pattern; that these regions cluster about the highest novel rates in the session.

In interview 205 (Table 6.4) the correlation coefficient obtained between insight density and novel rate is essentially zero ($r = 0.02$). Only two of the six insight regions (Segments 21–25 and 51–55) correspond with high novel-figurative rates; the other four are paired with average to low rates. As in Interview 143, the clustering of insight regions is again in proximity to high novel activity with the first four insight regions (Segments 11–15, 16–20, 21–25, and 26–30) following upon a dramatic increase in novel activity (3 novel figures per 100 words in Segment 6–10). These same regions correspond to a period of substantial and gradually increasing metaphoric activity which

TABLE 6.4
Combined Summary Table for Interview 205

Segment	Words	Novel-figurative rate	Frozen-figurative rate	Insight density	Insight region
1–5	629	0.64	4.13	2	–
6–10	158	3.16	5.69	1	–
11–15	266	1.89	4.14	3	1
16–20	296	1.69	7.43	4	1
21–25	129	3.23	3.10	1	1
26–30	560	2.14	5.17	5	1
31–35	256	0.78	4.69	2	–
36–40	318	1.26	2.52	2	–
41–45	283	0.78	4.44	1	–
46–50	348	2.02	1.21	0	–
51–55	138	3.62	1.45	4	1
56–60	127	0.00	0.79	0	–
61–65	809	1.49	6.18	1	–
66–70	176	1.71	11.93	0	–
71–75	207	2.41	5.31	0	–
76–80	110	2.73	3.64	0	–
81–84	912	0.54	2.52	4	1
Total	5722	–	–	30	6
Mean	–	1.43	4.42	1.76	–
SD	–	1.01	2.58	1.63	–

TABLE 6.5
Combined Summary for Interview 301

Segment	Words	Novel-figurative rate	Frozen-figurative rate	Insight density	Insight region
1–5	475	1.26	2.95	4	–
6–10	461	1.08	3.47	5	1
11–15	315	0.32	3.17	0	–
16–20	385	0.26	2.34	1	–
21–25	695	1.44	3.45	6	1
26–30	157	4.45	1.91	9	1
31–35	384	1.82	1.30	2	–
36–40	147	0.00	5.44	1	–
41–45	274	1.82	1.82	6	–
46–50	278	1.44	1.79	9	1
51–55	140	1.43	1.43	0	–
56–60	164	0.61	0.61	1	–
61–65	319	1.57	3.76	2	–
66–68	105	0.00	6.67	0	–
Total	4299	–	–	46	4
Mean	–	1.26	2.81	2.71	–
SD	–	1.09	1.82	3.08	–

peaks in Segment 21–25 and dramatically diminished thereafter. As the rate of novel figurative output subsides, so too did the judges' selection of insightful events. The fifth insight region obviously occurs during a period of intense metaphoric activity, while the final insight region (Segment 81–84) occurs within a segment containing only a few novel metaphoric expressions. It does, however, follow a period (Segment 71–80) during which there was a great deal of such activity.

In the next session (Interview 301) a new pattern emerges that seems to hold some promise for clarifying the relationship of figurative language to insight. All four insight regions correspond to at least average rates or better of novel-figurative activity. Even though there are some periods of high novel metaphoric rate (for example, Segments 51–55, 31–35, and 41–45) without insight, there are no low novel rates that cooccur with regions of insight. A correlation coefficient of .71 ($p < 0.01$) obtained between insight density and novel figurative rate also describes this result. A closer examination of novel-metaphor rates preceding and succeeding insight regions indicates a pattern similar to the two immediately previous sessions. Each insight region occurs either just before or just after a significant increase in figurative output. What is unique about this session is the greater degree of correspondence between insight and figurative language.

This same close cooccurrence of insight and novel figurative language also

TABLE 6.6
Combined Summary for Interview 373

Segment	Words	Novel-figurative rate	Frozen-figurative rate	Insight density	Insight region
1–5	689	3.05	3.48	6	1
6–10	236	2.97	1.70	1	–
11–15	267	4.12	1.87	4	1
16–20	337	0.89	6.53	0	–
21–25	194	1.55	3.09	2	–
26–30	208	1.44	4.81	1	–
31–35	157	4.46	5.09	1	–
36–40	132	0.00	5.30	1	–
41–45	105	5.66	3.81	2	–
46–50	227	2.20	4.85	1	–
51–55	243	1.23	5.35	1	–
56–60	113	0.89	6.19	0	–
61–65	163	1.23	3.07	2	–
66–70	141	2.84	3.55	0	–
71–75	253	5.14	5.14	2	–
76	2	0.00	0.00	0	–
Total	3467	–	–	24	2
Mean	–	2.57	4.18	1.50	–
SD	–	1.71	1.71	1.54	–

appears in the final interview (Interview 373, Table 6.6). Only two insight regions could be defined from the therapist–judge's selections, one within Communication Segment 1–5 and the other within Segment 11–15. Both insight regions cluster about the same period of very high metaphoric activity and diminish as the rate decreases. A correlation coefficient computed between rate of novel figurative activity and insight density produced a value of .45 ($p <$ .10), thereby lending weak quantitative support for the hypothesis of a coincidence of metaphor and insight.

Table 6.7 presents the roster of correlation coefficients computed between the three pairs of number arrays found in Tables 6.2–6.6; between novel-figurative rate and insight density; between frozen-figurative rate and insight density; and between novel-figurative rate and frozen-figurative rate. Several patterns are evident in the data presented by this table. First, when novel figurative rate and insight density are significantly correlated in a positive direction (as in Interviews 93, 301, and 373) novel and frozen figurative rates are significantly correlated in a negative direction. Second, insight density and frozen figurative rates are unrelated or inversely related across all five interviews. Finally, when there is an insignificant, but positive, correlation between novel and frozen rate, or if there is a zero correlation between novel and frozen rate, there is no correlation between novel figurative rate and insight density. It must be remembered, however, that insight occurred throughout each of these interviews even when uncorrelated with the occurrence of novel figurative expressions.

With this thought in mind and in light of the correlations obtained we are led to the following conclusions about figurative language and insight in these five interviews. Vis-à-vis, figurative language, therapist—judges tended to select two types of events as insightful: regions in which there is a great deal of novel metaphoric activity and regions in which insight is unrelated to both novel- and frozen-figurative activity. It is as if insightful events are judged as occurring either coincident with a high novel rate or within regions characterized by more literal language. Regions judged to indicate an insightful experience, however, are never concurrent with trite or frozen figurative activity. From this we infer that patients experience insight, or, more precisely, make conversation judged as insightful, either within the context of novel figurative language or within the confines of explicitly literal language.

One more aspect of this data need be mentioned before we move on to a specific examination of the metaphoric themes comprising a case study, and this concerns the use of insight density (I_D) values "uncorrected" for segment length. In order to avoid any possible argument as to the meaning of correlations computed over noncorrected values, I_D rates (I_D/words) were calculated for each segment. Following this, correlations were computed between the corrected I_D rates and novel usage and between corrected I_D rates and frozen usage. Results of these analyses produced only one change in any of the 10 correlations reported in the first two columns of Table 6.7; for Interview 93 the correlation between novel rate and I_D dropped from .65 to .26. All other correlations retained the same sign, while all remaining significant correlations increased in value. Correcting I_D for segment length essentially left the pattern of results basically as they were and suggests that it is meaningful to use the simpler, uncorrected, values as we have done in this chapter.

TABLE 6.7
Correlation Coefficients Obtained between Insight Density and Two Types of Figurative Language

Interview	Novel-figurative rate versus insight density	Frozen-figurative rate versus insight density	Novel-figurative rate versus frozen-figurative rate	Number of segments
93	0.65**	−0.63**	−0.56**	10
143	0.38	0.37	0.27	12
205	0.02	−0.07	0.05	17
301	0.70***	−0.21	−0.45**	14
373	0.45*	−0.15	−0.53**	16

*$p < 0.10$.   **$p < 0.05$.   ***$p < 0.01$.

METAPHORIC THEMES IN THE FIVE INTERVIEWS

Results of the preceding analyses suggest that it is no longer possible to maintain as correct the strong hypothesis developed in Chapters 4 and 5. Rather, present results suggest that the relationship of insight to figurative expression is not one of simple correspondence: rather, there seems to be two somewhat different patterns of relationship. The first pattern, which was documented best in Interviews 93, 143, and 301, is represented by the straightforward cooccurrence of figurative language and judgments of insight. The second pattern, which occurs to some degree in all 5 interviews, is represented by an alternation of figurative and literal statements in which the literal statements embodying an insightful experience often follows upon neighboring areas of high novel figurative activity. Although figurative language does seem to have a role in promoting insight in psychotherapy, it seems best to defer our final word on this matter until we have looked more carefully at the specific figurative themes about which the patient was thought to exhibit an insightful experience.

In order to do this two judges, working together, categorized each instance of novel figurative language from all five interviews into minimal groupings on the basis of their impressions of the most obvious themes. Table 6.8 presents the results of their sorting in rank order of how frequently a particular theme occurred across all five interviews.

In this table, the first column gives a descriptive label for the thematic category determined by the judges. The heading, "Session/total," indicates the total number of times the theme occurred in that session, while the heading "Patient" indicates the number of times the patient used it and the heading "Therapist" indicates the number of times the therapist used it. The final two columns give the total number of uses across all five sessions, as well as the total number of times a theme was used by patient and therapist separately. So, for example, the theme of personal self worth, and so on (Theme 1) occurred 43 times across all 5 sessions; with the patient responsible for 30 of these uses, and the therapist responsible for 13.

Given this way of presenting the data, the most conspicuous pattern to be noted in this table concerns the remarkable redundancy of metaphoric themes across the whole of therapy. In order to appreciate the significance of this finding, we need remember the amount of time intervening between each of the interviews. From Interview 93 to 143, 130 days passed. From Interview 143 to 205, 177 days elapsed. Intervening between Interviews 205 and 301 were 260 days, and finally, there were 217 days between Interviews 301 and 373. In terms of the data presented in Table 6.8 it is clear that there is a significant degree of stability and redundancy in at least 14 of the 27 novel figurative themes emerging during the course of all 373 interviews.

Some themes (like Themes 1, 2, and 8) were fairly constant across all interviews; some became more frequent as therapy progressed (like Themes, 4, 5,

6, and 7), while others diminished across time (like Themes 10 and 11). Several themes were unique to particular interviews (like Themes 15–26) while others showed a strong revitalization in later interviews after having disappeared subsequent to their first introduction in early interviews (like Themes 3, 13, and 14).

Another general feature which is easily noted concerns the initiator of each figurative theme. A cursory examination of the frequency of occurrence as partitioned for patient and therapist yields this information, and here results show that the patient initiated 16 of 26 themes in these interviews while the therapist introduced only five.[1] What is of interest here is the conclusion that the therapist utilizes the metaphoric content and productions of the patient more often than those that he himself has introduced. A brief description of the sequence of occurrence for each major novel figurative theme across interviews should surely clarify these patterns and it is to this matter which we now turn.

Metaphor Theme 1: Personal self worth or loss thereof. It is the patient who introduced this theme into the therapy in Interview 143. It is one of four patient-produced themes (1, 4, 5, and 13) that remained fairly stable throughout all of the interviews. It ranks first in frequency in Interview 143 and at least third in all of the remaining sessions. It is also one of two patient-introduced metaphors (1 and 5) which the therapist eventually adopted and appeared to use far more frequently than the patient in later sessions.

Metaphor Theme 2: Some feelings are experienced as overpowering. The patient's insistence that he is powerless in the face of his urges and intense desires is a crucial issue in this psychotherapy. It appears, however, to be more crucial to the patient in Interview 93, in which it is the most frequent novel figure, than in Interview 373, in which it ranks seventh in frequency. In terms of the changes that occur in psychotherapy we would conclude this pattern to be an excellent prognostic sign. In the early stages of therapy, patients often cast themselves into a role in which they can depict themselves as victims trapped in a cruel world neither of their own making nor choosing. The gradual demise in therapy of patient-introduced (and produced) themes that typify this attitude might indicate a positive change towards autonomy and self-activation.

Metaphor Theme 3: Analogy of physical strength–weakness to character strength–weakness. This is a patient-initiated metaphor which develops out of his felt inadequacies in regard to the self-control of impulses. To compensate for these feelings of helplessness the patient takes an overly active and conscientious interest in sports. His interests in athletics provides the analogue for expressing his anxieties and concerns about interpersonal experiences. Of particular interest here is the relative infrequency of this theme in the first four interviews and its

---

[1] Patient: Themes 1–5, 8, 13–15, 17–19, 22–24, and 26. Therapist: Themes 7, 10–12, and 20. Undetermined: Themes 6, 9, 16, 21, and 25.

TABLE 6.8
Metaphoric Themes in Five Psychotherapy Interviews

	Interviews											
	93		143		205		301		373		Row	Total
Theme title	Total	Patient/ Therapist	Total	Patient/ Therapist	Total	Patient/ Therapist	Total	Patient/ Therapist	Total	Patient/ Therapist		
1. Personal self-worth or loss thereof	—	—	16	15/1	11	10/1	4	2/2	12	3/9	43	30/13
2. Some feelings are experienced as overpowering	9	7/2	8	4/4	3	3/0	8	2/6	5	4/1	33	20/13
3. Analogy of physical strength/weakness to character strength/weakness	2	2/0	2	0/2	2	2/0	—	—	26	16/10	32	20/12
4. Patient perceived as passive object	1	1/0	—	—	19	7/12	4	2/2	6	3/3	30	13/17
5. Expressed problems with women	3	2/1	1	1/0	16	15/1	—	—	8	0/8	28	18/10
6. Patient's problems in postponing gratifications	—	—	7	4/3	7	2/5	8	5/3	1	1/0	23	12/11
7. Patient's relationship with the therapist	—	—	11	3/8	—	—	—	—	10	8/2	21	11/10
8. Felt negative influence of parents in present problems	7	6/1	1	1/0	3	0/3	3	3/0	5	3/2	19	13/6
9. References to the patient being self-centered or selfish	—	—	—	—	—	—	14	5/9	—	—	14	5/9
10. Personification of conscience	—	—	12	0/12	1	0/1	1	1/0	—	—	14	1/13
11. Patient fails to consider the consequences of his behavior	5	1/4	7	2/5	—	—	—	—	1	1/0	13	4/9
12. Patient's problems with perceiving himself as accountable for his behavior	—	—	10	0/10	3	1/2	—	—	—	—	13	1/12

13. Patient experiences a sense of "presence" about feelings or events of the past	2	2/0	1	1/0	–	–	3	3/0	7	6/1	13	12/1
14. Patient's difficulties in experiencing his feelings directly	–	–	7	6/1	–	–	–	–	2	1/1	9	7/2
15. Patient's changing attitudes about need fulfillments	–	–	–	–	7	6/1	–	–	–	–	7	6/1
16. Personification of thoughts, feelings or needs	–	–	6	3/3	–	–	–	–	–	–	6	3/3
17. Patient's experience of hopelessness about himself	–	–	6	5/1	–	–	–	–	–	–	6	5/1
18. Derogatory exaggerations of name calling	2	2/0	–	–	2	2/0	–	–	–	–	4	4/0
19. References indicating attempts at positive change	–	–	–	–	–	–	–	–	4	3/1	4	3/1
20. Problems of self-assertion in sexual terms	–	–	–	–	–	–	3	0/3	–	–	3	0/3
21. Therapy perceived as scientific analysis	–	–	3	2/1	–	–	–	–	–	–	3	2/1
22. Partitioning of self	–	–	–	–	2	2/0	–	–	1	1/0	3	3/0
23. Possession of another person as an object	–	–	2	2/0	–	–	–	–	–	–	2	2/0
24. Patient's experience of loneliness	–	–	2	2/0	–	–	–	–	–	–	2	2/0
25. Analogy of entitlement to legalism or rights	2	1/1	–	–	–	–	–	–	–	–	2	1/1
26. Attempt at making sense of various feelings	1	1/0	–	–	–	–	–	–	–	–	1	1/0
27. Miscellany	4	2/2	5	2/3	6	4/2	2	1/1	2	1/1	23	12/11
Col. Total	38	27/11	107	53/54	82	27/27	54	27/27	90	51/39	371	211/160

dominance in Interview 373. One wonders if the analogy of physical strength—weakness to character strength—weakness is not one of the most useful novel metaphoric themes within the whole of this therapy. It certainly is most apt in light of the patient's very active participation in sports and surely provides him with a readily available model by which to guide extratherapeutic activities. Its importance is also highlighted by the fact that this theme is the only one which dramatically increases throughout therapy. In the first three interviews it ranks fifth, ninth, and sixth respectively. In the final interview it ranks first.

Metaphor Theme 4: Patient perceived as a passive object. This theme, though introduced by the patient, reveals a great deal of variation. It does not appear in Interview 143, but is the most frequent theme in Interview 205. The therapist is chiefly responsible for this theme peaking in that session. Subsequent to this interview the theme appears to stabilize in its rate of occurrence.

Metaphor Theme 5: Expressed problems with women. The frequence of the patient's metaphoric comments about his problems with women bears a striking similarity to the previous theme. The theme ranks 4th in the Interviews 93 and 373, tenth in Interview 143 and second only to Theme Four in Interview 205. One context within which the patient reveals his problem about relating to women concerned his experience of having little control over these relationships. In this context it follows neatly upon the patient perceiving himself as a passive, manipulated object (Theme 4). This is the second of the patient-initiated metaphors that is adopted by the therapist in the final interview. In that interview the therapist responds with this theme to the patient's stated reluctance to marry.

Metaphor Theme 6: Patient's problems in postponing gratifications. This figure, referring to the patient's problems in tolerating frustrations, is introduced by him in Interview 143. The therapist's active interest in pursuing this line of conversation is clear from his participation in maintaining the topic for three widely separated interviews. The theme ranks sixth in frequency in Interview 143, fourth in the next interview, and second in Interview 301. In Interview 301 it is introduced by the patient early on and quickly evolves into a different theme (9) at the therapist's persuasion. This new theme, the patient's self-centeredness, then comes to dominate this interview.

Metaphor Theme 7: Patient's relationship with the therapist. In Interview 143 the therapist begins to comment on the ongoing relation with the patient, doing so in the context of a figurative communication. Surely this is not the first time in 143 interviews that the therapist has highlighted this particular manner of therapist—patient interaction. The absence of such comments in Sessions 93, 205, and 301 leads us to suspect this event to be relatively unique in therapy at this time. Of particular importance is that the therapist uses this theme more frequently in Interview 143 and that it was the therapist and not the patient who introduced it in this session. In contrast, it is the patient in Interview 373 who makes use of this figure in talking about his relationship with significant persons in the past. This figurative theme is the only one introduced by the therapist that has any degree of stability throughout the course of therapy. Every other theme introduced by the therapist (Themes 9–12) decreases dramatically over time.

Metaphor Theme 8: Felt negative influence of parents in present problems. The patient's comments regarding the influence of his parents in his present problems is a recurring theme which decreases in significance as time passes in therapy. It is introduced by the patient in Interview 93 in which it ranks second in frequency for that session. As time passes it diminishes in importance to where it ranks seventh by Interview 373. As with Themes 2 and 4, we would infer it is of major therapeutic significance that the patient is able to distinguish between the influence of those who reared him – thus contributing greatly to his present troubles – and his own capacity to transcend such an influence and become self-determining. Such a pattern of change is perhaps indicated by the diminished frequency of Theme 8.

Metaphor Theme 9: References to the patient being selfish or self-centered. Little can be said regarding this theme except that it was a therapist-introduced metaphor that evolved from a number of figurative comments (as in Theme 6) produced by the patient in Interview 301. Clearly it is unproductive in its own right, although it is closely related to a number of significant themes which did occur in the same interview (Themes 1, 2, 4, and 6). The overall concern of patient and therapist in this interview deals with the patient's passivity which is rooted in an unrealistic and infantile sense of entitlement. What the patient gains in being catered to and coddled is lost in self-esteem and autonomy.

Metaphor Theme 10: Personification of conscience. This is an excellent example of a theme introduced by the therapist which apparently served little overall purpose. It diminishes quickly in the sessions following its introduction and fails to recur at all in the last session. It lends some support to the idea that it is patient themes, expressed in novel metaphors, which are important to therapy. The themes which do not evolve from the patient's figures or those which are radically introduced by the therapist (with little reference to the patient's problems) seem to be of little use.

Metaphor Themes 11 and 12: Patient fails to consider the consequences of his behavior, and patient's problems in perceiving himself as accountable for his behavior. Again the therapist introduces these themes and both rapidly diminish in rank and importance. Interestingly enough Themes 9–12 form a cluster of therapist-initiated and therapist-dominated metaphors which decrease sharply over time and which seem to be concerned with what can be called the patient's intense narcissism. Selfishness, conscience, consequences, and accountability (Themes 10–12, respectively) all seem to belong to the same nexus of topics. One wonders if the therapist's own ethics are not showing in these unproductive metaphors.

Metaphor Themes 13–26. The remaining figurative themes do not occur frequently enough to merit specific discussion. None of these ranked higher than fourth in any interview. Their relations to more frequent themes and the significance of their occurrence is sufficiently unclear as to exclude them from further consideration.

It seems clear from the preceding discussion of the twelve most frequent themes that the patient's concerns with self-esteem (Theme 1) and character strength (Theme 3) form the focal points for his psychotherapy. The discussions of his feelings as overwhelming (Theme 2), his passivity (Theme 4), specifically with women (Theme 5), and his impulsivity (Themes 6, 9, and 11) in seeking gratifications all form a second complex of metaphoric themes out of which the two dominant themes of self-esteem and character strength evolve. This evolution is simple enough to describe. The patient came to therapy primarily concerned with his sexual problems, a topic that quickly led to a generalized discussion of his problems with women and his concerns about passivity. It is understandable that a person who feels "out of control" in the face of overwhelming forces — be they women, urges, or impulses — is going to feel helpless and passive. As passivity and helplessness intensifies so too does a sense of worthlessness. The patient's compulsive interest in sports provides an apt metaphor within which to discuss his lifelong feeling of being characterologically weak (helpless, passive, worthless). All of these themes are discussed within the context of the patient's relationship with the therapist (Theme 7) and as a consequence of his feeling that his parents were instrumental in establishing this character defect (Theme 8).

These themes, then, are the metaphoric content of the whole of therapy — a broad survey of topics discussed figuratively. If these thematic conclusions are representative of the therapy process, the structure on and by which therapy proceeds, then statements of insight which are figurative should fall within the same thematic domains and be of comparable rank. To make such a comparison the occurrence of each of 26 metaphoric themes *within* insight regions was tabulated and Table 6.9 reports the relative frequencies of themes occurring within the regions selected as insightful.

The values reported in this table represent the number of times a particular figurative theme occurred in a communication unit selected as insightful by our judges. In obtaining these values, instances of insight were listed in a roster for each therapist–judge. Beside each instance containing a novel figure the theme category to which that figure belonged was noted. To obtain values for Table 6.9, it was a simple matter of summing the totals for the four judges per session.

TABLE 6.9
The Number of Times across all Five Sessions a Given
Metaphoric Theme Occurred within an Insight Region

Theme	Interview number					
	93	143	205	301	373	Total
1	–	25	5	5	5	40
2	1	4	–	3	2	10
3	1	–	–	–	21	22
4	–	–	10	4	–	14
5	4	1	6	–	–	11
6	–	7	2	6	2	17
7	–	10	–	–	10	20
8	3	–	2	5	10	20
9	–	–	–	9	–	9
10	–	11	–	1	–	12
11	1	5	–	–	1	7
12	–	8	–	–	1	9
13	6	2	–	4	1	12
14	–	1	–	–	2	3
15	–	2	–	–	–	2
16	–	3	–	–	–	3
17	–	2	–	–	–	2
18	–	–	–	–	–	0
19	–	–	–	–	1	1
20	–	–	–	3	–	3
21	–	1	–	–	–	1
22	–	–	–	–	–	0
23	–	3	–	–	–	3
24	–	2	–	–	–	2
25	1	–	–	–	–	1
26	1	–	–	–	–	1

For example, in Interview 143, 25 represents the number of times Theme 1 occurred in regions chosen by our therapist–judges as insightful. In the same way, Theme 2 occurred 4 times in insight regions in Interview 143, while Theme 6 occurred 9 times and so on for all 26 themes.

From this table it is obvious that the metaphoric theme most frequently occurring within regions of insight is Theme 1, a theme concerned with the patient's sense of self-worth and loss of esteem. Most of these occurred in the 143rd interview and recurred at a lower rate thereafter. The second most frequent theme category within regions of insight occurred almost totally within Interview 373 and concerned the patient's strength and weakness (Theme 3). The third cluster of metaphors included within insight regions concerned the patient's relationship to the therapist and his feelings that, somehow, his parents were influential in his problems. The next six most frequent metaphor themes within insight statements are as follows: the patient perceived as a passive object (Theme 4); personification of conscience (Theme 10); the patient's sense of "presence" about some feelings or events of the past (Theme 13); his expressed problems with women (Theme 5); and his experience of some feelings as overpowering (Theme 2).

Using these data a general description of the content about which the patient experienced insight can be conjectured. Early in psychotherapy (Interview 93) the patient has become aware of the various problems he experiences in his relationships with women (Theme 5) and this insight evolves from an awareness that particularly stressful problems of the past are everpresent in his daily living (Theme 13). In Interview 143 the patient seems to understand a very basic dynamic in his personality makeup. He comes to realize just how his deeply rooted sense of worthlessness (Theme 1) is intimately tied to a harsh and relentless conscience (Theme 10) which damns him for his sense of entitlement (Theme 6), his impulsivity (Theme 11) and his irresponsibility (Theme 12). This awareness occurs within the context of the patient discussing his relationship to the therapist (Theme 7). In Interview 205 the patient has now come to see some relationship between his sense of worthlessness (Theme 1) and his passivity (Theme 4), specifically with women (Theme 5). Following this, in Interview 301, he begins to understand the role his parents have played (Theme 8) in contributing to his sense of entitlement and selfishness (Themes 9 and 6); and how such feelings repeatedly diminish his sense of self-esteem (Theme 1). Finally, in Interview 373 we observe that the patient seems to understand his dilemma in a very sophisticated manner. He senses how it is that he suffers from a defect in character (Theme 3), a fault which contributes to serious problems in modulating his self-esteem (Theme 1). He senses himself as a vulnerable man who behaves with his therapist (Theme 7) as he behaved in regard to his parents in the past (Theme 8).

Taking both the quantitative and the thematic data of the preceding analyses into account suggests that insightful experiences are related to figurative activity in a number of different ways. Regions judged as insightful occur either as coincident with high rates of novel figurative expression or in coincidence with strictly literal discourse. In none of the interviews examined is there any coincidence at all of frozen figurative activity and statements judged as insightful. What emerges here is a conclusion that insight can occur within the context of creative metaphor as well as within the context of explicit literal expression. Even though insight selections do not always cooccur directly with novel figurative output, they do seem to cluster on either side of periods during which high rates of novel figurative activity occur.

When insight does occur within the context of novel figurative language, it usually concerns the major themes discussed. These major themes would seem to form the topical structure upon which the fabric and process of insight — and thus therapy — proceeds. And yet one question remains: What is the relation between literal and metaphorical statements judged as insightful? To answer this, each insight region was inspected and four seemingly distinct patterns of relation emerged:

1. There are insight statements which are themselves figurative that report the patient's awareness of a connection or relation between past and present.
2. There are metaphorical insight statements which are general case statements. That is, they possess obvious implications and applications beyond their actual words and do not deal only with the specific topic under discussion.
3. There are literal insight statements which are highly specific to certain applications, as opposed to the general applicability of the previously described metaphorical statements.
4. An overall pattern was observed which best describes the relation between metaphor and insight as the "literalization of metaphors."

Within all of the insight regions examined we find three examples of the first type, that is, metaphorical relational statements.[2] In Interview 93, for example, the remark "Everything leads back to my mother" was selected by all four therapist—judges as an insightful event. It is apparent the patient here was using a figure of speech to express his awareness of a relationship between what he was communicating in therapy and particular features of his relationship with his mother. In addition to this awareness, there was the implication that his new found observation possessed a more global application; that is, applied to other aspects of his life. Another nonliteral statement selected by therapist—judges as an insightful event, which also indicated the patient's awareness of a relation between past and present, occurred somewhat later in the same interview when the patient says, "[I]t's almost like I'm still doing it — they're with me right now." In this statement the patient made a generally applicable figurative statement about a more particular revelation a few lines before. In his earlier comments he was talking about the ways in which he involved himself in violent family arguments between mother and father. As his report continued he became aware of his tendency to do similar things in his life now, and this awareness was expressed metaphorically. As in the previous case, the patient made a metaphorical statement implying an awareness of some connection between present and past behavior. A final illustration of this type of insight statement was presented in Interview 143. The patient, in commenting about the manner in which he confuses himself by never being satisfied in a relationship, and thereby punishing himself, said "Because when you're nice I don't want you. When you pitch me out I want you." He then continued with the comment, "This is what it is with Person X." Again we observe the patient stating metaphorically a relationship between one event in his present experience with another in his past.

The importance of "metaphorical generalities" — the second pattern of insight

---

[2] The total number of examples for these 4 patterns will be greater than 17 since some instances were counted more than once.

observed — has been stressed by Simpkinson (1972) in an indirect fashion. He hypothesized, after Bruner (1962b), that one function of metaphorical language in therapy was to provide "models of awareness." By this he meant a conceptual model which the patient was able to carry away from the therapy hour and which had relevance in his day to day problem setting and solving. Certainly the patient's awareness of his problematic behavior as containing vestiges of infantile ways of dealing with the world was a "model of awareness" for this particular case. There are four instances of these models of awareness, which we prefer to call metaphoric generalities since it avoids the implication of having a "thing in your head" that the idea of a "mental model" might conjure up. In Interview 205 the patient summed up a lengthy literal disclosure of his feelings about being pressured by his girlfriend in the metaphor, "It's like I seem to feel as though I am doing what [Person X] wants." This generality is used to express for the patient his awareness of a pervasive aspect of his relation to his girlfriend — his passivity and indecisiveness. Later in Interview 301 a similar pattern emerges. Here the patient made a long, but literal, comment about his acting out by coming late to therapy and summed the situation up with the statement, "I feel like there should be some punishment." Here again the statement clearly has an application far beyond the present therapy situation. It is a metaphorical generality which the patient is able to refer to after the hour has passed.

Interestingly enough the therapist also supplied such metaphorical generalities to the patient. In Interview 205, after the patient disclosed how he, in the past, felt that people, especially women, would not like him were it not for his physical and sexual prowess, the therapist commented "You felt it's a deceit, it's a fraud." Later, after the patient has made a series of insightful remarks, applicable only to particular problems in his life, the therapist says "You have always felt and thought of yourself as a passive object who is being manipulated by, particularly a woman, like mother."

One must conclude that this is one way in which metaphor relates to insight. There were no literal statements of insight which were also general statements. Within the context of therapy metaphors seem to possess a potential and economy for summing up and generalizing global insights about relationships and feelings. In all of the examples presented there seems to be a demand in the metaphor that both the patient and therapist search for further instances to which the general statement can be applied. The broad applicability of such general statements is what is meant by global insight.

The observation that literal statements of insight were typically concrete and particular (in contrast to general case statements of insight which were exclusively metaphorical) highlights a third pattern which emerged in this particular case. In this third class of literal insight statements the patient directly appropriated explicit feelings for himself. Four examples illustrate this point.

1. In Interview 143 the patient, who was crying, said "And uh — Where's my,

this is what — I'm uh, I'm very confused about this because at first I'm glad and then I cry." In this statement the patient made a direct reference to his experience, and he did so without recourse to figurative expression.

2. In Interview 205 the patient, in the midst of a series of literal statements (considered as insightful by all four therapist—judges), said "I am afraid because I dare not do this . . ."

3. Again in Interview 205 he said "The thing is I'm angry, I'm very angry at [Person X], I think as you were talking I became angry."

4. And again in the same Interview 205 he said about his mother, "I do feel I can handle myself. It's not as though I'm worried about not handling myself. It's just that I don't like her."

All of these statements were chosen by all four therapist—judges as indication of an insightful experience. In each case, it was a literal statement in which the patient directly appropriated a feeling for himself, that is, in which he made a first-person declarative statement about his internal affective experience.

The fourth and final category of insight events is by far the more pervasive throughout all the insight regions examined. Because of its frequency, we surmise it evidences a most crucial relation between figurative language and insight in psychotherapy. For this set of statements we find a pattern in which a metaphorical expression is first produced and then literalized by the patient. The first example of this pattern appeared in Interview 93. Here the patient said ". . . it's like, you talked one time about feeling for my mother being something from my mother, and masturbation could be something from my mother." This metaphorical statement was then followed by a literalization of the implicit ideas contained within it, "I'm not clear on that. I've thought about it before and it seems like it might sound all right but — yeah, wanting my mother — wanting more from my mother." Again in the same interview the patient made the metaphorical assertion "I want to stick my mother." A few lines later he explicated what we already implied from his statement, "Because it's my mother I want to have intercourse with."

In Interview 143 the therapist introduced a novel figure which subsequently was literalized by the patient. Towards the middle of the interview the therapist, talking about the manner in which the patient sought out punishment, said, "As though you'd like to cast off the responsibility onto something external to yourself." Moments later, the patient responded, "Yes. I'm becoming aware, I don't know what's taking me so long. I am becoming aware of the, I know that the pattern that follows is when I want something is when I'm also — be sneaky."

Later in the same interview the therapist responded in a literal restatement of a patient produced novel figure. In this instance the patient produced a figurative generality which captured his increased awareness of a tendency to sabotage his relationships with women: "It's like [Person Y] and everything else all this — all over again." To this the therapist responded, "And this is what you're trying to bring about in analysis with me too — to fail." Here again a novel metaphor was literalized and then extended to include other referents.

In Interview 205 the patient talked about his feeling of being a passive victim in relationships in life rather than an active pursuer. He expressed this metaphorically, "It's almost like I didn't choose [Person X]. I didn't exactly choose her, I, it's almost as though when I ran away from [Person Y] I, there was [Person X] and the only thing I could think of was I still wanted, I want love and I want, I wanted to be married and have intercourse. And there was [Person X]." The patient's next response made these "as if" statements quite explicit. "There was no choice. I didn't, I didn't — know I, I could make a choice or start to make a choice, think about choosing." This statement represented a strong affirmative appropriation of an experience. The similes "as if," and "as though," were succeeded by literal statements which clarified his experience.

In Interview 301 the patient responded in a long literal statement to three therapist-produced novel figures. The therapist used the simile, "As though you feel you don't deserve to succeed," the metaphor, "Bad little boy role," and the rhetorical question "Who's guilty and unreliable and all that?" These figures highlighted the patient's implicit self-concept as bad, crooked, weak, and even criminal. In response, the patient made a series of first-person statements, like, "Now I know that I'm fighting these things. I'm doing these things." These literal statements chronicled his growing acceptance of the therapist's more figurative description. These literal statements, in turn, were followed by a figurative generality, "I feel like [there] should be some punishment." This figure followed upon the patient's agreement with the therapist's figurative statements and developed out of it. Later in this same interview the patient made a literal, simple affirmation to another therapist metaphor. The therapist said, "As though this passive way is the way to get the pleasure. The active up and doing way is blocked for you, I guess, by fear." To which the patient responded "Yeah. Maybe what we were talking about yesterday." The next insight region of Interview 301 (Segment 46–49) also showed this same pattern. The patient used the novel figure, "makes me feel not in command," which was literalized into, "I was thinking, they're sort of controlling me," in his next response.

In both insight regions of interview 373 the same pattern also held. When the therapist—judges most generally agreed on an insightful event it was usually a statement which literalized the implications of a novel figure. For example, "It's almost as though this is what my father is saying to me when I was stealing from him and he never said anything about it or let me get away with it . . . just like this is what he was doing, laughing, or just calling me a little, little shit." Here the patient, increasingly aware of his feelings for the therapist being similar to his feelings for another significant people (his father), said of these feelings, "[they] make me angry at you."

Finally in the last region of insight the patient gently explicated what was implicit in two preceding metaphors. The direct statement "I felt all alone," evolved out of the novel figure, "I couldn't quite get my feelings," and "I felt sort of separate from everybody."

By way of summary then, we have found insightful events to be: (1) metaphorical statements affirming a relation between past and present experience; (2) figurative generalities which can be considered as general case statements; (3) literal statements which represent the patient's direct affirmation and acceptance of current experience; and (4) literal statements which closely follow and explicate some aspects of a preceding figurative statement.

Although it has been possible to describe four different patterns of relations among figurative language, literal language, and statements judged to reflect insightful experiences, the fourth pattern would seem to represent the best characterization of their mode of interaction. Stated in the most rudimentary form, insight as a process, involves the literalization of figurative statements into first-person affirmations about one's own experience which are then owned as appropriate to that experience. A useful figure seems to bring about insightful experiences because it relates diverse parts of a life to one another and then portrays these relations in their most general and/or revealing form. The final aspect of this process occurs when the patient makes these new perspectives his own in the present, and expresses this fact in the form of a simple literal statement.

SOME SUMMARY SPECULATIONS AND A GENERAL CONCLUSION

Just as in poetry and in more general problem-solving situations, metaphoric language within the context of psychotherapy provides the speaker and the listener with a model of awareness or a horizon, as Lonergan (1957) would call it. This in turn provides both speaker and listener with a perspective from which to work through or toward some or all of the implications of the model and it is this process of "explicating the implicit" which constitutes the essential aspects of the process usually called insight.

Integral and essential to such a process is figurative language, both as a chronicler of what has transpired and as a herald of what is to come. As we have seen, novel figures lead to insight insofar as they, as figurative generalities, provide a model of awareness from which viable behavioral applications can be, and are, drawn. What is witnessed then, is a continuous process of metaphorization to literalization and so on. When a novel metaphor is produced it provides a figurative model which suggests a number of possible ways to go. The communicating parties select any one (or several) of these routes, and then begins the process of explication. As the theme, or route, selected reaches a greater degree of precision in explication, other implicit statements also begin to emerge and suggest a hitherto unsuspected development. What happens, within and across sessions, is that the patient in psychotherapy communicates on several levels simultaneously. In order to understand and interrelate these various levels and themes, the therapist needs to take note of the novel figurative statements in current use. Such observation can reveal the various experiences that may be in the process of explication.

Literal, first-person declarative statements, on the other hand, reveal those experiences the patient feels safe in disclosing. These statements are clear, uncomplicated, and literal, and usually deal with experiences directly accessible to the patient; for example, "I hate her," or "I am angry." Such statements show that the patient has appropriated certain self-experiences and is now responding to them. Prior to these statements the patient only felt safe in communicating such experiences in implicit and/or disguised ways; sometimes in novel figures, sometimes in symbols, sometimes in body language, sometimes in dress, and often in symptoms.

The best example of this kind of process is provided in the cited case study in terms of the patient's metaphorical statements concerning the analogy of physical strength to character strength. This theme was first introduced in Session 93 when the patient reported an acute sensitivity to his girl friend's request that he carry some packages. Instead of complying with her request he got angry with her and expressed this in terms of the statement, "As though I was saying why are you questioning me. I am strong enough to carry all this. You don't have to ask me if I could carry it," seems to describe his experience of her questioning of him and also seems to provide early evidence of a much more important problem. It is noteworthy that his statement projected the responsibility for this unpleasant experience onto his girl friend; that is, it was her fault for making him feel weak or helpless.

In Interview 143 this same figurative analogy surfaced again in the context of the therapist making an observation that it "takes strength" to tolerate frustration and to control one's impulses. In the next session (Interview 205), the patient characterized his inability to respond to his girl friend in an assertive and straightforward manner with "It was a weak thought ... I couldn't say it strongly." He reports how this experience left him feeling childish and then angry with himself.

In Interview 373 the same theme resurfaced within an insight region in the context of the patient's comparison of his obsessive concerns with sports and his feeling of being characterologically deficient. In these figurative remarks the whole texture has changed. The patient now "sees" a sensible relation between his concerns with athletic prowess and his newly acquired awareness of his pervasive helplessness. In addition, his novel figures (well on their way to literalization) are now first person declarative statements. We conclude from this that he has begun to appropriate the responsibility for his experience and, in clinical terms, no longer projects them onto others.

Later in the same interview, in a second insight region, the patient selects another aspect of this analogy when he introduces the idea of "protecting" himself from character weakness. "I'm still protecting myself from the feeling of being weak." At the same time he provided the therapist with several literal examples of how he carried through with this defensive maneuver in his daily life. "I said in the last two or three weeks I felt sort of unfriendlier ... for a while I was practicing this friendliness, making an effort to be friendly and everything. Then I sort of stopped it or something the last couple of weeks." His new experience of "protecting" himself from his weakness draws upon another metaphorical dimension implicit in the original novel figure. Not only has he acquired an awareness of himself as a person who pretends to be strong when actually he feels helpless; he also has begun to make sense of the whole defensive structure which for years had prevented this insight.

The process of insight then, at least in "talking psychotherapy," is had by verbalizing implicit experiences in novel figurative expressions and then by describing the implication of these expressions. As this process unfolds and reverberates there seems to be a "rule" by which one metaphor rather than another is developed. The patient, seemingly in spite of certain intrusions by the therapist, begins to talk about those experiences he feels he can now express.

Does this mean that each figure is developed into a simple theme and then is no longer dealt with? The answer here seems to be that literalizing one particular aspect of a figure may not exhaust all of its implications, and the really good figure, therapeutically (and poetically) speaking, is one which has many varied and significant implications. If the patient pursues a second or a third implication, such implications come to take on new textures and meanings as a consequence of their interaction with other newly explicated insights. It is this open-ended feature of novel figurative expression which permitted our judges to categorize various novel figures into sensible and meaningful themes. It is this same feature which permits psychotherapy to be a viable enterprise and a continuous, dynamic process. It gains this vitality from the fact that one novel metaphor, or figurative implication, may be well on its way to literalization while another aspect of the same figure or a completely new figure is being introduced into the communication system involving patient and therapist.

Psychotherapy, like all problem solving, becomes an open-ended process largely because patient and therapist learn how to use figurative insights as a method or style of solving taxing problems in living. Such a heuristic is somewhat different from Bruner's "model of awareness" in that it is better construed as a style of behaving rather than as a relatively static frame of reference. Simpkinson's (1972) conclusion that the patient acquires a "model of awareness" from the metaphors used in psychotherapy which he "takes with him from the therapy room" to apply to problems in the extra-therapy world is correct but undynamic. What the patient learns in psychotherapy is a style of communication and a strategy for problem solving. He learns that the process of "explicating the implicit" in his experience is one way of maintaining contact with his experience of himself and others, and this often takes place within the context of working through the explication of a novel figure of speech.

Part III

FIGURATIVE LANGUAGE, CHILDREN, AND THE EDUCATIONAL CONTEXT

Part II

7
The Development of Figurative Language

The normal course of language development in children has been a source of interest to parents, educators, and psychologists. Although the primary focus of this research has been concerned with syntactics, a recent review has shown an increasing concern for the semantic side of language as well (E. Clark, 1973). Unfortunately, the development of figurative language per se has been largely ignored as a fruitful area of research but, like an uninvited guest, such language has crashed a number of good, clean linguistic parties. For example, Clark (1973) finds onomatopoeia ("bow-wow," "moo," "gee-gee") present at her semantic party, while J. Gardner (cited in Gardner, 1973) found hidden in the protocols collected by Brown that "Adam, when 2 years old, [saw] his cocoa 'dancing like cowboy coffee' . . ." (p. 145). Berko-Gleason (1973) likewise finds very rich use of expressive language in child–child interactions in which expressive child language not only makes use of onomatopoeia such as "yukk" or "blah," but comes complete with voice and diction changes for other people and creatures.

Figurative gate crashing is not limited to America alone. Werner (1948) long ago noted poetic language constantly present in young children's speech all around the world, while Chukovsky in the Soviet Union provides numerous examples of children's figurative usage. He mentions a 2-year-old girl who, while taking a bath, had her doll "drown in" and "drown out" of the water. As a matter of fact, in a section entitled "Children and Their Poetry," Chukovsky (1965) provides the following examples of poems produced by preschool children:

Little Rain
(by two-year-old Inna)

Little rain, little rain, where were you?
I was outside making the dew. [p. 80]

The Sun
(by three-year-old Tatia)

Open, open the gates —
The sun is coming up in the sky! [p. 80]

The Bashful Little Bear
(by four-year-old Olia)

The littel bear stands in the nook
Smiling at a little book —
He's ashamed indeed
That he cannot read. [p. 80]

By the age of 10, children's poetry has advanced enough so that a school child of this age in an American classroom can write:

What is an image?
A bright reflection in a pond?
A picture copy in the tinted glass?
No.

An image is a person reflected to other people,
A person seeing your senses.
That is an image.

A door in your mind
Where your thoughts leak through.
An image.

Your inner beauty.
Your inner senses,
Working to make friends,
Your image.

Not only Chukovsky, but most parents as well (at least those who are aware of it), can easily supply instances of figurative language drawn from verbalizations of their own preschool children. In spite of this fact, and in spite of the fact that figurative usage is an acknowledged language phenomenon, there have been few studies or systematic observations of the development of figurative language. Perhaps one of the reasons for this is the difficulties figurative language present when one tries to conceptualize a formal theory of semantics such as have been described in great detail in Chapter 2.

THE DEVELOPMENTAL TRENDS IN FIGURATIVE LANGUAGE USE

The one major exception to this, was provided by Asch and Nerlove (1960) who were interested in the developmental course of double-function terms, that is, those terms which refer both to the physical properties of things and to the psychological properties of people. In their study, Asch and Nerlove used only 50 children (5 groups with 10 subjects in each group), ranging in age from 3 to

12, with subjects coming from upper-middle-class homes in the Swarthmore, Pennsylvania area. Since the experimenters were "looking for trends, rather than norms," they felt that a sample of this size would be sufficient. Children were interviewed on a one-to-one basis and questioned about a limited number of double-function terms: sweet, hard, cold, soft, bright, deep, warm, and crooked.

The results of this study clearly indicated that mastery of double-function terms followed a regular developmental course, with young children tending first to use these terms strictly in reference to objects. The psychological sense of a double-function term seemed to come later and then apparently as a separate vocabulary item independent of its physical meaning (something on the order of a homonym). The realization of a double-function property to these terms was the last thing to occur; and then, usually not spontaneously within the age groups studied.

There is, however, some problem with this interpretation as it now stands and the crux of the problem revolves around the specific double-function terms used. All of the terms (at least all of the terms specifically mentioned in the study) have already been frozen into dead lexical entries. So, for example, if we look in as old a dictionary as *Webster's Universal Dictionary of the English Language* (1937) under the entry "hard," we find that the fifth definition (out of 14) runs as follows: "unfeeling, not easily moved by pity ... severe, obdurate ... as a hard landlord." Frozen metaphors (those that regularly appear in the dictionary) may be learned as separate lexical items and need not necessarily, in the minds of children, have any connection whatsoever with the meaning of the term as it might be applied to a physical referent. The questions of when (at what age) and in what manner children understand and/or deal with original or novel metaphors is therefore essentially left untouched by this study. Unfortunately, we cannot use Asch and Nerlove's (1960) trends with any certainty in describing the developmental course of novel figurative usage in children.

There is still a further problem involved in interpreting Asch and Nerlove's results and this has to do with the specific nature of the task used. Asch and Nerlove asked their subjects to explain the meaning of the double-function terms utilized in the study. Thus, they were looking for developmental trends in the ability to explain or analyze metaphoric language but were not concerned with the ability to produce or to comprehend such language independent of an ability to explain them. When dealing with language in general, and figurative language in particular, it would seem necessary to make a distinction between explication and use, especially in view of the fact that it is not uncommon to find use often precedes explication; that is, the ability to explain the "whys" and "wherefores" of a particular aspect of language often comes after the child's ability to use a word properly in context. Certainly few children are aware of, or could explain, the sentence structure and grammar of the language they now speak fluently.

When considered in this light, Asch and Nerlove's (1960) results are somewhat more comprehensible: children can analyze and explicate frozen metaphor (or double-function terms) only when older or perhaps, in Piagetian terms, at the stage of formal operations. Such a view is consistent with Elkind's (1970, 1974) view that an ability to analyze metaphor arises as a feature of adolescent reasoning. When younger, children seem to interpret language literally and may be unable to shift meanings and explain a metaphor or double-function term in a broader or nonliteral sense. An adolescent, according to Elkind (1974), on the other hand, "no longer takes everything literally and begins to sense the multiple meanings inherent in a given word, picture, or gesture" (p. 176). As their data indicated, only Asch and Nerlove's (1960) older subjects were able to explain the double-function meanings of their terms and this seems to make sense in terms of a developmental analysis such as Piaget's.

Gardner (1974), noting the contradiction apparent between the ability of children to produce figurative language and the research and theoretical analyses arguing that figurative language processes are among the last language capacities to develop, has conducted research designed to examine the comprehension aspects of figurative-language development in children. Working with polar adjectives exemplifying different sense domains, Gardner constructed what he termed "a simple test of metaphoric capacity." This test involves the novel application of adjectives from one domain to five other sense domains where they are not ordinarily used and, therefore, could only be used by metaphoric extension. Each set of adjectives had a literal exemplar and five sets of metaphoric uses, one in each of six sense domains. The six modalities, or sense domains, represented were: visual (color), visual physiognomic (facial expressions), visual abstract (line configurations), auditory (pitches), tactile (objects felt while blindfolded), and verbal kinesthetic (a general bodily feeling expressed in words). The five pairs of polar adjectives used were: cold—warm, hard—soft, happy—sad, loud—quiet, and light—dark.

The final test was constructed after a pilot study had been run in order to establish the "correct" metaphoric exemplar for each adjective pair within each modality. Ten college students participated in this pilot study and a criterion of eight out of the possible ten choices for any of the exemplars was used to define the correct matching. The major study involved 101 subjects from working and lower-middle socioeconomic classes, with approximately equal numbers of males and females at four different age levels, $3^1/_2$, 7, $11^1/_2$, and 19. Each subject was tested individually and given the literal exemplar of a particular adjective pair, like, "loud—quiet" paired with "two recorded samples of the same pitch differing only in loudness." After it was established that subjects did understand the literal meaning of the polar adjectives used, metaphoric projection sets of the adjectives were presented one at a time, like loud and quiet color samples, loud and quiet tactilely perceived objects, loud and quiet faces, etc. All subjects were first asked to choose an exemplar fitting each adjective and then to give their reasons for that choice. All remaining polar adjective pairs were presented in the same manner so that each subject had 25 pairs to match "metaphorically."

Results indicated a significant age effect (older children tended to select the "correct" pairing more frequently), no sex effect and no sex by age interaction.

Sheffe comparisons indicated that there were significant differences between all age levels except between the 11½- and 19-year-olds where differences were practically nonexistent. Analyses of the reasons supplied for the particular mappings chosen indicated that preschool children had considerably more difficulty in producing reasons for their choices than they had in making the appropriate or "correct" choice. When they did respond to questioning, preschoolers tended to give answers that were not necessarily based on an understanding of the metaphoric qualities of the matches made. Seven-year-olds tended to be quite literal and concrete while 11½-year-olds (and, of course 19-year-olds) were able to explain their metaphoric matches quite reasonably and well. Results indicate that on this particular task children can and do make metaphoric matches and that this ability does increase with age, at least, from 3½ to 11½ years of age.

If there is one difficulty with this study, it concerns the structure of the task itself. One cannot help but question the distinction of a "right" or "wrong" metaphoric matching. Given the nature of metaphor, the individuality involved in a person's choice in terms (or modalities) to compare, and the numerous metaphoric and nonmetaphoric reasons for any given choice, how can it be unequivocally stated that some matches are correct and that others are mismatches? Since this test was first developed using college students and the results formed the bases of right and wrong matches, Gardner (1974) would seem to have had a sound basis for his decisions. Unfortunately, however, what may be a "wrong" match for an adult may be a "right" match for a child and what may be a "bad" metaphor for an adult may be a "good" metaphor for a child. This is, of course, a very difficult distinction to make experimentally, and Gardner is well aware of the problem when he repeatedly reminds the reader that the categories of correct and mismatched apply only within the context of this experiment and are not meant in any absolute sense.

A second possible difficulty in this experiment involves the forced-choice nature of the response required: the child must map one of the polar adjectives onto one of the exemplars provided. After one adjective is matched to its exemplar, the other adjective must necessarily be mapped onto another exemplar whether it fits or not. A child could, therefore, mismatch the first adjective for perfectly good metaphoric reasons, and, because of a lack of any viable alternative, mismatch the second adjective. Finally there is a problem with the nature of the metaphors themselves. In this particular task, the child has little or no opportunity to make novel metaphors but must be content with selecting from frozen figurative possibilities (like "cold" with "blue;" "warm" with "red;" "hard" with "frown;" and "soft" with "smile"). Although this study provides us with some information concerning the developmental course of frozen metaphoric use, it still leaves the area of novel metaphoric use untouched.

The fact that frozen metaphors were used in this study might also explain the pattern of developmental data produced. Frozen figures might be learned as vocabulary items, and as a child gets older he or she would be likely to choose those (frozen) figures which he or she has heard and learned. A younger child, who might not be familiar with a particular (frozen) figure would have no special reason or training to choose the "correct" matching. Since items used in this test were developed from a pilot study done with college students, it is reasonable to assume that the older a child is — or the closer he is to the age of the criterion group — the closer his answers will conform to those of that criterion group.

Despite these problems, results of the Gardner (1974) study do confirm certain findings of the earlier Asch and Nerlove (1960) study; that young children cannot explain the nature of metaphoric matches while older children can. In addition, the Gardner study also shows that children as young as $3\frac{1}{2}$ years of age can and do make (frozen) metaphoric matches and this is an important finding vis-à-vis the developmental course of figurative expression.

In a second study, Gardner, Kircher, Winner, and Perkins (1975) were concerned with examining children's verbal metaphoric productions as well as metaphoric preferences. To this end, 84 subjects equally distributed over 4 age levels (7, 11, 14, and 19) and 47 preschool children (3- and 4-year-olds) were required to produce an ending and choose 1 of 4 endings to a series of 18 incomplete stories or sentences of the following type:

> Things don't have to be huge in size to look that way. Look at that boy standing over there. He look as gigantic as ... (Gardner, Kircher, Winner, & Perkins, 1975, p. 128)

Each story was written in both a neutral and a metaphor-inducing style (as well as simply as a short incomplete declarative statement) in order to determine whether the set of the story influenced the selection made; that is, could a "metaphoric set" increase the probability of a metaphoric response? Each story involved a different adjective including the following six common adjectives: "soft," "dark," "quiet," "short," "cold," "sad"; their antonyms, "hard," "light," and so on; and six adjectives related to the antonyms but stronger in nature, like "stony," "gigantic," and so on. The four endings created for the choice part of the experiment involved the same 18 stories and consisted of a literal ending, a conventional ending, a metaphorically appropriate ending (defined by Gardner, Kircher, Winner, & Perkins as an ending "transporting the adjective to a realm where it was not ordinarily applied but where, in the present context, it was appropriate" (p. 128)) and a metaphorically inappropriate ending ("transporting the adjective to a realm where it was not ordinarily applied and where, moreover, it was not appropriate" (p. 128)).

Each subject was tested individually over several sessions and was asked to respond to stories containing each of the 18 adjectives, to choose one of four supplied endings for each and to explain the reasons for their choice or preference. Preschoolers responded to only six of the stories. Guidelines for metaphorically appropriate endings were established and subject productions and preferences coded according to one of four types: literal, conventional, appropriate, and inappropriate.

Results of this study showed that there was a decline in the number of literal and trite endings preferred by the four groups (not including the preschoolers), an increase in the number of appropriate endings preferred, and no significant difference in the number of inappropriate endings preferred. Although preschoolers showed no dominant preference for ending type, all other groups did: The 7-year-olds preferred literal responses, the 11-year-olds trite responses; and the 14- and 19-year-olds, both trite and appropriate responses. The majority of metaphoric productions at each age level were coded as trite with no statistically significant differences found among the four older groups. Further analyses conducted on the appropriate responses produced at each age level indicated that the oldest subjects produced more appropriate endings than the two younger groups (7 and 11). When the data collected from preschoolers were adjusted and analyzed, it was found that preschoolers could not adequately explain the reasons for their choices. Seven-year-olds again were quite literal and concrete while 11-year-olds, although concrete, in general tended to reject literal responses. In keeping with earlier results, 14- and 19-year-olds could explain and compare metaphoric endings while even trite endings were more embellished. The "metaphoric-set" stems produced more metaphoric endings only in college-age subjects.

Although these results clearly extend our knowledge about the development of figurative expression, there are still some questions that need to be asked. One of these concerns the classification scheme used; most particularly in regard to judgments of "trite" for productions such as "thundering as the President making a speech on television." Although Gardner *et al.'s* (1975) definition for the "appropriate" category was clearly specified, what might be trite for an adult judge might be quite novel or appropriate for a younger child. Although less important, a different question concerns the use of only similes to represent all aspects of figurative language and only adjectives to represent all form classes; for this reason, the generality of Gardner, and co-workers' results for all metaphoric language may be a bit tenuous.

More positively, however, this study does indicate that there is an increase in preference for metaphoric usage with age, and again confirms the finding that only older children have the analytic ability necessary to explicate metaphor. Perhaps, the most interesting result of this study is that preschoolers produced an absolutely higher number of metaphors than any other group. Although reasons for this are unclear (is it true metaphoric ability or only the lack of an appropriate word or construction?) the possibility must be considered that metaphoric production, if not preference, may sometimes decrease with age.

In addition to this work by Gardner and his associates (1975), other studies have also examined the development of figurative language, most particularly in written work produced by children. Although these studies were not concerned primarily with such development, they do provide relevant data in this context. Hill (1972), for example, found that figurative language was produced in the written work of elementary school children in Grades 2 through 6. Although there was no significant increase in the use of figurative language over grade levels, sixth graders did seem to show a greater frequency of use than children in any other grade. Sweet (1974), in analyzing several genres of written work produced by fourth through sixth graders (243 papers in all), found that although the seven categories of figurative language for which he searched were present on all grade levels there were no discernable developmental trends.

In a more direct attempt to develop age trends for the use and production of figurative language, Pollio and Pollio (1974) examined the written work of third-, fourth-, and fifth-grade students. Their sample consisted of six classes (two per grade level) attending a school located in a middle- to upper-middle-class neighborhood containing a fairly homogeneous white population, one probably similar to that used by Asch and Nerlove (1960). In this study, children were asked by their teacher to provide written language samples for three different tasks. One of these involved asking the children to write a composition on one of five different imaginative topics, like, "What would you do if all the trees disappeared?" A second required them to write as many sentences as they could to sets of five different words capable of double-function use. A third task asked them to make comparisons between sets of three different pairs of words, like "clock" and "child." The specific words used in the second, or Multiple Sentences task included many of the same words used by Asch and Nerlove (1960) (with the addition of some verbs such as "jump," "sing," "climb") in the hope of providing some degree of comparability between results of the two studies. In order to control for special word effects there were three different forms of the Comparisons and Multiple-Sentences tasks (the second and third tasks), and all three forms were distributed randomly within each class with all orders of administration equally present throughout the class. The data for all forms of the test were pooled for each analysis so that any order effect or any differential word effect might be controlled. Both of these latter tasks were open ended (one word or word pair per half sheet of paper) so that children could write as little or as much as they desired.

Instances of figurative language were recorded using the Barlow, Kerlin, and Pollio (1971) method and reliabilities were established. Before any meaningful conclusions could be drawn about how frequently figurative language was used by these children, it was first necessary to determine if children in all three grades wrote compositions of equal length. The data on this point were quite unequivocal: the children did not. There were statistically significant differences between length of compositions at all grade levels with number of words increasing as grade advanced. It was, therefore, necessary to make a correction for composition length before direct comparisons could be made across grade levels. The statistic developed for this purpose was a simple one: all scores were converted to proportions; that is, the number of figures over the number of words times 100. The reason for multiplying by 100 was to get rid of decimal scores and to express the number of figures as some number per 100 words of text, as done in other studies.

Analyses of these data revealed that on the Composition task students produced a significantly higher number of frozen than novel figures at each of the three grade levels. The total number of figures, however, decreased significantly over successive grade levels although this decrease was more marked for novel than for frozen figures.

In order to insure comparability of data among tasks, and to examine the effects of task demand, the same conversion procedure was applied to Multiple-Sentences and Comparisons tasks. Results of the Multiple-Sentences procedure revealed that a significantly greater number of frozen than novel figures was produced although the number of frozen figures was considerably larger than occurred in the Composition task. There was also a significant increase in the total number of figures produced over all three grades. Analyses of the Comparisons task showed that this task elicited a significantly greater number of novel than frozen figures and that both types of figurative language increased markedly and significantly over grades.

The absolute value of figurative language usage was also of interest. The rate of novel figurative usage evoked by the Comparisons task was far in excess of that evoked by either of the other 2 tasks with the average for all 3 grades falling somewhere around 5.5 figures per 100 words. This was considerably higher than average novel values for the Multiple-Sentences task (1.5 per 100 words of text) and for the Composition task (1.0 per 100 words of text).

Results for frozen figures were somewhat different. The range of values across all 3 tasks for frozen figures was nowhere near as great as for novel figures, with the Composition task producing a mean value of about 1.5, the Comparison task a mean somewhat under 2.5, and the Multiple-Sentences task a mean value somewhat under 3.5. Ranking these procedures in terms of their ability to elicit figurative language, it becomes clear that the Comparison task was best in evoking novel usage and that the Multiple-Sentences task was best in evoking frozen usage. The Composition task, by contrast, seemed to depress the child's use of both frozen and novel figurative language. One other point of interest in these data concerns the progression of figurative usage over grades. For both the Multiple-Sentences and Comparison tasks there were moderate to strong increases in figurative language over grades, while the trend was exactly opposite for the Composition task. These results imply that there is a strong interaction between the task you ask a child to do and his seeming ability to use figurative language.

In interpreting these results, it can be seen that children can and do produce both novel and frozen figurative language as early as third grade (age eight) although their ability to explicate this language, as has been noted in the Asch and Nerlove (1960) and Gardner (1974) studies, may not be present. The differential age effects shown by the three different tasks is also of considerable interest in that a child's production of figurative usage appears to be influenced by task-specific constraints. On the Composition task, metaphoric language decreased over successive grades although informal examination of the compositions produced showed very little change in vocabulary used, but similar to results found by Loban (1963), profound changes in the child's control of grammar and spelling. The Composition task seemed to be one in which a school child was very concerned about getting a good grade and that meant: don't take chances with either spelling, grammar, or word choice. In short, writing a composition seemed to suggest to the child: do the best you can, but don't rock the boat. Perhaps it is for these same reasons that both Hill and Sweet (see pages 167–168 of this chapter) found no development increase in figurative usage in the written work examined in their studies. Experimentally, this may mean that a more accurate way in which to assess developmental trends in connected discourse would be to have children "speak their compositions" rather than write them. In this way, it might be possible to remove demand characteristics that go along with the writing of a composition in an elementary-school classroom.

The data from the Pollio and Pollio (1974) study suggest that composition tasks as they are presently construed in the public-school system are not conducive to the production of either novel or frozen figurative language and that creative writing may in fact be a misnomer, at least when measured from the perspective of how frequently children used figurative language in their compositions. In the elementary-school context, compositions seem best construed not as a task in creative writing but rather as a task in the control and use of grammar and word choice. On the basis of this analysis, something needs to be done in order once again to make creative writing creative.

Taking these results in conjunction with data produced by the Gardner, Kircher, Winner, and Perkins (1975) study, it might be appropriate to say that the educational process appears to suppress the use of novel figurative language. This point is equivocal, however, since the Comparisons task, which is less school related than the Composition task — it requires the child to do something that he or she would not ordinarily do in the classroom — did seem to enable students to produce novel figurative language with such production increasing over grade. In this context, however, it is also important to bear in mind that a Comparisons task may force the production of novel figures since what is a novel figure but a new or unusual way of connecting or relating two initially disparate terms or ideas?

THE DEVELOPMENTAL COURSE OF FIGURATIVE LANGUAGE: SOCIO-CULTURAL EFFECTS

In order to determine the developmental level of figurative output in school-age children across a wide variety of socioeconomic and sociocultural levels M. Pollio (1973) has analyzed the performance of elementary school children on a variety

7. THE DEVELOPMENT OF FIGURATIVE LANGUAGE

of figurative use tasks. The subjects used in these studies were enrolled in five diverse elementary schools within the Knoxville, Tennessee, city school system. Within each school two classes in Grades 3 through 6 were examined. All classes were arranged by the principal of each school into heterogeneous groups prior to the beginning of the academic year. At each grade level, within each school, one of the two classes (depending upon the size of the school) were designated as a control class(es). For this study, there were a total of 19 experimental and 21 control classes. Teachers were randomly selected to be either experimental or control teachers. (Only the data for control classes were analyzed for developmental trends. For a description of the experimental teaching procedures used and the results of the second portion of this study, see Chapter 9 of this volume).

The five schools used in this study were quite different and can be described as follows:

School 1: a minimally integrated school located in an upper-middle to middle-income area. (There were no fully integrated schools of this type available.) The students in this school, in general, scored above average on standardized intelligence and achievement tests.

School 2: an integrated school located in a middle-income area. The students in this school also scored above average on intelligence and achievement tests.

School 3: a completely white school located in a lower- to lower-middle-income area. The students scored approximately at the mean on standardized tests.

School 4: a completely black school located in a lower-income area. Both the intelligence and the achievement test scores of children in this school were well below average, with the exception of the reading and language scores of the third grade. Achievement test scores seemed to become progressively lower in the upper grades.

School 5: an integrated school located in a lower income area. The children in this school scored approximately the same as those in School 4.

Because of the small number of children in Schools 4 and 5, the proximity of location between the schools and the equality of neighborhoods, the data for these schools were collapsed and treated as if provided by a single school (subsequently labeled School 4).

The three tasks used in this study were the same as those employed in the earlier Pollio and Pollio (1974) study, that is, a Composition task, a Comparison task, and a Multiple-Sentences task. All tests were administered by the regular classroom teacher. Developmental trends were derived from the data produced by control classes. In addition, all children were excluded who were "over age" for the grade they were in, that is, those who had repeated grades thereby making them over 1 year older than the average age for that grade. This was done in order to insure that the development levels represented those of children of normal age for the different grades assessed. The final sample was randomly selected from all subjects meeting this criteria. The total sample used in this part of the study consisted of 240 students, 60 per school, 15 at each grade level for Grades 3, 4, 5, and 6.

Three raters were trained by the Barlow, Kerlin, and Pollio (1974) method, until rater reliability exceeded the criterion of 80% for 2 + 1 (or better) ratings. Acceptance rates for all tests were quite high while rejection rates were quite low. (See Chapter 3, this volume, for specific details.)

Composition Test Results

In order to determine if the number of words contained in the compositions increased over schools and grades, an analysis of variance was computed over the data for all grades for all schools. The results of this analysis revealed that the mean number of words per composition per grade did differ significantly ($F_{3,224} = 7.16$; $p < .001$) with number of words per composition increasing as grade level increased. There was also a significant difference between the mean number of words produced in the different schools ($F_{3,224} = 15.54$; $p < .001$) with children in School 1 producing the longest compositions, and children in School 4 producing the shortest compositions. In general, the number of words per composition increased between Grades 3 and 6, although scores were quite variable within schools. It was noted, however, that the mean number of words produced in Grade 3 for School 1 was greater than the mean number of words produced in Grade 6 for all other schools.

In keeping with procedures established in the Pollio and Pollio (1974) study all figurative rates were converted to percentages. This conversion was executed for all children in all grades, in all schools, for frozen and novel figures separately. Figure 7.1 presents these trends for all schools combined. An analysis of variance computed over these data showed a significant difference between the rate of production of novel and frozen figures ($F_{1,224} = 24.47$; $p < .001$) with more frozen than novel figures produced per 100 words. In addition, there was a significant difference in the rate of production across grades ($F_{3,224} = 4.23$; $p < .01$) with total figures (frozen and novel combined) showing a general upward trend. There were no significant differences found between schools. All double-order interactions were not significant, but the triple-order interaction was found to be significant ($F_{9,224} = 2.48$; $p < .05$).

In order to explore the meaning of the triple-order interaction, as well as to examine the specific pattern of figurative output in each of the schools, separate plots were done for each school and separate analyses of variance computed. Figure 7.2a–d presents these school-by-school results. As can be seen in Figure 7.2a, the rate of novel figures increased from Grades 3 to 4 and then decreased slightly until Grade 6 in which the mean of .87 was not much above the Grade 3 mean of .75. The results of an analysis of variance done over these data showed that children in this school produced a greater number of frozen than novel

7. THE DEVELOPMENT OF FIGURATIVE LANGUAGE   173

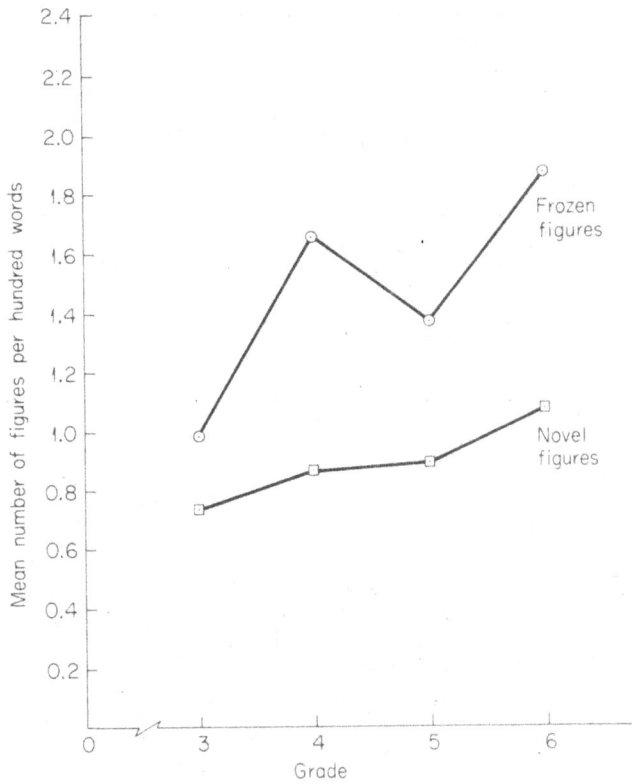

FIGURE 7.1 Compositions – All schools combined.

figures ($F_{1,56}$ = 8.79; $p < .01$), that there was no significant differences between grades on total figurative production, and that there was no significant interaction.

The results of an analysis of variance for School 2 showed no significant difference between the production of frozen and novel figures and no significant difference between grades but a significant interaction of grade by frozen and novel usage ($F_{3,56}$ = 6.38; $p < .01$). Figure 7.2b shows the pattern of metaphoric production for this school. It should be noted that where frozen production was highest (Grade 4), novel production was lowest; and that where novel production was highest (Grade 3), frozen production was lowest.

Results of an analysis of variance for School 3 was in agreement with the original analysis computed over all schools combined. Figure 7.2c presents this pattern, in which results indicated a significant difference between rates of production of frozen and novel figures ($F_{1,56}$ = 4.95; $p < .05$) with children producing more frozen than novel figures in their compositions. There was also a

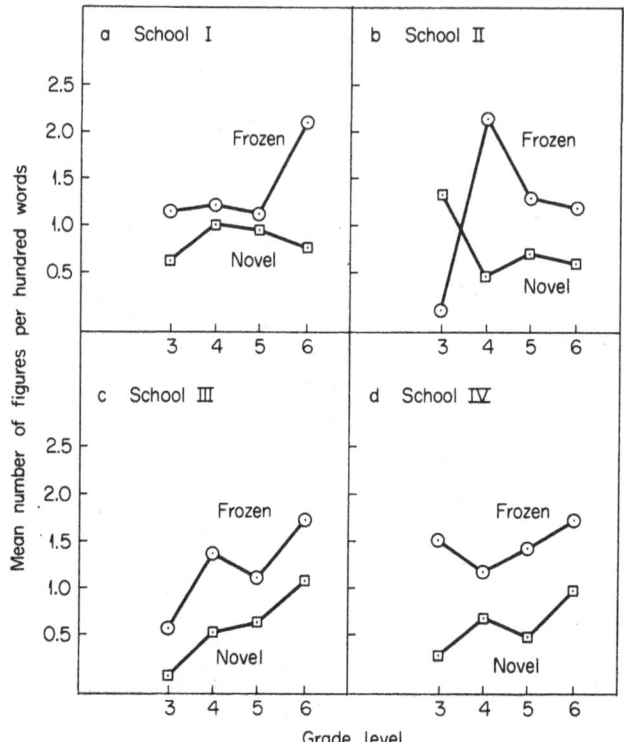

FIGURE 7.2 (a–d) School-by-school trends in the production of figurative language on a composition task.

significant increase over grades ($F_{3,56} = 4.60; p < .01$), with both novel and frozen usage showing such increase, and there was no significant interaction.

The results for School 4 (see Figure 7.2d) showed that these children tended to produce more frozen than novel figures ($F_{1,56} = 7.98; p < .01$). Unlike results for School 3, there were no significant differences between grades and no significant interaction. Inspection of the means for this school showed few differences between grades in frozen usage and a slight upward trend in novel usage.

In agreement with the Pollio and Pollio (1974) study, children in this study used more frozen than novel figures on a composition task. If frozen figures are considered as part of the lexicon and are learned in the same manner as other vocabulary items, then this result is to be expected. Children use established lexical items such as frozen figures more frequently than they use more difficult and innovative lexical items such as novel figures of speech.

In contrast to the general downward trend in figurative usage from Grade 3 through Grade 5 found by Pollio and Pollio (1974), these results showed a general upward trend from Grades 3 through 6. This seeming difference, however, is clarified by a closer examination of results for individual schools. The children sampled in the Pollio and Pollio study were all from one middle- to upper-middle-class school and had mean intelligence and achievement-test scores all well above average; the range of means for intelligence test scores were from 114 to 118, while the range of means for achievement-test scores varied from the 66th to the 75th percentile. It would not be appropriate, therefore, to compare trends found in the combined data of four intellectually and economically varied schools with those found for one high-intelligence, high-achievement school. A better procedure would be to compare results found for schools used in this study that were somewhat comparable to the school used in the other study. The mean intelligence and achievement test scores for School 1 were, in fact, directly comparable to those found in the Pollio and Pollio (1974) study, and although somewhat lower, the mean intelligence and achievement test scores for School 2 were also somewhat comparable.

Turning now to results for School 1, it can be noted that there was no significant grade effect for total figurative production. Looking more closely at the trend for frozen figures, it can be seen that children produced approximately the same number of frozen figures in Grades 3 through 5 although they showed a sharp increase in Grade 6. In the Pollio and Pollio (1974) study, it was found that frozen usage declined from Grade 3 to 4, and increased slightly in Grade 5. The data for novel usage, however, showed a different pattern. Looking again at Figure 7.2a, it can be noted that after an initial increase in usage from Grade 3 to 4, novel production declined slightly, but steadily, from Grades 4 through 6. This pattern is not unlike that found in the earlier study, where novel usage declined from Grades 3 through 5, although the decline in the earlier study was somewhat more dramatic.

Looking now at results found for School 2 (see Figure 7.2b) it can be noted that after an initial increase in frozen production between Grades 3 and 4, frozen usage again declined. Novel usage, on the other hand, declined from Grade 3 to 4, increased slightly in Grade 5, but declined again in Grade 6.

From these data for comparable schools it can be seen that novel figures show a somewhat downward trend not unlike that found in the Pollio and Pollio (1974) study. The important point, however, is not the slight downward trend found in novel figurative language for these schools, but rather the obvious lack of increase over grades. If the source of these data is taken into consideration (as derived from a composition task), then an explanation like that offered by Pollio and Pollio must be reiterated: when children are placed within a normal classroom situation, especially in a middle- to upper-middle-class school, grades are extremely important and a "don't rock the boat" philosophy seems to prevail, thereby depressing the use of novel figurative language in these schools.

What then are the patterns like in lower- to lower-middle-class schools? Turning now to Figures 7.2c and d, it can be noted that figurative usage, in general, and novel usage, in particular, showed an upward trend. These schools, especially School 3, were in fact responsible for the significant upward grade trend found in the overall analysis presented in Figure 7.1. It may be that children in these schools simply do not care and use whatever language they wish, or it may be that these schools are actually teaching creative writing in a manner that best encourages a creative product, by allowing children to write whatever they like in whatever manner they like and thereby teaching them to write in a natural, relatively gradefree way.

A qualitative examination of the mechanics of language, the use of syntax, spelling, punctuation, and so on, revealed that children in Schools 1 and 2 were appreciably better than children in Schools 3 and 4. If, however, novel usage can be taken as an indication of creative expression, then children in Schools 3 and 4 came generally to surpass those in Schools 1 and 2 as grade level increased. It is interesting to note that at the third-grade level novel figurative usage was higher for Schools 1 and 2 than for Schools 3 and 4, but by the time the sixth grade was reached, novel usage was higher in Schools 3 and 4 than in Schools 1 and 2. In effect, what seemed to happen is that children in middle- to upper-middle-class schools come to suppress their use of novel figurative terms in a normal classroom situation while children in lower- to lower-middle-class schools do not. Whether this is the direct result of teaching procedures or teacher/parent attitudes is unknown; what is known, is that overconcern for classroom achievement seems to render creative writing a clear misnomer.

Comparisons Test Results

A second task done by all children asked them to make as many comparisons as they could between pairs of randomly selected words. In order to determine if children of different ages tend to use comparisons of differing lengths, an analysis of variance was computed over the number of words used in the total Comparisons task (it should be remembered here that the Comparisons Task consists of 3 word pairs). The results of this analysis showed a significant difference in number of words used between schools ($F_{3,224} = 2.98; p < .05$) with children in School 2 producing the greatest number of words, and with children in School 3 producing the smallest number of words. There was also a significant difference between grades ($F_{3,224} = 14.27; p < .001$) with results indicating, for all schools combined, a significant increase between Grades 3 and 4; a gradual decrease between Grades 4 and 5; and a larger decrease between Grades 5 and 6.

The analysis of variance also revealed a significant interaction between school and grade ($F_{9,224} = 3.40; p < .001$). An inspection of the data indicated that while Schools 2 and 3 followed the general trends described above, Schools 1 and 4 did not. In both of these schools the number of words increased through Grade 5, and then dropped sharply in Grade 6.

In keeping with our by now standard procedure, the number of rated metaphors produced in response to the Comparisons task was divided by the number of words and multiplied by 100, thus producing a percentage score directly comparable to those used in evaluating the Composition task. Means and standard deviations were then computed separately for frozen and novel usage for all grades within all schools and these data are presented graphically in Figure 7.2. A complex analysis of variance computed over these results revealed that children tended to produce more novel than frozen figures of speech for the Comparisons task ($F_{1,224} = 36.38; p < .001$). In addition, there was a significant difference between schools ($F_{3,224} = 4.59; p < .01$) with Schools 1 and 2 producing significantly higher rates of figurative usage than School 4. There was no significant grade effect for the Comparisons task, although there was a significant frozen–novel by school interaction ($F_{3,224} = 4.81; p < .01$), and a significant triple order interaction ($F_{9,224} = 2.18; p < .05$).

In order to learn more about these interactions, as well as to examine the specific output of figurative usage for the different schools, separate analyses of variance were computed for each school. The results of this kind of analysis for School 1 (see Figure 7.4a) revealed that children in this school produced a greater number of novel than frozen figures for the Comparisons task ($F_{1,56} =$

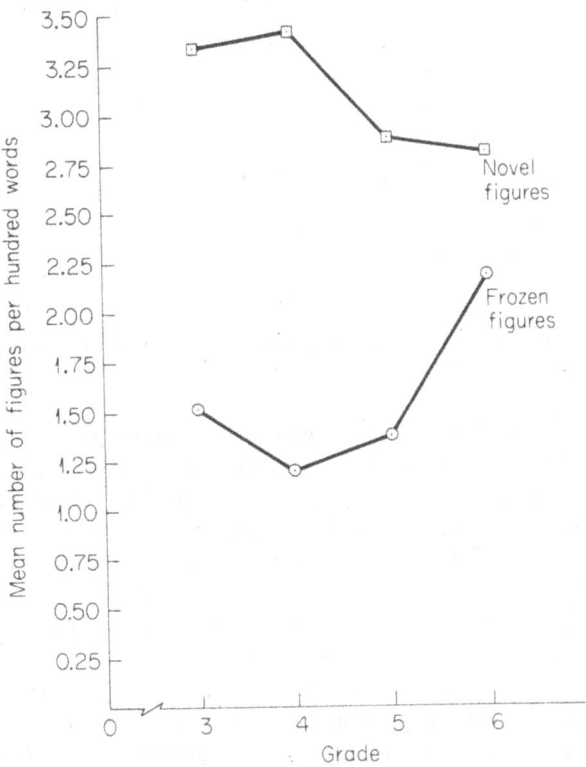

FIGURE 7.3 Comparisons – All schools combined.

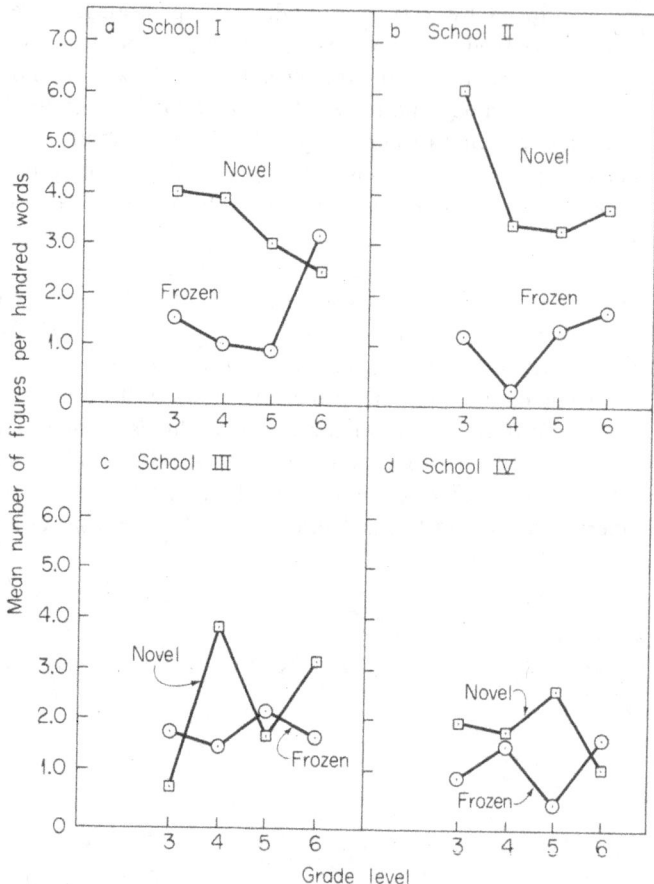

FIGURE 7.4 (a–d) School-by-school trends in the production of figurative language on a comparisons task.

11.74; $p < .01$). In addition, there was no significant grade effect and no significant grade by frozen–novel interaction, although the interaction did approach statistical significance ($F_{3,56} = 2.38$; $p < .07$). As can be seen from Figure 7.4a, the interaction was due to the tendency of novel figurative usage to decrease from Grades 3 through 6, and the tendency of frozen usage to decrease from Grades 3 through 5 and, then increase from Grade 5 to 6. It is interesting to note, however, that the greatest total rate of figurative output occurred in Grade 3 while the lowest rate occurred in Grade 5.

The data for School 2 are presented in Figure 7.4b. Results of an analysis of variance computed over these results again revealed that children tended to produce more novel than frozen figures on the Comparisons task ($F_{1,56} = 33.33$; $p < .001$). No other comparison was significant although the grade effect did approach significance ($F_{3,56} = 2.58$; $p < .06$). An inspection of means for this school showed that novel figurative usage decreased from Grade 3 to 4 and remained fairly constant through to Grade 6; while frozen usage decreased from Grade 3 to 4 and increased slightly from Grade 4 onward.

For School 3, the results of a similar analysis of variance revealed no significant grade or frozen–novel effects and only a significant interaction between the two ($F_{3,56} = 3.34$; $p < .05$). These data are presented in Figure 7.4c. An examination of the means produced by children in this school showed that each grade varied quite a bit with Grades 3 and 5 producing a higher rate of frozen figures; and Grades 4 and 6 producing a higher rate of novel figures. In general, the data for School 3 are extremely noisy.

The results of an analysis of variance computed for School 4 (see Figure 7.4d) revealed no significant differences on any variable. As is obvious, this pattern of statistical results is quite different from that reported for all other schools. As can be seen from the figure, results for this school were quite variable and even "noisier" than those obtained for School 3.

In summary, the data obtained for the Comparisons task produced a significant difference between frozen and novel usage with novel figures predominating. As shown by statistical analysis, this difference was carried primarily by Schools 1 and 2. Present data indicate that Schools 3 and 4 showed no significant differences between frozen and novel usage on the Comparisons task. These results, therefore, help clarify the significant school by frozen–novel interaction found for the combined analysis. The triple-order interaction can be ascribed to the significant grade by frozen–novel interaction found on the analysis computed over the data of School 3 and the high (but not significant) grade effects found on the analyses computed for Schools 1 and 2.

The results of this study again confirmed, in part, results found in the Pollio and Pollio (1974) study. Children use more novel than frozen figures in a task that demands comparisons between originally disparate words. Unlike results of the Pollio and Pollio (1974) study, there was no significant grade effect in this study.

Looking at results for Schools 1 and 2 (see Figures 7.4a and b), a general downward trend in novel figurative usage can be noted. In the Pollio and Pollio (1974) study, the Comparisons task, which is somewhat different from a normal school assignment, seemed to "release" upper-middle-class children from their "inhibitions" and thereby allow them to use novel figures in a relatively free and unrestrained manner. In Schools 1 and 2 this apparently was not true. Although this task did elicit more novel than frozen figures, novel usage still decreased as grade increased. These results did show, however, that children in these schools used more novel figures on a task requiring comparison of two words than on one requiring connected prose.

Results for Schools 3 and 4 (see Figures 7.4c and d) were quite variable. For both of these schools, there was no significant difference between frozen and novel usage. A qualitative examination of results obtained for the Comparisons test for both schools, but particularly for School 4, showed that children seemed either unable or unwilling to perform this task and gave few meaningful comparisons. The ability to relate two unlike words, such as those used in comparisons, requires productive thinking. One hypothesis concerning the results found for these schools may be that little productive thinking is required or encouraged in these children. Teaching and learning may be confined to the rote-performance level, making tasks requiring nonrote manipulations of symbols and words meaningless and, therefore, partially rejected.

What these data suggest, then, is that in high-achievement schools children are able to and do make use of novel figurative language in helping them describe the way(s) in which two words are similar. Children in lower-achievement schools show very little difference in their use of novel or frozen figurative language on the Comparisons task, although unlike children in the higher-achievement schools there is no generally downward trend in the use of novel figures. Without belaboring the point: higher-achievement schools progressively surpress the use of novel figurative language not only on a composition task, but in some cases on other tasks as well. This is true despite the fact that children from these schools are better able to, and do, use all kinds of figurative language more easily than children in lower-achievement schools.

Multiple-Sentence Test Results

The third task asked of all children in this study was to write as many different sentences as they could to sets of double-function words. In order to determine whether children wrote differing amounts on the Multiple-Sentences task an analysis of variance was computed over the number of words produced for all grades and schools. The results of this analysis revealed a significant grade effect ($F_{3,224} = 11.91; p < .001$) with number of words produced first increasing from Grade 3 to 4, and then decreasing through Grade 6. There were no significant differences between schools although there was a significant grade by school interaction ($F_{9,224} = 2.62; p < .01$). An inspection of the data revealed that in Schools 1 and 2 the number of words produced increased from Grades 3 through 5 and then decreased in Grade 6; while in Schools 3 and 4 the number of words produced increased from Grade 3 to 4, and then decreased through Grade 6.

In keeping with these results, and in order to allow comparisons between the Multiple-Sentence and the Composition and Comparisons tasks, a rate per 100 words conversion was also applied to these data (see Figure 7.5). Again, a complex analysis of variance was computed over these data, and revealed that children produce a greater number of frozen than novel figures on this task ($F_{1,224} = 157.20; p < .001$). There was also a significant between-school difference ($F_{3,224} = 5.57; p < .01$), with Schools 1, 2, and 3 using significantly more figures than School 4. A significant grade effect was also noted ($F_{3,224} =$

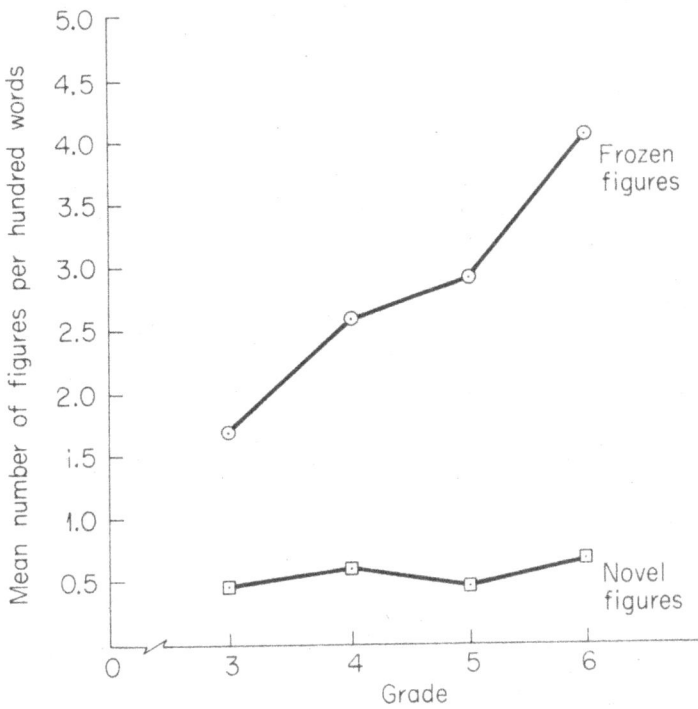

FIGURE 7.5 Multiple sentences — all schools combined.

7.94; $p < .001$), with total figurative usage increasing as grade increased. The grade by frozen–novel interaction was also significant ($F_{3,224} = 6.32; p < 001$), while all other interactions were not. In order to look further at trends within specific schools, separate graphs were plotted for each of the schools and separate analyses of variance computed.

Results of the analysis of variance computed for School 1 revealed that the rate of production of frozen figures was significantly greater than that of novel figures ($F_{1,56} = 59.85; p < .001$) while all other comparisons were not significant. As can be seen from Figure 7.6a, novel usage remained fairly constant and quite low across all grades.

For School 2 (see Figure 7.6b), the analysis showed that children produced significantly more frozen than novel figures on the Multiple-Sentences task ($F_{1,56} = 43.03; p < .001$). In this school there was a significant grade effect ($F_{3,56} = 6.26; p < .01$) with total figurative usage increasing significantly as grade increased. This conclusion, however, must be moderated in terms of the significant grade by frozen–novel interaction ($F_{3,56} = 5.75; p < .01$). An inspection of the results for School 2 shows that while frozen figurative usage increased in every grade from Grades 3 through 6, novel figurative usage

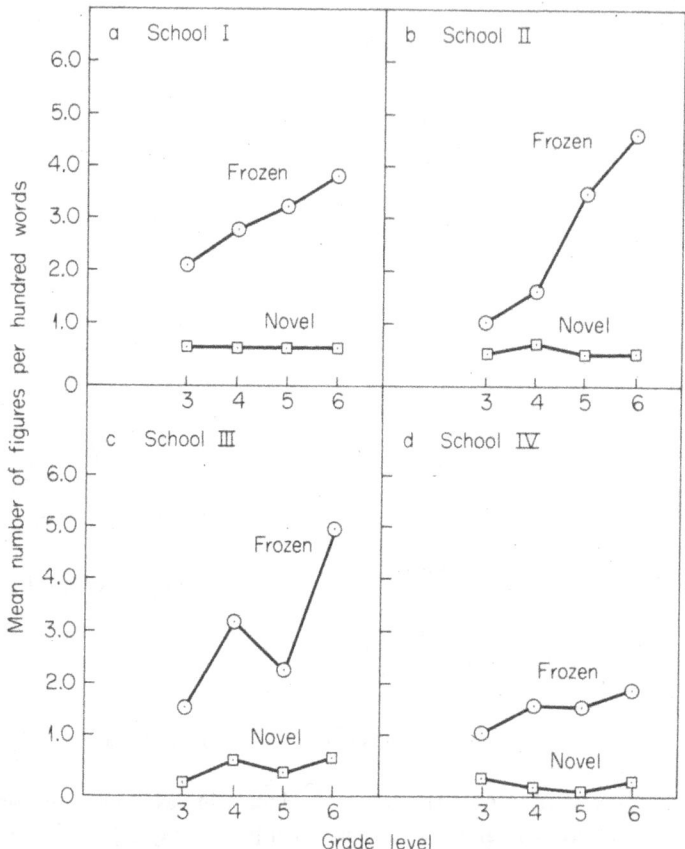

FIGURE 7.6 (a–d) School-by-school trends in the production of figurative language on a multiple-sentence task.

increased only slightly from Grades 3 to 4, and then remained constant (and very low) through Grade 6.

The analysis of variance computed over the data for School 3 (see Figure 7.6c) again revealed that students produced a significantly higher rate of frozen than novel figures ($F_{1,56} = 39.61; p < .001$) for this task. There was also a significant grade effect ($F_{3,56} = 3.80; p < .05$) with total figurative usage, in general, increasing between Grades 3 and 6. Unlike results for School 2, the interaction was not significant.

For School 4 (see Figure 7.6d), results again confirmed the finding that on a Multiple-Sentences test children produced significantly more frozen than novel figures ($F_{1,56} = 20.70; p < .001$). All other comparisons were not significant.

The results of the present analyses again confirm and extend conclusions reached in the Pollio and Pollio (1974) study. On this task children produced more frozen than novel figures, with such production increasing over grade. Unlike the Pollio and Pollio (1974) study where both frozen and novel usage increased with grade, in this study, only frozen usage increased while novel usage remained low and at approximately the same level across grades and schools, with this pattern holding true for all schools. Although this task did stimulate a fairly high rate of frozen figures, novel figures again seemed to be suppressed, with only School 3 showing any trend toward increasing novel usage across grades.

Since many of the words used in this final task were the same as those used by Asch and Nerlove (1960), it is interesting to note that primarily frozen usage increased with age. One may hypothesize that the higher rate of frozen usage was brought about by the stimulus words themselves; that is, older children were progressively better able to use words such as "cold," "hard," and so on in their frozen double-function sense. It is not at all clear that had a different set of words been randomly selected, the pattern of figurative production might not in fact be somewhat different.

Conclusion

Since each task used in this study evoked different patterns of figurative usage, the absolute levels of figurative production can also be compared. For frozen usage, the Multiple-Sentences task seemed to evoke a higher rate of figurative production than did either the Comparisons or the Composition tasks. This pattern was also true for the Pollio and Pollio (1974) study which utilized these same tasks. For novel figures, on the other hand, the Comparisons task produced a higher rate of figurative production than did either the Composition or the Multiple-Sentences tasks. This again is in agreement with results reported by Pollio and Pollio (1974). It can be seen that figurative production, in general, and novel production, in particular, was considerably higher for all tasks in the Pollio and Pollio (1974) study than in this one. Inspection of the means for School 1 (comparable to the school used in earlier studies) showed that only in the Composition task was School 1 approximately equal in both production and pattern to that earlier school. From this data, it can be concluded that a Multiple-Sentences task elicits frozen usage; a Comparisons task novel usage; and that a Composition task tends to suppress both.

The production of metaphor on written tasks by children in the stage of formal operations has also been studied by Schonberg (1974). In her doctoral dissertation, Schonberg analyzed the metaphoric production of 40 high-school seniors (20 males and 20 females) on several written tasks. Her student subjects were all drawn from a single high school in a middle- to upper-middle-class neighborhood. These subjects, therefore, were comparable in intelligence to students in the Pollio and Pollio (1974) study, as well as to subjects in the Asch and Nerlove (1960) study and to subjects in Schools 1 and 2. In Schonberg's experiment each subject responded in writing to 2 forms of 2 different tasks.

The objective Comparisons task included the same 6 word pairs utilized in the Pollio and Pollio (1974) and M. Pollio (1973) studies. The self-referent Comparisons task was experimenter-constructed and contained 6 pairs of words such as "my life" and "a clock;" "my thoughts" and "a play;" "my friends" and "a mirror," and so on. In addition, there were also two Composition tasks: an objective composition entitled "My Favorite Literary Character," and a self-referent composition entitled "Who Am I?"

Three raters, including one female high school senior, were trained by the Barlow, Kerlin and Pollio (1971) procedure, until rater reliability was established. All instances of figurative language were converted to a rate per 100 words of text score so that this data might be integrated with earlier findings. Mean rates for each task were established. Table 7.1 presents the mean rates of metaphoric production for these data, as well as comparable values for the Pollio and Pollio (1974) and M. Pollio (1973) studies. The first thing to note about Table 7.1 is that means for novel metaphors in the Schonberg (1974) study are much lower than those found in other studies. On the other hand, frozen metaphoric production is quite high. One possible explanation for what may have happened here is that raters in the Schonberg study were quite adept at detecting metaphors but quite stringent in judging metaphors as novel. For this reason it would be more valid when making cross-study comparisons with this particular study to consider total metaphoric output, rather than attempting specific within-category comparisons (see Chapter 3, pp. 70–73 for a more extended discussion of cross-sample comparisons). Because of this, comparing results obtained by different rating groups ought be treated with caution.

As can be seen from Table 7.1, adolescents do appear to produce a higher total rate of metaphoric usage on both Composition and Comparisons tasks than do comparable elementary school children. Results of t tests computed between the

TABLE 7.1
Mean Rates of Metaphoric Production

Subject sample and task	Novel	Frozen	Total	Study
Adolescents				
Compositions: self	.44	6.73	7.17	Schonberg (1974)
Compositions: objective	.10	7.04	7.14	Schonberg (1974)
Comparisons: self	1.95	9.40	11.35	Schonberg (1974)
Comparisons: objective	.63	7.72	7.35	Schonberg (1974)
Children (Grades 3–6)				
Compositions (School 1)	.98	1.57	2.55	M. Pollio (1973)
Compositions (School 2)	1.00	1.42	2.42	M. Pollio (1973)
Composition	.95	1.44	2.39	Pollio and Pollio (1974)
Comparisons (School 1)	3.61	1.82	5.43	M. Pollio (1973)
Comparisons (School 2)	4.32	1.27	5.59	M. Pollio (1973)
Comparisons	5.50	2.28	7.78	Pollio and Pollio (1974)

objective comparison data obtained from the Schonberg (1974) study and data obtained from Schools 1 and 2 demonstrated significant differences between these groups with adolescents producing higher rates of figurative usage than children. There is, however, only one exception to these overall trends, and this concerns Comparison test data from the Pollio and Pollio (1974) study. There is no obvious explanation for this difference except to note the extremely high values found for this task relative to all other studies on comparable children.

Schonberg also examined the total rates of metaphoric production for self-referent and objective tasks and found that on the Comparison task students used more metaphors (both frozen and novel) for self-referent than for the objective comparisons. In addition, she found an overall significant difference in the rate of production of novel and frozen metaphors with the rate of frozen metaphors exceeding that of novel. In analyzing her composition data, Schonberg found a significant difference between frozen and novel metaphors. There was also a significant difference between the rate of novel metaphoric production on self-referent and objective compositions, with students producing more novel metaphors on self-referent compositions.

What is of most interest in the Schonberg (1974) study is, of course, the increase in the production of metaphoric language shown by the adolescent. This is in keeping not only with earlier studies but also with earlier analyses of figurative development. Also of interest is that different tasks continued to produce different patterns of figurative usage. Not only do adolescents produce more figurative language on a Comparisons task than on a Composition task; the specific topic of the task (objective or self-referent) also appears to effect their total outputs.

The development of figurative language, then, is by no means an uncomplicated topic to evaluate experimentally. Distinctions must always be made between novel and frozen figurative usage, between explicative and productive tasks, between open-ended and restricted tasks, between school-related and nonschool-related tasks and so on. Where comparisons are made, or a developmental continuum (or more likely, many developmental continua) established, it is feasible only to juxtapose groups sharing a common set of task demands and a somewhat common set of personal attributes. Taking all of these factors in account, Figure 7.7 presents one possible developmental continuum using mean total rates of figurative production as its metric. The data used in constructing this figure were taken from the Comparisons- and Composition-test data produced by students in the Pollio and Pollio (1974) study, in Schools 1 and 2 (M. Pollio, 1973) as well as from the particular high school studied by Schonberg (1974). Figure 7.7 also contains mean total rates of figurative production for college students using the TAT as a stimulus for written work (Lockwood, 1974) so as to provide one final point for older respondents.

As can be seen from Fig. 7.7, task demands clearly affect figurative production. Across all grades, the Comparisons task elicits a higher rate of figurative output (with frozen and novel usage combined) than does any written-prose

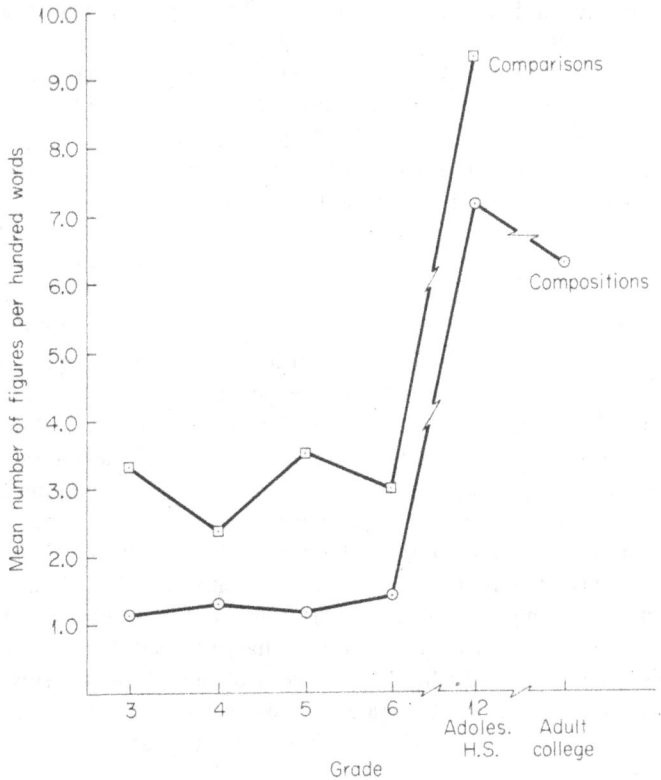

FIGURE 7.7 A developmental continuum for figurative production.

task. The most obvious conclusion one can draw concerns the differential rates of production across grades. For both tasks, the mean total rate of figurative usage for Grades 3—6 remains approximately the same; there is little noticeable increment in metaphoric output over these grades. By the time a child has reached Grade 12, however, figurative usage has more than doubled. Although the rate does drop slightly for college students, it should be remembered that these subjects were unselected University of Tennessee students who might very well be slightly different from the high-school and elementary-school students used in other studies. It should also be remembered that the task given to the college-age subjects was somewhat different from that given to the other groups, and the demand properties of that particular task may account for the difference in rates.

What results presented in this figure dramatically and clearly demonstrate is that differences in the productive capacities of people at different ages are clearly in evidence. If we turn to a Piagetian analysis of intellectual development, it can be seen that children in the concrete operational stage (Grades 3—6) utilize metaphoric language to a much lesser degree than adolescents who are in the stage of formal operations. What this research does is provide support for a Piagetian analysis in the productive realm: in particular, it supports the notion of a genuine discontinuity in figurative language production somewhere between the ages of 11 and 16.

THE DEVELOPMENTAL COURSE OF FIGURATIVE LANGUAGE COMPREHENSION AND EXPLANATION

The original study done by Asch and Nerlove (1960) concerned the child's ability to understand and explain figurative usage. Although there has been some further work on this topic by Gardner et al. (1975), it remained for Winner and Rosenstiel (1975), working within Gardner's laboratory, to clarify the developmental course of the child's ability to understand and explain figurative language. In their experiment, 30 subjects (15 males and 15 females) were asked to do two different tasks at each of six age levels: 6, 7, 8, 10, 12, and 14 years. The first task, explication, required subjects to explain the meaning of a short metaphoric sentence. The second task, comprehension, required the subjects to choose among four possible meanings for the same sentences and paraphrase their choice of answer.

The four alternatives used in the comprehension task were composed of a literal interpretation, a thematic interpretation, (associating two parts of the metaphor into a single narrative dealing with a single theme; for example, a prison guard who "had become a hard rock" was seen as working in a "rocky prison"), a concrete interpretation ("which might entail the engulfing of one domain of the metaphor by the other, i.e., the guard like the rock is physically hard"), and a metaphoric interpretation. Responses to the explication task were also classified according to this scheme which the authors felt might constitute the stages a child passes through on the way to mature figurative understanding. Two other categories were also used in answers given in response to the explication task: incomplete and inappropriate metaphors.

In addition to these analyses, Winner and Rosenstiel (1975) were also interested in determining the relative difficulty of four different types of figurative expression: novel, frozen, cross sensory, and psychological—physical. To this end their 16 stimulus sentences were partitioned into the following four classes: novel cross sensory, frozen cross sensory, novel psychological—physical, and frozen psychological—physical. For all four groups, subjects were asked to explain the metaphoric relation linking elements of the figure with the adequacy of such explanations being evaluated by two independent raters.

Results for the comprehension-choice task showed significant differences among ages for each type of response, with literal, thematic, and concrete responses more in evidence at the lower ages (6, 7, and 8) and metaphoric responses more in evidence at the upper years (10, 12, and 14). Literal responses were chosen most frequently by 7-year-olds (could they be joking with the experimenters?), thematic responses by 6-year-olds, and concrete responses by 8-year-olds. Beyond 8 years of age, there was an increase in metaphoric choice with 10-year-olds choosing figurative expression more frequently than 8-year-olds and 12-year-olds more than 10-year-olds.

Results of the explication task were quite similar to those reported for the comprehension task: 6- and 7-year-olds used thematic explanations; 8-year-olds used concrete explanation, while there was a progressively increasing tendency toward metaphoric explanation at all age levels beyond 8 years of age. In addition, 6 year-olds used significantly more incomplete explanations.

Although there were no differences between sexes on the choice task, sex differences were in evidence on the explication task in which males produced more literal responses than females, except in the case of 14-year-olds, in which males used more metaphoric explanations than females. In comparing the comprehension and explication conditions, Winner and Rosenstiel (1975) state that younger subjects more frequently chose a literal interpretation than they supplied one in explaining a given figure. Similarly, results also showed that younger subjects more often chose a thematic response than they offered one. In general, concrete responses were the most favored mode of answer in the explication task with 7-, 10-, and 12-year-olds providing more concrete explications than choices.

In interpreting their results Winner and Rosenstiel (1975) claim some modest support for their hypothesized sequence of stages in the development of metaphoric comprehension. Although the literal stage was dropped, these authors claim some evidence for thematic, concrete, and metaphoric stages in the explication task with thematic responses peaking at 7, concrete responses at 8, and metaphoric responses peaking at 10 years of age, respectively. An informal examination of strategies and reasoning also showed that there were qualitative differences in metaphoric reasoning at the ages studied and that this reasoning was more truly figurative as the age of the children increased.

In analyzing the influence of metaphor type on ease of explanation, Winner and Rosenstiel found that cross sensory items produced more metaphoric explications than items in the psychological–physical domain. This was explained by hypothesizing that psychological–physical metaphors are more difficult for youngster subjects due to "an unfamiliarity with psychological domains as compared to sensory ones." In addition, these authors argue that psychological–physical figures require a greater "leap" because of the difference in domain inherent in this type of metaphor when compared to cross sensory metaphors which are completely within the physical domain.

In contrast to other analyses, Winner and Rosenstiel (1975) found no differences in ease of explication between frozen and novel items. They explain this by stating that either the novel metaphors used were too conservatively chosen or that the novel—frozen distinction is a relatively unimportant one. Although specific examples of the novel metaphors used were not provided with their report, the weight of prior evidence suggests the first of these explanations. In addition, the results of a recently completed study using a multiple-choice technique (Pollio, 1976), revealed a significant difference in the total number of novel and frozen metaphors understood by children in Grades 4 through 8. In this experiment, children were able to choose the correct alternative far more frequently for frozen than for novel figures and these differences were maintained consistently across grades. Whether a metaphor is frozen or novel ought make a difference in comprehension as well as in use, and Winner and Rosenstiel's (1975) "conservative" explanation is probably the correct one for their particular experiment.

One further comment need be made about the Winner—Rosenstiel study and this concerns their definition of "the concrete interpretation stage" which they seem to feel is not metaphoric in any sense of the term. While this definition may be appropriate in terms of formal poetry, their example of concrete interpretation − interpreting the sentence "After many years of working at the jail, the prison guard had become a hard rock that could not be moved" as "the guard, like the rock, is physically hard and muscular" − is certainly somewhat metaphoric and not totally literal. Some interpretations of metaphor (and indeed some metaphors themselves) may be more abstract, sophisticated, and apt than others; yet that does not make these "others" any less metaphoric. Perhaps a better designation for their category might be "simple metaphoric," indicating some degree of figurative comprehension, while a more advanced stage might be designated as "complex metaphoric," indicating a respondent's appreciation of all of the different nuances and ramifications of a particular figure.

On the basis of their results, the authors feel that the period between 8 and 10 years of age is a very crucial one in which there is a radical increase in metaphoric comprehension. Nonmetaphoric comprehension, according to Winner and Rosenstiel (1975), may be due either to "an inability to interpret words on multiple levels (a linguistic immaturity) or to an inability to perceive multiple kinds of similarity between disparate objects (a cognitive deficiency) or to some amalgam of these factors [p. 25]." Although they have no sure data on this point the authors hypothesize that the latter is the case. In terms of a timetable for the development of figurative activity Winner and Rosenstiel propose that the ability to produce metaphor precedes the ability to understand it and that the ability to explain metaphor occurs in late preadolescence and is probably not complete until well into adolescence.

In order to study more directly the relationship of cognitive development to metaphoric comprehension, Billow (1975), studied such comprehension in 50 above-average intelligence boys, ages 5 through 13. Billow (1975) reasoned that metaphoric comprehension might be considered as a type of classificatory activity and as such there "should be a relationship between comprehension of that kind of metaphor which is based on similarity and concrete operational thinking and between comprehension of that kind of metaphor which is based on proportionality and formal operational thinking [p. 415]."

In order to study these relationships, Billow divided his experiment into 2 different phases. Phase 1 used 12 similarity metaphors derived from published anthologies of children's poetry and chosen for their relative concreteness. In order to determine the developmental level of thinking in these subjects, a "quantification of inclusion task" was used with the 12 metaphors as stimuli.

In Phase 2, a subset of 30 boys, ages 9 through 13, was used to study the relationship of proportional metaphors and proverbs to formal operational thinking. Proverbs were considered to be more abstract than proportional metaphors and, therefore, even more difficult to understand. The proportional metaphor test was followed by the proverb test and both tasks were followed by a combinatorial-reasoning task involving the use of 4 color disks. A scoring system and interscorer reliability were established for this latter task.

The results of Phase 1 indicated that children can and do solve similarity metaphors before the so-called stage of concrete operations (at age 5); and that "a stable use of concrete operations (as measured by the inclusion test) is not a necessary condition for metaphor comprehension" (Billow, 1975, p. 419). Billow (1975) also notes, however, that as a child reaches and passes 7 years of age, the number of metaphors solved intuitively (without the use of concrete operations) stabilizes and then declines, suggesting "that whereas evidence of operational mechanisms is not a necessary condition for metaphor comprehension, it is a sufficient one [p. 421]."

Results of Phase 2 showed that the proportional metaphor test and the test of combinatorial reasoning were significantly related, with "progressively more adequate performance on the combinatorial task ... matched by a progressively greater number of proportional metaphors solved" (Billow, 1975, p. 422). All of this leads to the conclusion that there is a strong relationship between comprehension of proportional metaphors and the attainment of formal operations. There was no evidence of a direct relationship between the proverb test and the combinatorial-reasoning tests although proverb comprehension did increase with age.

Billow's study clearly shows that although younger children do understand figurative language before the stage of concrete operations, they do so less regularly than is true for older children. It is unfortunate that Billow did not include his 5- and 7-year-old subjects in Phase 2. It would certainly be interesting to see how some of the younger children would have handled the proportional metaphor test especially given the finding that they were able to handle similarity metaphors. Although Billow's (1975) study supposedly handled the "comprehension" aspect of figurative language, subjects were actually asked to give the meaning of the metaphors presented. This does indeed handle the issue of comprehension but at a very advanced level — almost that of explication.

In terms of explication, Billow found that children of above average intelligence could, as early as five years of age, explicate the meaning of similarity metaphors. This finding is important, and one that differs from earlier results by Asch and Nerlove (1960). Perhaps the difference between these two studies may be explained in terms of the stimulus items used. Whereas Asch and Nerlove used frozen double-function terms Billow used more novel figures derived from children's poetry, like "A butterfly is a flying rainbow," "The stars are a thousand eyes," "A flower is a grounded bird," and so on. Although these figures may be somewhat familiar (and, therefore, frozen) to adults, they would seem to be very much more novel to children than terms such as "hard" and "sweet." Children may, therefore, be able to explain the meaning of novel metaphors far earlier than their ability to explain frozen figures or at least frozen double-function terms. This possibility also lends some support to the hypothesis that Winner and Rosenstiel (1975) chose their novel metaphors too conservatively. If indeed there is no difference in the comprehension of frozen and novel figures, then why should Billow's (1975) subjects understand and explain novel metaphors, while Asch and Nerlove's (1960) subjects could not do the same for frozen figures.

Taken together, the results of the studies reviewed and presented in this chapter are all compatible with a stagewise analysis of linguistic development. By usual definition, most children used in the M. Pollio (1973) and in the Pollio and Pollio (1974) studies were in the so-called stage of concrete operations — that is, ranged in age from 8 to 11 years — and results show that children at these ages can and do make use of metaphoric language. According to results reported in the Winner and Rosenstiel (1975) and Billow (1975) studies, children within this stage (and sometimes even younger) can and do understand figurative expression in some manner or other. Such children according to both Asch and Nerlove (1960) and Gardner (1974) are unable to *explain* frozen metaphoric language and are able to do so only when somewhat older; or in Piagetian terms, are in the stage of formal operations. What this suggests is that younger children (8–11 years of age) are able to *use* frozen (and novel) figurative language within a specific context but may be unable to explain why the elements related in a frozen figure make a sensible combination until they move — as Gardner's (1974) data show — from the stage of concrete operations to the stage of formal operations. This would seem to be the case even though Winner and Rosenstiel (1975) did find that some children were able to explain figurative expression at a somewhat earlier age.

On the other hand, children can give the meanings of somewhat novel similarity metaphors at a much earlier age; definitely within the stage of concrete operations. This is as it should be in terms of a Piagetian analysis; for in the stage of concrete operations, children are able to apply highly abstract rules to concrete situations but are unable to talk about these rules in perfectly abstract terms. The child's ability to use figurative language seems to show these same trends. Children are able to produce figurative language in specific contexts far in advance of their ability to analyze (frozen) figurative language abstractly. The case for novel figurative language, however, does not seem to be quite as clear cut. On the basis of Billow's (1975) results, children can tell the meanings (and almost explain) novel figures at a much younger age. Before a definitive statement can be made, however, a clearly explicative task using novel figures must be done.

SUMMARY AND CONCLUSIONS

Beginning with onomatopoeia and finishing with total literate figurative usage, the speech and writing of children provide evidence for the occurrence of figurative language as early as 2–3 years of age. To be sure, such usage is not poetic in any profound sense, but just as surely it exists not only in the poetic attempts of a few special children, but in the writing and speaking of more ordinary child language users as well.

Although one of the earliest studies by Asch and Nerlove (1960) came to the correct, but limited, conclusion that children younger than 11 years of age cannot explain frozen figurative usage, more recent research has shown that children well under 11 years can and do produce, and make use of many different types of figures of speech. This is not surprising for it is a relatively well-established linguistic (cognitive) fact that usage precedes explanation and the domain of figurative language is no exception. Other recent studies have also shown that children younger than 11 years do comprehend both frozen and novel language, and can perhaps even explain novel figures.

The results of a number of different studies involving children's writing make a number of finer discriminations. For one, these studies show that in writing compositions, school-age children from 8 to 12 years old use more frozen than novel figures, and somewhat contrary to expectation, the rate of usage for novel figures (for children at the higher socioeconomic and achievement levels) seems to decrease over grade level. This somewhat surprising (and troubling) fact has made its appearance in studies involving children writing compositions in high socioeconomic, high-achievement schools, and the general conclusion of this work seems to be that children do not write creatively when asked to do creative writing; at least not if the production of novel figurative language is used as a criterion of such writing.

Contrary to such findings for high socioeconomic high-achievement schools is the result that low socioeconomic low-achievement schools show an increase in use of novel figurative language over grades, so that by Grade 6 children in these "poorer" schools have higher absolute rates than children in the "better" schools. Given this result, one question that arises is whether novel usage is just suppressed by a Composition task, or if, in fact, it is lost. Developmental results obtained for other tasks seem to suggest a suppression explanation, in that novel figurative usage increased over grades for both a Multiple-Sentences and a Comparisons task in one study (although not in a second study) involving different schools.

Results obtained from the Comparisons task also revealed that under the conditions of this task, children of all ages produce more novel than frozen usage. This finding makes good sense if we consider what it is that novel figurative language has always been thought to do: make sensible novel juxtapositions between initially disparate elements. Under task conditions in which subjects are required to make comparisons it is perfectly reasonable to expect a good deal of novel usage, and such, in fact, is the case.

Carrying this data beyond the sixth-grade level, so as to include written work done by high-school students, produced a rather marked discontinuity in the data obtained. Not only did high-school students use somewhat more figurative language; their total rates were between three to seven times as large as elementary-school children. Such a result is, of course, perfectly congruent with a stagewise interpretation of more general cognitive and linguistic development, such as has been developed by Piaget, and suggests that although young children may use and, even to some degree, understand poetic diction, such language does not fully come of age until adolescence when not only must the child try to make sense of his world, but must also try to make sense of himself. In this way do the increased cognitive abilities characteristic of adolescent thinking make possible unusual comparisons and the concomitant stretching of human language use.

8
Figurative Language and the Educational Process

Every young adult nearing graduation from high school knows what a metaphor is. Or does he? A student can usually give a vague definition and supply a few examples of metaphor from the domain of poetry; but is that enough? More importantly, does the average high-school or college graduate know what a metaphor can do? Does the graduate recognize the importance of metaphor in the world around him?

Educationally, as elsewhere, figurative language has been viewed as the province of literature and rhetoric: metaphors are linguistic devices encountered and dealt with almost exclusively within the context of novels and poetry and only later applied to the area of written composition. The purpose of many of our previous chapters has been to dispel this notion and to stress the importance of metaphoric usage as a heuristic for problem solving and creative thinking in many diverse fields. If indeed this is the case, then an evaluation of educational attitudes toward such language assumes great importance.

The reason for teaching students to use figurative language in creative writing would seem quite apparent: plain, bare facts written in a plain, cold manner are boring. As Mulder (1959) and Ferguson (1958) both suggest in terms of the educational context, metaphors tend to hold the student's attention and to be remembered as would the facts and truths they present. In learning to write, attention must be given to the use of metaphor for, as Mulder (1959) puts it, children must be taught to "wrap (their) ideas in cellophane" (p. 85). Ferguson also feels that metaphors are both compelling and unforgettable, and advocates the use of words as pictures, suggesting that as school children come to use and appreciate novel metaphors they come to discover new relationships and this, in fact, would seem to be the major reason for teaching figurative language in a program of creative writing.

Despite scattered interest such as that shown by Mulder and Ferguson, there seems to be a general lack of concern over the metaphoric process in education.

Emig (1972), for example, has noted:

> If comprehending and creating metaphor form "one of the pillars of human cognition" such a major mode for learning would seem an essential subject for research, perhaps particularly by those of us in English education. Yet the literature surprises. The few direct efforts to describe how children deal with metaphor tend to be anecdotal, with little conceptual anchoring... [p. 163]

What then is the relationship between figurative language and education? What have educators learned about figurative language, what questions do they raise about such language, and how do they incorporate this knowledge into educational process and curriculum?

In an article entitled "Children and Metaphor," Emig (1972) notes that people who study metaphor usually share some or all of four basic assumptions:

1. While everyone agrees that metaphor is worthy of serious study no one can decide on a common definition.
2. A somewhat pernicious assumption is that we should be wary of metaphor, for people (particularly children) tend to equate the similarity implied in metaphor with literal reality.
3. Any would-be user or teacher should make the metaphor explicit, making sure to note its limitations, because of the conceptual difficulties involved in using figurative language.
4. Figurative language is complex and should not be treated as purely decorative.

The second assumption — be wary of metaphor — is the one that has been explicitly singled out and discussed in the educational literature. So, for example, Watts (1944) cautioned teachers against using analogy as a teaching device because he feels children up to the age of $6^1/_2$ do not know the difference between living and nonliving objects and therefore will confuse metaphors based on this distinction. He also provides some data (although the sources of, and the procedures used to gather, these data are sketchily presented at best) to show that children up to the age of 10 cannot do logical analogies of the type "up is to down as ceiling is to ____ [given 4 choices of answers]." The message of his chapter, "Metaphor and Analogy" can be summarized best as: Teachers beware. Do not under any circumstances use metaphor and/or analogy; they are dangerous and possibly harmful to children!

In addition to presenting her four basic assumptions, Emig (1972) also deals with the question of whether metaphor is an optional or intrinsic feature of language usage. Emig (1972) suggests that "for very young children first comprehending and creating metaphor, metaphor may well be a constitutive form of language, an absolutely necessary feature of discourse" (p. 168). This line of argument is extended by saying that whenever anyone, child or adult, deals with a new concept, metaphor may be a necessity and only becomes a genuine option rather than a necessity once the concept is mastered. The functions of the metaphoric process for people of different ages and stages of development is, therefore, an area of research very much in need of exploration, particularly in so far as it relates to the educational process.

Emig also raises questions for research which she feels are vital to the study of metaphor in children. Her primary concerns deal with the development of metaphor although she is also quite concerned about the role of metaphor in both emotional and moral development. In terms of the educational context, Emig (1972) concludes her discussion of the role of figurative language in the curriculum with a significant and straightforward question: "Do textbooks deal with metaphor importantly — that is, say, as a possible shaper and controller of our world view?" (p. 175). An answer to this question provides one of the central themes of this chapter.

STUDENT TEXTBOOKS AND THE TEACHING OF FIGURATIVE LANGUAGE

Emig's question is an important one and in an attempt to provide an answer M. Pollio (1971) examined three series of language arts textbooks for children published between 1960 and 1970. She found that metaphor (when treated at all) was still taught largely as a neglected stepchild of a slightly less neglected parent, poetry. The student's introduction to metaphor usually began no earlier than the third grade. There he or she was presented with a somewhat simplified definition of the terms *simile* and *metaphor* and was promptly given an example of each, primarily drawn from poetry included in the textbook. Finally, the child was asked to create a few original similes and metaphors. The complete lesson appeared on a single page and a review lesson occurred somewhat later in the book. So entered and so exited figurative language for the year. In the following years, the frequency of lessons on metaphor in the textbooks examined did not increase and those lessons that did occur, followed the same general format.

In order to determine how extensively figurative language is treated in more recent and/or different language arts textbooks for children, two other well-known and widely used textbook series have been carefully examined: one by Laidlaw and the other by Follett.

The Laidlaw series, written by Hard, Harsh, Ney and Shane (1972), consists of four books designed for use in Grades 3 through 6. In the third grade textbook, *Adventures in English,* which contains 320 pages, only 8 deal with figurative usage, although there is no explicit mention of figurative language as such. Four of these pages deal with personification in the writing of riddles involving either objects or pets as people. These pages are noted in the index under the title, "Compositions, sense impressions." The other 4 pages concern the use of onomatopoeia in words that repeat sounds. On the fourth-grade level the textbook, *Exploring in English,* also 320 pages long, contains 9 pages dealing in some manner with figurative usage. Of these 9 pages, 4 deal with onomatopoeia (2 with choosing specific words in compositions and 2 with sounds in language); 2 deal with personification (pretending to be a machine and writing as such); while 3 deal with metaphor (indexed under "colorful expressions," concerned primarily with the meanings of idioms or other frozen figures such as "green thumb").

In the fifth-grade book, *Discovery in English,* 9 of the 384 pages have something to do with figurative language. Of these 9 pages, 3 make use of personification in writing from different points of view; while 6 deal with frozen figurative usage in terms of jargon or slang. Finally, of the 384 pages contained in the sixth-grade book, *Progress in English,* 9 pages are again devoted to figurative language. Of these 9 pages, 5 deal with hyperbole in the writing of tall tales while 4 deal with metaphor: two in descriptions from verse and 2 in extending the meaning of words. All in all, for this series, 35 out of 1,408 pages, or .025%, deal in some way with figurative language. Specific figures are neither defined nor discussed and figurative language, as such, is never explained nor developed as an important topic in its own right.

The second set of books considered, the Follett series (Meshover and Robinson, 1970), consists of six books for use in Grades 1 through 6. The first book (127 pages) has 1 page dealing with figurative language (simile and metaphor from poetry) while 4 pages are devoted to this topic in the teacher's edition. Of the 4 pages contained in the teacher's edition, 1 deals with onomatopoeia and 1 with personification (both from poetry). The remaining 2 pages deal with simile: one in the form of simile stems and one in the discussion of a simile which occurs in one of the stories. There is no explicit identification of figurative language as such.

In the second-grade book, containing 159 pages, there are only 3 pages in the student's book and 15 in the teacher's edition that deal with figurative language. All of the pages in the child's book deal with simile, 1 from poetry, 1 in creating poetry, and 1 in explicating what similes mean. Of the 15 pages in the teacher's edition, all cover various figures (simile, metaphor, hyperbole, personification, and onomatopoeia) primarily drawn from poetry, with some examples of simile stems and poetic creation. Again there is no explanation or explicit naming of the various figures of speech, nor any discussion of their significance in contexts other than poetry.

In the third-grade book (225 pages), 9 pages contain figurative usage with 1 of these dealing with onomatopoeia and 1 with similes from poetry. The remaining 7 pages deal with frozen figures, primarily in terms of idioms. The teacher's edition contains 14 pages dealing with figurative language: five deal with idioms and 9 with writing similes using "like" and "as" in their stems. The fourth-grade textbook (319 pages) contains only 1 reference to figurative language and that in the teacher's edition only. This is an important reference, however, because it involves the specific introduction of the term, simile, and provides for the production of similes by students. The fifth-grade book (383 pages) has 9 pages dealing with figurative language (6 pages on simile and 3 on personification) while the teacher's edition has only 4 (referring to those pages in the children's book). In the sixth-grade text (383 pages) there are 3 pages dealing with figurative language in the children's book and 8 pages in the teacher's edition. It is in this sixth-grade book that the term, metaphor, is finally introduced. All in all then, in this series, 25 out of 1,626 pages, or .015% of the material, deal with figurative language and in no case does the discussion touch on the possible significance of metaphor as a tool for conceptual analysis.

The treatment of figurative language in children's language arts textbooks, therefore, has changed somewhat in these more recent books. Unfortunately, the explanation of figurative terms still either does not appear at all or appears at, or after, the fourth-grade level even in the teacher's edition. Teaching, itself, is usually confined to examples (again, or still, drawn primarily from the realm of poetry) or to the production of a small number of figurative types such as personifications and similes. This latter emphasis would seem to be a good innovation especially since research has shown that children are able to produce figures of speech in advance of their ability to explicate such usage (see Chapter 7). The texts, however, do not deal with metaphoric language as a possible "shaper or controller of our world view" as Emig (1972) somewhat dramatically suggested, nor do they present it as a possibly useful heuristic in problem solving or as a tool for conceptual use.

This relative lack of concern over the formal teaching of figurative usage in the language-arts curriculum is in marked contrast to the actual occurrence of figurative expression in children's reading materials (and as noted in Chapter 7, in child language). As early as 1961, in an analysis of the figurative content of two reading and one social studies series designed for use in the third, fourth and fifth grades, Grosbeck (1961) found 582 figures present in the third grade, 837 in the fourth, and 1,337 in the fifth. This would seem an extraordinary number, considering that little direct instruction was then, or is now, given to help the child in learning how to use or interpret such usage.

Robertson (1973) also discussed the large number of figures of speech found in texts for children and concluded that reading comprehension may be adversely affected by the child's possible lack of understanding of figurative language. Robertson noted that direct teaching lessons given in conjunction with practice activities are rare and that practice activities alone are often expected to do the requisite teaching. In a more constructive vein, she feels that children should be encouraged to discuss interpretations of metaphoric language with adults and should be shown how to check out their interpretations with the surrounding context in which the figure of speech occurred. Expansion of the figure, using a paraphrase method and vocabulary expansion, are also recommended. The use of figures of speech in their own writing may also aid children in the comprehension of reading materials. Young readers, according to Robertson, need teacher help to ensure the understanding of figurative language.

8. FIGURATIVE LANGUAGE AND THE EDUCATIONAL PROCESS

Running somewhat contrary to this trend of the nonteaching of figurative language, the Synectics Company has developed a series of workbooks, called *Making It Strange* (1968), designed for use in Grades 3 through 6. The workbooks are constructed specifically to foster creative writing and thinking, and to help the child develop the operational mechanisms shown to be valuable for adult users of the synectic process. This series, it is hoped, will help increase the child's use of figurative language and help the student internalize a metaphorical way of thinking. According to the rationale of this series, increasing command of figurative expression will further prepare the child for the use of metaphor as a heuristic in thinking.

In the *Making It Strange* series, each workbook begins with a statement more or less informing the child that there are no right or wrong answers to any of the exercises in the book. The child is free to create and use language in any way desired. In using these books for creative writing, the "don't rock the boat" philosophy should not and cannot prevail. The exercises in all four workbooks are similar increasing only in difficulty from book to book. Contained in each book are items such as:

1. Stretching exercises:

    "A picket fence is like a dragon's tail because_____
    _____ [Book I, p. 8]."
    "Which weighs more — a cough or a sneeze?_____
    Why?_____ [Book I, p. 12]."
    "Is 3 funnier than 4?_____
    Why?_____[Book II, p. 37]."
    "A magnet is like fishing bait because_____
    _____[Book III, p. 8]."
    "What animal is like a parachute?_____
    Why?_____[Book IV, p. 9]."

2. Being the thing (Writing a story with the author telling the story as if he were the object named in the title):

    "The Gypsy Dollar" (Book I);
    "A Bullet" (Book II); and
    "Zero" (Book IV).

3. Compressed conflicts:

    "Peaceful terror describes what animal?_____
    _____ [Book III, p. 64];
    "An example of pleasing pain is_____
    because_____[Book IV, p. 49]."

Exercises such as these are thought to enable the child to use metaphor and the metaphoric process in thinking as well as in writing. They help the child "make the familiar strange," that is, see the everyday world in a different, unusual way; and "make the strange familiar," see unusual things and puzzling problems in a way that will reduce their unusual character and make them more comprehensible. In this manner these workbooks are designed not only to increase metaphoric usage but to provide a means of using metaphor in its heuristic function.

TEACHER-EDUCATION TEXTS AND THE TEACHING OF FIGURATIVE LANGUAGE

How do textbooks for teachers or prospective teachers deal with the teaching of metaphoric language? In order to answer this question, several recent texts in the areas of language arts, in general, and reading, in particular, were examined.

In *The Language Arts in Childhood Education* (Burns, Broman, & Lowe, 1971) figurative language is briefly listed as necessary for vocabulary and as a part of the understanding and development of oral expression. These authors state that figurative language is often problematic for children but that they (children) can be helped to identify and interpret it. The book gives examples of personification, metaphor, and simile and encourages the use of paraphrase both as a method of developing an understanding of figures of speech and as a test of whether or not the figure is understood. The authors also provide simile stems as exercises for teaching figurative language and provide references to literary examples (primarily poetry) that would be helpful in teaching metaphor.

In *Developing Language Skills in the Elementary Schools* (Greene & Petty, 1971) part of only one page is devoted to similes. This page explains what a simile is and encourages its use (for children) as a means of adding interest and meaning to oral and written expression. Four suggestions for teaching figurative language are given by Greene and Petty (1971):

1. Encourage children to list interesting comparisons they encounter . . .
2. Encourage children to watch for opportunities to use examples, figures of speech, and interesting comparisons in their written and oral expression.
3. Have the children maintain a column on the bulletin board similar to the "Patter" in the *Reader's Digest*.
4. Have the children practice completing sentences such as the following with the most interesting phrase:
   The boat rocked as _____. (p. 350)

In *Adventures in Communication, Language Arts Methods* (Smith, 1972) metaphor is mentioned briefly along with abstraction, as part of a later ability to conceptualize. Suggestions for teaching involve the use of slang which is rich in metaphor as part of language development.

In *Experiences in Language, Tools and Techniques for Language Arts Methods* (Petty, Petty, & Becking, 1973), figures of speech are explained and examples given. The authors state that children are interested in figurative language and may want to keep charts of such language. Art activities, such as illustrating the literal meaning of a figure of speech, are also suggested for vocabulary building. In the literature section of this book, figurative language is again discussed and it is suggested that children compose figures of speech in order to appreciate their difficulty and the amount of work required to produce such figures.

Miles V. Zintz (1970), in *The Reading Process, The Teacher and the Learner* places figures of speech in a section called "Extending Language for Critical Reading Ability." He contends that knowing the source of a common figurative expression or allusion will make that expression more meaningful to the reader. He defines figures of speech and notes that the literal interpretation of any figure is a cause of misinterpretation in reading. Finally, he defines several figures of speech and gives examples of each. Knowledge of these figures is necessary, he feels, for critical reading.

Emerald V. Dechant (1970) treats figurative and idiomatic language in a section of a chapter entitled "Developing a Meaningful Vocabulary" in his book *Improving the Teaching of Reading*. Using numerous examples of common (frozen) figurative usage both from everyday speech and children's classroom readers, Dechant shows the need for elementary school pupils to master metaphoric language in order to understand what they read. According to Dechant, however, children interpret figurative expressions literally and often are unaware of their mistakes in interpretation. After presenting a table containing definitions of the major types of figurative language, specific recommendations for teaching figurative reading skills are given. These include multiple-choice exercises which require the child to pick from three phrases the phrase that correctly explains a given metaphor; using simile stems; underlining figurative expressions in poetry or prose; identifying different kinds of figures of speech; completing sentences such as "I'm hungry enough to eat a ____;" and explaining common figures of speech, illustrated by pictures of the literal meaning as contrasted with pictures of the figurative meaning. The use of such exercises is designed to familiarize the child with figurative expressions and thereby to enable him or her to deal more effectively with such expressions in the course of reading.

In *Reading-Language Instruction: Innovative Practices* Robert B. Ruddell (1974) deals with comparisons and specifically with simile. He feels that children should utilize mental images drawn from their own experiential background to create descriptions. He provides a simple, but interesting, activity for helping children develop comparisons in the early grades. In this regard he suggests placing sets of pictures on the board, discussing similarities and differences in the pictures and finally developing comparisons based on these observed similarities and differences. For more advanced students, Ruddell suggests that they be encouraged to explain the meaning of the term, simile, and that the teacher make use of simile stem exercises for this purpose.

Delores Durkin (1970), in *Teaching Them to Read,* includes figurative language as a means of studying variability in the meaning of a word. She feels that as reading material increases in difficulty the frequency of metaphoric language also increases, thereby making the comprehension of such usage that much more important. The study of such language, therefore, ought to begin in the early school years by including figures of speech in the oral language used by teachers. She suggests two books, *A Hog on Ice* (1948) and *Heavens to Betsy* (1955), both by Charles Funk, that would be useful to teachers to remind them of the many idiomatic and figurative expressions found in the English language. In these books, Funk traces the historical development of frozen figurative expressions such as "spick and span," "to chew the rag," and so on.

In summary, textbooks for teachers seem to have comparatively little to say about figurative language or how to teach it. Treatment of this topic ranges from nothing at all (Spache & Spache, 1973) to one sentence urging the study of such usage (Dallman, Rouch, Change, & Deboer, 1974). Dechant (1970) provides the most complete treatment and this covers only five pages of the text. In almost every one of these books figurative language or particular figures of speech such as simile and metaphor are found neither in the table of contents nor in the index but must be located by a careful page by page search of those sections of the book devoted to vocabulary development, composition, comprehension, and/or critical reading. Discussions of figurative usage are devoted to the need to teach such language and some simple exercises to use in that instruction. Nowhere is metaphorical language treated as a potential cognitive tool.

READING AND THE TEACHING OF FIGURATIVE LANGUAGE

Teachers and prospective teachers, however, use sources other than their college textbooks for ideas and information about teaching and it seems reasonable to ask what is contained in magazines and journals used by people in the field of education and what research dealing with the teaching of figurative language has been presented in these sources? By way of introduction, we might note that most of the literature dealing with this topic concerns either the need to teach metaphoric language and/or a description of methods potentially useful for the teaching of such language.

Figurative language according to many authors must play an important role in the reading and language arts taught by schools today. Upton (1964a) has argued that if reading can be defined as the ability to interpret significant symbols then an ability to understand metaphor must be one of the highest forms of intelligent behavior, for it involves the capacity to see both similarities and differences. He feels that an inability to deal with figurative usage is one of the major reasons why effective communication via reading is hindered. More specifically, Upton notes that readers often have trouble with figurative expression largely because they have been taught to regard such usage simply as literary ornament. He notes (1964b) that metaphor is one of the most fruitful types of semantic adaptation and that creativity involves the ability not only to see analogies but also to see similarities where others see only differences. Upton also feels that the heuristic and creative functions of metaphor have long gone unappreciated in educational circles and that rigorous training in the interpretation of metaphor is a necessity not only for critical reading but for intelligent and creative thinking as well. For this reason, he includes metaphor exercises as an integral part of his own reading courses at the college level.

Upton is not alone in his view of metaphor as necessary for reading comprehension. As early as 1945, Armstrong stated that one of the major reading problems of high school students was their inability to interpret allusions; unfortunately, however, he let it go at that. Cooper (1954), concerned more specifically with reading improvement in the secondary school, suggests using various different concepts from the field of semantics, one of which is that of metaphor, to achieve reading improvement. Cooper feels that students should be able not only to recognize metaphor but should also be able to judge the applicability of the metaphor to the context and to identify those elements that can be applied to new situations. In order to accomplish these ends he proposes a four-year program for the high schools in which an analysis of semantic concepts play an important role.

Burkland (1964), more specifically concerned with the teaching of poetry, feels that teachers should provide students with the means for understanding figurative language. To this end he suggests a tripartite approach. Teachers should first show that the students commonly use figurative language in slang and that metaphoric usage abounds in advertising. After this, the teacher ought to point out that poetic metaphor is different only in that it is more original than the stereotypic figurative language characteristic of the advertiser or student. Finally, Burkland suggests using exercises in imaginative association. This technique, he feels, will make the strange (poetry) familiar and approachable for the student.

Somewhat figuratively, Newton (1964) characterizes figurative language as "an Achilles Heel in reading comprehension." The ability to understand figurative language is a necessary element of comprehension according to Newton. On this basis she suggests that the study of such language be part of a planned, systematic, and sequential program of reading and provides some suggestions as to the goals of such a program for Grades 10–16.

Similar curricular suggestions have been made many times over in the area of language arts teaching and curriculum. Burmeister (1973) stresses the need for the public school curriculum to handle figurative language largely because of the major role it plays in advertising and propaganda. Proll (1972) even recommends beginning such instruction in Grade 1, while Curtis (1972) suggests that a careful analysis of figurative usage begin in Grade 3. In this regard he outlines a program to contrast literal and metaphoric language and then goes on to suggest the development of an abstract—figurative scale by which children could come to learn how to evaluate the appropriateness of figurative usage. All of these suggestions stress figurative-language training as an integral part of a developmental reading program from primary school through college.

In terms of specific teaching techniques, Ferguson (1958) has suggested that students refer to all of their experiences on a certain day in terms of the specialized vocabulary used in a particular field, making sure to change fields each day. In this way, Ferguson feels that new uses for words and new relationships might be revealed. Hughes (1967) feels that students should not be taught figurative language by being given definitions of the different figures of speech. Through personal experience, students should become so sensitized to metaphoric usage that they discover it everywhere — in science, in slang, in advertising, as well as in literature. Such personal experience should begin in the primary grades and in order to help in this regard Hughes provides practical (although commonplace) methods such as simile stems and similar tools to be used in the early school years. The results of such activities would result in both creative writing skills and in an increased sensitivity to literature.

In order to help expand and teach vocabulary, and, indeed, language itself, Heiman (1967) also suggests the use of slang. He feels that slang expressions can be related to four different areas of linguistics, only one of which need concern us here: the classification of various figures of speech. Using slang expressions which are themselves figures of speech can enable a teacher to help students identify, define, differentiate and remember the different types of figurative expressions. All the teacher need do is listen to the language of his or her students, record and classify the slang and then use it as a teaching tool. Since slang is current and meaningful to students it may, according to Heiman, "even help them ace the course, man!"

Some specific procedures for teaching idiomatic expression have been suggested by Foerster (1974) in an article entitled "Idiomagic!" In this article, Foerster discusses the frequency of use and the comparative difficulty students have in understanding idioms. As a remedy she suggests having students collect idioms, making sure they understand them, and then place them in a writing center for use in creative work. Another procedure is to collect expressions that could make humorous or unusual pictures, have the students illustrate these idioms independently and let the rest of the class guess which idiom was used. Pantomiming some idioms in a charades-type game could also be an effective teaching device. Finally, Foerster suggests developing an idiom baseball game in which two teams are used. The pitcher gives the idiom and the batter explains it to get a hit. Three outs retire a side. These direct teaching procedures may help children understand and use idiomatic expressions and, through them, all of figurative language.

All of these techniques are motivated by pedagogic desire to help the child learn not only to appreciate figurative language but to help more specifically with increasing reading vocabulary. Sometimes, however, when figurative language is not understood or appreciated children have great difficulty in comprehending what they read. This is particularly true for some bilingual children for whom idiomatic or metaphoric expressions can present an almost insurmountable obstacle largely because these expressions do not translate easily from one language to the other. In the same way, an idiomatic, or frozen, expression can cause difficulty for any child who has never had experience with that expression and, so, subsequently interprets it literally.

In one attempt to determine the difficulties different ethnic groups have with idiomatic expressions found in standard fourth-, fifth- and sixth-grade reading texts Yandell and Zintz (1961) constructed a 90-item multiple-choice idioms test using common idioms taken as exact quotations from intermediate-grade reading books. For this test, four alternatives were designed for each item which consisted of the correct answer, a literal interpretation of the idiom and two related but incorrect answers. Thirty items from each grade level (fourth, fifth, and sixth) were included on the test. In order to extablish norms for comparison and to determine some of the difficulties nonnative speakers might have with idioms, the test was first administered to 390 Anglo sixth graders. Following this, it was given to 516 sixth-grade students composed of Anglo, Spanish, Navajo, and Zuni ethnic groups. A small subsample of 20 students for the Anglo and Navajo groups and one of 10 students each for the smaller Zuni and Spanish groups was then randomly selected from the larger sample for purposes of more intense analysis.

Reliabilities for the Yandell–Zintz (1961) test for each group were established and here it is interesting to note that reliabilities for the non-Anglo groups were extremely high (Spanish, .916; Navajo, .912; and Zuni, .906) while that of the Anglo group, although high (.754), was considerably lower than for the other groups. Following this evaluation of test reliability, scores were tabulated in raw scores and percentiles established for each ethnic group. Results showed that the performance of each of the minority ethnic groups was significantly lower than that of the control Anglo group. Percentile ranks prepared for the control group showed that the 50th percentile corresponded to a raw score of 71 (of 90). When compared to this control group, the median score for Spanish-American children ranked in the fifth percentile, the median score for Zuni children ranked in the second percentile, while the median score for the Navajo children ranked in the 1st percentile. Unfortunately these results may be biased as the reading-achievement scores of these groups were also quite low and those results for the idiom test could in part have been an artifact of poorer reading ability in the non-Anglo groups.

On the basis of these results, Yandell and Zintz (1961) argue that there is a clear need for the direct teaching of idiomatic expressions to bilingual children and that some experimental studies of direct teaching methodology ought to be conducted. It is obvious, however, that the same idiomatic or frozen metaphoric expressions could and do cause difficulty for English–speaking children as well. No child, regardless of ethnic group, scored perfectly on the idioms test and it seems to be the opinion of almost all of the authors reviewed in this chapter that interpretation of metaphoric language is a necessity for reading comprehension. Perhaps a direct teaching method for idiomatic and figurative language needs to be established for all children.

WRITING AND THE TEACHING OF FIGURATIVE LANGUAGE

Turning now from reading to writing, Stewig (1966) has noted that teachers often are unaware of good creative writing and, therefore, cannot instruct their students in it. Children, he says, can profit from an awareness of metaphor as a form, from acquaintance with (and a chance to analyze) metaphor as well as from an opportunity to create new figures. He suggests that children should search for and share metaphors in order to increase their critical judgment and advocates these as specific activities for children in the intermediate grades.

Children's ability to use figurative language in writing was also the concern of Groff (1962), who examined figures of speech found in poetry written by children in Grades 4, 5, and 6. In this study there were 540 subjects in all: 132 in the fourth grade; 220 in the fifth; and 188 in the sixth. Of these subjects, covering 61 different elementary schools, 385 were girls (71.3%) and 155 boys (28.7%). The poems evaluated by Groff were volunteered by the children and therefore not collected in an experimentally controlled manner.

For the poetry examined, seven different types of figures of speech were found: personification, simile, hyperbole, metaphor, metonymy (including synecdoche), symbolism, and irony. In all, children produced 170 different figures of speech; 42 by boys and 128 by girls, with simile and personification representing approximately 75% of all figures produced. Results also showed that girls produced 6% more figures of speech per poem than did boys. From this study, Groff concluded that children in the intermediate grades can, and do, use figurative language in their poetry and that emphasis on the teaching of metaphoric expression in these grades should improve the quality of such poetry. Unfortunately, he leaves the question of figurative usage in prose essentially untouched.

A study by Hill (1972), however, was directed toward identifying the specific literary devices used in prose writing by children in Grades 2–6. In addition, Hill was also interested in determining the frequency of such devices and the grade level at which they occurred. To this end, he collected stories volunteered by children at each of the 5 grade levels for a total of 175 stories. Each story was analyzed in terms of a checklist of literary devices divided into two categories, structure and texture. The latter category consisted of different figures of speech: alliteration, apostrophe, hyperbole, irony, metaphor, personification, and simile; and the former category consisted of syntactic variations. Results showed that all literary devices appeared to varying degrees at each grade level with the structure category appearing more frequently than the texture category. In addition, Hill found that there was a greater frequency of figurative usage at the sixth-grade level, with clichéd, or frozen, figurative usage the most common.

A further study of children's writing and figurative language was done by Sweet (1974). His analysis was guided by four questions:

1. Is there more evidence of figurative usage in one genre of composition than in another, where these genres consisted of narrative description, poetry and tall tales?
2. Is there a natural growth in figurative usage from Grades 4 through 6?
3. Do teachers rate writing as better if it contains more figurative language?
4. Is the amount of reading a child does related to his production of figurative language?

Three samples of writing (one of each type) were collected from 81 students: 24 in the fourth grade; 28 in the fifth; and 29 in the sixth. These were then analyzed by the investigator alone, using a checklist for figurative language. This checklist included the same 7 figures of speech used by Hill (1972). On the basis of preliminary results, Sweet selected 10 students who had the highest frequency of figurative usage and 10 who had the lowest, and then submitted their writing to 3 different fourth-grade teachers to rate independently. Finally, Sweet prepared a class roster for all classes used and asked the teacher to rate each child on a 3-point scale ("avid reader," "average reader," "reads little or nothing that is not required").

Across the total set of 81 descriptive compositions analyzed, Sweet found 90 instances of figurative usage, with only four of the seven literary devices appearing. Simile was the most frequently used figure (76 instances), while apostrophe, irony, and personification were not used at all. Fifth graders produced more figurative expressions than either of the other two grades. In the poetry samples obtained, 130 instances of metaphoric language appeared. Again simile appeared most frequently (102 instances), while irony was the only figurative possibility that was never used. As in descriptive compositions, fifth-grade children produced the greatest amount of figurative language. On tall tales, only 34 figures were utilized, with all devices appearing at least once. For this genre, sixth-grade children used the greatest number of figures of speech. At the fourth and sixth-grade level, students who used more figurative language were judged to be the more able writers, while at the fifth-grade level, use of figures of speech was unrelated to writing ability. Amount of reading done (as judged by teachers) had no relationship to the number of figures produced.

From these results, Sweet concluded that the type of composition the child is asked to write does affect both the frequency and type of figurative expression used. While reading seems to have only little relationship to the production of figurative expression, the use of such expression does seem to affect teacher judgment as to the quality of the written product.

In addition to this work on reading and writing, figurative language has also been taught in other areas of study. In the field of science, for example, metaphor and visual imagery have been presented to college-level students as an heuristic. In a two-year experimental study, conducted by Gordon (1965) at Harvard University, synectics procedures were used to train freshman science majors in problem solving and hypothesis formation. Gordon describes three different attempts at using this procedure and concludes that training in figurative usage did help students develop the habit of constructive hypothesis formation.

Phelan (1971) has also tried to teach metaphor as a problem-solving device by developing a program designed for use by high-school students. This program cut across the fields of art, English, and the humanities and dealt with the theme "What is man?" Activities were designed by small groups of students. These activities were viewed and analyzed in terms of the metaphors they presented, as well as in terms of the relation of these metaphors to the overall theme and to the experiences of the students. In general, student response was favorable although a quantitative evaluation was not undertaken.

With these two exceptions, extensions to other fields are rare. Figurative language, even within the context of language education, itself, is still a neglected topic. Although some suggestions as to how to teach it are being made, the overall impact on both student and teacher-education texts is quite negligible. Figurative language still belongs to poetry, and that's all there is to it — at least as far as the educational context is concerned.

SUMMARY AND CONCLUSIONS

The importance of figurative language as a heuristic for creative problem solving and thinking, as an integral part of rhetoric, literature, and creative writing, as well as a necessity for reading comprehension and vocabulary development has been stressed by many educators. Student textbooks, however, show very few lessons dealing specifically with figurative usage and tend to include such lessons (when included at all) almost as an afterthought. Reading textbooks and textbook series, on the other hand, seem to abound in nonliteral phrases and sentences. Children therefore apparently are supposed to be able to produce, comprehend, and interpret figurative language without any direct teaching in the mastery of such usage. Research studies have shown that children do indeed have difficulty with metaphoric and nonliteral language, and need and can profit from direct instruction.

8. FIGURATIVE LANGUAGE AND THE EDUCATIONAL PROCESS 209

Do teachers themselves, however, receive instruction on how to teach figurative language? An examination of teacher-training texts in the field of language arts and reading shows that instruction for teachers is almost as scanty as instruction for children. Magazines and journals prepared for teachers do give some suggestions for direct teaching methodology, while at the same time stressing the importance of incorporating such teaching practices within a planned sequential program. The one published sequential program for teaching figurative processes to children, the *Making It Strange* (Synectics, Inc., 1968) series, has not found wide adoption. Although the idea of incorporating a program such as this into the curriculum pervades much of the literature, there is as yet no consensus on how this aim is to be accomplished.

The overall conclusion suggested by these facts must be that all protestations to the contrary, figurative language is not, even now, viewed as an important aspect of the educational process except by a small number of educators none of whom, unfortunately, manage to write a best-selling series of textbooks. This is all the more lamentable in view of the clear importance of such language for a wide variety of educational skills and goals. Although we can only guess as to why figurative language continues to be outside the pale of educational respectability, our best guess would be that educators are no different from other practitioners and that most still cling to the view that figurative expression is simply an ornament in language. For this reason we suspect that not until the myth of ornament is finally sent packing will there be any (or many) attempts to develop techniques designed to teach teachers and students alike how to deal with this significant, but neglected, aspect of the public-school curriculum.

9
Making It More: Evaluating Methods for Teaching Figurative Language

On page 48 in the fourth workbook of the *Making It Strange* (Synectics, Inc., 1968) series, children are asked to respond to the compressed conflict, "disciplined freedom." This oxymoron, more than any other single phrase, perhaps captures the way in which figurative language should be taught in the schools. Children should have the freedom and opportunity to express anything they wish, in whatever way they wish, while maintaining the discipline that effective communication demands. As a matter of fact, one of the older children using these materials in a classroom context did respond to this phrase with the word "school," while another responded with the word "creativity." Of the first child we may say "lucky boy," while of the second we may say "how fitting," but in either case both responses are appropriate to the purpose of this chapter: to discuss the possibility of teaching one aspect of creative writing and thinking within the confines of that public institution known as the school.

Now the teaching of creativity, or creative writing, or creative thinking or, for that matter, creative anything is a difficult proposition at best. Still, the attitudes expressed by our two students correctly pose the problem: how to permit and even encourage the occurrence of a creative and possibly chaotic process within the confines of good form, be such good form social order or literary style. A more general aspect of this problem was best stated long ago by Alfred North Whitehead who defined progress as "the ability to preserve order amid change and change amid order" and this definition is no less true of creative teaching and learning than of social progress.

What this chapter is about, then, is not the presentation of an algorithm guaranteed to produce creative writers and/or thinkers; rather what it is about is the presentation and evaluation of a few selected teaching techniques designed to encourage the child in using that most precious of commodities, disciplined freedom. If we can reawaken the child's desire to innovate with good form, then we may have moved both him and the school in an appropriate and productive direction. Make no mistake, these techniques, even those that work, cannot and do not guarantee anything more than a framework within which creative learning and thinking can occur. They are not, and must not be thought to be, a magic mechanical panacea capable of turning children automatically into creative problem solvers on any and all occasions. We say this despite our confidence in the relationship of figurative language to creative problem solving.

EXPERIMENTAL PROCEDURES FOR TEACHING FIGURATIVE LANGUAGE

With these limitations in mind, what are some of the experimental procedures that have been used in schools to augment figurative language as an important and necessary subject and not simply as a supplement to the main curricular areas? In one early study done on this topic, Groesbeck (1961) evaluated the ability of students in the third, fourth and fifth grades to transfer their ability to interpret figurative language from one task to another. In order to equate experimental and control subjects, Groesbeck used tests of reading, vocabulary, and intelligence. Following an initial evaluation involving specially designed tests of figurative interpretation, students in an experimental group were given ten 20-min. classroom lessons on the interpretation of figurative usage. At the conclusion of this phase of the experiment, both experimental and control subjects were posttested on a similar test of figurative-language interpretation.

Results showed that subjects who received the experimental treatment scored significantly higher on the posttest than those who did not. Groesbeck (1961) suggests that teachers should make sure that all children understand the figurative expressions they encounter; and that specific instruction in interpretation of figurative expressions be given to children in the intermediate grades. She also strongly recommended that textbook manufacturers give greater consideration to nonliteral meanings in the construction of elementary texts.

In another study, Horne (1966) used children's literature as a focal point for developing activities designed to measure sixth-grade pupils' use and understanding of figurative language. She also studied the effects of these activities on reading comprehension and vocabulary, taking sex, IQ, age, and socioeconomic status into account. In order to assess these interrelationships, a special test of how well children understand metaphoric language was devised and administered to a large group of sixth-grade students. Seventy-three sixth-grade pupils then served as members of an experimental group; 72 students served as members of a control group. All students were pretested on the special test. In addition, a sample of writing was gathered and analyzed for total number of figures produced. Twenty-four sessions using lesson plans designed to increase the comprehension of figurative language and relating this language to children's literature were then conducted. All subjects were posttested on a second version of the specially developed test, as well as on a test of reading ability. Finally, a second sample of the children's writing was collected.

Results showed that the experimental group was significantly higher than the control group in both comprehension and production of figurative language. Reading comprehension and vocabulary, however, were not affected by experimental procedures. Although this latter finding is potentially of interest, it may be construed as an artifact of the tests used. Since very little figurative language is included on standardized tests of reading comprehension and vocabulary, procedures designed to increase the production and comprehension of figurative language should have little or no effect on such tests.

Additional results also revealed that sex, age, and socioeconomic status were largely unrelated to increases in figurative usage. High IQ scores, however, were related to the comprehension of figures of speech, but not to their production. This result is in keeping with work reported by Wallach and Kogan (1965) and by Getzels and Jackson (1962). As they note, children with high intelligence may indeed be able to comprehend figures of speech but may not be highly original and therefore may not be able to produce figures of speech as easily as they understand them. A second interpretation of this finding may be consistent with the "don't rock the boat" philosophy discussed in Chapter 7. High-intelligence students may know that using figurative language can be dangerous and, therefore, deliberately do not use such expression in written work. Unfortunately it is impossible to decide between these alternative explanations, given the nature of the data provided. As it now stands, Horne's (1966) study seems to indicate that experience and instruction in figurative usage is valuable for sixth-grade students although the effect of such instruction on reading level is still somewhat unclear.

In more recent times, Holstein (1972a) used a case-study approach in order to induce figurative thinking in fourth-grade children. The materials used in this study involved a series of metaphorical activities designed by her which were similar to items appearing in the *Making It Strange* series created by Synectics, Inc. (1968). Each child worked individually with the experimenter on 8 lessons of 30 min. each for a period of 4 weeks, with student progress evaluated on the basis of differences in a pre- and posttest consisting of both oral and written responses.

Among other things, Holstein's (1972a) results indicated that: "the exercises utilizing metaphorical language served the purpose of improving free and innovative writing and speaking, although some of the empathetic and spontaneous responses were lacking in the written situation" (p. 59). Since this study was limited by the relatively small size of the sample and by the fact that these children received individual instruction, Holstein suggests that a study of metaphorical experiences conducted in a classroom situation with a larger sample would be advisable before more definitive conclusions could be offered.

9. EVALUATING THE TEACHING METHODS 213

In a second article derived from data collected in the same study, Holstein (1972b) presents three specific case studies of children exposed to her experimental procedures. These case studies, and the oral and written language reported, provide interesting data showing not only the productive metaphoric ability of the students but their elaborative abilities as well. Such ability, as it manifested itself in one student, as reported by Holstein (1972b), may be seen in the following:

> When asked what the ticking of a clock was like, Stacey replied, "Well, the revolving of the earth around the sun." Asked why, she answered, "Because it just keeps going on and on." When asked, "The sunset is like what feeling?" she said, "Glamorous." Asked to elaborate, she said, "Most of the time when the sun sets there is pink and orange and all different kinds of different colors near it and it looks pretty." (p. 49)
>
> One of Stacey's most profound answers was when she was asked, "Which will last longer this smell or a bird's chirp?" She said, "A bird's chirp. Well, their birds have babies and those babies will chirp and it will go on and on."
> "What about the smell?"
> "It won't have babies and you might use the smell for a seasoning and run out of it." (p. 49)

Stacey's ability to explain figurative language is quite advanced, given both her age (most fourth graders are between nine and ten years of age) and the results of research discussed previously (see Chapter 7). The other two children, whose case studies were also reported by Holstein, did not do quite as well, although both of them did show productive ability and some beginning elaborative ability. The techniques used by Holstein, as reported in both studies did enable these particular children to shake free of some restrictive bonds and thereby to innovate or create.

Motivated by their earlier studies on the development of figurative language, Winner and Gardner (1974) investigated three different means of training 10- and 11-year-olds to think metaphorically. In the Winner and Gardner (1974) study, 3 different kinds of metaphor were used: visual (the ability to make visual connections and comparisons unmediated by language), scientific (the use of skills related to scientific creativity), and verbal (using words in new ways, and applying them to domains where they were not ordinarily found). The basic purposes of this study were to determine relationships among these three different kinds of metaphoric thinking and to determine the effects of various training procedures on performance. The subjects were 57 fifth-grade students randomly chosen from their classrooms. Four groups, one control and three training, were formed with all groups receiving both a pretest and a posttest. The three training groups each received one of the three different types of training (visual, scientific, or verbal) while the control group received no training whatsoever.

Two different pretest probes were used. The first was a story written in class as a classroom exercise; as a normal ongoing activity that was part of the regular curriculum and which elicited a spontaneous sample of language. For these stories 5 different titles were supplied, one for each classroom. The second probe was a more structured one and involved the completion of a 3-sentence vignette in which the last sentence was incomplete. There were ten such vignettes. The subject completed each vignette and was asked to explain his production. Following this, the child chose one of four endings, supplied by the examiner, to complete the same vignette. These endings were coded into the same categories as those used in the earlier study (Gardner, Kircher, Winner, & Perkins, 1975) and consisted of the 4 categories, metaphoric—appropriate, literal, trite, and metaphoric—inappropriate.

The posttest was identical to the pretest except that composition topics were rotated among classes. Ten additional verbal vignette items were added as were visual and scientific test questions. On this basis it was possible to assess the effects of the three different training procedures on a wide variety of tasks controlling for normal developmental growth.

Each experimental group received two months of intensive training. The visual method consisted of presenting the child with three different types of exercises, two of which involved an unusual or "metaphoric" pairing of two pictures. A third exercise used abstract photographs and encouraged the child to see different categories of things within the picture. The science-training procedure was designed to help the child break out of clichéd thinking and see a problem from a different perspective, "to make it strange." For this training, four different exercises were used: an unusual or creative-uses task in which the child tried to think of different or atypical uses for a concrete object; solving puzzles, the solution of which depended upon recentering and seeing the puzzle in a new manner; "being the thing," thereby asking the child to see the world from the perspective of an animal or other object; and finally, asking the child to describe the world in which something strange had happened, like "a world in which buildings could move of their own accord." Verbal training procedures involved the use of the same kinds of items as those used on the pretest (the vignettes) with the addition of a discussion of the different ways in which words could be used. The concept of originality in general, and of verbal originality in particular, was specifically introduced and explained.

After training was completed a posttest was administered to all groups including the control group. In between the two halves of the verbal test (which was given in two sessions) a matched subgroup, derived from all groups except the verbal training group, was given explicit training in verbal metaphors. Results showed, not surprisingly given the training tasks, that the verbal-training group progressed from literal or trite usage on the pretest to original or metaphoric usage on the posttest. Both scientific- and visual-training procedures seemed to have no effect on metaphoric use on the posttest, suggesting that such training does not spontaneously transfer to the verbal realm.

After explicit training given between the verbal posttests, Gardner (personal communication, 1975) found that neither science nor visual training enabled subjects with explicit verbal training to do better on verbal metaphor than controls. Although the science group did somewhat better, results were not statistically significant. From further analyses of the data, Gardner and Winner (Gardner, personal communication, 1975) conclude that any and all of their three procedures will lead to a somewhat higher performance on many different kinds of metaphor tests but that their length of treatment was probably not long enough to produce significant effects.

On all of the various metaphor posttests, the control group consistently did the worst. For visual metaphor tasks, verbal training seemed to help; that is, the verbal group paired pictures metaphorically as a first choice more often than the science and control groups did, although this was not statistically significant. For the science posttest, visually-trained children were able to think of more new and original uses for familiar objects. According to Gardner and Winner, this may have occurred because of the similarity of the abstract visual photo task to these posttest problems. Verbal training seemed to help in the science task in which the world had to be described from a new perspective. Whether this was because of the verbal nature of this task or because verbal training helped children see things in a new way is unclear. What is clear from their study, however, is that children do possess considerable potential for metaphorical thinking and expression and that such potential can be increased by exercises such as those used in this study.

MAKING IT STRANGE TRAINING PROCEDURES

In order to evaluate the effects of the *Making It Strange* (Synectics, Inc., 1968) workbook series, which contains exercises similar to those used both by Holstein (1972a,b) and Winner and Gardner (1974), M. Pollio conducted two separate studies. The first study (M. Pollio, 1971) used children in the third through fifth grades in one high-intelligence, high-achievement, upper-middle-class school. Developmental baseline data were collected on three different probes: a Composition task, a Multiple-Sentences task, and a Comparisons task and were reported in a study by Pollio and Pollio (1974). Following this, an instructional period of four weeks was undertaken during which time experimental groups used the *Making It Strange* (Synectics, Inc., 1968) series and control groups proceeded with the normal ongoing curriculum. Finally, a posttest, containing composition topics identical to those used in the pretest, was administered. All data produced by students in this study were rated using the Barlow, Kerlin, and Pollio (1971) procedure. After interrater reliability had been established scores were converted to percentages (rate per 100 words of text) and means computed for the various conditions.

Figure 9.1 presents a comparison of the pretest and the posttest means for both control and experimental groups for novel usage. This figure shows that while control groups, which on the pretest showed a higher percentage of novel

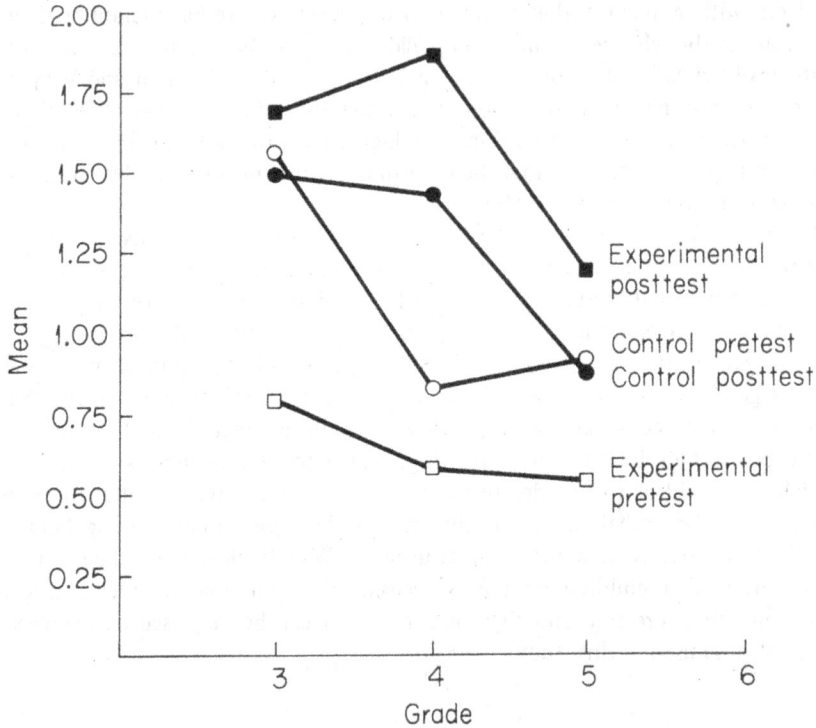

FIGURE 9.1 Pretest versus posttest over all grades, control versus experimental — novel usage.

usage, remained approximately the same experimental groups improved markedly in all three grades. Statistical analyses showed that there was a significant increase in novel usage from the pretest to the posttest and that there was also a significant interaction between pretest and posttest and the experimental and control groups. Looking at Figure 9.1 it can be seen that although all groups did increase in novel usage, experimental groups showed a markedly larger gain. The pretest level for control groups was initially higher than for experimental groups (although not significantly so) while the posttest level for experimental groups was higher than that of control groups.

Figure 9.2 presents results for these same groups for frozen usage. As can be seen from this figure, subjects in both experimental and control groups increased in their use of frozen figurative language from the pretest to the posttest although this increase was not statistically significant. The only group whose results differed markedly from this pattern was the Grade-3 Control Group which showed an unusually high pretest and an unusually high posttest. An analysis of variance comparable to that used for novel figures was computed for frozen usage and showed that there was a significant decrease in usage over grades as well as a significant interaction between grade level and experimental and control groups.

A further analysis using a matched pairs sign test was also done in order to determine if there was a significant directional change in usage from pre- to posttest. This procedure was used to assess individual changes in language behavior that perhaps were masked by group scores such as those used in an analysis of variance. In order to make use of this test, difference scores were computed for each subject, with the results of this computation presented in Table 9.1. As these results show, there was a significant number of students who increased their use of novel figures of speech in both the fourth- and fifth-grade experimental groups. In addition, there was a significant difference between experimental and control groups collapsed over all three grades. On the other hand, no comparison involving frozen figures was significant. Thus, experimental groups in all three grades showed a greater increase in instances of novel usage on the posttest than comparable control groups. In contrast to these results for novel usage, frozen usage showed very little difference between experimental and control groups.

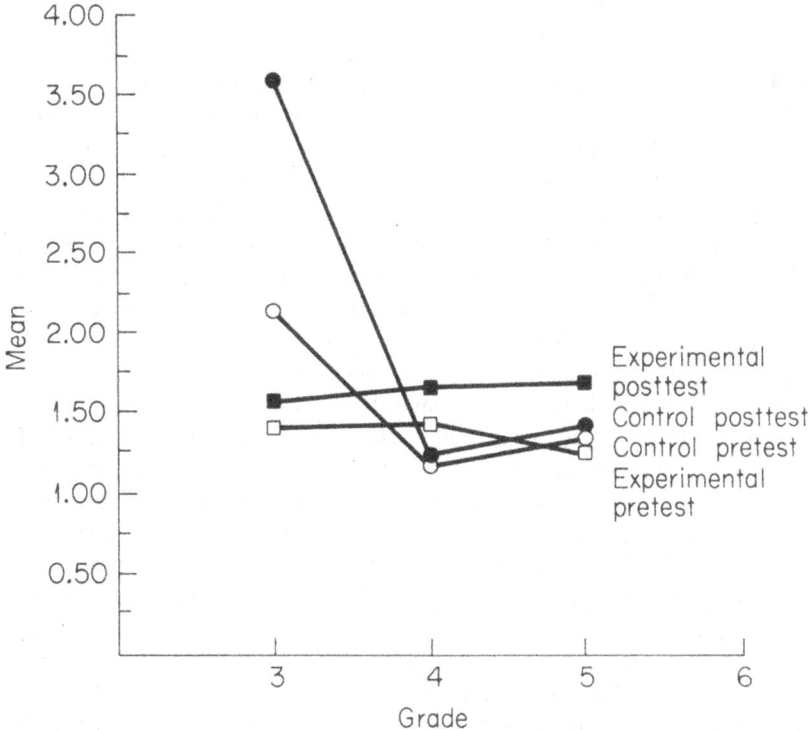

FIGURE 9.2 Pretest versus posttest over all grades, control versus experimental — frozen usage.

TABLE 9.1
Sign Test over all Three Grades, Control Versus Experimental—Frozen and Novel

	3		4		5		Total	
	Frozen	Novel	Frozen	Novel	Frozen	Novel	Frozen	Novel
A. Experimental condition Number of positive instances[a]	9	11	10	14**	10	13*	29	38*
N^b	17	16	17	17	17	18	51	51
B. Control condition Number of positive instances[a]	13	5	10	9	10	7	33	21
N^b	19	14	17	15	19	17	55	46

*$p < 0.05$.   **$p < 0.01$.

[a] A positive instance is one in which the posttest score is larger than the pretest score.

[b] N values are uneven due to the dropping of all zero-difference cases as required by a sign test.

Starting out somewhat negatively, these results suggest that the *Making It Strange* (Synectics, Inc., 1968) series had no effect on the use of frozen figurative language. And this is not too surprising, for a training procedure designed to initiate "strange" or unusual patterns of viewing the world or talking about it should have little or no effect on a child's ability to produce frozen figures of speech, especially if we consider such items simply as additional vocabulary. The sharp decrease between the third-grade class and the other two grades in the use of frozen figures can, perhaps, again be attributed to the Composition task itself. A frozen figure may be considered by the child as a slightly inappropriate or even slanglike expression and children literally may be trained not to use such language on composition tasks.

In contrast to this, the use of the *Making It Strange* series did affect the production of novel figures of speech. This fact, however, seems to be influenced by grade level, with fourth- and fifth-grade students showing a significant increase in novel usage and with third-grade students showing only a marginally significant trend. What then does this series do? Does this series, in training a child to think differently, make him more aware of unusual relationships or does it give him tacit permission to exhibit strange language use in a restrictive composition task? Did use of the series teach the child how to look at the world metaphorically or did it free the fourth- and fifth-grade children from the "don't rock the boat" philosophy? If the former is true, then there is no question of the value of this series in promoting metaphoric thinking. If the later is true, then would one or two short lessons by the teacher, or, more simply, the reinforcement of unusual language behavior by the teacher, produce the same results? On the basis of this study it is impossible to specify exactly how the *Making It Strange* books brought about the results obtained.

MAKING IT STRANGE ACROSS SOCIO-ECONOMIC LEVELS

In order to answer these questions, M. Pollio (1973) used the *Making It Strange* series as training materials in alternate second- through sixth-grade classes in each of the four schools used in the developmental study reported in Chapter 7. In this new study, the first instructional phase lasted approximately six months, or until all classes had time to complete the *Making It Strange* workbook. All students in these experimental classes were then evaluated using three tests identical to those given (at the same time) to developmental subjects, which, for purposes of this study were designated as control classes. As may be remembered, these tests include a Composition test, a Comparisons test, and a Multiple-Sentences test. For this study, 160 children (10 per class) served as experimental subjects.

A second instructional phase of four-weeks duration then followed this initial training and testing period. During this second period, students in the control groups used a different set of instructional materials. These consisted of three specially designed lesson plans together with appropriate follow-up activities. Motivational devices, reinforcement techniques and discussion-sharing follow-ups were explicitly developed and demonstrated for participating teachers. In general, motivating devices stressed the use of descriptive language while reinforcement techniques involved the writing of complimentary remarks like "good," and so on, near all instances of figurative language and then sharing the children's writing with the class while verbally complimenting them on any unusual usage. Figurative language was used by the teachers in explaining the task but was not identified as such.

Following this second phase, all children in all groups were tested again using the same three tests as before. For this testing period, children were asked to choose a different composition topic although this requirement was not stringently enforced since language usage, not content, was of interest. Since there were three forms of the Comparisons and Multiple-Sentences tests, all three forms were varied for the posttest, so that no child took the same test twice. All orders of administration were present equally throughout each class. The data for all forms of the test were pooled for each analysis, so that any order effect or any differential in test effectiveness that might be present could be counterbalanced. At the completion of testing, ten children per control class were randomly selected from the 15 used in the developmental part of the study. A total of 320 subjects, therefore, were used for this study. Achievement- and intelligence-test data of both groups were compared and found approximately equal. In addition, teachers were never told nor were they aware of which children were being studied.

Composition Test Results

Experimental versus control group   In order to determine if the experimental training procedure (the *Making It Strange* series) had any effect upon the rate of metaphoric production, the first test data, consisting of compositions for both experimental and control groups, were examined. Means for frozen usage produced by experimental and control groups for all schools and grades are presented in Table 9.2. Comparable means for novel usage are presented in Table 9.3. In these tables, the data are presented separately for each of four different schools. As mentioned in Chapter 7, these schools differed both in socioeconomic and achievement levels. In general, both socioeconomic and achievement levels decreased from School 1 through School 4 (see page 171 for a more complete description).

The results of an analysis of variance computed for frozen usage revealed only two significant interactions while all main effects were not statistically significant. It is interesting to note that there were no experimental–control differences for frozen usage. For novel figurative usage, on the other hand, an analysis of variance revealed a significant grade effect ($F_{3,288} = 3.23; p < .05$) with novel usage increasing from Grade 3 to 4, decreasing in Grade 5, and increasing again in Grade 6. More importantly the comparison between control and experimental groups was also significant ($F_{1,288} = 14.82; p < .001$) with

TABLE 9.2
Mean Rates of Frozen Figurative Usage Control and Experimental Groups (Compositions Task)

School	Group	Test	Grade				Total
			3	4	5	6	
1	Control	1	1.17	1.60	1.45	2.28	1.62
	Experimental	1	0.99	1.20	2.17	2.59	1.74
2	Control	1	0.25	2.85	1.55	1.42	1.52
	Experimental	1	0.95	1.38	1.21	1.48	1.25
3	Control	1	0.40	1.68	0.89	1.46	1.11
	Experimental	1	2.29	0.88	2.64	1.55	1.84
4	Control	1	1.63	0.99	1.30	0.83	1.19
	Experimental	1	1.55	1.29	1.80	1.58	1.56
Total	Control	1	0.84	1.78	1.30	1.50	1.36
	Experimental	1	1.45	1.19	1.96	1.80	1.60

TABLE 9.3
Mean Rates of Novel Figurative Usage Control and
Experimental Groups (Compositions Task)

			Grade				
School	Group	Test	3	4	5	6	Total
1	Control	1	0.64	0.86	0.86	0.93	0.82
	Experimental	1	0.51	1.53	1.72	1.81	1.39
2	Control	1	1.32	0.62	1.11	0.61	0.91
	Experimental	1	0.93	1.74	0.97	2.63	1.56
3	Control	1	0.14	0.77	1.08	1.01	0.75
	Experimental	1	1.24	1.96	1.19	1.30	1.42
4	Control	1	0.62	1.03	0.51	0.86	0.76
	Experimental	1	0.48	1.66	0.99	0.58	0.93
Total	Control	1	0.68	0.82	0.89	0.85	0.81
	Experimental	1	0.79	1.72	1.21	1.58	1.33

experimental groups producing more novel figures than control groups. All other comparisons were not significant.

In order to examine more closely the effects of the training procedure, two further analyses of variance were computed for each school, one for frozen usage and one for novel usage. As the significant interaction effects reported for frozen figures in the major analysis suggest, there were few consistent effects within each of these separate analyses. The most important of these concerned a significant increase over grades in frozen figurative output for Schools 1 and 2 and rather inconsistent or nonsignificant effects for the more "messy" data produced by Schools 3 and 4. Results also showed a significant experimental–control effect for School 3. For novel figures the results of these separate analyses of variance showed significant differences between experimental and control groups for Schools 1, 2, and 3, with School 4 again showing essentially random differences across grades and training conditions.

In agreement with the earlier M. Pollio (1971) study, results of this study show that *Making It Strange* (Synectics, Inc., 1968) materials do not effect frozen figurative usage but do seem to increase the production of novel figurative language in children using the series. Since the children who participated in that earlier study were all from one high-intelligence, high-achievement school most comparable to School 1, it is interesting to note that data produced by students in School 1 also yielded the same pattern of results. Here, as before, there were no significant differences in frozen usage but a significant difference, higher rates of production, in novel figurative usage for children using the *Making It Strange* series. For School 2, also somewhat comparable to the school used in the earlier study (M. Pollio, 1971), results again were the same. In School 3, however, experimental groups surpassed control groups in frozen figurative usage as well as in novel usage, while in School 4, there were no significant differences between groups in any regard.

The fact that the *Making It Strange* series, in general, has little or no effect on frozen figurative usage makes sense if we again consider frozen figures simply as vocabulary items. Creative thinking or activities designed to increase creative thinking and writing (as is the case for these books) should have little or no effect on vocabulary choice, particularly in schools such as Schools 1 and 2 in which children would seem initially to have an above average vocabulary. Perhaps the significant difference between control and experimental groups favoring experimental groups found in School 3 for frozen usage was due to the fact that these children need vocabulary stimulation, with the *Making It Strange* series providing a sufficient (if minimal) amount of such work and, therefore, increasing frozen as well as novel production.

Taken as a whole, the *Making It Strange* series does seem to increase the production of novel figurative language on a composition task although the effects of these books are different for schools having students with differential achievement and socioeconomic levels. In middle- to upper-middle-income, high-achievement schools such as Schools 1 and 2, this series trains children to use novel figures of speech and, perhaps by extension, to think creatively. In schools such as School 3 (a lower-middle to middle-income, average-achievement school) the series seems to help children produce both more frozen and more novel figures thereby increasing vocabulary as well as perhaps engendering creative thinking. In schools such as School 4 (a lower-income, low-achievement school) the *Making It Strange* series seemed to have had no effect whatsoever. One possible explanation for this may be that the workbooks were too difficult (in terms of reading level) for the grades in which they were used. An alternate explanation, particularly since we found that achievement test percentiles decrease as grade increases in this school, is that children in schools of this type do not seem to learn much from anything or anyone as they spend more time in school. The *Making It Strange* materials would seem to present no exception to this sad "general rule." Whether this is the fault of the teaching techniques or of the materials is unknown. What is known, however, is that children in these schools generally achieve test scores within the average range in the early grades and thereafter show a progressive decrease in academic achievement in the later elementary school grades.

Composition test results: Lesson plans. In order to determine if the *Making It Strange* series makes children more aware of unusual relationships by teaching them to look at the world metaphorically, or whether it tacitly gives them permission to use unusual language by freeing them from the usual "don't rock the boat" philosophy we need to look at results produced by two further conditions of this experiment. Basically, these involve a special instructional phase which was instituted for students in the control groups. During this phase, students were exposed to a series of lesson plans specifically developed to teach them figurative language while teachers were asked to make a special attempt to reinforce all instances of unusual language. In order to evaluate the effectiveness of these procedures, differences between the rates of figurative language used on the first test were compared with rates produced after this instructional phase had been completed for all control groups.

Table 9.4 presents the appropriate results for all 4 grades for both frozen and novel usage. In this table, the groups designated as Control 2 provide data appropriate for evaluating the effectiveness of the teaching program. An examination of frozen figurative usage presented in this table shows, with the exception of Grade 3, relatively small and insignificant differences among the grades as well as a small and relatively insignificant difference between Control 1 and 2 conditions. Although not apparent from this table, an examination of frozen rates for the 4 participating schools did show much larger differences between Schools 1 and 2 and Schools 3 and 4. As these patterns might suggest, results of an analysis of variance computed over frozen figurative rates showed a significant school effect ($F_{3,144}$ = 4.90; $p < .01$) and a significant triple-order interaction ($F_{9,144}$ = 2.12; $p < .05$), with all other comparisons being not significant.

Turning now to novel usage, results again present a very inconclusive pattern. Although three of the four grades do show slightly more novel figurative output

TABLE 9.4
Mean Rates of Frozen and Novel Figurative Usage for
Control 1 and Control 2 Groups: Composition Test

Grade	Group	Type of figure	
		Frozen	Novel
3	Control (Test 1)[a]	.84	.68
	Control (Test 2)	1.36	1.37
4	Control (Test 1)[a]	1.78	.82
	Control (Test 2)	1.47	.95
5	Control (Test 1)[a]	1.30	.89
	Control (Test 2)	1.74	.91
6	Control (Test 1)[a]	1.50	.85
	Control (Test 2)	1.53	1.03
Total	Control (Test 1)[a]	1.36	.81
	Control (Test 2)	1.51	1.01

[a] All values for Control 1 groups are the same as those reported in Tables 2 and 3. Control 2 values reflect the effects of interpolated teaching procedures described in the text.

under Control 2, differences are not large, even discounting the reversal found for the fifth grade. An examination of the school by school results revealed a similar patchy pattern and, so, it comes as no surprise that an analysis of variance computed over these data revealed only a significant school-by-grade interaction ($F_{9,144}$ = 2.50; $p < .05$). No significant teaching effects were found for any other of the comparisons made.

Separate analyses of variance computed over novel and frozen rates for all four schools separately did not at all change the picture obtained from these larger analyses. The overall conclusion must be that the specific teaching and reinforcement procedures instituted in this study were relatively ineffective in increasing figurative usage, both novel and frozen, in tests given control students.

In order to examine more precisely the role of written reinforcement on Test 2 compositions, the number of papers as well as the number of written reinforcements per paper were counted, and means computed. As a consequence of this analysis, it was discovered that not only did some teachers not use reinforcement; some did not even return the lessons. Using values obtained from this evaluation as a guide, 7 classes were selected for further study: Grade 4, School 1, ($\bar{X}$ = 2.10); Grades 3 ($\bar{X}$ = .88) and 4 ($\bar{X}$ = .60), School 2; Grades 4 ($\bar{X}$ = .29) and 6 ($\bar{X}$ = 3.23), School 3; and Grades 5 ($\bar{X}$ = 2.61) and 6 ($\bar{X}$ = 2.11), School 4. Values in parentheses following each class represent the mean number of reinforcements given by the teacher across all papers turned in by the class. In general, the criterion used to select these classes was that reinforcement be given at least some of the time on all three of the corrected lessons. As can be seen in some cases the number of reinforcements was quite small (.29) while in others it was quite large (3.23).

For School 1, t tests for paired differences were computed separately for frozen and novel usage for Test 1 versus Test 2 and no significant differences were found. For School 2, two analyses of variance were computed over the data of Grades 3 and 4 for frozen and novel usage separately and again no significant differences were found between tests. For School 3, no significant comparisons were found on the analysis for frozen usage; for novel usage, however, there was a significant test effect ($F_{1,18}$ = 9.09; $p < .01$) with both groups producing more novel figures on Test 2 than on Test 1. For this school, a significant grade by test interaction ($F_{1,18}$ = 4.52; $p < .05$) was also found. An inspection of the means showed that while the rate of novel usage increased somewhat for Grade 4, the increase for Grade 6 was much greater. For School 4, two separate analyses of variance were computed for frozen and novel usage on the data produced on Test 1 and Test 2. As before, no significant differences were found on any comparison. From all of these analyses of novel usage it becomes apparent that only one class, Grade 6 in School 3, showed any effect of reinforcement on the production of figurative language, and that this class was given considerably more reinforcement than any of the other classes.

This control training procedure was developed in order to answer the question raised by the M. Pollio (1971) study; viz, would one or two short lessons by a teacher produce the same results as the *Making It Strange* (Synectics, Inc., 1968) series and thereby show that this series simply frees children from restrictions placed upon them in a composition task? The results of the control training procedure seem to indicate that this is not the case. In almost all of the schools the lesson plans did not produce a significant difference between Test 1 and Test 2 in favor of Test 2. In contrast to this, there was a significant difference between students in the experimental (using the *Making It Strange* workbooks) and control groups on Test 1.

The data generated by this experiment also allow for other comparisons between the various teaching techniques. One of the more obvious of these concerns differences between the prepared lessons used by teachers and the use of the *Making It Strange* workbooks by students. One way in which to make such an evaluation is to compare Test 1 compositions of experimental groups exposed to the *Making It Strange* series with Test 2 scores produced by control groups who had been exposed only to the newly developed lesson plans. For frozen usage, analyses of variance computed over these data showed only a significant school by experimental—control interaction ($F_{3,288} = 3.92; p < .01$) with all other comparisons being not significant. A comparable analysis computed over novel figurative usage revealed that the test performance of students exposed to the *Making It Strange* series (Test 1) was significantly more predictive of novel figurative expression than the Test 2 performance of students in the control group exposed to lesson plans ($F_{1,288} = 3.70; p < 0.05$). In addition, results also revealed a significant grade by experimental—control interaction ($F_{3,288} = 3.46; p < .05$) and a significant triple-order interaction $F_{9,288} = 2.33; p < .05$). It therefore seems reasonable to conclude that experimental groups produced more novel figures on Test 1 than control groups did on Test 2. An examination of the school-by-school results showed that children in School 2 produced the highest rate of novel figures while, not surprisingly, those in School 4 produced the lowest.

Summarizing all of these data suggest the following conclusions: The control training procedure (the lessons) was sometimes as effective, and sometimes not as effective, as the experimental procedure (using the *Making It Strange* series) in increasing novel figurative production in compositions. A comparison of control and experimental groups on novel figurative language for all schools and grades was significant although comparisons for individual schools were not. In School 2, in fact, control groups surpassed experimental groups in the production of frozen figurative expression.

The exact interpretation of these results is a bit more complicated than would appear from a simple listing of significance levels obtained between groups. One complicating factor is the difference in time and amount of treatment. Experimental groups used the *Making It Strange* series for a period of six months while control groups used the prepared lessons for a period of only four weeks. The control training program, however, was more concentrated and Test 2 results obtained from control groups were secured four weeks later than Test 1 results gathered from experimental groups.

Another factor complicating an interpretation of these data has to do with the fact that control group results reflect not only the specific lesson training given but the effects of the prior six months normal curriculum. Thus, given any differences between experimental and control at Test 1, we can only ask whether additional training narrows the gap. It is impossible to assume that the two groups were equal at the beginning of the second training program. They clearly were not.

With these reservations in mind, the results can be used to provide some suggestions as to the relative success of the *Making It Strange* series vis-à-vis the lesson plans. Here, it seems reasonable to suggest that lessons such as those developed for these children did improve the figurative production of control groups on compositions to some degree. This increase in production apparently did not bring all control groups up to the level of students who had used the *Making It Strange* series although both procedures did achieve levels higher than that attained by children in the appropriate control conditions.

But what of the experimental groups? Did their production of figurative language change from Test 1 to Test 2, and if so, what was the direction of such change? In order to answer these questions separate analyses of variance were computed for both frozen and novel usage for all experimental groups over both testing sessions for all schools and grades. The results of these analyses indicated that while the *Making It Strange* series did seem to promote novel figurative usage and free children from restraints placed upon them in a composition task when they were tested immediately upon the completion of these materials, such effects did not last over a 4-week period. As a matter of fact, novel usage was significantly ($F_{1,144} = 17.92; p < .01$) higher across all 4 schools (1.33) on Test 1 than on Test 2 (.82).

One can only wonder what happened in these classrooms during the month between tests, and here our best guess would seem to be that our teachers reverted back to their old ways, strenuously imposing restrictions on spelling and grammar, but, most especially, on "strange" language use. Test 1 results indicated that these children certainly were capable of using more figurative language, yet at the second testing they did not. Perhaps these materials succeeded only in freeing the children, yet left the teacher untouched when such materials were withdrawn. The sad fact may be that perhaps our teachers weren't made strange enough.

There is still one further speculation possible to explain why the effects of *Making It Strange* did not last. Perhaps we do not naturally play with language simply because using language conventionally is easier and less demanding. For most tasks there is no *necessity* to use novel language. Because it is not demanded, it may not be elicited. The educational solution to this is to construct tasks in which novel language is *needed* rather than one in which it is simply one possible way of handling it.

In addition to these considerations we need to find out if there were differences between control and experimental groups on the second test after control students had received some specific training in figurative usage. To answer this point, Test 2 results of both groups, for novel and frozen usage separately, were compared. The analysis for all schools for frozen usage revealed a significant difference between control and experimental groups ($F_{1,144} = 5.44; p < .05$) with experimental students producing more frozen figures than control students. In addition, there was a significant school effect ($F_{3,144} = 5.62; p < .01$) with School 1 producing the greatest total number of figures and School 4, the least. As might be expected, there were no significant differences on Test 2 between experimental and control groups in terms of their relative ability to produce novel figures.

The results of these analyses suggest the following summary. The effects of the *Making It Strange* series on the production of novel figures does not seem to endure over a 4-week period. The picture for frozen production is somewhat brighter in that students in the experimental groups produced more frozen figures on Test 2 than on Test 1 or than any of the control groups at either testing period. Thus whatever effects there are, seem to endure for frozen figures but not for novel figures. Such, sadly, is the conclusion we must reach in regard to the effects of the *Making It Strange* scores on compositions written by children within the context of four vastly different public elementary schools.

Effects of Training on Comparisons and Multiple-Sentence Tasks

In a further attempt to determine the effects of the *Making It Strange* (Synectics, Inc., 1968) series on figurative language we also analyzed the results of both the Comparisons task and the Multiple Sentences task for all groups. The first analysis involved a comparison of experimental groups with control groups on Test 1 in order to determine if the *Making It Strange* series had any effect on figurative production in the Comparisons task. As may be remembered, the Comparisons task required children to suggest how randomly paired items such as *clock* and *baby* were similar. As before, answers were rated for novel and frozen usage and means established for all classes for all schools for both experimental and control groups. The same subjects were used for these analyses as were used for the Composition task.

Table 9.5 presents the means for frozen figurative usage for all groups and schools, while Table 9.6 presents the data for novel figurative usage for these same groups and conditions. An analysis of variance computed for frozen usage over these data for all schools and grades showed no significance whatsoever. The analysis for novel figurative usage also failed to show any significant effect of any of the *Making It Strange* series and only revealed a significant school

TABLE 9.5
Mean Rates of Frozen Figurative Usage Control and Experimental Groups (Comparisons Task)

School	Group	Test	\multicolumn{4}{c}{Grade}	Total
			3	4	5	6	
1	Control	1	1.39	0.92	1.52	1.71	1.39
	Experimental	1	1.86	0.95	1.07	1.33	1.30
2	Control	1	1.48	0.41	1.50	2.12	1.38
	Experimental	1	1.61	2.36	0.75	0.97	1.42
3	Control	1	2.33	1.88	2.40	1.33	1.99
	Experimental	1	0.71	2.85	2.21	3.64	2.35
4	Control	1	1.46	1.88	0.71	2.53	1.64
	Experimental	1	0.41	1.84	0.94	1.81	1.25
Total	Control	1	1.67	1.27	1.53	1.92	1.60
	Experimental	1	1.15	2.00	1.24	1.94	1.58

effect ($F_{3,144} = 6.41$; $p < .001$) with Schools 1 and 2 producing the greatest number of novel figures and with Schools 3 and 4 producing the least. In order to look further at each school, separate analyses of variance were computed. The results of these further analyses showed no significant differences among any of the various experimental and control groups. Because prior work (see Chapter 7) had shown a greater use of novel than frozen figures on this type of task, novel–frozen differences were also evaluated statistically. Here results showed a significant difference between frozen and novel usage for Schools 1 and 2, with students in both schools producing more novel than frozen figures on this task.

What these results seem to suggest is that the *Making It Strange* series had no effect whatever on the production of figurative language, either novel or frozen, on the Comparisons task. Although these data did corroborate the fact that Comparisons task elicits more novel than frozen figurative usage for middle- to upper-middle-class children, this is nothing new. What is interesting, however, is that a series such as *Making It Strange* adds nothing to novel production. Perhaps the hypothesis that this series frees children from the "don't rock the boat" philosophy on a composition task is a more feasible hypothesis than the alternative hypothesis that it serves, in general, to promote novel figurative usage.

In order to explore the effects of the lesson plans on the Comparisons task, the Test 1 data for control groups were compared to their Test 2 data. The results of an analysis done over all schools for frozen data revealed no significant differences, while results for novel usage showed only a significant school effect with School 1, as usual, producing the greatest number of novel figures and School 4, again as usual, the fewest. In order to explore this result further, separate analyses for each school were also computed. The results of these analyses revealed only significant novel versus frozen comparisons with children producing more novel than frozen usage on this task in Schools 1, 2, and 3. The results for classes receiving appropriate reinforcement showed no significant differences in either novel or frozen production for any class or grade in any school. All of these results seem to indicate that lesson plans and reinforcement techniques have little effect on the production of either frozen or novel figures of speech on the Comparisons task.

In order to examine the residual effects of the *Making It Strange* series over a four-week period, the results of Tests 1 and 2 for the experimental groups were examined. The results of all of the analyses undertaken seem to give little indication of any differential effects of the *Making It Strange* series over time. Again, the only consistency that emerged was that the Comparisons task elicited more novel than frozen figurative usage.

Finally, analyses were computed comparing both experimental and control groups after a delay of four weeks. The results of an analysis for frozen usage revealed no significant comparisons, while an analysis for novel usage showed only a significant school effect, with School 1 again producing the greatest number of novel figures, and with School 4 producing the fewest. In general, then, it can be seen that neither using the *Making It Strange* series nor being exposed to a series of specially designed lesson plans had any special effect on metaphoric usage on the Comparisons task. Only one thing is clear — students produce more novel than frozen figures on this type of task and that none of our teaching procedures had any effect at all.

Another way in which to test the efficacy of the present training procedures involves the Multiple Sentences task. As previously explained, this task requires children to use a word in as many different sentences and senses as possible. Using statistical techniques identical to those used in regard to the Comparisons

TABLE 9.6
Mean Rates of Novel Figurative Usage Control and Experimental Groups (Comparisons Task)

School	Group	Test	Grade				Total
			3	4	5	6	
1	Control	1	4.84	4.66	2.91	2.83	3.81
	Experimental	1	2.05	2.54	3.62	3.53	2.94
2	Control	1	5.23	3.65	2.43	4.35	3.92
	Experimental	1	2.85	2.33	3.27	5.96	3.60
3	Control	1	0.50	4.49	1.83	3.36	2.55
	Experimental	1	3.04	3.93	2.61	1.82	2.85
4	Control	1	3.18	1.26	1.72	1.46	1.93
	Experimental	1	1.27	2.31	1.41	3.74	2.18
Total	Control	1	3.44	3.52	2.22	3.03	3.05
	Experimental	1	2.30	2.78	2.73	3.76	2.89

TABLE 9.7
Mean Rates of Frozen Figurative Usage Control and Experimental Groups (Multiple-Uses Test)

School	Group	Test	Grade 3	4	5	6	Total
1	Control	1	1.96	3.12	2.84	4.13	3.01
	Experimental	1	3.08	2.62	2.58	6.11	3.60
2	Control	1	1.48	2.47	2.94	4.59	2.87
	Experimental	1	2.74	2.84	3.97	4.78	3.58
3	Control	1	2.13	3.59	2.64	4.94	3.33
	Experimental	1	1.35	2.46	4.59	5.24	3.41
4	Control	1	0.94	1.70	2.61	1.94	1.80
	Experimental	1	0.86	2.35	1.93	3.07	2.05
Total	Control	1	1.63	2.72	2.76	3.90	2.75
	Experimental	1	2.01	2.57	3.27	4.80	3.16

test, an evaluation was made of the effectiveness of both the *Making It Strange* series and the lesson plans/reinforcement procedures on the production of frozen and novel figures within this task. The specific means for frozen figurative usage for all schools, grades, and conditions are presented in Table 9.7, while comparable means for novel usage are presented in Table 9.8.

The first set of analyses involved comparisons between control and experimental groups at the close of the experimental training condition. An analysis of variance computed over the means for frozen figures showed no significant differences between experimental and control groups although there were signifi-

TABLE 9.8
Mean Rates of Novel Figurative Usage Control and Experimental Groups (Multiple-Uses Test)

School	Group	Test	Grade 3	4	5	6	Total
1	Control	1	0.63	0.64	0.58	0.26	0.53
	Experimental	1	0.00	0.85	0.28	0.42	0.38
2	Control	1	0.43	0.71	0.64	0.93	0.68
	Experimental	1	0.88	1.01	0.72	0.45	0.77
3	Control	1	0.44	1.15	0.66	1.53	0.95
	Experimental	1	0.90	0.83	0.00	0.15	0.47
4	Control	1	0.61	0.37	0.14	0.00	0.28
	Experimental	1	0.00	0.32	0.12	0.76	0.30
Total	Control	1	0.53	0.72	0.51	0.68	0.61
	Experimental	1	0.45	0.75	0.28	0.45	0.45

cant differences between schools ($F_{3,144} = 5.95; p < .01$) with School 4 producing far fewer frozen figures than any of the other schools. These analyses also indicate significant differences among grades ($F_{3,144} = 13.90; p < .001$) with the number of frozen figures increasing as grade increased. All other comparisons were not significant. For novel usage (see Table 9.8) the *Making It Strange* series again failed to produce a significant effect. The only significant comparison was that among schools ($F_{3,144} = 2.91; p < .05$) with School 4 again producing the least amount of figurative language.

Separate analyses computed over each of the four schools all showed similar results and lead to the summary statement that the *Making It Strange* series seemed to have no effect on figurative production — either novel or frozen — for the Multiple-Sentences task, as was also the case for the Comparisons task. Whereas the Comparisons task seemed to evoke more novel than frozen figures, the Multiple-Sentences task seemed to elicit far more frozen than novel figures. As a matter of fact, novel metaphoric usage appeared only infrequently across all grades whereas frozen figurative usage seemed to increase over grade.

Other analyses similar to those reported in connection with the Composition and Comparisons tasks were also undertaken for the Multiple-Sentences task. In these analyses no differences were found on any of the comparisons done between experimental and control groups. What these analyses showed instead were the usual grade and school effects which by now are quite familiar for this set of results. The only psycholinguistic or educationally relevant result concerns the fact that significant differences were found in favor of frozen figurative usage for all schools on the Multiple-Sentence task.

All in all, then, both the school-by-school and overall analyses done on the Multiple-Sentences task showed that neither the lesson plans nor the workbook-series procedures seemed to influence the production of figurative language. In all cases there were the usual and predictable differences between novel and frozen figurative language (novel greater than frozen for Comparisons, and frozen greater than novel for Multiple Sentences) as well as the by now familiar differences among the four schools. Although there is some comfort to these facts in that they replicate the results of the Pollio & Pollio (1974) study, it is also quite clear that neither the special lesson plans nor the *Making It Strange* series significantly increased the use of either novel or frozen figurative language on either of these two final tasks. The effects of the *Making It Strange* series were quite specific to the Composition task and did not seem to extend to the Comparisons or Multiple-Sentences tasks.

TEACHERS, TEACHING, AND TEACHING TECHNIQUES

Now that the statistical dust has settled and the last number has found its appropriate interpretive niche, several comments must be made and a general conclusion drawn. First, all of the teaching techniques used to stimulate figurative language are similar — they provide children with activities that are different from those normally used in a classroom. Children are encouraged to risk, to use their imaginations, to make the world strange. Secondly, the consequences to the child for being creative — for this is what such activities encourage — are all positive. In the context of these tasks children can do no wrong for they are in a world in which no one cares about, nor even pays attention to, mistakes. Strange writing, odd symbols and unusual thoughts are not only what is wanted; they are also what is, and becomes, expected. Freed from ordinary restraints the child is allowed to play with words, symbols, and ideas in whatever way desired.

In most general terms all of the experimental procedures used in this study are best construed as removing pedagogic barriers set up in the name of educating children to do the "right thing." When the task is one the child has never done before, the child's performance reflects a more immediate response to the demands of the task unaffected by the filter of rigid pedagogical stricture. For novel tasks, such as Comparisons or Multiple-Sentences, the child needs no freeing for they were never properly restricted in the first place. In the case of more usual classroom tasks, in which a proper response has been taught, using the *Making It Strange* series had its most pronounced effect. Writing a composition in the context of a classroom made strange is not the same as writing a composition in the context of an ordinary classroom and it is this difference in outlook which may account for results produced on the Composition task.

Our conclusion is derived primarily from an analysis of statistical data and only secondarily from our experiences with children in the classroom. In a book entitled *Wishes, Lies, and Dreams,* Kenneth Koch (1970) describes his first-person experiences in attempting to teach the children of Public School 61 how to write poetry:

> Teaching really is not the right word for what takes place. It is more like permitting the children to discover something they already have. I helped them to do this by removing obstacles, such as the need to rhyme . . .
> There are other barriers besides rhyme . . . that can keep children from writing freely and enjoying it. One is feeling they have to spell everything correctly. Stopping to worry about spelling a word can cut off a fine flow of ideas. So can having to avoid words one can't spell. Punctuation can also be an influence, as can neatness. (pp. 25–26)

What general conclusion then can we draw from this research? What is it that helps the child achieve the disciplined freedom necessary for figurative language usage and creative writing, thinking and/or problem solving? Obviously, it cannot be a particular teaching technique: there is no clean cookbook solution to the problem of teaching figurative language and/or creative expression. All that appears to be necessary for, and conducive to, increased creative production is the proper teacher, teaching in the proper atmosphere, or atmospheres, of disciplined freedom. For this reason, it seems reasonable to suggest that the teaching techniques utilized in these studies had their greatest effects not on the students but on the teachers themselves. These techniques may have freed the teachers from the demands a school curriculum normally makes: teach facts and make sure kids give the "right" answers. In the freer atmosphere created by relaxing or denying these pedagogic demands both teacher and student could create and be responsive to innovation. It was not that students were freed from the "don't rock the boat" philosophy; rather there no longer was a boat to rock, It vanished when the teacher's concern for the right answer was removed.

That children can and do use novel figurative language when allowed, or encouraged to, has clearly been demonstrated. It has also been shown that such usage decreases as grade increases in what are usually known as the "better" schools. In lower socioeconomic schools, however, this does not occur, and we are tempted to ask what are the real differences among these schools? By their very nature, better schools are more achievement oriented – they want all of their students to know the right answers, for knowing the right answer is thought to be a guarantee of success. In lower socioeconomic schools children are not pushed quite as hard. Although this may have its disadvantages in terms of academic achievement and success, it may provide a freer atmosphere to create.

Does this mean, then, that facts are unimportant, that they have no proper value? Here again, the phrase, "disciplined freedom" provides a clue: facts are part of the discipline and if we may be permitted yet another pun, the discipline needed for creativity as well as for success. It is every individual teacher in each and every classroom, however, who must determine the appropriate mix of fact and freedom for the children and the activity at hand.

The conclusion that is inevitable, then, is that techniques for teaching figurative usage are perhaps unimportant in and of themselves. What is important is the teacher, how he or she teaches, and the classroom atmosphere that this combination creates. In an atmosphere of disciplined freedom, in which the freedom to create really exists, and where the teacher is free, open, encouraging, accepting and disciplined, novel figurative usage and creative student response will occur. In the last analysis, it is the teacher who matters, not the technique: it is the teacher who must know what freedom entails as well as how and when to impose the discipline that such freedom demands in order to insure creative, articulate, and satisfactory products.

SUMMARY AND CONCLUSIONS

Figurative language, as an integral part of both creative teaching and learning and developmental language usage has usually been considered as supplemental to a normal school curriculum. The importance of figurative language, however, has been recognized and procedures for teaching such usage developed. Most of these procedures involve the use of fanciful figurative activities that encourage unusual thinking, speaking and/or writing. In two reports of one large study,

Holstein (1972a,b) found that such metaphorical exercises increased not only the productive capacities of children but their elaborative capacities as well. Winner and Gardner (1974) gave metaphoric training to students in three domains, visual, scientific, and verbal, and measured verbal output for creative usage. Results indicated that specific exercises in the verbal domain increased metaphorical thinking and expression when tested on a similar verbal task.

In the first of two larger studies, M. Pollio (1971) using commercially available materials (the *Making It Strange* series) found that novel figurative production was facilitated on a Composition task for upper-middle-class students. In a second study (1973), reported extensively in this chapter, it was found that these same materials again increased novel production in middle- to upper-middle-class schools but had no effect on lower socioeconomic-class schools. In a lower-middle-class school, frozen figurative production was also increased.

Contrasting these results with results obtained after a series of lessons and reinforcement techniques designed specifically to teach metaphoric use, Pollio found that the *Making It Strange* series seemed to be more effective in augmenting the production of novel figurative usage than these specially devised lessons. In further analyses evaluating the effects of both the *Making It Strange* series and the lessons and reinforcement techniques on Comparisons and Multiple-Sentences tasks, it was found that neither teaching technique served to augment frozen or novel figurative production on either of these tasks.

On the basis of such results, it seems reasonable to conclude that effects brought about by the use of these materials is predominantly one of freeing both the teacher and the child from the restraints imposed upon them by the normal school curriculum in its demand for factual knowledge. This kind of freeing may indeed have its greatest impact on the teacher rather than on the student. Although teaching figurative language is, in and of itself, important as part of the language-arts curriculum, its effect in helping promote creative process in class would seem to be more important for the teacher than for the student. If the teacher is enabled, by whatever method, to establish an accepting, encouraging, and restraint free atmosphere in the classroom then the disciplined freedom needed for creative process, for figurative language, for communication, and for real learning, itself, will be established and the general values of an educational process thereby encouraged and promoted. In the end, it is the teacher rather than the technique that really matters.

References

Aleksandrowicz, D. R. The meaning of metaphor. *Menninger Clinic Bulletin*, 1962, *26*, 92–101.
Alexander, F. *Psychoanalysis and psychotherapy.* New York: Norton, 1956.
Alexander, F. The dynamics of psychotherapy in light of learning theory. *American Journal of Psychiatry*, 1963, *20*, 440–448.
Alston, W. P. *Philosophy of Language.* Englewood Cliffs, N.J.: Prentice-Hall, 1964. Pp. 64–106.
Anderson, C. C. The psychology of metaphor. *Journal of Genetic Psychology* 1964, *105*, 53–73.
Aristotle. *The poetics* (translation by Ingram Bywater). Oxford: Oxford University Press, 1909.
Armstrong, D. T. Literary allusions. *English Journal* 1945, *34*, 218–219.
Arnheim, R. *Visual thinking.* Berkeley: University of California Press, 1970.
Arnold, J. E. Education for innovation. In S. J. Parnes & H. F. Harding (Eds.), *A source book for creative thinking.* New York: Scribner's, 1962. Pp. 127–138.
Arthos, J. Figures of speech. In A. Premminger (Ed.), *Encyclopedia of Poetry.* Princeton: Princeton University Press, 1965. Pp. 273–274.
Asch, S. E. On the use of metaphor in description of persons. In H. Werner (Ed.), *On expressive language.* Worcester, Mass.: Clark University Press, 1955. Pp. 29–38.
Asch, S. E. The metaphor: A psychological inquiry. In R. Tagiuri & L. Petrullo. (Eds.), *Person perception and interpersonal behavior.* Stanford, Calif.: Stanford University Press, 1958. Pp. 86–94.
Asch, S. E., & Nerlove, H. The development of double-function terms in children. In B. Kaplan & S. Wapner (Eds.), *Perspectives in psychological theory.* New York: International Universities Press, 1960.
Austin, J. L. *How to do things with words.* New York: Oxford University Press, 1965.
Baker, S. J. The sexual symbolism in language. *International Journal of Sexology*, 1948, *2*, 13–18.
Barclay, J. R. The role of comprehension in remembering sentences. *Cognitive Psychology*, 1972, *2*, 229–254.
Barlow, J. M. *Metaphor and insight in psychotherapy.* Unpublished doctoral dissertation, University of Tennessee, 1973.

REFERENCES

Barlow, J. M., Kerlin, J. R., & Pollio, H. R. *Training manual for identifying figurative language* (Technical Report #1). Metaphor Research Group, University of Tennessee, Knoxville, 1971.
Barlow, J. M., Pollio, H. R., & Fine, H. J. Insight, metaphor and psychotherapy. Unpublished manuscript, University of Tennessee, 1971.
Barron, F. *Creativity and psychological health: Origins of personality and creative freedom.* Princeton, N. J.: Van Nostrand, 1963.
Bartlett, C. F. *Remembering.* Cambridge, England: Cambridge University Press, 1932.
Baym, M. The present state of the study of metaphor. *Books Abroad, 25,* 1961, 215–219.
Beck, S. J., Beck, A. G., Levitt, E. E., & Molish, H. B. *Rorschach's test: Vol. I. Basic processes.* (3rd ed.) New York: Grune & Stratton, 1961.
Bellak, L., & Small, G. *Emergency psychotherapy and brief psychotherapy.* New York: Grune & Stratton, 1965.
Berggren, D. *An analysis of metaphorical meaning and truth.* Unpublished doctoral dissertation, Yale, 1959.
Berggren, C. C. The use and abuse of metaphor. *The Review of Metaphysics, 1962, 26,* 237–258.
Berko-Gleason, J. Code switching in children's language. In *Cognitive development and the acquisition of language.* Timothy E. Moore (Ed.), New York: Academic Press, 1973. Pp. 159–168.
Bickerton, D., Prolegomena to a linguistic theory of metaphor. *Foundations of Language, 1969, 5,* 34–52.
Billow, R. M. A cognitive developmental study of metaphor comprehension. *Developmental Psychology,* 1975, *11,* 415–423.
Black, M. *Models and metaphors: Studies in languages and philosophy.* Ithaca, New York: Cornell University Press, 1962.
Black, M. Metaphor. In W. E. Kenick (Ed.), *Art and philosophy.* New York: St. Martin Press, 1964. Pp. 449–65.
Bloomfield, M. W. A grammatical approach to personification and allegory. *Modern Philology,* 1963, *55,* 161–171.
Blos, P. *On adolescence.* New York: Free Press, 1962.
Blumenthal, A. L. *Language and psychology.* New York: Wiley, 1970.
Bolinger, D. L. The atomization of meaning. *Language,* 1965, *41,* 533–573.
Bransford, J. D., Barclay, J. R., & Franks, J. J. Sentence memory: A constructive versus interpretive approach. *Cognitive Psychology,* 1972, *3,* 193–209.
Bransford, J. D., & Franks, J. J. The abstraction of linguistic ideas. *Cognitive Psychology* 1971, *2,* 331–350.
Bransford, J. D., & Johnson, M. K. Contextual prerequisites for understanding: Some investigations of comprehension and recall. *Journal of Verbal Learning and Verbal Behavior,* 1972, *11,* 717–726.
Bransford, J. D., & McCarrell, N. S. A sketch of a cognitive approach to comprehension: Some thoughts about understanding what it means to comprehend. In W. Wimer & D. Palermo (Eds.), *Cognition and the symbolic process.* Englewood Cliffs, N. J.: Prentice-Hall, 1974.
Breger, L. *From identity to instinct.* Englewood Cliffs, N. J.: Prentice-Hall, 1973.
Brill, A. A. Poetry as an oral outlet. *The Psychoanalytic Review,* June 1931, 357–378.
Brooke-Rose, C. *A grammar of metaphor.* London, 1958.
Brown, J. I. Vocabulary – Key to Communication. *Education,* 1959, *80,* 80–84.
Brown, N. O. *Life against death.* New York: Random House, 1959.
Brown, R. W. How shall a thing be called? *Psychological Review,* 1958, *65,* 14–21.
Brown, R. W. *Words and things.* Glencoe, Ill.: The Free Press, 1958. (a)

Brown, R. W. Is a boulder sweet or sour? *Contemporary Psychology*, 1958, *3*, 113–115. (b)

Brown, R. W. *Social psychology*. New York: The Free Press, 1965.

Brown, R. W. *A first language: The early stages*. Cambridge, Mass.: Harvard University Press, 1973.

Brown, R. W., Leiter, R. A. & Hildum, D. C. Metaphors from Music Criticism. *Journal of Abnormal and Social Psychology*, 1957, *54*, 347–352.

Brown, S. J. M. *Image and truth: Studies in the imagery of the Bible*. Rome: Oficium Libri Catholici, Catholic Book Agency, 1955. P. 161.

Brown, S. J. M. *The world of imagery: Metaphor and kindred imagery* (2nd ed.). New York: Russell & Russell, 1966.

Bruner, J. S. Going beyond the information given. In H. E. Gruber (Ed.), *Contemporary approaches to cognition*. Cambridge, Mass.: Harvard University Press, 1957. Pp. 41–69.

Bruner, J. S. The conditions of creativity. In W. E. Henry (Ed.), *Contemporary approaches to creative thinking*. New York: Atherton Press, 1962. (a)

Bruner, J. S. *On Knowing: Essays for the left hand*. Cambridge, Mass.: Belknap Press of Harvard University, 1962. (b)

Burke, K. *A grammar of motives*. Berkeley: University of California Press, 1969.

Burkland, C. E. The presentation of figurative language, *Quarterly Journal of Speech*, 1964, *41*, 383–390.

Burmeister, D. The language of deceit. *Media and Methods*, 1973, *52*, 22–25.

Burns, B. *Some Psychological aspects of anomalous sentences*. Unpublished masters' dissertation, University of Tennessee, 1975.

Burns, P. C., Broman, B. L., & Lowe, A. L. *The language arts in childhood education* (2nd ed.). Chicago: Rand McNally, 1971.

Butler, J., Rice, H., Laure, B., & Wagstaff, F. On the naturalistic definition of variables: an analogue of clinical analysis. In Strupp, H. & Luborsky, L. (Eds.) *Research in Psychotherapy*. Washington: American Psychol. Assn., 1962. Pp. 178–205.

Cain, A. C., & Maupin, B. M. Interpretation within the metaphor. *Bulletin of the Menninger Clinic*, November 1961, *XXV: 6*.

Carlson, R. K. Recent research in originality. *Elementary English*, 1963, *40*, 583–589.

Caruth, E., & Ekstein, R. Interpretation within the metaphor: Further considerations. *American Academy of Child Psychiatry Journal*, 1966, *5*, 35–45.

Cassirer, E. *The philosophy of symbolic forms*. New Haven: Yale University Press, 1953.

Cerf, B. *A treasury of atrocious puns*. New York: Random House, 1966.

Chafe, W. L. *Meaning and the structure of language*. Chicago: University of Chicago Press, 1970.

Chafe, W. L. Discourse structure and human knowledge. In J. Carroll & R. Freedle (Eds.), *Language comprehension and the acquisition of knowledge*. New York: Harcourt, Brace, & World, 1972.

Chapman, J. W. The perception and expression of a metaphor as a function of cognitive style and intellectual level. Unpublished doctoral dissertation, Georgia State University, 1971.

Chessick, R. D. *How psychotherapy heals: The process of intensive psychotherapy*. New York: Science House, 1968.

Chomsky, N. *Syntactic structures*. The Hague: Mouton, 1957.

Chomsky, N. *Aspects of a theory of syntax*. Cambridge, Mass.: M.I.T. Press, 1965.

Chomsky, N. *Language and mind*. New York: Harcourt, Brace & World, 1969.

Chukovsky, K. [*From two to five*.] (Morton Ed. and trans.) Berkeley and Los Angeles: University of California Press, 1965.

REFERENCES

Clark, E. What's in a word? On the child's acquisition of semantics in his first language. In T. Moore (Ed.), *Cognitive development and the acquisition of language.* New York: Academic Press, 1973. Pp. 65–110.

Clark, H. H., Carpenter, P. A., & Just, M. A. On the meeting of semantics and perception. Paper presented at the 8th Carnegie Conference on Cognition, Pittsburgh, Pa. May, 1972.

Coleman, E. The meaning of metaphor. *The Gordon Review,* 1965, *8,* 151–163.

Cooper, D. Concepts from semantics as avenues to reading improvement. *English Journal,* 1954, *53,* 85–90.

Corbett, E. P. J. *Classic rhetoric for the modern student.* New York: Oxford University Press, 1965. Pp. 438–448.

Craddick, R. A., & Miller, J. A. Investigation of the symbolic self using the concentric circles method and animal metaphor. *Perceptual and Motor Skills,* 1970, *31,* 147–150.

Crutchfield, R. The creative process. In *Conference on the Creative Person.* Berkeley: University of California, Institute of Personality Assessment and Research, 1961.

Curtis, D. The measure of the metaphor. *Elementary English,* 1972, *49,* No. 7, 1053–1055.

Daiches, D. Myth, metaphor and poetry. In *Royal Society of Literature of the United Kingdom,* London. Vol. 33, 1961.

Dallman, M., Rouch, R. L., Change, L. Y. C., & DeBoer, J. J. *The teaching of reading* (4th ed.). New York: Holt, Rinehart & Winston, 1974.

Davitz, J. *The language of emotion.* New York: Academic Press, 1969.

Day-Lewis, C. *The poetic image* (2nd ed.). London: Jonathan Cape, 1961.

Dechant, E. V. *Improving the teaching of reading* (2nd ed.). Englewood Cliffs, N. J.: Prentice-Hall, 1970.

Deese, J. E. *The structure of associations in language and thought.* Baltimore, Md.: Johns Hopkins Press, 1965.

Deese, J. E. Meaning and change of meaning. *American Psychologist,* 1967, *22,* 641–651.

Deutsch, F., & Murphy, W. F. *The clinical interview. Volume one, diagnosis.* New York: International Universities Press, 1955.

Dickey, J. Metaphor as pure adventure. Lecture delivered at the Library of Congress, December 4, 1967.

Downey, J. E. The psychology of figures of speech. *The American Journal of Psychology,* 1919, *30,* 103–115.

Downey, J. E. The metaphorical consciousness. In J. E. Downey (Ed.), *Creative imagination: Studies in the psychology of literature.* New York: Harcourt, Brace, 1929.

Drange, T. *Type crossings.* The Hague: Mouton, 1966.

Deisdadt, R. An analysis of the use of analogies and metaphors in science. *Journal of Psychology,* 1968, *68,* 97–116.

Durkin, D. *Teaching them to read.* Boston: Allyn & Bacon, 1970.

Edie, J. M. Expression and metaphor. *Philosophy and Phenomenological Research,* 1963, *23* (June), 538–561.

Ehrenwald, J. *Psychotherapy, myth and metaphor.* New York: Grune & Stratton, 1966.

Ekstein, R., & Wallerstein, J. Observation or the psychotherapy of borderline and psychotic children. *Psychoanalytic study of the child,* 1956, *11,* 303–311.

Ekstein, R. Cross-sectional views of the psychotherapeutic process with an adolescent recovering from a schizophrenic episode. *American Journal of Ortho-psychiatry, 31,* 1961, 757–775.

Ekstein, R. *Children of time and space of action and impulse.* New York: Appleton-Century-Crofts, 1966.

Elkind, D. *Children and adolescents: Interpretive essays on Jean Piaget.* New York: Oxford University Press, 1970.

Elkind, D. *A sympathetic understanding of the child: Birth to sixteen.* Boston: Allyn & Bacon, 1974.

Embler, W. *Metaphor and meaning.* Deland, Fla.: Everett-Edwards, 1966.
Emig, J. Children and metaphor. *Research in the Teaching of English,* 1972, 6 (No. 2), 163–175.
Empson, W. *The structure of complex words.* London: Butterworths, 1951.
Empson, W. *Seven types of ambiguity.* New York: Meridian Books, 1955.
Erikson, E. H. *Childhood and society.* New York: Norton, 1950.
Erikson, E. H. *Young man Luther.* London: Faber & Faber, 1954.
Erikson, E. H. Identity and the life cycle. *Psychological Issues,* 1959, *1* (Whole monograph).
Erikson, E. H. *Identity: Youth and crisis.* New York: Norton, 1968.
Ervin, S. M. & Foster, G. The development of meaning in children's descriptive terms. *Journal of Abnormal and Social Psychology,* 1960, *2,* 271–275.
Farber, E. Chemical discoveries by means of analogies. *Isis, 41,* 1956, 20–26.
Ferguson, C. W. Words as pictures. *National Parent Teachers,* 1958, *52,* 14–16.
Fillmore, C. J. The case for case. In Bach, E., & Harms, R. T. (Eds.), *Universals in linguistic theory.* New York: Holt, Rinehart & Winston, 1968.
Fillmore, C. J. Verbs of judging: An exercise in semantic description. In C. J. Fillmore, & D. T. Langendoen (Eds.), *Studies in linguistic semantics.* New York: Holt, Rinehart & Winston, 1971.
Fillmore, C. J., & Lungendoen, D. T. (Eds.) *Studies in linguistic semantics.* New York: Holt, Rinehart & Winston, 1971.
Fine, H. J., Pollio, H. R., & Simpkinson, C. H. Figurative language, metaphor and psychotherapy. *Psychotherapy: Theory, Research and Practice,* 1973, *10,* 87–91.
Foder, J., & Katz, J. J. (Eds.). *The structure of language.* Englewood Cliffs, N. J.: Prentice-Hall, Inc., 1964.
Fodor, N. Psychopathology and the problem of oral libido in the use of language. *American Image,* 1956, *13,* 347–381.
Foerster, L. M. Idiomagic. *Elementary English,* 1974, *51,* 125–127.
Foss, M. *Symbol and metaphor in human experiences.* Princeton, N. J.: Princeton University Press, 1949.
Foss, M. *Symbol and metaphor.* Lincoln: University of Nebraska Press, 1966.
Freud, S. [*Psychopathology of everyday life.*] London: Liveright, 1905.
Freud, S. [*A general introduction to psychoanalysis.*] New York: Boni & Liveright, 1920.
Freud, S. [*Jokes and their relation to the unconscious.*] New York: Norton, 1960.
Friedman, M. H. *Stream of consciousness: A study in literary method.* New Haven: Yale University Press, 1955.
Friedman, N. Imagery. In A. Premminger (Ed.), *Encyclopedia of poetry and poetics.* Princeton: Princeton University Press, 1965. Pp. 363–370.
Fry, W. F. *Sweet madness: A study of humor.* Palo Alto, Cal.: Pacific Books, 1963.
Funk, C. E. *A hog on ice.* New York: Harper and Brothers Publishers, 1948.
Funk, C. E., *Heavens to Betsy!* New York: Harper and Brothers Publishers, 1955.
Gardner, H. *The arts and human development.* New York: Wiley, 1973. (a)
Gardner, H. Children's metaphoric productions and preferences. Unpublished manuscript, Harvard University, 1973. (b)
Gardner, H. Metaphors and modalities: How children project polar adjectives onto diverse domains. *Child Development,* 1974, *45,* 84–91.
Gardner, H., Kircher, M., Winner, E., & Perkins, D. Children's metaphoric productions and preferences. *Journal of Child Language.* 1975, *2,* 125–141.
Gendlin, E. T. A theory of personality change. In J. T. Hart & T. M. Tomlinson (Eds.), *New directions in client-centered therapy.* New York: Houghton Mifflin, 1970. Pp. 129–173.
Getzels, J. W., Jackson, W., & Phillip, W. *Creativity and intelligence: Explorations with gifted students.* New York: Wiley, 1962.

REFERENCES

Gislason, H. B. Elements of objectivity. In Wendell Phillips *Quarterly Journal of Public Speaking,* 1917, *3,* 125–134.

Goldiamond, I., & Dyrud, J. E. Some applications and implications of behavioral analysis for psychotherapy. In J. M. Shlien (Ed.), *Research in Psychotherapy* (Vol. 3). Washington, D.C.: American Psychological Association, 1968. Pp. 80–81.

Goldman-Eisler, F. *Psycholinguistics: Experiments in spontaneous speech.* New York: Academic Press, 1968.

Goodman, N. *Languages of art.* Indianapolis: Bobbs-Merrill, 1968.

Gordon, W. J. J. *Synectics: The development of creative capacity.* New York: Harper, 1961.

Gordon, W. J. J. The metaphorical way of knowing. In G. Kepes (Ed.), *Education of vision.* New York: George Braziller, 1965. Pp. 96–103.

Greene, H. A., & Petty, W. T. *Developing language skills in the elementary schools* (4th ed.). Boston: Allyn & Bacon, 1971.

Groff, P. J. Figurative speech in poems by children. *Elementary School Journal,* 1962, *63,* 136–140.

Groesbeck, H. The comprehension of figurative language by elementary children: A study in transfer. Unpublished doctoral dissertation, University of Oklahoma, 1961.

Guilford, J. P. Creativity in the arts. *Psychological Review,* 1957, *64,* 110–118.

Guilford, J. P. *The nature of human intelligence.* New York: McGraw-Hill, 1967.

Guntrip, H. *Schizoid phenomena, object relations, and the self.* New York: International Universities Press, 1969.

Hall, R. A. Why a structural semantics is impossible. *Language Sciences,* 1972, *21,* 1–6.

Hallmann, R. J. The necessary and sufficient conditions of creativity. In J. C. Gowan, G. D. Demos, & E. P. Torrance (Eds.), *Creativity: Its educational implications.* New York: Wiley, 1967.

Hard, J. S., & Harsh, W., Ney, J. W., & Shane, H. G. *Laidlaw language experience program.* River Forest, Ill.: Laidlaw Brothers, 1972.

Harding, D. W. The hinterland of thought. In L. C. Knights & B. Cottle (Eds.), *Metaphor and symbol.* London: Butterworths, 1960.

Harrower, M. R. Organization in higher mental processes. *Psychologische Forschung,* 1932, *17,* 56–120.

Harrower, M. R. *The therapy of poetry.* Springfield, Ill.: Charles C Thomas, 1972.

Hartmann, H., Kris, E., & Lowenstein, R. M. Comments on the formation of psychic structure. *The psychoanalytic study of the child.* New York: International Universities Press, 1947. Pp. 11–38.

Harvey, O. J., Hunt, D. E., & Schroder, H. M. *Conceptual systems and personality organization.* New York: Wiley, 1961.

Harvey, O. J. *Motivation and social interaction, cognitive determinants.* New York: Ronald Press, 1963.

Harvey, O. J. System structure, flexibility and creativity. In O. J. Harvey (Eds.), *Experience, structure and adaptability.* New York: Springer Publ., 1966. Pp. 39–65.

Heese, M. The explanatory function of metaphor. Paper presented at the Congress of the International Union for the Logic, Methodology, and Philosophy of Science, Jerusalem, April 1964.

Heiman, E. The use of slang in teaching linguistics. *English Journal,* 1967, *56* (February), 249–252.

Henle, P. Metaphor. In P. Henle (Ed.), *Language, thought and culture.* Ann Arbor: University of Michigan Press, 1958. Pp. 173–195.

Hersch, C. The cognitive functioning of the creative person: A developmental analysis. *Journal of Projective Techniques,* 1962, *26,* 193–200.

Hester, M. B. *The meaning of poetic metaphor: An analysis in light of Wittgenstein's claim that meaning is use.* The Hague: Mouton, 1967.

Hill, J. D. *An analysis of the writing of elementary children, grades 2–6, to determine the presence, frequency of use, and development by grade level of specified literary devices.* Unpublished doctoral dissertation. Indiana University, 1972.

Holstein, B. I. Use of metaphor to induce innovative thinking in fourth grade children. *Education,* 1972, *93,* 56–60. (a)

Holstein, B. I. A case study analysis of several children's responses to metaphorical experiences. *Journal of Education,* 1972, *154,* 45–69. (b)

Hormann, H. *Psycholinguistics: An introduction to research and theory.* New York: Springer-Verlag, 1965.

Horne, R. N. *A study of the use of figurative language by sixth grade children.* Unpublished doctoral dissertation, University of Georgia, 1966.

Hughes, T. Linguistic approaches to figurative speech. *Instructor,* 1967, *77,* 58–59.

Husserl, E. *Ideas.* (translated by W. R. Boyce Gibson) New York: Collier, 1931.

Hutchinson, E. D. Varieties of insight in humans. *Psychiatry,* 1939, *2,* 323–332.

Hutchinson, E. D. The period of frustration in creative endeavor. *Psychiatry,* 1940, *3,* 351–359.

Hutchinson, E. D. The nature of insight. In P. Mullahy (Ed.), *A study of interpersonal relations.* New York: Hermitage Press, 1949.

Inhelder, B., & Piaget, J. *The growth of logical thinking from childhood to adolescence.* New York: Basic Books, 1958.

Isenberg, A. On defining metaphor. *Journal of Philosophy,* 1963, *60,* 609–622.

Issacs, S. The nature and function of fantasy. In J. Riviere (Ed.), *Developments in Psychoanalysis.* London: Hogarth, 1952. Pp. 67–121.

Jakobson, R. Linguistics and poetics. In T. Sebeok (Ed.), *Style in Language.* Cambridge, Mass.: M.I.T. Press, 1960.

Jenkins, J. J., Russell, W. A., & Suci, G. An atlas of semantic profiles for 360 words. *American Journal of Psychology,* 1958, *71,* 688–699.

Jennings, J. G. *An essay on metaphor.* London: Blackie, 1915.

Johnson, M. G. A cognitive feature model of compound free associations. *Psychological Review,* 1970, *77,* 282–293.

Johnson, M. G. Language flexibility and theories of meaning. Paper presented at meetings of the Psychonomic Society, St. Louis, November 1972.

Johnson, R. Imaginative sensitivity in schizophrenia. *Review of Existential Psychology and Psychiatry,* 1964, *4,* 255–264.

Jordan, W. J. A reinforcement model of metaphor. *Speech Monographs,* *39,* 1972, 223–26.

Kaplan, B. Some psychological methods for the investigation of expressive language. In H. Werner (Ed.), *On expressive language.* Worcester, Mass.: Clark University Press, 1955.

Kaplan, B. Radical metaphor, aesthetic and the origin of language. *Review of Existential Psychology and Psychiatry,* 1962, *1* (2), 72–84.

Karwoski, T., Odbert, A., & Osgood, C. Studies in synaesthetic thinking II: The role of form in visual responses to music. *Journal of Genetic Psychology,* 1942, *26,* 199–222.

Katz, J. J., & Fodor, J. A. The structure of a semantic theory. *Language,* 1963, *39,* 170–210.

Katz, J. J., & Postal, P. M. *An integrated theory of linguistic descriptions.* Cambridge, Mass.: M.I.T. Press, 1964.

Kelly, G. *The psychology of personal constructs: Vol. 1.* New York: Norton, 1955.

Kelly, G. A. *A theory of personality: The psychology of personal constructs.* New York: Norton, 1963.

Klopfer, B., Ainsworth, M. D., Klopfer, W. G., & Holt, R. R. *Developments in the Rorschach technique: Vol. I, technique and theory.* Yonkers, N. Y.: World Books, 1954.

Knapp, R. H. A study of metaphor. *Journal of Projective Techniques,* 1960, *24,* 389–395.

Knapp, R. H., & Green, H. N. Personality correlates of success imagery. *Journal of Social Psychology,* 1964, *62,* 93–99.
Koch, K. *Wishes, lies, and dreams: Teaching children to write poetry.* New York: Chelsea House, 1970.
Koen, F. An intra-verbal explication of the nature of metaphor. *Journal of Verbal Learning and Behavior,* 1965, *4,* 129–133.
Koestler, A. *Insight and Outlook.* London: Macmillan, 1949.
Koestler, A. *The act of creation.* London: Macmillan, 1964.
Koffka, K. *Principles of Gestalt psychology.* New York: Harcourt, Brace, 1935.
Kohler, W. *Gestalt psychology.* New York: Liveright, 1929.
Kraus, S. *The great debates.* Bloomington, Ind.: Indiana University Press, 1962.
Kris, E. O. On preconscious mental processes, *Psychoanalytic Quarterly,* 1950, *19,* 23–51.
Kris, E. *Psychoanalytic explorations in art.* New York: International Universities Press, 1952.
Kris, E. On some vicissitudes of insight in psychoanalysis. *International Journal of Psychoanalysis,* 1956, *37,* 45–59.
Kuhn, T. S. *The structure of scientific revolutions.* Chicago: University of Chicago Press, 1962.
Laffal, J. *Pathological and normal language.* New York: Atherton Press, 1965.
Lakoff, G. On generative semantics. In L. Jakobovitz & D. Steinberg (Eds.), *Semantics: An interdisciplinary reader.* Cambridge, England: The University Press, 1971.
Lakoff, G. The role of deduction in grammar. In C. J. Fillmore and D. T. Langendoen (Eds.), *Studies in linguistic semantics.* New York: Holt, Rinehart & Winston, 1971.
Lakoff, R. If's, and's and but's about conjunction. In C. J. Fillmore & D. T. Langendoen (Eds.), *Studies in linguistic semantics.* New York: Holt, Rinehart & Winston, 1971.
Lakoff, R. Language in context. *Language,* 1972, *48,* 907–927.
Langendoen, D. T. *Essentials of English grammar.* New York: Holt, Rinehart & Winston, 1970.
Langer, S. *Philosophy in a new key.* Cambridge, Mass.: Harvard University Press, 1957.
Lasswell, L. Verbal references and physiological changes during the psychoanalytic interview. *Psychoanalytic Review,* 1936, *22,* 13–24.
Leder, S. Psychotherapy: Placebo effect and/or learning. In R. Porter (Ed.), *The role of learning in psychotherapy.* New York: International Universities Press, 1968. Pp. 114–123.
Leech, G. N. *Meaning and the English verb.* London: Longmans, 1971.
Leech, G. N. *Semantics.* Baltimore: Penguin Books, 1974.
Leedy, J. J. *Poetry therapy.* Philadelphia: Lippincott, 1969.
Lenrow, P. B. The uses of metaphor in facilitating constructive behavior change. *Psychotherapy,* 1966, *3* (4), 145–148.
Loban, W. *The language of elementary school children.* Champaign, Ill.: National Council of Teachers of English, 1963.
Lockwood, B. R. Figurative language as a function of cognitive style. Unpublished doctoral dissertation, University of Tennessee, 1974.
Lonergan, B. *Insight: A study of human understanding.* London: Longmans, Green, 1957.
Ludovici, A. M. *The secret of laughter.* London: Constable, 1932.
Lyons, J. *Introduction to theoretical linguistics.* New York: Cambridge University Press, 1968.
Maclay, H. Overview. In D. D. Steinberg & L. A. Jakobovitz (Eds.), *Semantics.* Cambridge: Cambridge University Press, 1971. Pp. 157–182.
Madge, C. Myth, metaphor and world picture. *Manchester Literary and Philosophical Society* (Proceedings), 1963, *105,* 53–63.

Madge, C. Metaphor. In S. Spender & D. Hall (Eds.), *The concise encyclopedia of English and American poetry.* New York: Hawthorne Books, 1963. Pp. 198–202.

Maier, N. R. F. A gestalt theory of humor. *British Journal of Psychology,* 1932, *23,* 69–74.

Margolis, J. Notes on the logic of simile, metaphor and analogy. *American Speech,* 1957, *32,* 186–189.

Martin, A. R. The dynamics of insight. *American Journal of Psychoanalysis,* 1952, *12,* 24–38.

Maslow, A. H. Cognition of being in the peak experience. Presidential address at the American Psychological Association, Chicago, September 1956.

Maslow, A. H. *Toward a psychology of being.* Princeton, N. J.: Van Nostrand, 1962.

Mawardi, B. *Industrial invention: A study in group problem solving.* Unpublished doctoral dissertation, Harvard University, 1959.

Mawardi, B. Creative use of the metaphor in a cognitive impasse. Paper read at the American Psychological Association, New York, September 1961.

McCawley, J. D. The role of semantics in a grammar. In E. Bach & R. T. Harms (Eds.), *Universals in linguistic theory.* New York: Holt, Rinehart & Winston, 1968.

McCawley, J. D. Where do noun phrases come from? In D. D. Steinberg & L. A. Jakobovitz (Eds.), *Semantics.* Cambridge: Cambridge University Press, 1971. Pp. 217–231.

McGhee, P. E. Development of the humor response: A review of the literature. *Psychological Bulletin,* 1971, *76,* 328–348.

McNemar, Q. Lost: Our intelligence. Why? *American Psychologist,* 1964, *19,* 871–882.

Meshover, L., & Robinson, V. *The world of language.* Chicago: Follett Education Corporation, 1970.

Michael, F. S. *Semantic properties of metaphor: An investigation into the meaning of non-literal expressions.* Unpublished doctoral dissertation, University of Pennsylvania, 1974.

Miller, G. A. *Language and communication.* New York: McGraw-Hill, 1951.

Miller, G. A., & Isard, S. Some perceptual consequences of linguistic rules. *Journal of Verbal Learning and Behavior,* 1963, *2,* 217–228.

Miller, J. *The applications of the metaphor as an approach to the study of personality.* Unpublished master's thesis, Georgia State University, 1970.

Morris, C. *Signification and significance: A study of the relation between signs and values.* Cambridge, Mass.: M.I.T. Press, 1964.

Mulder, A. Wrap your ideas in cellophane. *Education,* 1959, *80,* 85–87.

Muller, F. M. Metaphor as a mode of abstraction. *Fortnightly Review,* 1886, *46,* 617–632.

Murphy, W. F. *The tactics of psychotherapy.* New York: International Universities Press, 1965.

Murray, H. A. *Thematic apperception test manual.* Cambridge, Mass.: Harvard University Press, 1943.

Myden, W. Interpretation and evaluation of certain personality characteristics involved in creative production. *Perception and Motor Skills,* 1959, *9,* 139–158.

Nash, H. Freud and metaphor. *Archives of Psychiatry,* 1962, *7,* 25–29.

Nash, H. The role of metaphor in psychological theory. *Behavioral Science,* 1963, *8,* 336–345.

Neisser, U. *Cognitive psychology.* New York: Appleton-Century, 1967.

Nemetz, A. Metaphor, the Daedalus of discourse. *Thought,* 1958, *33,* 417–442.

Newton, E. S. Figurative language: An Achilles heel in reading comprehension. *Journal of Reading,* 1964, *8,* 65–70.

Odell, G. C. D. *Simile and metaphor in the English and Scottish ballads.* New York: Columbia College Press, 1892.

Ogden, C. K., & Richards, I. A. *The meaning of meaning* (10th ed.). London: Routledge & Kegan Paul, 1960.
Olson, D. R. Language and thought: Aspects of a cognitive theory of semantics. *Psychological Review*, 1970, *4*, 257–273.
Olson, D. R. Language use for communication, instruction, and thinking. In J. Carroll, & R. Freedle (Eds.), *Language comprehension and the acquisition of knowledge*. New York: Harcourt, Brace, & World, 1972.
Osborn, M. M. *The function and significance of metaphor in rhetorical discourse*. Unpublished doctoral dissertation, University of Florida, 1963.
Osborn, M. M., & Ehninger, D. The metaphor in public address. *Speech Monographs*, 1962, *29*, 223–234.
Osgood, C. E. The nature and measurement of meaning. *Psychol. Bull.*, 1952, *49*, 197–237.
Osgood, C. E. *Method and theory in experimental psychology*. New York: Oxford University Press, 1953.
Osgood, C. E. Toward a wedding of insufficiencies. In T. R. Dixon & D. L. Horton, (Eds.), *Verbal behavior and general behavior theory*. Englewood Cliffs, N. J.: Prentice-Hall, 1968.
Osgood, C. E., Suci, G. J., & Tannenbaum, P. H. *The measurement of meaning*. Urbana, Ill.: University of Illinois Press, 1957.
Owen, G. E. L. Logic and metaphysics in some earlier works of Aristotle. In T. During, & G. Owen (Eds.), *Aristotle and Plato in the mid-fourth century*. Goteborg: Almquist & Wicksell, 1957. Pp. 163–190.
Paivio, A. *Imagery and verbal processes*. New York: Holt, Rinehart & Winston, 1971.
Pap, A. Types and meaninglessness. *Mind*, 1960, *69*, 41–54.
Pearson, P., & Maddi, S. R. The similes preference inventory: Development of a structured measure of the tendency toward variety. *Journal of Consulting Psychology*, 1966, *30*, 301–308.
Peckman, M. Metaphor: A little plain speaking on a very weary subject. *Connotation*, 1962, *1* (2), 29–46.
Pederson-Krag, G. The use of metaphor in analytic thinking. *Psychoanalytic Review*, 1956, *25*, 66–71.
Percy, W. Metaphor as mistake. *Sewanee Review*, 1958, *66*, 79–99.
Perls, F. S. *Ego, hunger and aggression*. New York: Vintage Books, 1947.
Perls, F. S. *In and out of the garbage pail*. New York: Bantam Books, 1969. (a)
Perls, F. S. *Gestalt therapy verbatim*. New York: Bantam Books, 1969. (b)
Petty, W. T., Petty, D. C., & Becking, M. F. *Experience in language, tools and techniques for language arts methods*. Boston: Allyn & Bacon, 1973.
Phelan, R. Readers are metaphor makers. *Claremont Reading Conference Yearbook*, 1971, *35*, 44–50.
Piaget, J. *The origin of intelligence in children*. New York: International Universities Press, 1952.
Piaget, J. *The Language and thought of the child*. New York: MacMillan, 1955.
Pine, F., & Holt, R. R. Creativity and primary process: A study of adaptive regression. *Journal of Abnormal and Social Psychology*, 1960, *61*, 370–379.
Pitts, M. *Anomaly and verbal behavior*. Unpublished doctoral dissertation, University of Wales, 1975.
Polanyi, M. *The tacit dimension*. New York: Doubleday, 1966.
Pollio, H. R. *The structural basis of word association*. The Netherlands: Mouton, 1966.
Pollio, H. R. The whys and hows of metaphors and their measurement. Paper presented at Southeastern Psychological Association Meetings, Atlanta, Georgia, 1972.
Pollio, H. R. *The psychology of symbolic activity*. Reading Mass.: Addison-Wesley, 1974.
Pollio, H. R., & Barlow, J. M. A behavioral analysis of figurative language in psychotherapy: One session in a single case study. *Language and Speech*, 1975, 236–254.

Pollio, H. R., & Burns, B. The anomaly of anomaly. Paper presented Psychonomics Society meetings, 1974. St. Louis, November 1974.
Pollio, H. R., & Francisco, E. Figures in public debate. Paper presented at Southeastern Psychological Association, April, 1974. Miami, Florida.
Pollio, M. R. *Figurative language in the elementary school.* Unpublished master's thesis, University of Tennessee, 1971.
Pollio, M. R. *The development and augmentation of figurative language.* Unpublished doctoral dissertation, University of Tennessee, 1973.
Pollio, M. R. Children's Comprehension of Figurative Language, Unpublished manuscript, 1976.
Pollio, M. R., & Pollio, H. R. The development of figurative language in school children. *Journal of Psycholinguistic Research, 1974, 138*–143.
Porter, C. M. *Figures of speech, divergent thinking and activation theory.* Unpublished doctoral dissertation, North Texas State University, 1969.
Prince, G. M. The operational mechanisms of synectics. *Journal of Creative Behavior,* 1968, *2* (1), 1–13.
Proll, E. Teach figurative speech. *Instructor,* 1972, *82,* 143.
Ransom, J. C. *The world's body.* New York: Scribner's, 1938.
Ransom, J. C. *The new criticism.* Norfolk, Conn.: New Directions, 1941.
Rapaport, D. The history of the awakening of insight. In M. M. Gill (Ed.), *The collected papers of David Rapaport.* New York: Basic Books, 1967.
Reinsch, N. L., Jr. An investigation of the effects of the metaphor and simile in persuasive discourse. *Speech Monographs,* 1971, *38,*142–45.
Richards, I. A. *The philosophy of rhetoric.* New York: Oxford University Press, 1936.
Richards, I. A. *Interpretation in teaching.* London: Kegan, Paul, French & Trubner, 1937.
Robertson, J. E. Figurative language. *Instructor,* 1973, *83,* 50–51.
Rommetveit, R. *On message structure.* London: Academic Press, 1974.
Rorschach, H. *Psychodiagnostics.* Berne, Switzerland: Huber, 1942.
Ross, J. R. On declarative sentences. In R. A. Jacobs & P. S. Rosenbaum (Eds.), *Readings in English transformational grammar.* Waltham, England: Ginn, 1970.
Royce, J. R. Metaphorism and humanistic psychology. In J. T. F. Bugental (Ed.), *Challenge of humanistic psychology,* New York: McGraw-Hill, 1967. Pp. 28–41.
Ruddell, R. B. *Reading-language instruction: Innovative practices.* Englewood Cliffs: Prentice-Hall, 1974.
Runion, H. An objective study of the speech style of Woodrow Wilson. *Speech Monographs,* 1936, *3,* 75–94.
Ryle, G. *The concept of mind.* New York: Barnes & Noble, 1949.
Sagan, E. "The Case of Audrey." American Academy of Psychotherapy Tape Library, Philadelphia. 1962.
Sarbin, T., Anxiety: Reification of a metaphor. *Archives of General Psychiatry, 10,* 1964, 630–638.
Schon, D. A. *Displacement of concepts.* London: Tavistock Publ., 1963.
Schonberg, R. B. Adolescent thought and figurative language. Unpublished doctoral dissertation, University of Tennessee, 1974.
Scott, G. The 18th century philosophy of metaphor. Unpublished master's thesis, Vanderbilt University, 1943.
Searle, J. R. *Speech acts: An essay in the philosophy of language.* Cambridge, England: Cambridge University Press, 1969.
Sewell, E. *The human metaphor.* South Bend, Ind.: University of Notre Dame Press, 1964.
Shaed, E. Figurative language: An Achilles heel in reading comprehension. *Journal of Reading,* 1964, *8,* 65–69.

Shahn, B. Imagination and intention. *Journal of Existential Psychology and Psychiatry,* 7 (1), 1967, 13-17.
Shapiro, D. *Neurotic Styles.* New York: Basic Books, 1965.
Sharpe, E. F. An examination of metaphor. *International Journal of Psychoanalysis.* 1940, *21,* 201-213.
Sharpe, E. F. *Collected papers on psychoanalysis.* London: Hogarth, 1950.
Sheehan, D. Wallace Stevens' theory of metaphor. *Papers on Language and Literature,* 1966, *2,* 57-66.
Shibles, W. A. *Metaphor: An annotated bibliography and history.* Whitewater, Wis.: The Language Press, 1971.
Shultz, T. R. The role of incongruity and resolution in children's appreciation of cartoon humor. *Journal of Experimental Child Psychology,* 1972, *13,* 456-477.
Shultz, T. R. Development of the appreciation of riddles. *Child Development,* 1974, *45,* 100-105.
Shultz, T. R., & Horibe, F. Development of the appreciation of verbal jokes. *Developmental Psychology,* 1974, *10,* 13-20.
Shultz, T. R., & Pilon, R. Development of the ability to detect linguistic ambiguity. *Child Development,* 1973, *44,* 728-733.
Silberer, H. On symbol-forming. In D. Rapaport (Ed.), *Organization and pathology of thought.* New York: Columbia University Press, 1951. Pp. 208-233.
Simpkinson, C. H. *Explorations into figurative language in psychotherapy.* Unpublished doctoral dissertation, University of Tennessee, 1972.
Singer, E. *Key concepts in psychotherapy.* New York: Random House, 1965.
Skeat, W. W. *An etymological dictionary of the English language.* Oxford, England: Clarendon Press, 1898.
Skinner, B. F. *Verbal behavior.* New York: Appleton-Century-Crofts, 1957. P. 92.
Smith, J. A. *Adventures in communication, language arts methods.* Boston: Allyn & Bacon, 1972.
Snider, J. G., & Osgood, C. E. *Semantic differential technique.* Chicago: Aldine, 1969.
Spache, G. P., & Spache, E. B. *Reading in the elementary school* (3rd ed.). Boston: Allyn & Bacon, 1973.
Staehlin, W. Zur psychologie and statistik der metaphor. *Archives of General Psychology,* 1914, *31,* 397-425.
Steenburgh, E. W. Metaphor. *Journal of Philosophy,* 1965, *62,* 22-41.
Steinberg, D. D., & Jakobovitz, L. A. *Semantics: An interdisciplinary reader in philosophy, linguistics, and psychology.* Cambridge, England: Cambridge University Press, 1971.
Stelzer, H. Analysis by metaphor. *Quarterly Journal of Speech,* 1965, *51,* 52-61.
Stern, G. *Meaning and change of meaning.* Bloomington, Ind.: Indiana University Press, 1931.
Sterzinger, O. Die grume des gefallens und misfallens in poetischen bilde. *Archives of General Psychology,* 1913, *29,* 16-91.
Stewig, J. W. Metaphor and children's writing. *Elementary English,* 1966, *43,* 121-123, 128.
Strachey, J. The nature of the therapeutic action of psychoanalysis. *International Journal of Psychoanalysis,* 1934, *15,* 127-159.
Strang, B. M. *Metaphors and models.* Newcastle-Upon-Tyne: University of Newcastle-Upon-Tyne, 1965.
Sullivan, H. J. *Conceptions of modern psychiatry.* Washington: W. A. White Psychiatric Foundation, 1947.
Suzuki, D. T. Zen. In D. T. Suzuki, E. Fromm, & R. Martino (Eds.), *Zen Buddhism and psychoanalysis.* New York: Harper, 1960.
Sweet, J. A. Playing with a simile. *Viewpoints.* 1974, *50,* 45-51.

Synectics, Inc. *Making it strange*. New York: Harper & Row, 1968.
Tarachow, A. *Introduction to psychotherapy*. New York: International Universities Press, 1963.
Thomas, O. *Metaphor and related subjects*. New York: Random House, 1969.
Torrance, E. P. *Torrance tests of creative thinking*. Princeton, N. J.: Personnel Press, 1966.
Truscott, I. Contextual constraints and schizophrenic language. *Journal of Consulting and Clinical Psychology*, 1970, *35*, 189–194.
Turbayne, C. M. *The myth of metaphor*. New Haven: Yale University Press, 1962.
Turner, J. Maxwell on the method of physical analogy. *British Journal of Philosophy and Science*, 1956, *6*, 226–239.
Ullmann, S. *The principles of semantics* (1st ed.). New York: Barnes & Noble, 1946.
Ullmann, S. *The principles of semantics: A linguistic approach to meaning* (2nd ed.). London: 1957.
Ullmann, S. Semantic universals. In Greenberg, J. H. (Ed.). *Universals of language* (2nd ed.). Cambridge, Mass.: M.I.T. Press, 1966. Pp. 217–262.
Upton, A. *Design for thinking*. Stanford: Stanford University Press, 1961. Pp. 75–81.
Upton, A. Reading and intelligence. *Claremont Reading Conference Yearbook*, 1964, *28*, 137–143. (a)
Upton, A. A linguistic approach to problems of analysis and interpretation. *Journal of Communication*, 1964, *14*, 118–122. (b)
Upton, A., & Samson, R. *Creative analysis*. New York: Dutton, 1963.
Urban, W. M. *Language and reality*. New York: Macmillan, 1961.
Valenstein, A. F. The psychoanalytic situation: Affects, emotional reliving, and insight in the psychoanalytic process. *International Journal of Psychoanalysis*, 1962, *43*, 315–324.
Valery, P. *The art of poetry*. New York: Vintage Books, 1961. P. 72.
Wallach, M. A., & Kogan, N. *Modes of thinking in young children*. New York: Holt, Rinehart & Winston, 1965.
Walpole, H. R. *Semantics: The nature of words and their meaning*. New York: Norton, 1941. Pp. 141–158.
Warburg, J. Review of Brooke-Rose's *A grammar of metaphor*. *Modern Language Review*, *55*, 1960, 97–98.
Warringer, J. E. *English Grammar and composition*. New York: Harcourt, Brace, 1951. Pp. 265–269.
Watts, A. F. *The language and mental development of children*. Boston: Heath, 1944. Pp. 195–217.
Weinreich, U. Explorations in semantic theory. In T. A. Sebeok (Ed.), *Current trends in linguistics* (Vol. 3). The Hague: Mouton, 1966.
Weissman, A. D. *The existential core of psychoanalysis*. New York: Brown, 1965.
Welsh, R. A. A critique of the use and abuse of metaphor. *The Review of Metaphysics*, 1962, *16*, 258–259.
Werner, H. *Comparative psychology of mental development*. New York: Follett, 1948.
Werner, H. Review of Ullmann' *Semantics*. *Language*, *28*, 1952, 256–257.
Werner, H. (Ed.) *On expressive language*. Worcester: Clark University Press, 1955.
Werner, H. The concept of development from a comparative and organismic point of view. In D. B. Harris (Ed.), *The concept of development*. Minneapolis: University of Minnesota Press, 1957. Pp. 125–148.
Werner, H. *Die ursprunge der metaphor*. Leipzig: Englemann, 1919.
Werner, H., & Kaplan, B. *Symbol formation*. New York: Wiley, 1963.
Wheelis, F. The place of action in personality change. *Psychiatry*, 1950, *13*, 135–362.
Wheelwright, P. *The burning fountain: A study in the language of symbolism*. Bloomington: University of Indiana Press, 1959.

Wheelwright, P. *Metaphor and reality.* Bloomington, Ind.: University of Indiana Press, 1962.

Wiersma, M. Ceiling unlimited. *Education,* 1959, *80,* 76–79.

Wild, C. Creativity and adaptive regression. *Journal of Personality and Social Psychology,* 1965, *2,* 161–169.

Wilson, D. *Presuppositions and non-truth conditional semantics.* London: Academic Press, 1975.

Wimsatt, W. K. Review of Foss's, *Symbol and metaphor. Review of Metaphysics,* 1950, *4,* 279–90.

Wimsatt, W. K. Poetic tension: A summary. *New Scholasticism,* 1958, *32,* 73–88. (a)

Wimsatt, W. K. *The verbal icon: Studies in the meaning of poetry.* New York: Noonday Press, 1958. (b)

Winner, E., & Gardner, H. Training children in metaphoric thinking (A Preliminary Report). Cambridge, Mass.: Harvard Project Zero, 1974.

Winner, E., & Rosenstiel, A. K. The development of metaphoric understanding. Unpublished manuscript, 1975.

Winterowd, W. R. *Rhetoric: A synthesis.* New York: Holt, Rinehart & Winston, 1967.

Wittgenstein, L. *Philosophical investigations.* (G. E. M. Anscombe, Transl.) New York: Macmillan, 1953.

Wittgenstein, L. *The blue and brown books.* Oxford: Basil Blackwell, 1958.

Wolberg, L. R. *The technique of psychotherapy.* Parts 1 and 2. New York: Grune & Stratton, 1954.

Wolman, B. *The unconscious mind: The meaning of Freudian psychology.* Englewood Cliffs: Prentice-Hall, 1968.

Yandell, S., & Zintz, M. Some difficulties which Indian children encounter with idioms in reading. *The Reading Teacher,* 1961, *14,* 356–59.

Ziff, P. *Semantic analysis.* Ithaca, New York: Cornell University Press, 1960.

Zilboorg, G. The emotional problem and the therapeutic role of insight. *Psychoanalytic Quarterly,* 1952, *21,* 1–53.

Zintz, M. V. *The reading process, the teacher and the learner.* Dubuque, Iowa: Brown, 1970.

Author Index

A

Aleksandrowicz, D. R., 107, 108, 115, *235*
Alexander, Franz, 119, *235*
Anderson, C. C., 104, 105, 106, *235*
Aristotle, 18, 20, *235*
Armstrong, D. T., 203, *235*
Asch, S. E., 59, 60, 162, 163, 164, 166, 168, 169, 183, 187, 191, 192, *235*

B

Baker, S. J., 105, *235*
Barlow, J. M., 6, 7, 67, 68, 69, 70, 71, 74, 75, 76, 83, 110, 111, 112, 115, 133, 136, 168, 172, 184, 215, *235*
Bartlett, C. F., 105, *236*
Becking, M. F., 200, *244*
Bellek, L., 103, *236*
Berko-Gleason, J., 161, *236*
Bickerton, D., 49, 50, 51, *236*
Billow, R. M., 189, 190, 191, *236*
Black, M., 21, 22, *236*
Bolinger, D. L., 51, 65, 93, *236*
Boswell, J., 33
Breger, L., 113, *236*
Brooke-Rose, C., 67, *236*
Broman, B. L., 200, *237*
Brown, N. O., 11, 18, 19, 40, 105, 161, *236*
Bruner, J. S., 101, 152, 157, *237*
Burkland, C. E., 203, *237*
Burmeister, D., 203, *237*

Burns, B., 94, 95, 96, *237*
Burns, P. C., 200, *237*
Butler, J., 108, *237*

C

Cain, A. C., 107, *237*
Carlson, R. K., 88, *237*
Cassirer, E., 28, 30, 63, *237*
Cerf, B., 32, 34, 35, *237*
Change, L. Y. C., 202, *238*
Chapman, J. W., 85, 86, 88, *237*
Chessick, R. D., 103, *237*
Chukovsky, K., 161, 162, *237*
Clark, E., 161, *238*
Cooper, D., 203, *238*
Corbett, E. P. J., 38, 39, *238*
Curtis, D., 203, *238*

D

Dallman, M., 202, *238*
Darwin, C., 13
Deboer, J. J., 202, *238*
Dechant, E. V., 201, 202, *238*
Deese, J. E., 41, 55, *238*
Descartes, Rene, 13
Deutsch, F., 102, 103, *238*
Dickey, J., 27, 28, *238*
Dickinson, Emily, 48
Downey, J. E., 106, *238*
Dreisdadt, R., 13, *238*

Author Index

Dryud, J. E., 108, *240*
Durkin, D., 201, *238*

E

Edie, J. M., 13, *238*
Ehninger, D., 16, 41, 42, 43, 44, 84, *244*
Einstein, A., 13
Ekstein, R., 15, 16, 107, 115, *238*
Elkind, D., 164, *238*
Emig, J., 195, 196, 198, *239*
Empson, W., 20, *239*
Erikson, E. H., 105, 112, *239*

F

Ferguson, C. W., 194, 204, *239*
Fillmore, C. J., 52, 53, *239*
Fine, H. J., 15, 109, 115, 130, *239*
Fleming, Ian, 9
Fodor, N., 45, 46, 51, 53, 93, 105, *239*
Foerster, L. M., 204, *239*
Foss, M., 23, 24, 31, *239*
Francisco, E., 6, 8, 71, 72, 78, 79, 81, 83, *245*
Freud, S., 16, 92, 102, 113, 116, 123, *239*
Funk, C., 202, *239*

G

Gardner, H., 161, 164, 165, 166, 167, 169, 170, 187, 191, 213, 214, 215, 234, *239*
Gendlin, E. T., 124, 125, 126, 127, 128, 129, *239*
Getzels, J. W., 212, *239*
Goldiamond, I., 108, *240*
Goldman-Eisler, F., 8, *240*
Gordon, W. J. J., 14, 15, 87, 128, 208, *240*
Greene, H. A., 200, *240*
Groesbeck, H., 198, 211, *240*
Guntrip, H., 113, *240*

H

Hard, J. S., 196, *240*
Harrower, M. R., 63, 109, *240*
Harsh, W., 196, *240*
Hartmann, H., 113, *240*
Harvey, O. J., 85, 86, 88, *240*
Heiman, E., 204, *240*
Hester, N. B., 17, 24, 26, 27, *240*
Hill, J. D., 167, 170, 206, 207, *241*

Hobbes, Thomas, 33
Holstein, B. I., 212, 213, 215, 234, *240*
Hood, Thomas, 33
Horibe, 36
Hormann, H., 62, *241*
Horne, R. N., 88, 211, *241*
Hughes, T., 204, *241*
Husserl, E., 27, *241*
Hutchinson, E. D., 127, 128, *241*

I

Isard, S., 93, 94, *243*
Isenberg, A., 20, *241*
Issacs, S., 105, *241*

J

Jackson, W., 212, *239*
Jakobavitz, L. A., 52, *242*
Jenkins, J. J., 41, *241*
Johnson, M. G., 55, 56, 57, *241*
Jordan, W. J., 42, *241*

K

Kaplan, B., 61, 62, 63, 64, *241*
Katz, J. J., 45, 46, 51, 53, 57, 93, *241*
Kelly, G., 86, *241*
Kennedy, John F., 4, 5, 6, 7, 8, 10, 71, 72, 78, 79, 80, 81, 82, 83, 84
Kerlin, J. R., 67, 168, 172, 184, 215, *236*
Kircher, M., 166, 170, 214, *239*
Knapp, R. H., 105, 106, *241*
Koch, K., 232, *242*
Koen, F., 41, 42, 44, *242*
Koestler, A., 32, 35, 36, 87, 127, 128, *242*
Koffka, K., 35, 36, 63, *242*
Kogan, N., 212, *247*
Kohler, W., 58, 59, 62, 63, 64, 66, *242*
Kris, E., 103, 113, 122, 123, 128, *242*

L

Lakoff, R., 52, 54, 96, *242*
Langendoen, D. T., 52, *242*
Langer, S., 28, 29, 30, 63, *242*
Lasswell, L., 117, 128, *242*
Laure, B., 108, *237*
Leder, S., 118, 119, *242*
Leech, G. N., 52, *242*

Leedy, J. J., 15, 109, *242*
Leibniz, G. W., 20
Lenrow, P. B., 15, 108, 109, 115, *242*
Loban, W., 170, *242*
Lockwood, B. R., 6, 8, 83, 89, 90, 185, *242*
Lonergan, B., 126, 127, 128, 129, 155, *242*
Lowe, A. L., 200, *237*
Lowenstein, R. M., 113, *240*
Ludovici, A. M., 34, *242*

M

Maclay, H., 51, 52, *242*
Maier, N. R. F., 35, 36, *243*
Martin, A. R., 121, 122, *243*
Maslow, A. H., 87, 88, 92, *243*
Maupin, B. M., 107, *237*
Mawardi, B., 15, 32, 34, 36, *243*
McCawley, J. D., 52, 54, 96, *243*
McGhee, P. E., 36, *243*
McKuen, R., 56
McNemar, Q., 80, *243*
Meshover, L., 197, *243*
Michael, F. S., 53, *243*
Miller, G. A., 8, 93, 94, *243*
Mulder, A., 194, *243*
Murphy, W. F., 102, 103, 120, 121, *243*

N

Nash, H., 16, 19, 33, *243*
Neisser, U., 65, *243*
Nerlove, H., 162, 163, 164, 166, 168, 169, 183, 187, 191, *236*
Newton, E. S., 203, *243*
Ney, J. W., 196, *240*
Nixon, Richard M., 4, 5, 6, 7, 8, 10, 71, 72, 78, 79, 80, 81, 82, 83, 84

O

Ogden, C. K., 19, 42, *244*
Olson, D. R., 93, *244*
Osborn, M. M., 16, 41, 42, 43, 44, 84, *244*
Osgood, C. E., 40, 41, 42, 44, 64, *244*

P

Paivio, A., 41, *244*
Pap, A., 93, *244*
Pederson-Krag, G., 105, *244*
Percy, W., 20, 21, 24, *244*
Perkins, D., 166, 170, 214, *239*
Perls, F. S., 120, *244*
Petty, W. T., 200, *244*
Phelan, R., 208, *244*
Pilon, R., 36, *246*
Pitts, M., 95, 96, *244*
Pollio, H. R., 6, 7, 8, 15, 41, 44, 67, 68, 69, 70, 71, 72, 74, 75, 76, 78, 79, 81, 83, 109, 110, 111, 112, 115, 130, 133, 168, 170, 171, 172, 174, 175, 179, 182, 183, 184, 185, 215, *231, 244, 245*
Pollio, M. R., 6, 71, 72, 83, 168, 170, 171, 172, 174, 175, 179, 182, 183, 184, 185, 189, 196, 215, 219, 221, 225, 231, 234, *245*
Porter, C. M., 88, 89, *245*
Proll, E., 203, *245*

R

Rapaport, D., 122, *245*
Reinsch, N. L., Jr., 42, *245*
Rice, H., 108, *237*
Richards, I. A., 15, 21, 23, 42, *245*
Rilke, R., 101
Robertson, J. E., 198
Robinson, V., 197, *243*
Rommetviet, R., 54, 107, 108, *245*
Rosenstiel, A. K., 187, 188, 189, 191, *248*
Rouch, R. L., 202, *238*
Ruddell, R. B., 201, *245*
Russell, W. A., 41, 121, 122, *241*
Ryle, G., 13, *245*

S

Sagan, E., 112, *245*
Sartre, J. P., 14
Schon, D. A., 12, *245*
Schonberg, R. B., 6, 71, 83, 90, 91, 92, 183, 184, 185, *245*
Sewell, E., 28, 101, *245*
Shakespeare, W., 33, 56
Shane, H. G., 196, *240*
Shapiro, C., 85, 87, *246*
Sharpe, E. F., 16, 106, *246*
Sheehan, D., 27, *246*
Shultz, T. R., 36, *246*
Simpkinson, C. H., 6, 15, 71, 78, 109, 115, 130, 152, *246*

Author Index

Sharpe, E. F., 105, *246*
Silberer, H., 105, 106, *246*
Skeat, W. W., 33, *246*
Singer, E., 116, 129, *246*
Small, G., 103, *236*
Smith, J. A., 200, *246*
Southern, Terry, 9, *246*
Spache, E. B., 202, *246*
Spache, G. P., 202, *246*
Steinberg, D. D., 52, *246*
Stelzer, H., 12, *246*
Stevens, W., 27, 28
Stewig, J. W., 206, *246*
Strachey, J., 117, *246*
Suci, G., 40, 41, *241*
Sullivan, H. J., 113, *246*
Suzuki, D. T., 3, 4, 9, 10, *246*
Sweet, J. A., 168, 170, 207, *246*

T

Tannenbaum, P. H., 40, 41, *244*
Tennyson, Alfred Lord, 3, 4, 10
Thomas, Dylan, 54
Thomas, W., 34, 46, 47, 48, 49, *247*
Torrance, E. P., 89, *247*
Truscott, I., 94, *247*

U

Ullmann, S., 12, 60, *247*
Upton, A., 202, 203, *247*

V

Valenstein, A. F., 121, *247*
Valery, P., 29, 58, *247*

W

Wagstaff, F., 108, *237*
Wallach, M. A., 212, *247*
Watts, A. F., 195, *247*
Weinreich, U., 46, 51, *247*
Weissman, A. D., 108, *247*
Welsh, R. A., 20, *247*
Werner, H., 60, 61, 62, 63, 64, 66, 161, *247*
Wheelis, F., 117, *247*
Wheelwright, P., 23, 24, 25, 26, 31, *247*
Wilson, D., 52, 54, *248*
Wimsatt, W. K., 25, 26, *248*
Winner, E., 166, 170, 187, 188, 189, 191, 213, 214, 215, 234, *248*
Winterowd, W. R., 20, *248*
Wittgenstein, L., 26, 27, 30, *248*
Wolberg, L. R., 103, 118, *248*

Y

Yandell, S., 205, *248*

Z

Zilboorg, G., 120, *248*
Zintz, Miles V., 201, 205, *248*

Subject Index

A

Analogy
  as mechanism in figurative language 18 ffg
  cautions about in Education, 195
Anomaly
  and context-free lexicon, 96
  and figurative usage in verbal learning, 95–96
  and metaphor, 97–98
  as cognitive process, 93–94
  as logical problem, 93
  interpretation of, 96
  relationship to nonsense and metaphor, 92–93
  role in theory of metaphor, 49
Apostrophe, defined, 38
Associative anamnesis, 102
Association theory
  and theories of metaphor, 43–45
Audrey, Case of, 68–70, 74–75
  episodic quality of figurative usage in, 80–81
  figurative themes in, 110–111

B

B-Cognition
  and figurative expression, 87–88
Bad faith, in language usage, 21
Blocking role in sematic-feature theory, 47–48

C

Cognitive style and figurative usage, 85–87
Communication, intersubjective nature of, 20–21, 54, 107–108
Comparisons task
  and frozen figurative usage, 227–228
  and lesson plans, 228–229
  and *Making It Strange* study general results, 219, 227–229
  novel figurative usage in, 170, 227–229
  explanation of, 180
  results for sociocultural groups, 176–180
  with adolescents, 184–185
Composition task
  and frozen figurative usage, 174
  and *Making It Strange* study,
    general results, 219–227,
    residual effects, 226
  and results of special lessons, 222–225
  explanation of, 168
  high socioeconomic groups, 221
  Making It Strange and lessons,
    conclusions, 225–226
  problems with, 170
  results for sociocultural groups, 172–176
  with adolescents, 184–185
Concepts, displacement of, 12–13
Concrete-universal, 25, 26
Connotation, role in meaning, 28
Construal rule, 46

254 Subject Index

Context
   role in definition of anomaly, 93–94
   role in semantic theory, 96
Contradiction
   role in anomaly and figurative language, 53
Corrective emotional experience, 119
Creative problem-solving,
   role of figurative language in, 32
Creativity,
   and teachers, 233
   teaching of, 210–211

D

Dancing of poetry, 29
Denotation, role in meaning, 28
Depth-language, 23
Diaphor, 24
"Don't Rock the Boat" philosophy
   and *Making It Strange* series, 218
   and teachers, 233
   description of, 175, 212
   explanation of, 170
Double-function terms
   cross language effects, 59–60
   definition of, 162
   development of, 162–164
   examples of, 163
Dreams and poetic symbolism, 106
Dynamic schematization,
   role in the development of symbols, 61–63

E

Elementary cognitive characteristic (ECC), 55–56
Epiphor, 24
Epoche
   role in understanding poetry, 27
Epistemology
   and insight, 126–127
   and poetry, 28–29

F

Feature hierarchy
   critical analysis of, 49
   role in Thomas' theory, 48–49

Feature matrix, defined, 47
Feature, sematic
   cross-category effects, 50–51
   relationship to mediational responses, 44–45
   rules of assignment for, 50–51
Figure-ground role in figurative language, 22–23
Figurative comprehension, possible stages in, 187–189
Figurative language
   absolute values for in production tasks, 3, 169
   alternations of in psychotherapy, 142
   and adolescent reasoning, 164
   and bilingual problems in reading, 205
   and I Q, 211–212
   and personality variables, 85 ffg
   and reading comprehension, 211–212
   and reading problems, 202–203
   and rule violations, 96
   and teachers, 231–233
   and teacher ratings of creative writing, 207–208
   Aristotle's view, 18–19
   as ornament, 209
   as part of literature and rhetoric, 194
   Barlow, Kerlin and Pollio technique, 168, 172, 215
   Brown's view, 19
   case study teaching approach, 212–213
   caveats in intepreting functions of, 9–10, 11–16, 17–18
   children's use of different literary genres, 207–208
   children's use in poetry, 206–207
   children's use in prose, 206–207
   cross-sample comparisons, 184
   developmental continuum of, 185–186
   development of; comprehension and explanation, 187–191
   development of; conclusions, 191–192
   development of in different sociocultural groups, 171–172
   development of elaborative ability, 213
   development of in explanation task, 163–164
   development of in school children, 168–187
   development of in written work, 167–168

Figurative language *(contd.)*
　development of in Piagetian theory, 186–187
　development of productive capacity in adolescense, 183–185
　development of in different sociocultural groups, 170–183
　developmental trends, general, 162–170
　episodic properties in psychotherapy, 76–78
　experimental procedures for teaching of, 211–215
　formal categories of, 37–40
　gestalt hypothesis of, 63 ffg
　in adolescent compositions, 90–92
　in children's writing, 211–212
　interpretation of in children's literature, 211
　lack of concern for in education, 194
　neglect in semantic theory, 161
　Ogden and Richard's view, 19–20
　ornamental view of, 30
　output properties of, 96–97
　Piagetian analysis, 163, 164
　public debate, theoretical role in, 16–17
　quantitative estimates of frequency, 5 ffg
　quantitative estimates of role in psychotherapy, 84–85
　quantitative results, writing, 8
　rates of occurrence in speech, 6–8
　reasons for teaching, 194
　reasons for use, 30 ffg
　relations to amount of reading done, 207–208
　reliability of ratings, 68–73
　results of different training procedures, 214–215
　scientific training procedures, 213–215
　special lessons and reinforcement procedures, 219
　teaching of and problem-solving, 208
　teaching of and reading, 202–206
　teaching of and slang, 203, 204
　teaching of and socioeconomic levels, 233
　teaching of and student reading books, 198
　teaching of and student textbooks in language arts, 196–198
　teaching of and teacher education texts, 200–202

Figurative language *(contd.)*
　teaching of and writing, 206–208
　teaching of in science, 208
　teaching of, conclusions, 232–233
　teaching of in classroom writing, 213–215
　teaching suggestions, 200–204
　training procedure for raters, 67 ffg
　ubiquity of, 28–30, 63–64, 98
　verbal training procedures for, 213–215
　visual training procedures, 213–215
Figures in speech
　clinical results, 73–78
　public rhetoric, 78–82
Figure of speech
　different types of in children's writing, 206–207
　fresh or living, defined, 43
　predictions of goodness, interpretability, etc., 56–57
Figures of speech, frozen 43, 68
　and Comparisons task, 227–228
　and Composition task, 220–222
　and *Making It Strange*, 216–218
　and Multiple Sentences task, 230–231
　as vocabulary items, 165–166
　defined, 7
　development of, 165
　in ordinary language use, 9
　perception of in rating data, 72–73
　quantitative relationship to novel figures, 82–84
　relationship to double function terms, 163
　relationship to utterance length, 82–84
　role in public oratory, 83–84
　role in puns, 33
　role in theory of metaphor, 49
　thematic independence, 81–82
Figures of speech, novel 68
　and Composition task, 221–222
　and Comparison task, 227–229
　and *Making It Strange*, 215–218
　and Multiple Sentences task, 230–231
　as ego process, 130
　as problem solving and wish fulfillment, 130
　clustering in psychotherapy, 150
　differences with frozen figures, 97
　episodic output properties, 97
　perception of in rating data, 73

Subject Index

Figures of speech *(contd.)*
  quantitative relationship to frozen figures, 82–84
  relationship to utterance length, 82–84
  thematic inter-relatedness, 81–82
  unwitting use in psychotherapy, 102–103
Focus, 21
Focusing, 124–125
Follett Reading Series, 196
Frame, 21

G

Gestalt Therapy (see Audrey, Case of)
  number of words per session, 7
  use of figurative language in, 74–75, 120
  and ego, 123
  and emerging conflicts, 122–123
  and figurative language in psychotherapy, 136–141
  and mutative interpretations, 117–118
  and the urge to question, 126–127
  as a patient process, 118–120
  as emotional process, 119, 122
  as emotional-integrative model, 120, 121
  as experiencing, 124–127
  as experiential acquaintship, 121
  as knowing by description, 121
  as literal statements, 151, 155
  as "literalization of metaphors", 151, 153–154, 155–157
  as metaphoric generalities, 151, 152
  as problem-solving, 127–128
  as unfolding, 128
  contemporary views of, 124–129
  co-occurrence with figurative language, 142
  descriptive, 122
  Murphy's views, 121
  ostensive, 122
  regions of agreement, 134–135
Gestalt theory
  analysis of jokes and figurative language, 35–36
Global applications, 125–126

H

Haiku-poem, 3
Homonym, 163
Humor and laughter theories of, 33–34
Hyperbole, defined, 38–39

I

Iconic thread
  role in poetry, 28
Images
  role in poetry, 26
Incomplete stories
  use of, 166
  use of in comprehension and explanation tasks, 187
  use of in training study, 214
Insight
  and early analysts, 116, 117
  research and empirical findings, 132, 133 ffg
  stages of, 127–128
Interpretation
  Speaker/Hearer Agreement in, 96
Interpretative act
  role in understanding metaphor, 57
Inter-subjectivity role in communication, 20–21, 54, 107–108
Irony,
  defined, 39

J

Jokes
  relationship to figurative expression, 35–36
  relationship to problem-solving, 37

K

Kennedy-Nixon debates
  distribution of inter-sentence intervals,
    for Kennedy, 79
    for Nixon, 78
  frozen figures, 78, 79, 80
  novel figures, 78, 79, 80
  rates of figurative use in, 7–8, 79
  reliability of ratings, 72
  thematic interrelatedness, frozen and novel figures, 81–82
Knowing
  two ways, 121

L

Laidlaw Reading Series, 196
Language, literal 49; 50–51
  contrasted with figurative, 30
  relationship to figurative, 29
Language, propositional
  relationship to emotional, 28–29
Language, rational
  as distinct from emotional, 19
  as inseparable from emotional, 19, 20
Laughter
  relationship to figurative expression, 32–37
Lexicon
  context-free assumption, 96
  in feature model, 55–56
  psychological definition, 66
  relationship to "knowing" a word, 57–58
Literal use systems, 22
Litote, defined, 38–39

M

Making It Strange
  across socio-economic levels, 219–231
  compressed conflict, 210
  description of workbooks, 199–200
  training procedures, 215–231
  training procedures and frozen figurative language, 216–218
  training procedures and novel figurative language, 215–218
  training procedures with high socio-economic groups, 215–219
Maluma, 58–59; 62
Mediated generalization,
  role in metaphor, 41
Metaphor
  and anomaly, 92–96; 97–98
  and education, 195
  and educational research, 196
  and Gestalt theory, 58 ffg
  and psychotherapy, 15–16
  as additional vocabulary, 11
  as cognitive process, 23
  as conflict, 113–114
  as heuristic, 14–16, 101
  as interactive Gestalt, 31
  as intellectual history, 11–12

Metaphor *(contd.)*
  as libidinal discharge, 105
  as forgotten experience, 105
  as mask, 16–17, 30
  as mistake, 20–21
  as ornament, 17–18
  as semantic destruction, 24
  as shaper of "world view", 196, 198
  as symbolic disguise, 104
  as unstructured tension, 105
  as violation of language system, 58
  as vital synthesis, 24
  Black's views on, 21–23
  constructive theory of, 65
  contrast between perceptual and response theories, 64 ffg
  Darwin's tree, 13
  Einstein's mirror, 13
  feature models of, 45–58
  feature theories compared to perceptual theories, 65–66
  formal definition of, 37
  Freud's "play within a play", 16–17
  functions of in psychotherapy, 108, 109
  Gestalt theory, relationship to feature theories, 63–64
  high and low users of, 89–90; 91–92
  in borderline and psychotic patients, 107
  in ego psychology and object relations, 113
  in psychotherapy, 108, 109, 110, 111
  interpretation, relationship to judgments of quality, 57
  in schizophrenia, 107, 108
  in student language arts texts, 196–198
  linguistic analysis of, 49–51
  measurement of, 67, ffg
  Osborn and Ehninger's model, 42 ffg
  perceptual models of, 53–64
  psychoanalytic interpretation of, 16–17
  psychological feature model of, 54 ffg
  purpose in child language, 195
  response theory of, 40 ffg
  role in evoking imagery, 105
  role in philosophy, 13–14
  role in psychotherapy, speculations on, 155
  semantic feature models, 44; 45 ffg
  specific theoretical models of, 32–66

Metaphor *(contd.)*
  Stelzer's hypothesis, 12
  taxonomic aspects of, 48
  Thomas' semantic feature theory of, 46 ffg
  Valery's analysis, 29, 58
Metaphoric capacity
  Gardner test, 164
  Gardner test, critique of, 165–166
Metaphoric comprehension
  and cognitive development, 189–191
  and frozen and novel figures, 191
  and Piagetian Stages, 190–192
Metaphoric language
  high and low users, 97
Metaphoric preferences
  age trends, 167
  and production categories, 166
  and production, development of 166–167
Metaphoric production
  age trends, 167
Metaphoric style
  Chapman's study, 88
  Lockwood's study, 89–90
  negative picture of, 87
  personality sketch of, 89
  Porter's study, 88–89
  positive picture of, 87, 88
  Schonberg's study, 90–92
Metaphoric transfer
  in poetry, 60–61
Metaphorically appropriate endings
  definition of, 166
Metaphorically inappropriate endings
  definition of, 166
Mixed metaphor, 32, 34
Models of awareness, 101, 157
"Mouse that roared", 5
Multiple Sentences task
  and double-function terms, 183
  and frozen figurative language, 230–231
  and *Making It Strange* study, 219, 229–231
  explanation of, 168
  results of sociocultural groups, 180–183

N

Namer and Hearer
  role in figurative language, 20–21
"Need for symbolization", 28–29; 63

Nonsense, Anomaly and figurative language, 93–94
Non-sense
  role of Speaker/Hearer agreement in, 53

O

Onomatopoeia 39, 161
  Werner and Kaplan's views, 61
  in language arts texts, 196–198
Ornament
  role in figurative language, 17–18
Oxymoron, defined, 38

P

Periphrasis
  defined, 38
Personal constriction
  and low use of figurative language, 91–92
Personality
  and figurative usage, 85 ffg
Personification
  defined, 38
  in children's poetry, 206
  in language arts texts, 196–198
Physiognomic-definition task, 62
Physiognomic perception
  defined, 61
  role of body in, 62–63
Physiognomic process
  relation to symbol formation, 61
Poem
  and poetic vision, 25 ffg
Poetic language
  and psychotherapy, 4–5
  transfer/analogy postion, 18–23
Poetry
  and creation of "reality", 27 ffg
  and politics, 4
  and psychotherapy, 15–16
  and teaching, 4
  children's, U.S.A., 162, 232
  children's, Soviet Union, 161–162
  difficulty for association theory, 44
  epistemic significance of, 27 ffg
  Hester's views, 27
  obstacles to in children's writing, 233
  relationship to world view, 31
  role of figurative language in, 25 ffg

Poetry *(contd.)*
  role of iconic symbolism in, 25
  role of reading in, 27
Poetry Therapy, 109–110
Presupposition
  contextual, 52–53
  critical analysis of, 53–54
  defined, 52
  logical, 52, 53
  role in figurative language, 51 ffg
Problem solving
  AMIO pattern in groups, 15
    relationship to humor and figurative language, 36–37
  role of trace in, 63
Psychoanalysis
  and Zen Buddism, 3
  role of metaphor in, 104–105
Psychoanalytic psychotherapy
  metaphoric themes in, 142–143, 146–151
  words per session, 7
Psychosocial development
  and figurative language usage, 90–92
Psychotherapy
  and metaphor, 101–104
  role of figurative language in, 74, 130 ffg
  student therapists, 7
Public debate
  and figurative language, 97
Pun
  defined, 39
  etymology of, 33
Puns, 32–33

Q

Qualifiers
  role in Osborn and Ehninger's theory, 42–43

R

Rating procedures,
  effects of different groups, 73
  rejection and acceptance rates, 71–73
Ratings of figurative language, summary of 16 different samples, 71
Rational language,
  as related to emotional language, 28–29
  contrasted with expressive language, 23–24

Reality
  relationship to figurative expression 23–24
Reference movement, 125
Resemblence in difference
  definition of in metaphor, 20
Riddles
  developmental course of, 36
  examples of, 34–35
  relationship to figurative language, 35
  relationship to problem-solving, 35
  relationship to puns, 35
Rorschach test
  as predictor of metaphoric style, 89–90

S

Schizophrenia
  and metaphoric interpretation, 16
"Seeing as"
  role in poetic understanding, 27
  Wittgenstein's views, 26, 27
Semantic differential
  role of metaphor in, 40–41
Semantic feature models,
  linguistic, 45–54
  psychological, 54–58
Sense
  role of Speaker/Hearer agreement in, 52–53
Sense and sensa, 26–27
Senses, hierarchy of
  role in poetic expression, 60–61
Shipley-Hartford Scale, 88
Simile
  defined, 37
  in children's poetry, 206
  in student language arts texts, 196–198
Simile stems
  in teaching, 200, 201
Slip of the tongue, 102
Speaker-Hearer
  tacit bond in speech, 96
Sperber's Law, 30
  and frozen figurative language, 12–13
Steno-language, 23
Structure bound experiencing, 125, 127
Superiority
  role in figurative language and humor, 34
Symbolic transformation
  Langer's views, 28–29

Synechdoche,
  defined, 38
Synectics, 14–15
  analysis of group communication patterns, 15
Synesthesia
  and metaphor, 40, 41
  and metaphor in children, 164
  in poetry, 60–61
Syntax
  role in figurative expression, 48–49

T

Task constraints
  role in figurative production, 169–170
Tenor, 21, 42
Tension
  in concrete-universals, 25–26
  in figurative language, 31
  in poetry, 28
  role in figurative expression, 23–25
Thematic interpretation
  explanation of, 187
Therapy, child analytic
  use of figurative language in, 77
Therapy, existential
  use of figurative language in, 77
Therapy, rational-emotional
  use of figurative language in, 76

This I Believe Test, 86, 88
Thorndike-Lorge List, 95
Tuckatee, 58–59, 62

U

Unfolding, 124
Universals, poetic, 26
Utterance length
  relation to frozen and novel figures, 82084

V

Vehicle, 21, 42

W

Walking
  of prose, 29
Word-association
  role in psychological feature model, 55
  role in theory of metaphor, 41–42
Word compounds
  role in metaphor, 55–57

Z

Zen Buddism
  and psychoanalysis, 3